Policing UK Honour-Based Abuse Crime

"This book fills an important gap in the academic literature on honour based abuse (HBA), by looking at the specific challenges of policing HBA. Drawing on extensive and original material, Aplin addresses issues of crime, harm and language; and how some policing practises around HBA may disadvantage victims of HBA. Aplin's work is challenging, and innovative, and provides valuable insights in policing HBA in the UK."

—Dr Geetanjali Gangoli, *University of Bristol, UK*

"This book adds an interesting and provocative dimension to existing literature. The focus on police culture(s) and practices gives a unique insight into differentiated responses to particular forms of violence against women from minoritised communities and provides a unique lens through which to critically unpack the phenomenon. Its comprehensive examination of the subject makes it compulsory reading for practitioners, policy makers, researchers and students."

—Dr Ravi Thiara, Associate Professor, *University of Warwick, UK*

Rachael Aplin

Policing UK Honour-Based Abuse Crime

palgrave
macmillan

Rachael Aplin
Leeds Beckett University
Leeds, UK

ISBN 978-3-030-18429-2 ISBN 978-3-030-18430-8 (eBook)
https://doi.org/10.1007/978-3-030-18430-8

Cover illustration: Alamy: FCJMBC

This Palgrave Macmillan imprint is published by the registered company Springer Nature Switzerland AG
The registered company address is: Gewerbestrasse 11, 6330 Cham, Switzerland

This book is dedicated to my little brother Joe Ashworth. Miss you and loving you always.

Foreword

I am delighted to write this foreword, not only because Rachael Aplin is a valued colleague with whom I have shared many platforms but also because I believe deeply in this book, which is rooted in real-life cases, underpinned by Rachael's experience of over 20 years of policing. The author has the credibility of being at the coalface of policing, and this book critically, objectively and constructively explores policing and other professional practices to educate for the protection of the most vulnerable of victims. As a survivor of honour-based abuse and founder of the national charity Karma Nirvana, I recognise that the protection of victims very much depends on whether the professional has an understanding of the issues at the point of reporting. I was informed of the "one chance" rule by a detective sergeant who was challenged by a complex honour killing investigation and was astonished at how professionals often only have one opportunity to "get it right." The consequences of poor decision-making can mean that victims of honour abuse experience a raft of criminal offences explored in the forthcoming chapters.

This book provides a broad and useful compilation of concepts and cases, as well as innovative approaches and practical strategies to expose under-discussed areas of criminality. As an advocate, I am a firm believer that victims and survivors must shape and inform policy and practice. The book achieves this by rooting the research in real-life testimonies excavated through the examination of 100 police classified case records and magnified further by interviews with specialist officers. This study is an important resource for frontline police officers, investigators, social workers, teachers, those with safeguarding responsibilities, health practitioners and third sector agencies providing support to victims recovering from honour-based abuse. It explores how victims experience honour codes and how they are controlled by community norms, social policing and collective decisions, leading to acts of punishment for those that courageously report.

Forced marriage is not a "cultural" issue, and this work is liberating for those who fear treading on "cultural toes". The author provides a refreshing and bold account. She is not afraid to highlight the realities of how mothers play a fundamental role in the perpetration of honour-based abuse, one I can personally attest to on the basis of my own childhood experiences growing up in Britain, and corroborated by the many thousands of victims calling Karma Nirvana's helpline. The author explores how victims' wishes are overridden and they are sometimes returned to abusive situations by the very professionals entrusted to protect them. During my years of campaigning, I sought to address "honour crimes" as a violation of human rights and, given their gendered nature, a manifestation of violence against women. This research is an educational resource and of importance in the fight against honour crimes. There is a widespread lack of knowledge and awareness of the subject matter and this book goes a long way in redressing that balance.

Founder, Karma Nirvana, Leeds, UK Jasvinder Sanghera CBE

Acknowledgements

I remain utterly grateful to the 15 police officers who willingly took the time to be interviewed about this complex crime, despite their busy schedules. Your anonymity is assured and your dedication to the difficult job of policing is without question. Thanks also go to the Chief Constable and Force Intelligence Branch senior leaders who allowed me access to the electronic documentary data. I am indebted to my supervisors Doctor Tom Cockcroft and Professor Colin Webster. Colin, you have been incredibly supportive throughout. Thank you for your faith in me.

Warm thanks to Gaynor Lewis, Andrea Fitton and Ivy Ashworth-Crees, for the support afforded with interview transcription; Winnie Innes, for painstakingly proofreading my work; and Mike Gristwood, senior police analyst, for providing advice on the presentation of graphs and charts. My appreciation is also extended to Emeritus Professor Terry Thomas and friend and fellow lecturer Nicola Groves, who provided advice on two draft chapters, and friend Doctor Lisa Long, for her patience in affording advice on the "process" of writing a book.

Love goes to my family Ivy, John, Bev, Ed and Winnie—thanks for believing in me. Most of all, my unequivocal love to my husband Charlie and our children Joe and Emily. You have had to sacrifice precious family time so I could squirrel myself away in my office to work on this book. I owe you the most precious of gifts—time itself.

Contents

List of Figures

1
Introduction

The chapter opens by identifying the prevalence of honour-based abuse (HBA) and honour killings internationally. It rationalises why the crime is heavily gendered against women. Honour-based abuse (HBA) is defined, as are the key triggers prompting the abuse. The aim, objectives and overarching purpose of the study are delineated. As this study centralises on policing HBA, concepts of discretion and how police organisational culture(s)[1] develop are explored, along with storytelling as a mode of officer learning. This is followed by comparing the orthodox view of police culture(s) against contemporary more fluid perspectives. The challenges of policing of HBA are introduced, which highlights the need for the research. Latter sections draw on the cultural distinctions between HBA and traditional forms of domestic abuse, as these in turn provide additional barriers inhibiting victims from reporting or pursuing prosecutions. The chapter considers the advantages and limitations of retaining HBA within the mainstream domestic abuse framework and concludes with a structural outline of all chapter contents.

R. Aplin, *Policing UK Honour-Based Abuse Crime*,
https://doi.org/10.1007/978-3-030-18430-8_1

Introducing Honour-Based Abuse

Honour-based abuse is a serious yet largely hidden form of abuse. The United Nations General Assembly (UNGA) (2006) declares that about 5000 women worldwide lose their lives each year due to victim's transgressing family "honour" (Welden 2010: 381; Cihangir 2013). UK research highlights that 18 "honour" killings and 11 attempt murders occurred in the UK in the period 2010–2014 (Dyer 2015: 6). Although these statistics may appear small, this study will evidence that cases of non-lethal honour-based abuse (HBA) are more widespread than has been previously believed. Moreover, honour crimes are precursors to serious and sometimes lethal violence. Therefore, in improving the policing and multi-agency responses to HBA lies the opportunity to preserve life and safeguard victims of crime.

Although a small proportion of victims are male, HBA is unquestionably a highly gendered crime, with mostly female victims (Sen 2005; Gill 2013; NPCC policing strategy 2015). According to England and Wales statistics, 83% of females and 17% of males are victimised (ONS 2018: 32). Similarly, honour killing is statistically highlighted as a crime against young Muslim women (Gill 2013: 242; Chesler 2010; Chesler and Bloom 2012; Gill and Brah 2014: 74). Of the HBA cases prosecuted by the UK Crown Prosecution Service, 74% involve female victims (CPS 2015: 73). Chesler's worldwide study involving 230 honour killings (2010) concluded that men represent 7% of victims, which is identical to a United Nations study finding (Roberts 2014). Current figures identify that many defendants being prosecuted for domestic abuse are men (92%) (ONS 2018).

There are various definitions of HBA across international boundaries. The UK National Police Chiefs' Council (NPCC) definition for England, Wales and Northern Ireland is non-gender specific and accepts the possibility of male victimisation and female perpetration (2015). Since this research focuses on policing HBA and a prevalent finding was female perpetration, the UK NPCC definition is herein adopted (Fig. 1.1).

The key justification for perpetrating HBA is based on protecting a value system predicated on social norms and traditions. "Honour" is not about individual men controlling individual women but is a group entity,

> **Definition of honour-based abuse:**
>
> An incident or crime involving violence, threats of violence, intimidation, coercion or abuse (including psychological, physical, sexual, financial or emotional abuse), which has or may have been committed to protect or defend the honour of an individual, family and or community for alleged or perceived breaches of the family and/or community's code of behaviour
>
> (NPCC policing strategy, 2015:5)

Fig. 1.1 Definition of honour-based abuse

built on collective decision-making and community values, social policing and conformity with social and gender norms (Sen 2005). Honour relates to the behaviours that are expected of members of a community, while shame is associated with transgressing those expectations (Gill and Brah 2014). The heavy burden of preserving family honour becomes tied to the behaviour of women (Yuval-Davis 1998: 29; Shahid and Hyder 2008; Jafri 2009: 58). Women are used as the "vehicle" for transmitting social values from one generation to the next in ensuring the continued survival of the tribe and family institution (Wilford 1998: 15; Gupta 2003: 8; Jafri 2009). Extant literature tells us that abuse precipitated due to perceived honour violations is not about "honour"—albeit that is the pretext—but about the need to subjugate women to defend the status quo and preserve a traditional but essentially patriarchal way of life (Balzani 2011; Chesler and Bloom 2012), what Pitt-Rivers termed "honour as precedence" (1971). HBA is invoked when communities feel they are losing control (Razack 2004: 165).

The control of women is a key symbol of male power in societies with honour-centric value systems (Gill 2013; Gill et al. 2012), with concepts of honour and shame revolving around the control of female sexuality (Akpinar 2003; Reddy 2008; Bano 2011), particularly in ensuring sexual purity and virginity before marriage (Jafri 2009; Cihangir 2013; Baldry et al. 2013). Perceived dishonourable acts committed by women include sex outside marriage; adultery; illegitimate children (Meetoo and Mirza 2011; Belfrage et al. 2012; Eisner and Ghuneim 2013); appearing in a public place with someone other than her husband or relative (Eisner and Ghuneim 2013; The Muslim Council of Great Britain n.d.); a woman seeking a divorce regardless of any abusive relationship suffered (Jafri 2009; The Muslim Council of Great Britain n.d.); marrying without the consent of parents (Eisner and Ghuneim 2013; Belfrage et al. 2012); wanting to prevent or terminate an arranged marriage; engaging in homosexual acts or even involvement in a non-sexual relationship that is perceived as inappropriate (Belfrage et al. 2012; Roberts 2014). Heterosexual men face no or much less severe consequences in terms of abuse (Siddiqui 2005), possibly due to the uneven power relations and higher status enjoyed by men within the family dynamic (Gangoli et al. 2009: 427). When daughters are perceived as deviating from such norms, they are deemed by kin and community as responsible for their own victimisation (Jafri 2009; Welden 2010) and are therefore punished—hence the term "honour-based abuse." Paradoxically they are labelled as transgressors or "outsiders" (Becker 2008; Balzani 2011: 87). Families go to extreme lengths to prevent women from violating tradition to preserve family honour (Niaz 2003; Gill 2013).

Study Aim and Objectives

The aim of this study was to critically explore discretionary policing practices at honour-based abuse incidents. The objectives of the study were as follows:

1. To examine police decision-making, behaviours and discretionary practices when investigating HBA incidents
2. To determine the factors that influence and shape those policing decisions and practices
3. To assess the impact of those practices on service provision to victims of crime

In addressing these objectives, an accumulated set of questions emerged, such as how does policing HBA compare or align with policing "traditional" domestic abuse? What interactions take place between victims, perpetrators and professionals[2] in shaping the outcomes in HBA investigations? To what extent are police supervisors aware of the discretionary decisions made by officers? What stratagems do officers use in effecting non-enforcement discretionary decisions, and more pointedly what factors contribute to shaping those non-enforcement decisions? To what extent is there evidence of a universal or "monolithic" police culture? What partnership working arrangements are in place to police HBA, and are these effective in safeguarding victims? What impact do professional interventions have on the service provided to victims? However, it must be emphasised that this was a grounded theory approach and therefore many additional and unanticipated themes emerged as the study progressed—such is the nature of research.

Purpose of the Present Study

The purpose of this study was to critically explore discretionary policing practices and decision-making at reported HBA incidents in one police force. The study aimed to generate insights into the behaviour and decision-making of specialist and frontline police officers and, to a lesser extent, children's social care professionals as "social policers" (Thomas 1988: 7), to locate the best explanations for decisions made. The primary research design comprised a dual-phase methodology. This incorporated a case study comparison of 100 HBA incidents reported to police and taken from archived classified police electronic computer systems (qualitative and quantitative). Interview questions were devised after the initial coding of the case data in order to progressively build theory from the data (Glaser and Strauss 1967; Charmaz 2014; Miles and Huberman 1994). Semi-structured interviews took place with 14 specialist public protection police detectives and one Neighbourhood Policing Team (NPT) uniformed officer, inclusive of ranks from constable to inspector. A convergent parallel mixed method design was adopted for the first phase, which involved designing an instrument to capture both qualitative and quantitative elements simultaneously, analysing these separately, then comparing and integrating these within the findings. In fully interpreting the material, the researcher moved cyclically back and forth comparing electronic case records and interview transcripts, which is the constant comparison method and involved the theoretical sampling of fresh contexts (Glaser and Strauss 1967). The rationale for adopting a mixed method design was to undertake a comprehensive analysis of the research problem (Creswell 2014: 133). Grounded theory was applied, in which recurring patterns were categorised to encourage theory building (Strauss and Corbin 1998). As interactionist studies indicate, formal accounts of institutions seldom reflect the informal realities of that "living world" (Atkinson and Housley 2003: 169) and therefore the aim was to unmask the backstage reality (Punch 2009).

Introducing Organisational Police Culture(s)

Culture is "invisible" (Schein 1999: 8) and notoriously difficult to define but is evident within the attitudes, behaviours and practices of any workforce (Anthony 1994). Cultural cognitions are held by groups rather than individuals and modified over time due to critical evaluation and experience (Sackmann 1991; Schein 1999; Deal and Kennedy 1999). Edgar Schein defines organisational culture as:

> [a] pattern of shared basic assumptions invented, discovered or developed by a given group as it learns to cope with its problems of external adaptation and internal integration, that has worked well enough to be considered valid, and to be taught to new members as the correct way to perceive, think, and feel in relations to those problems. (Schein 1997 [1985]: 6)

Organisational culture is found in the shared beliefs and assumptions that gradually come to be "taken for granted" and which bind organisational members together akin to "social or normative glue" (Lewis 1980 as cited in Smircich 1983; Balthazard et al. 2006: 711). Culture has positive attributes in that it is stable, predictable (Schein 1999) and comforting to the rank and file providing "continuity and identity" (Hampden-Turner 1990: 21) and a sense of belonging to the group. Yet, police culture is often described in disparaging terms and is deemed to be "the source of all policing ills" (Rowe 2014: 125). Police culture is largely associated with negative values and attitudes (Chan 1996, 2005) and is often used to explain why "nothing seems to work" (Hampden-Turner 1990: 1).

How Culture(s) Develop

Organisational culture can be located within institutional practices that develop through people formulating informal working rules. Reiner suggests that such "craft rules" are manifested through stories, myths, legends and jokes (Reiner 2010). Practitioners follow "scripts" in given situations which they add to the practical tool kit and communicate to each other through storytelling (Shearing and Ericson 1991). The stories that police officers exchange are not simply "war stories" (Van Maanen 1978b: 297; Smith and Gray 1985) which exemplify impressive heroic encounters or exciting car chases. Through the use of concrete and specific examples, stories carry meaning (Crank 2016: 216–217) and are passed from officer to officer, serving to guide and initiate the newer recruits into the prevailing culture (Holdaway 1983; Deal and Kennedy 1999; Waddington 1999a). In a world of uncertainty, stories provide vicarious learning and "common sense direction" for officers (Holdaway 1983: 139), guiding them as to the "way we [police] do things" around here (Van Maanen 1978b: 301; Schein 1999: 24).

Officers rely on storytelling, "trial and error" and repetitive experience (Barnard 1976: xiv; Bayley and Bittner 1984: 50) in the making of decisions. They learn how to manage their workload and "what works" (Crank 2016: 213–214), improvising (Shearing and Ericson 1991) and modifying their approach when strategies prove ineffective. In this way officers continually refer to and update their back catalogue or "reference library," utilising the toolkit to problem-solve and make sense of situations that they encounter. This process has been termed as establishing a "vocabulary of precedents" (Mills 1940 as cited in Crank 2016). Therefore beliefs, craft rules and "precedent" guide decision-making and in turn structure action or inaction.

Earlier work suggests that frontline officers and management cops represent *two* separate subcultures (Reuss-Ianni and Ianni 1983; Van Maanen 1978c). Yet since then further research has proffered that there are numerous segmented and specialised subcultures within police units (Manning 1978: 244; Paoline 2003) which divide along departmental or professional lines, each with a partisanship towards their own group (Chan 1996; Hannagan 2005; Coliandris and Rogers 2008).

The Socialisation of New Recruits

Through this process of socialisation, new recruits are susceptible to organisational influences, particularly in the first four years (Van Maanen 1978b). From the perspective of the new recruit, established frontline operational officers have the highest credibility because they routinely interpret policies, procedures and legislation, reflected in Deal and Kennedy's "heroic figures" (1999). Socialisation not only influences new inductees but involves a "grooming" process of "dismantling the incoming identity of the new recruit" in order to "rebuild" (Manning and Van Maanen 1978: 269). Such socialisation imbues new recruits with a "blueprint" (Cole 2010: 92) of how to behave in order to achieve internal "fit," which is not necessarily aligned with that individual's value system. A further consideration is the dichotomy between the "old guard and the new guard" (Graef 1989: 12), with established police officers or "dinosaurs" (Crank 2016: 318) resisting the unknown that is "change" and new recruits possibly accepting that progression is needed, yet often acquiescing to the perceived competent voice of experience.

Consequently, the training of new recruits is said to be "limited" by the influence of strong "street cop" culture (Chan 1996). Referred to as "plastics," police trainers are often derided by operational officers unless they are active practitioners in the field. New recruits often hear experienced officers deriding formal police training as "bullshit," suggesting officers should "forget everything you've learned" at training school (Van Maanen 1978b: 306; Bittner 1978: 49; Crank 2016: 270). Furthermore, such cultural influences make new recruits vulnerable to "unlearn" because once out in the field they "become indoctrinated with the old culture" (Hannagan 2005: 228), with old habits and traditions remaining largely intact, despite the existence of better educated officers (Manning 1978). Charman's research findings reinforce this, with new recruits eager to culturally assimilate to their new group and affording a superior status to "on the job" learning, as opposed to training school (2017: 319).

Discretion and Selective Enforcement

Such is the "low visibility" nature of their work which is often unsupervised (Goldstein 1960: 543; Holdaway 1983: 165; Klockars 1985: 94), frontline officers have the latitude to wield broad powers of discretion, making relatively "unfettered choices" (Brown 1981: 131) as to how to deal with an incident. Discretion is the freedom that officers have to make choices about which laws will be enforced and when (Brown 1981; Klockars 1985). Klockars refers to police discretion as "selective enforcement," because officers have a degree of freedom concerning which laws will be enforced (Klockars 1985: 93; also, Goldstein 1960 and Waddington 1999b: 331). However, it must be noted that the use of discretion is not always inappropriate. Skolnick suggests that if an officer is influenced by their own *personal views* when making decisions, then this is deemed to be unauthorised discretion (1994). Because of this freedom, first, officers rarely have to defend the selective decisions they make from any comeback or criticism (Klockars 1985); and second, without censure this means they are able to deviate from law or organisational policy (Reiner 2010). Third, academics advance the view that by officers refusing to enforce some laws they wrongly act as judge and jury (Brown 1981; Edwards 1986: 232). In this way, police officers act as a street "bureaucrat" in making political decisions (Lipsky 2010 [1980]). Fourth, because informal working rules are developed from the bottom, this thwarts the ability of forces to successfully initiate policing reforms from the top (Bellingham 2000; Chan 2005; Punch 2009). Within an HBA context, this study will explore the gap between the corporate vision the organisation wants to achieve[3] (its service ideals) and the "reality of practice" (Lipsky 2010 [1980]: xvi).

Policing: Bad Apples or Rotten Orchards?

Whether police officers are perceived as *individually* responsible for their actions (bad apple) or situated within a systemically corrupt system or "rotten orchard" (Punch 2003 as cited in Punch 2009: 2) largely depends on whether the reader accepts the classic or more fluid interpretations of police cultures(s). The orthodox perspective of police culture suggests there is a deterministic universality about the attitudes and behaviours of police officers in all sharing similar structural patterns (Reiner 2000) and possessing a monolithic organisational mindset (Sklansky 2007). To this end, classic police culture scholars have attempted to map particular behaviours to officers by advocating that they align to a particular "type." For instance, the "professional" has the emotional intelligence to use violence where necessary in a principled way and is adept at verbal communication without the use of coercive force, which is a latent power. The enforcer, like Reiner's "new centurion," is a responsive individual who is effective in acting in the heat of conflict but who does not always appreciate the need for restraint (Muir 1977; Reiner 2010). Reiner's "uniform carrier" and Muir's (1977) "avoider" are similar in type in representing the cynical and disillusioned workshy officer (Manning 1977) that is lazy and incompetent (Muir 1977; also, Brown 1981: 94). Such officers "shirk the work as much as possible" (Reiner 1978 as cited in Reiner 2010: 137). Punch refers to these officers as "ducker and diver(s)" because they try not to work too hard and he contends that they joined the police for instrumental reasons (2009: 23). Such "loafers" fail to "back-up" others when there is a call for assistance and often the more competent officers are left having to tidy up the neglectful officers' "mess" in terms of crime enquiries (Van Maanen 1978a).

Contemporary scholars have departed from the contention that there is one monolithic police "culture" arguing that such typologies and schemas are reductionist and tend to overly simplify, making it difficult to recognise the "differences" in officers' decisions and behaviours, which obscures the complexity of the police identity. In effect "all we see is blue" (Sklansky 2007: 21; also, Waddington 1999a). Sklansky attributes this "blind spot" to those who tend to pool ideas about the police subculture, rather than showing evidence of it (2007: 22). This assumed homogeneity and universality of police officers also leaves little prospect for any organisational change (Chan 2005). The orthodox approach depicts officers as passive bystanders within a socialisation process that appears to override their will and individual agency (Chan 1997, 2005). Officers are not passive recipients collectively indoctrinated into adhering to cultural practices. They are active participants in constructing, shaping (Shearing and Ericson 1991) and reproducing (Sewell 1992; Chan 1996; Crank 2016) such structures. It is incumbent on individuals to accommodate or "reject" the "monolithic" influence of police culture (Loftus 2009: 72; Chan 1996: 111). Moreover, labelling an entire group (police officers) as imbued with the *same* characteristics is problematic and undoubtedly results in "crude generalisations" (Hobbs 1991: 606). This is far too simplistic an interpretation of police culture(s).

Like Chan, Brown promotes individualism in suggesting that officers react differently to the demands and pressures of their role. He suggests that officers combine value and empirical judgements based on their experience, and thus their decisions are structured by their own belief system (1981). Equally, Shearing also distinguishes that ethical hard-working officers focused on doing the "right thing" often "recognise the police subculture, but do not identify with it" (1981: 33). As alluded to by HMIC (Her Majesty's Inspectorate of Constabulary; 1999: 29), it is contradictory to suggest that all officers share the same "collective attitude," as those nominated for bravery awards who go above and beyond the call of duty are apparently part of this same (sometimes problematic) "culture."

Latterly, academics advocate that a more fluid interpretation is necessary, which illustrates the complex and multifaceted nature of police culture(s) (Chan 1997; Foster 2003; Sklansky 2007; Cockcroft 2007, 2013). Orthodox conceptions overlook factors such as the differences across internal departmental areas, policing across jurisdictions and the external impact of wider social change on police officers (Chan 1997, 2005). Officers are nestled within a time and social context, which shapes not only their views but the way they police (Cockcroft 2007). Some scholars have been inclined to accept that both propositions can coexist. They recognise the variation and complexity of cultures along with a "stubborn" endurance of some classic cultural patterns (Loftus 2009: 198), supporting the contention that police culture is "neither monolithic nor unchanging" (Reiner 2000: 106).

Policing and Researching Honour-Based Abuse

HBA is a specific form of domestic abuse and the operational policing of this crime falls under the auspices of public protection. Domestic abuse is both high volume and high risk, with 12% of all crimes across England and Wales' 43 police forces being domestic abuse related, which is a 1% increase from 2016 (ONS 2016, 2018). Over two-thirds (69%) of cases flagged as domestic abuse related are for violence against the person offences. This correlates with Police Recorded Crime figures whereby violence makes up many domestic abuse crimes dealt with by the police (77%) (ONS 2018: 59). Police were asked to attend over 1.1 million domestic abuse-related incidents in the year ending March 2018. Of these incidents only 50% were subjected to a crime report (ONS 2018: 11). Despite the volume of domestic abuse cases attended by officers, only 4% of the police budget is spent on public protection, which equates to just over 9000 officers and staff across England and Wales (HMIC 2014b: 84).

Prior research suggests that police officers display unsympathetic attitudes when attending HBA incidents (Belur 2008; Gill 2011; Hanmer et al. 2013 [1989]). Of concern is the contention that HBA victims are left in greater danger as a result of policing interventions (Patel 2003; Phillips and Dustin 2004; Gill et al. 2012). Southall Black Sisters suggest that the problem lies not necessarily in the absence of UK laws and policies to support HBA victims, but in the poor application of these by some frontline police officers (HMIC 2014b: 122). Poor policing has hitherto been evident in high-profile UK honour killings, where a lack of recognition of HBA, coupled with inept and unsympathetic interventions, has resulted in police officers under-protecting victims, for example, Shafilea Ahmed (2003), Banaz Mahmod (2006), Rania Alayed (2013), Fakhanda Younis (2013) and Sabeen Thandi (2013) (Dyer 2015). Banaz Mahmod reported harassment and death threats from family members to police officers on five separate occasions, and yet a frontline officer relayed the information back to perpetrators and dismissed her claims of impending death as "melodramatic", failing to safeguard her based on her unwillingness to prosecute (Silvestri and Crowther-Dowey 2008: 95; Payton 2011; Gill 2011). Reluctance to prosecute is a recurring theme fully explored in

Chap. 4. Research also suggests that police officers, social workers and other professionals often collude with perpetrators in accepting their interpretation of a situation (Siddiqui and Patel 2003; HMIC 2014b: 52) and this concept is critically assessed in Chap. 3.

There has been a growing concern that police forces fail to identify and record HBA crimes (Dyer 2015: 8). This is exacerbated in that HBA has no single crime type. HBA can be crimed under a gamut of disparate offences ranging from murder, unexplained death (suicide), fear of or actual forced marriage, controlling sexual activity, domestic abuse (including psychological, physical, sexual, financial or emotional abuse), child abuse, rape, kidnap, false imprisonment, threats to kill, assault, harassment and forced abortion (NPCC policing strategy 2015: 15). Consequently, determining the national statistical scale of HBA is problematic and it is contended that government figures reflect the tip of an iceberg. The massaging of UK police crime figures across the 1980s and 1990s led to the creation of the National Crime Recording Standards in 2002, in which officers were obligated to follow guidance on when and whether to record crimes (Home Office 2003). The pressure to "get tough on crime," increase detections and improve police efficiency led to New Labour's development of Police Performance indicators (2000). And yet little research has been conducted in the last 20 years about how these influences might have shaped the routine construction of a "crime" (Reiner and Newburn 2008: 363). Despite a recent increase in Forced Marriage referrals, charges and prosecutions (2017–2018), there has been a recent fall in HBA-flagged referrals, charges, prosecutions and convictions across 2017–2018 (CPS 2018: 12). Chapter 4 will critically explore police crime recording in an HBA context.

Government reports demonstrate numerous examples of police cultural practices in action (HMIC 2014a, 2015; House of Commons PASC 2014) and yet these often attribute poor domestic abuse outcomes to insufficient officer training and lack of awareness. Although there have been several illuminating ethnographic studies on police organisational culture and discretionary practices (Young 1991; Westmarland 2001; Loftus 2009), such studies have often demonstrated discretion across a wide range of policing activities and crime types. As acknowledged by Myhill and Johnson, there has been little research focus on how police construct and administer domestic violence (2016) and certainly none in relation to the specificities of HBA. Furthermore, Schein suggests that a cultural assessment of an organisational setting such as the police is valuable when tied to a specific organisational problem (Schein 1999: 86). Therefore, this research is specific in its focus on police discretionary practices applied solely within an HBA context.

The present research makes a significant contribution to research in its unique analytical inclusion of classified police data, which was not a feature of previous HBA studies. This research study will benefit police forces in England and Wales, the Home Office, the College of Policing and other public bodies involved in safeguarding such as social services, health and the education sector. Non-government organisations can also use the research findings to feedforward into prevention practices. As female victims push the boundaries by becoming more empowered and asserting their equal rights, such as obtaining educational qualifications or economic independence, they face more violence, repression and punishment (Niaz 2003; Jafri 2009: 7; Chesler and Bloom 2012). This is termed the backlash hypothesis (Barkan 2012). The Centre for Policy on Ageing suggested that by 2016 the ethnic minority population of England and Wales would increase to 12.1 million, constituting 21% and by 2051 this figure will increase to 27% of the total UK population (Lievesley 2012). Given the cultural and ethnic nature of this crime type, it is imperative that there is a more effective framework for policing and safeguarding HBA victims. It is vital not only that this crime type is understood by practitioners, but that they recognise the impact and implications that ineffective policing interventions can have on victims of crime.

HBA and Domestic Abuse: Cultural Distinctions and Barriers to Reporting

There are notable features differentiating HBA from traditional constructs of violence against women which provide a distinctively cultural nuance to the crimes. First, statistically honour killings are predominantly "Muslim-on-Muslim" crimes, representing 91% of perpetrators worldwide (Chesler 2010). Chesler and Bloom are critical of those who treat honour crimes as a "universal problem, not an Islamic issue" (2012).

Racial differences and fear of racist practices from professional bodies, including the police, also make this crime distinctive from traditional forms of domestic abuse. This can inhibit HBA victims from reporting incidents or pursuing prosecutions. It was the Macpherson report (1999), concerning the UK race hate murder of Stephen Lawrence (1993), which challenged whether officers were effective in policing ethnic minority groups (Reiner and Newburn 2008: 353). Unlike Scarman's report into the Brixton riots, Macpherson went further in labelling all police forces as "institutionally racist," diagnosing the cultural failure of the structural institution (1999: 56) and discrediting the notion of a few "rotten apples" amongst police officers (Macpherson 1999: 43). Researching deaths in police custody, in which 38% of victims (2011) were from Black and Minority Ethnic (BME) communities (Baker 2016), and the disproportionate and discriminatory application of stop and search procedures, in which six times as many Black Britons are unnecessarily searched compared to their white counterparts (Bowling and Phillips 2007), all strongly point towards discriminatory practices by some officers. Despite intensive diversity training and systematic monitoring of police practices since the advent of Macpherson's recommendations, rather than eradicate racism, this has precipitated "covert racism" (Holdaway 2013: 226), which has gone "underground" (Foster et al. 2005; Loftus 2009: 74), with some officers choosing their words, and their audiences, much more carefully (Morant and Edwards 2011: 287; Loftus 2009). There is also a perception of racism from victims, even if it is not palpable. Women fear racist attitudes may be levelled at their community should they complain of domestic abuse. Approaching mainstream authorities is perceived by the community as an "act of betrayal" (Mama 2008: 296; Haj-Yahia 2011: 33), with victims being accused of being traitors to their race (Thiara 2013). This was evident when the Manchester domestic abuse helpline reported reduced rates of contact from Muslim women in the aftermath of the 9/11 terrorist attacks (2001–2002). This supports the contention that domestic abuse is intimately connected with broader social structures that implicate all kinds of intersections with race, class, culture and gender relations (Burman et al. 2004).

As representatives of the dominant group, the police are said to engender stereotypical images of minority groups. This can result in unbalanced and unfair policing and distances the police from forging relationships with minority communities (Huisman et al. 2005; Hasisi 2008; Belur 2008). Minority communities can feel both over-policed as suspects and under-policed as victims, which can reduce their confidence in and willingness to cooperate with the police (Chakraborti 2007: 119; Mclaughlin 2007; Hasisi 2008). HBA victims are inherently mistrustful of "outsiders" and tense relations between police and minority communities can inhibit victims from reporting crimes and pursuing prosecutions (Gill 2004; Pease and Flood 2008; Hasisi 2008). Equally, since many immigrants have maintained cultural codes from their homeland, many will hesitate to contact police in the host country, as they may have experienced a poor relationship with police in their country of origin (Hasisi 2008).

Black women perceive that they receive an "inferior service" comparable to white victims of domestic abuse (Belur 2008: 436; also, Yarrow 2005), which can prevent victims from accessing services (Burman et al. 2004: 338). Victims are perceived by the host nation as "less authentic 'sons of the soil', less reliable and patriotic than the rest" (Parekh 2006: 234). This exacerbates victim reluctance to report crimes and damages police and community relations (Belur 2008). Although domestic abuse is often deemed a "soft" policing arena (McCarthy 2012), Patel argues that this "soft" approach very much depends on which section of the community is being policed (2003: 165). Poor policing interventions can often be interpreted along racial lines, with victims feeling "doubly victimised," first, by the perpetrator based on their gender, and second, along race lines when authorities fail to provide support and interventions (Gill 2004: 466; Patel 2008: 33; also, Gupta 2003):

> We're different, we're treated differently by our own because we're women, we're treated differently outside because we're Asian. (Chew-Graham et al. 2002: 342)

The very existence of honour codes and the fact that honour is "reclaimed" by abuse or killing (Sen 2005: 61; Chesler 2009) distinguishes it from the traditional domestic abuse framework. Ballard is categorical in labelling honour abuse as a "cultural crime" because notions of honour in English law and contemporary Britain are not similar to South Asian notions of honour (2011). To exemplify, in the 1999 murder case of female Pal Kaur, preserving her sexual morality, in terms of establishing the victim was *not* having an affair with her brother-in-law (the murderer), was more important to relatives than the murder of the female victim herself (Johal 2003). Thus, preserving the chastity of women and retaining male "honour" is prioritised above the life of women (Eisner and Ghuneim 2013; Jafri 2009: 138).

Ironically, victims are not only preoccupied about damaging family honour (Pease and Flood 2008; Siddiqui 2005) but about further jeopardising their *own* honour by reporting the abuse (Gill 2014). South Asian women are socialised into believing they are to blame for the violence and perceive it as "self-inflicted" (Burman et al. 2004: 339; Pease and Flood 2008; Gill 2013). Seeking outside help can highlight their own feelings of shame and exacerbates the perceived dishonour heaped on families (Osterman and Brown 2011; Gill 2014). This is particularly so when the case involves sexual assault. Because women are seen as items of male property (Niaz 2003; Dogan 2011; Payton 2011), any violation, such as a rape or sexual assault, symbolically taints the victims as unclean "carrier[s] of pollution" (Gorringe 2006: 237; Jafri 2009: 58). In some countries, the family resolves for the victim to marry the rapist,[4] which paradoxically restores family honour and reflects the low value placed on women (Okin 1999). Becoming pregnant as a result of rape or incest could warrant the death of the woman in order to expunge the violation (Meetoo and Mirza 2011). On these grounds it is therefore unsurprising that women retract sexual assault allegations, due to the adverse cultural stigma associated with being a victim of sexual assault. Police and Crown Prosecution Service (CPS) advocates certainly need to be aware of such complex cultural factors when trying to rationalise and manage a victim retraction.

A further distinction with traditional domestic abuse is that HBA perpetrators are often not the intimate partners (NPCC 2015: 14). Over half of the cases in a study of 124 BME women involved perpetrators that were family relatives (Thiara 2013). It should therefore be anticipated that victims do not want to prosecute close relatives that they love. In these situations, family members often pressurise the victim into remaining and accepting the abuse (ibid), which exacerbates the isolation felt by the victim. This is not a feature of traditional domestic abuse where victims often have *someone* to trust when fleeing the perpetrator.

HBA is often condoned and facilitated by multiple family or community members, making it a collective crime (Chesler 2009; Payton 2011; Thiara 2013; NPCC 2015). This is certainly apparent in the research. This aids in "legitimising" the act. Such co-opting does not occur in traditional domestic violence settings (Oberwittler and Kasselt 2011: 2). In traditional Western domestic abuse cases, a husband who kills his wife is rarely assisted by members of his family of origin or by his in-laws (Chesler 2010) and it is rare for brothers to kill sisters or for male cousins to kill female cousins (Chesler 2009). Furthermore, whilst fathers may kill infants and children in child abuse cases, there is no cultural pattern and it is very rare for Western fathers to specifically target, hurt or kill their teenage daughters (Chesler 2009, 2010).

The attitude of perpetrators in HBA situations differs greatly from traditional domestic abusers. The extremes of honour killing are often valourised with perpetrators proudly displaying their handcuffs on arrest (Jafri 2009: 11; Gill 2013; Gill and Brah 2014: 75). The act itself is ascribed a heroic status (Chesler 2009, 2010) and for the benefit of a presumed audience, what Payton alludes to as "violence as theatre" (2011: 74). Equally, a failure to maintain order and control in the house affects the reputation of the household head, and he will be recognised as "emasculated" (Reddy 2008: 307; Welden 2010: 385; Eshareturi et al. 2014: 372) or "weak" if he fails to remedy the situation. Daughters must be "brought into line." Comparably in traditional forms of domestic abuse, the perpetrator is not seeking any collective recognition and those behaviours are often confined to the secretive private sphere involving "one word against the other" (Brandon and Hafez 2008). Finally, the role of women in "policing" the behaviour of other women, as well as the potential for female participation in violence or murder (Sen 2005; Rew et al. 2013), is a distinctive feature not identified in traditional forms of domestic abuse research. Such complexities and hidden agendas in HBA create complex minefields for both victim and law enforcement to navigate through.

HBA is a distinct form of abuse and should not be conflated with traditional forms of domestic abuse. This was evident when survivors, activists, professionals and academics raised collective opposition to a Private Members Bill (Aggravated Murder of and Violence Against Women) due for a scheduled second reading in the House of Commons (24 March 2017). The proposal was to prohibit the widely used term of "honour" within HBA. Doing so could have simplified the complexities of HBA and aligned it with traditional forms of domestic abuse. This may have led to cultural specificities being overlooked and as a result the bill was withdrawn (IKWRO 2017).

Belur is critical of subsuming HBA within the traditional domestic abuse framework because Asian women are being "conveniently pushed into the box labelled domestic violence" rather than being given "special attention" in terms of examining existing institutionally racist effects of police practices and policies (2008: 429). However, this argument works from the premise that officers' practices are systemically "racist." Black's research, by comparison, did not show that race was an issue in officers' selective enforcement decisions (1971). Waddington suggests that entrenched racist views are prevalent within wider culture rather than being distinctive to the police setting and he argues there is an absence of comparative data to establish that police officers, more than other occupations, exhibit such prone behaviours (1999a). Indeed, the rationale behind integrating HBA within a wider domestic abuse framework was to *avoid* a racist reaction from the state (Welchman 2014: xi).

Yet isolating HBA as a "cultural" phenomenon can be equally dangerous, as it inadvertently engenders a "hands off" (Carens 2006: 8) distancing approach by professionals within public institutions. Professionals, keen to embrace diversity and multiculturalism, tend to prioritise cultural and religious practices over the individual human rights of women (Okin 1999; Phillips and Dustin 2004; Burman et al. 2004; Gill and Mitra-Khan 2010). Furthermore, academics suggest that professionals fear being accused of "interfering in the culture" and being labelled as "racist" (Siddiqui 2003: 80; Burman et al. 2004; Gill 2013) and therefore such cultural tolerance has led to avoidance behaviours and self-policing. Race anxiety[5] by professionals engenders the misconception that Asian women can "sort their own problems out" (Hanmer 2013

[1989]: 103) and that minority communities are essentially "self-governing" (Burman et al. 2004: 344; Southall Black Sisters 2001: 1; Siddiqui 2005). State *over* preoccupation with culture can therefore act as a barrier to effective public service provision (Burman et al. 2004; Meetoo and Mirza 2011: 43).

It is critical therefore to understand the relational aspects of black and white women's experiences, rather than address these as different experiences. Focusing on race and culture "difference" may address diversity but crucially overlooks the power, control and inequality (Thiara and Gill 2010) evident within the mainstream debate on the gendered nature of domestic abuse. In Burman et al.'s study, statutory services applied a "blanket approach" in which there was a tendency to "treat everyone the same" (2004: 348). We should not "splinter" and divide women's experiences (Thiara and Gill 2010: 35), but neither should we conflate the two crime areas as the same by overlooking cultural specificities. There is a danger that in doing so public policy will concede to the practices of the majority as unquestioned norms (Phillips and Dustin 2004: 531). Cultural practices should not be used by professionals to provide a two-tier set of policing requirements that cater differently between dominant and minority groups. When providing services, police officers must be sensitive and adjust accordingly to the cultural distinctiveness of minorities (Hasisi 2008). It is therefore argued that a balancing act is required between overlooking culture and over preoccupation with it. Cultural nuances should be *considered* without using culture as a justification or shield for criminal practices. HBA is a distinct phenomenon (Chesler 2009), clearly delineated from traditional constructs of domestic abuse (Sen 2005: 61), although, as the research will highlight, there are some key overlapping commonalities. Such commonalities are not only about the treatment, power and control wielded against victims, but in the manner of policing and professional responses to violence against women. HBA is undoubtedly a complex crime (Roberts et al. 2014: 39) and without considering both the cultural and gendered elements found in "traditional" domestic abuse, this crime category, as well as its victims, will be fundamentally misunderstood. It is therefore argued that it would be a mistake to separate HBA from the mainstream domestic abuse policing framework, as this would strategically "quarantine" it, which generates more problems than it solves.

Structure of the Book

Chapter 2 focuses on the research design methodology applied to this study. It outlines the philosophical approach of symbolic interactionism. The rationale for utilising electronic documentary data from police systems and semi-structured interviews with police detectives is explored. The benefits and limitations of the two phases are probed. Latter sections reflect on the key ethical considerations; the use of grounded theory as a means of analysis and the positionality of the researcher. Chapters 3, 4, 5, 6 and 7 comprise of the empirical findings which address all three objectives by examining police decision-making and stratagems applied when investigating HBA incidents. Equally, all chapters determine the impact that such discretionary practices have on the service provision to victims and isolate what factors appear to influence and drive officer practices.

Chapter 3 establishes those at heightened risks of HBA and the triggers which precipitate the crime. It distillates the extent to which professionals[6] are influenced by perpetrator narratives. The obscure arena of vulnerable adult abuse is examined and how professionals sometimes deny vulnerability, attributing "freewill" and consent to those lacking capacity. Conversely, the poor mental health of HBA victims is exaggerated by perpetrators, with illogical explanations sometimes left unchallenged by professionals. Findings expose goal displacement and the medicalising of victims. Labels are traded, with the perpetrators depicted as reasonable and acting in the "best interests" of victims. Conversely, teenage girls are portrayed as precipitating problems due to their perceived "wayward" behaviour. Whether officers can distinguish "genuine" from "non-genuine" victims and "truth" from "lies" is critically assessed.

Chapter 4 assesses crime recording decisions made by police officers at HBA incidents. It exposes the "grey figure" of crime, which are incidents reported to officers but not necessarily subjected to a crime report. Incident to crime conversion rates are surveyed across a four-year period (2011–2014 inclusive) followed by an in-depth examination of crime recording decisions for the 100 cases analysed, complemented by interview data. In justifying no-crime decisions, officers rely on perceived legalities and formal rules, such as the National Crime Recording Standard (NCRS) requirement for "victim confirmation" of crimes, as well as bias and subjective judgement. Performance target pressures and pre-empting CPS no-charge decisions are also explored. Overwhelmingly, findings illustrate that victim reluctance adversely impacts on officers' no-crime decisions. Manufacturing victim reluctance is effective in validating police inaction and in officers circumventing perceived "wasted workload." If it is not crimed, it has technically "not happened," which abrogates officers of responsibilities around investigation, prosecution and safeguarding.

Chapter 5 unearths the centrality of the craft of language, particularly the written word, in providing a convincing veneer for some officers to justify inappropriate "no-crime" decisions. It examines the disparity between the initial report made to call handlers and the final documentary "write-off." It establishes the extent to which supervisors are complicit in officers' discretionary decisions. Such discretion is accomplished through the use of quasi-legal and procedural rules and subjective judgements; omissions in data and alterations to language. The "family dispute" theme and the unwillingness of victims in disclosing offences replicate traditional domestic abuse explanations. This was demonstrated through the examination of DASH risk assessments and other related electronic documentation. Such stratagems dilute or entirely negate the risks to victims, stifle legitimate lines of enquiry, decriminalise cases and wrongly justify officers' no-crime decisions.

Chapter 6 is an excursus and explores the relatively obscure arena of females who commit or facilitate HBA, which transpired to be a prevalent theme. Although academics confirm the tacit involvement of women in honour abuse (Roberts 2014: 71; Eisner and Ghuneim 2013; Balzani 2011; Sen 2005), extant literature does not explain the functions and manifest behaviours exhibited by female perpetrators. Therefore, the roles played by women, specifically mothers, mothers-in-law and sisters, are explored. Abuse is categorised into six themes: violence; violence due to pregnancy; hard *and* soft psychological abuse; ostracism of victims; women being complicit and turning a "blind eye" to violence. This chapter identifies that mothers play a fundamental role in perpetrating HBA, largely against teenage daughters. The extent to which women act under duress or are willing participants in abusing other women is examined. The chapter reconsiders whether professionals should automatically trust mothers to safeguard children.

The final empirical chapter assesses the efficacy of professional interventions (predominantly police and children's social care) when HBA against children is reported. The prevalent theme of mediation and reconciling child victims back home to risk situations is evident in 73% of cases (16/22), which has adverse long-term impacts. Children's social care apply working agreements and section 20 voluntary arrangements. Professionals attest to making decisions out of deference to victims' wishes by suggesting that perpetrators cooperate with advice imparted during mediation. Yet, these stratagems serve to justify professional decision-making. The impact is that children's wishes are often overridden; the care system is circumvented; victims are retained with abusers and internal organisational demands are prioritised above children's best interests. The cost of care and extant workloads affect the selective preferences of some professionals.

Chapter 8 presents the central findings of the study along with key recommendations. Police officers do not reflect one monolithic police culture, with classic depictions failing to reflect the nuanced and complex interactions between victims, perpetrators and professionals. The dominant factors shaping professional decision-making revolved around whether the victim was deemed as blameworthy, whether professionals mistrusted victims as "non-genuine" or whether the victim was reluctant to prosecute. It is argued that many of the patterned inappropriate discretionary practices identified were functional strategies and centralised on unscrupulous officers providing rationale to decriminalise incidents and support their "no-crime" decisions, which included "accepting" the narratives advanced by perpetrators. The most salient trait was the pragmatism of officers in their preoccupation with personal workload reduction. The impact of these decisions left victims, including children and vulnerable adults, exposed to secondary victimisation; under-policed, underprotected and with unmet needs.

Notes

1. Also referred to as occupational culture.
2. The word "professionals" in this book refers mainly to police officers, but in other situational contexts (particularly Chap. 7), it can include social workers, teachers, healthcare professionals and housing officials.

3. Such as force priorities, vision and mission statements.
4. This was the same position under the English common law (1782) where the rape victim was deemed as "damaged goods" and rape convictions were nullified if the victim agreed to wed the rapist (Alexander 1995).
5. Professionals fear accusations of racism being levelled and therefore do not proactively manage the case. This can also be referred to as reverse racism or possessing cultural sensitivities.
6. The word "professionals" in this book refers mainly to police officers, but in other situational contexts (particularly Chap. 7), it can include social workers, teachers, healthcare professionals and housing officials.

References

Akpinar, A. (2003). The honour/shame complex revisited: Violence against women in the migration context. *Women's Studies International Forum, 26*(5), 425–442.

Alexander, D. (1995, Winter). Twenty years of Morgan: A criticism of the subjectivist view of mens rea and rape in Great Britain. *Pace International Law Review, 7*(1), 207–246.

Anthony, P. (1994). *Managing culture*. Buckingham: Open University Press.

Atkinson, P., & Housley, W. (2003). *Interactionism*. London: Sage Publications.

Baker, D. (2016). *Deaths after police contact: Constructing accountability in the 21st century* (Critical Criminological Perspective). London: Palgrave Macmillan.

Baldry, A., Pagliaro, S., & Porcaro, C. (2013, May). The rule of law at time of masculine honor: Afghan police attitudes and intimate partner violence. *Group Processes & Intergroup Relations, 16*(3), 363–374.

Ballard, R. (2011). Honour killing? Or just plain homicide? In L. Holden (Ed.), *Cultural expertise and litigation: Patterns, conflicts, narratives* (pp. 124–147). London: Routledge.

Balthazard, P., Cooke, R., & Potter, R. (2006). Dysfunctional culture, dysfunctional organisation: Capturing the behavioural norms that form organisational culture and drive performance. *Journal of Managerial Psychology, 21*(8), 709–732.

Balzani, M. (2011). Masculinities and violence against women in South Asian communities: Transnational perspectives. In R. Thiara & A. Gill (Eds.), *Violence against women in South Asian communities: Issues for policy and practice* (pp. 80–101). London: Jessica Kingsley.

Bano, S. (2011). Tackling crimes of honour: Evaluating the social and legal responses for combating forced marriages in the UK. In M. Idriss & T. Abbas (Eds.), *Honour, violence, women and Islam* (pp. 201–217). Oxfordshire: Routledge.

Barkan, S. (2012). *Criminology: A sociological understanding* (5th ed.). Upper Saddle River, NJ: Pearson Education Limited.

Barnard, C. (1976). Foreward. In H. Simon (Ed.), *Administrative behavior: A study of decision-making processes in administrative organisations* (3rd ed.). London: Collier Macmillan Publishers.

Bayley, D., & Bittner, E. (1984). Learning the skills of policing. *Law and Contemporary Problems, 47*(4), 35–59.

Becker, H. (2008). Outsiders. In E. Mclaughlin, J. Muncie, & G. Hughes (Eds.), *Criminological perspectives* (2nd ed., pp. 239–247). London: Sage Publications.

Belfrage, H., Strand, S., Ekman, L., & Hasselborg, A. (2012, Spring). Assessing risk of patriarchal violence with honour as a motive: Six years experience using the patriarch checklist. *International Journal of Police Science & Management, 14*(1), 20–29.

Bellingham, T. (2000). Police culture and the need for change. *Police Journal, 73*, 31–41.

Belur, J. (2008). Is policing domestic violence institutionally racist? A case study of south Asian women. *Policing and Society, 18*(4), 426–444.

Bittner, E. (1978). The functions of the police in modern society. In P. Manning & J. Van Maanen (Eds.), *Policing: A view from the street* (pp. 32–50). Santa Monica, CA: Goodyear Publishing Company Inc.

Black, D. (1971). The social organisation of arrest. *Stanford Law Review, 23*, 1087–1111.

Bowling, B., & Phillips, C. (2007). Disproportionate and discriminatory: Reviewing the evidence on police stop and search. *The Modern Law Review, 70*(6), 936–961.

Brandon, J., & Hafez, S. (2008). *Crimes of the community: Honour-based violence in the UK*. London: Centre for Social Cohesion.

Brown, M. (1981). *Working the street: Police discretion and the dilemmas of reform*. New York, NY: Russell Sage Foundation.

Burman, N., Smailes, S., & Chandler, K. (2004). Culture as a barrier to service provision and delivery: Domestic violence services for minoritized women. *Critical Social Policy, 24*(3), 332–357.

Carens, J. (2006). *Culture, citizenship and community: A contextual exploration of justice as evenhanded-ness*. Oxford: Oxford University Press.

Chakraborti, N. (2007). Policing Muslim communities. In M. Rowe (Ed.), *Policing beyond Macpherson: Issues in policing, race and society* (pp. 107–127). Devon: Willan Publishing.

Chan, J. (1996). Changing police culture. *British Journal of Criminology, 36*(1), 109–133.

Chan, J. (1997). *Changing police culture: Policing in a multicultural society.* Cambridge: Cambridge University Press.

Chan, J. (2005). Changing police culture. In T. Newburn (Ed.), *Policing: Key readings* (pp. 338–361). Devon: Willan.

Charman, S. (2017). *Police socialisation, identity and culture: Becoming blue.* London: Palgrave Macmillan.

Charmaz, K. (2014). *Constructing grounded theory* (2nd ed.). London: Sage Publications.

Chesler, P. (2009, Spring). Are honor killings simply domestic violence? *Middle East Quarterly, 16*(2), 61–69.

Chesler, P. (2010, Spring). Worldwide trends in honor killings. *Middle East Quarterly, 17*(2), 3–11.

Chesler, P., & Bloom, N. (2012, Summer). Hindu vs. Muslim honor killings. *Middle East Quarterly, 19*(3), 43–52.

Chew-Graham, C., Bashir, C., Chantler, K., Burman, E., & Batsleer, J. (2002). South Asian women, psychological distress and self-harm: Lessons for primary care trusts. *Health & Social Care in the Community, 10*(5), 339–347.

Cihangir, S. (2013, May). Gender specific honor codes and cultural change. *Group Processes & Intergroup Relations, 16*(3), 319–333.

Cockcroft, T. (2007). Police culture(s): Some definitional, methodological and analytical considerations. In M. O'Neill, M. Marks, & A. Singh (Eds.), *Police occupational culture: New debates and directions* (pp. 85–102). Bingley: Emerald.

Cockcroft, T. (2013). *Police culture: Themes and concepts.* New York, NY: Routledge.

Cole, K. (2010). *Management: Theory and practice.* Frenchs Forest, NSW: Pearson.

Coliandris, G., & Rogers, C. (2008). Linking police culture, leadership and partnership-working. *Police Journal, 81*(2), 111–125.

Crank, J. (2016). *Understanding police culture* (2nd ed.). London: Routledge.

Creswell, J. (2014). *Research design: International student edition. Qualitative, quantitative, and mixed methods approaches* (4th ed.). London: Sage Publications.

Crown Prosecution Service (CPS). (2015). *Violence Against Women and Girls Crime Report (2014–2015).* London: CPS. [Online]. Retrieved February 27, 2016, from https://www.cps.gov.uk/publication.

Crown Prosecution Service. (2018). *Delivering justice: Violence Against Women and Girls Report (2017–2018)*. London: CPS. [Online]. Retrieved February 6, 2019, from https://www.cps.gov.uk/publication.

Deal, T., & Kennedy, A. (1999). *The new corporate culture*. London: Orion Business books.

Dogan, R. (2011). Is honor killing a Muslim phenomenon? Textual interpretations and cultural representations. *Journal of Muslim Minority Affairs, 31*(3), 423–440.

Dyer, E. (2015). *Honour killings in the UK*. London: The Henry Jackson Society.

Edwards, S. (1986). Police attitudes and dispositions in domestic disputes: The London study. *Police Journal, 59*(3), 230–241.

Eisner, M., & Ghuneim, L. (2013). Honour killing attitudes amongst adolescents in Amman, Jordan. *Aggressive Behaviour, 39*(5), 405–417.

Eshareturi, C., Lyle, C., & Morgan, A. (2014). Policy responses to honor-based violence: A cultural or national problem? *Journal of Aggression, Maltreatment & Trauma, 23*(4), 369–382.

Foster, J. (2003). Police cultures. In T. Newburn (Ed.), *Handbook of policing* (pp. 196–227). Devon: Willan.

Foster, J., Newburn, T., & Souhami, A. (2005). *Assessing the impact of the Stephen Lawrence Inquiry* (Home Office Research Study, 294). London: Home Office.

Gangoli, G., McCarry, M., & Razak, A. (2009). Child marriage or forced marriage? South Asian communities in North East England. *Children & Society, 23*(6), 418–429.

Gill, A. (2004). Voicing the silent fear: South Asian women's experiences of domestic violence. *Howard Journal of Criminal Justice, 43*(5), 465–483.

Gill, A. (2011). Reconfiguring 'honour'-based violence as a form of gendered violence. In M. Idriss & T. Abbas (Eds.), *Honour, violence, women and Islam* (pp. 218–231). Oxfordshire: Routledge.

Gill, A. (2013, October). Feminist reflections on researching so-called 'honour' killings. *Feminist Legal Studies, 21*(3), 241–261.

Gill, A. (2014). All they think about is honour: The murder of Shafilea Ahmed. In A. Gill, C. Strange, & K. Roberts (Eds.), *Honour killing and violence: Theory, policy and practice* (pp. 177–198). Hampshire: Palgrave Macmillan.

Gill, A., Begikhani, N., & Hague, G. (2012). Honour-based violence in Kurdish communities. *Women's Studies International Forum, 35*, 75–85.

Gill, A., & Brah, A. (2014). Interrogating cultural narratives about 'honour'-based violence. *European Journal of Women's Studies, 21*(1), 72–86.

Gill, A., & Mitra-Khan, T. (2010). Moving towards a 'multiculturalism without culture.' Constructing a victim-friendly human rights approach to forced marriage in the UK. In R. Thiara & A. Gill (Eds.), *Violence against women in South Asian communities: Issues for policy and practice* (pp. 128–155). London: Jessica Kingsley.

Glaser, B., & Strauss, A. (1967). *The discovery of grounded theory: Strategies for qualitative research*. Mill Valley, CA: Sociology Press.

Goldstein, J. (1960). Police discretion not to invoke the criminal process: Low-visibility decisions in the administration of justice. *The Yale Law Journal, 69*(4), 543–594.

Gorringe, H. (2006). Banal violence? The everyday underpinnings of collective violence. *Identities: Global Studies in Culture and Power, 13*, 237–260.

Graef, R. (1989). *Talking blues: The police in their own words*. London: Collins Harvill.

Gupta, R. (2003). Some recurring themes: Southall Black Sisters, 1979–2003-and still going strong. In R. Gupta (Ed.), *From homebreakers to jailbreakers: The work of Southall Black Sisters* (pp. 1–27). London: Zed Books.

Haj-Yahia, M. (2011, July–August). Contextualizing interventions with battered women in collectivist societies: Issues and controversies. *Aggression & Violent Behavior, 16*(4), 331–339.

Hampden-Turner, C. (1990). *Corporate culture: From vicious to virtuous circles*. Somerset: Business Books.

Hanmer, J. (2013 [1989]). Women and policing in Britain. In J. Hanmer, J. Radford, & E. Stanko (Eds.), *Women, policing, and male violence: International perspectives* (pp. 90–124). London: Routledge.

Hanmer, J., Radford, J., & Stanko, E. (2013 [1989]). *Women, policing, and male violence: International perspectives* (Routledge Revivals). London: Routledge.

Hannagan, T. (2005). *Management concepts and practices* (4th ed.). Essex: Prentice Hall; Pearson Education Limited.

Hasisi, B. (2008). Criminology: Police, politics, and culture in a deeply divided society. *Journal of Criminal Law & Criminology, 98*(3), 1119–1145.

Her Majesties Inspectorate of Constabulary (HMIC). (1999). *Police integrity England, Wales and Northern Ireland. Securing and maintaining public confidence*. Swindon: Swindon Press.

Her Majesty's Inspectorate of Constabulary (HMIC). (2014a). *Crime-recording: Making the victim count. The final report of an inspection of crime data integrity in police forces in England and Wales*. London: TSO.

Her Majesty's Inspectorate of Constabulary (HMIC). (2014b). *Everyone's business: Improving the police response to domestic abuse*. London: TSO.

Her Majesty's Inspectorate of Constabulary (HMIC). (2015). *The depths of dishonour: Hidden voices and shameful crimes. An inspection of the police response to honour-based violence, forced marriage and female genital mutilation.* London: TSO.

Hobbs, D. (1991). A piece of business: The moral economy of detective work in the east-end of London. *British Journal of Sociology, 42*(4), 595–608.

Holdaway, S. (1983). *Inside the British police.* Oxford: Basil Blackwell Publisher Limited.

Holdaway, S. (2013). Police race relations in the Big Society: Continuity and change. *Criminology & Criminal Justice, 13*(2), 215–230.

Home Office. (2003). *National Crime Recording Standard (NCRS): An analysis of the impact on recorded crime.* Companion volume to crime in England and Wales 2002/2003. Part One: The National Picture.

House of Commons Public Administration Select Committee (PASC). (2014). *Caught red-handed: Why we can't count on police-recorded crime statistics.* Thirteenth report of session 2013–14, HC 760.

Huisman, K., Martinez, J., & Wilson, C. (2005, June). Training police officers on domestic violence and racism: Challenges and strategies. *Violence Against Women, 11*(6), 792–821.

Iranian and Kurdish Women's Rights Organisation (IKWRO). (2017). *Campaign success: Nusrat Ghani MP withdraws her bill which proposed to ban the term "honour" based violence and conflate it with domestic violence.* [Online]. Retrieved May 5, 2017, from http://ikwro.org.uk.

Jafri, A. (2009). *Honour killing: Dilemma, ritual, understanding* (2nd ed.). Oxford: Oxford University Press.

Johal, A. (2003). Struggle not submission: Domestic violence in the 1990s. In R. Gupta (Ed.), *From homebreakers to jailbreakers: The work of Southall Black Sisters* (pp. 28–50). London: Zed Books.

Klockars, C. (1985). *The idea of police.* Beverly Hills, CA: Sage Publications.

Lievesley, N. (2012). Population ageing in central and Eastern Europe: Societal and policy implications. *Ageing and Society, 32*, 1081–1083.

Lipsky, M. (2010 [1980]) *Street-level bureaucracy: Dilemmas of the individual in public services* (Expanded ed.). New York, NY: Russell Sage Foundation.

Loftus, B. (2009). *Policing culture in a changing world.* Oxford: Oxford University Press.

Mama, A. (2008). Woman abuse in London's Black communities. In B. Spalek (Ed.), *Ethnicity and crime: A reader* (pp. 275–300). Maidenhead: McGraw-Hill and Open University Press.

Manning, P. (1977). *The social organisation of policing*. Cambridge, MA: MIT Press.

Manning, P. (1978). Lying, secrecy and social control. In P. Manning & J. Van Maanen (Eds.), *Policing: A view from the street* (pp. 238–255). Santa Monica, CA: Goodyear Publishing Company Inc.

Manning, P., & Van Maanen, J. (1978). *Policing: A view from the street*. Santa Monica, CA: Goodyear Publishing Company Inc.

McCarthy, D. (2012). Gendering 'soft' policing: Multi-agency working, female cops, and the fluidities of police culture/s. *Policing & Society, 23*(2), 261–278.

Mclaughlin, E. (2007). *The new policing*. London: Sage Publications.

Meetoo, V., & Mirza, H. (2011). There is nothing 'honourable' about honour killings. In M. Idriss & T. Abbas (Eds.), *Honour, violence, women and Islam* (pp. 42–66). Oxfordshire: Routledge.

Miles, M., & Huberman, A. (1994). *Qualitative data analysis: An expanded sourcebook* (2nd ed.). London: Sage Publications.

Morant, N., & Edwards, E. (2011, July–August). Police responses to diversity: A social representational study of rural British policing in a changing representational context. *Journal of Community & Applied Social Psychology, 21*(4), 281–296.

Muir, W. (1977). *Police: Streetcorner politicians*. Chicago: University of Chicago Press.

Myhill, A., & Johnson, K. (2016). Police use of discretion in response to domestic violence. *Criminology and Criminal Justice: An International Journal, 16*(1), 3–20.

National Police Chiefs' Council (NPCC). (2015). *Honour-based abuse, forced marriage and female genital mutilation: A policing strategy for England, Wales and Northern Ireland-eradicating honour-based abuse, forced marriage and female genital mutilation together*. London: Home Office.

Niaz, U. (2003). Violence against women in South Asian countries. *Archives of Women's Mental Health, 6*, 173–184.

Oberwittler, D., & Kasselt, J. (2011). *Honour killings in Germany (1996–2005): A study based on prosecution files* (pp. 1–4). Max Planck Institute for Foreign and International Criminal Law. [Online]. Retrieved January 30, 2016, from https://www.mpicc.de/en/forschung.

Office for National Statistics (ONS). (2016). *Statistical bulletin: Domestic abuse in England and Wales, year ending March 2016*. [Online]. Retrieved January 14, 2017, from https://www.ons.gov.uk.

Office for National Statistics (ONS). (2018). *Statistical bulletin: Domestic abuse in England and Wales, year ending March 2018*. Released 22 November 2018. [Online]. Retrieved February 1, 2019, from https://www.ons.gov.uk.

Okin, S. (1999). *Is multiculturalism bad for women?* Princeton, NJ: Princeton University Press.

Osterman, L., & Brown, R. (2011, December). Culture of honor and violence against the self. *Personality & Social Psychology Bulletin, 37*(12), 1611–1623.

Paoline, E. (2003). Taking stock: Toward a richer understanding of police culture. *Journal of Criminal Justice, 31*(3), 199–214.

Parekh, B. (2006). *Rethinking multiculturalism: Cultural diversity and political theory* (2nd ed.). Basingstoke: Palgrave Macmillan.

Patel, P. (2003). The tricky blue line: Black women and policing. In R. Gupta (Ed.), *From homebreakers to jailbreakers: The work of Southall Black Sisters* (pp. 160–187). London: Zed Books.

Patel, P. (2008). Faith in the state? Asian women's struggles for human rights in the UK. *Feminist Legal Studies, 1*, 9–36.

Payton, J. (2011). Collective crimes, collective victims: A case study of the murder of Banaz Mahmod. In M. Idriss & T. Abbas (Eds.), *Honour, violence, women and Islam* (pp. 67–79). Oxfordshire: Routledge.

Pease, B., & Flood, M. (2008). Rethinking the significance of attitudes in preventing men's violence against women. *Australian Journal of Social issues, 43*(4), 547–561.

Phillips, A., & Dustin, M. (2004). UK initiatives on forced marriage: Regulation, dialogue and exit. *Political Studies, 52*(3), 531–551.

Pitt-Rivers, J. (1971). Honour and social status. In J. Peristiany (Ed.), *Honour and shame: The values of Mediterranean society* (pp. 19–77). Chicago: University of Chicago Press.

Punch, M. (2009). *Police corruption: Deviance, accountability and reform in policing*. Devon: Willan.

Razack, S. (2004). Imperilled Muslim women, dangerous Muslim men civilised Europeans: Legal social responses to forced marriages. *Feminist Legal Studies, 12*(2), 129–174.

Reddy, R. (2008). Gender, culture and the law: Approaches to honour crime in the UK. *Feminist Legal Studies, 16*(3), 305–321.

Reiner, R. (2000). Crime and control in Britain. *Sociology, 34*(1), 71–94.

Reiner, R. (2010). *The politics of the police* (4th ed.). Oxford: Oxford University Press.

Reiner, R., & Newburn, T. (2008). Police research. In R. King & E. Wincup (Eds.), *Doing research on crime and justice* (2nd ed., pp. 340–364). Oxford: Oxford University Press.

Report of an inquiry by Sir William Macpherson of Cluny. (1999). *The Stephen Lawrence Inquiry*. [Online]. Retrieved October 2014, from www.gov.uk/government.

Reuss-Ianni, E., & Ianni, F. (1983). Street cops and management cops: The two cultures of policing. In M. Punch (Ed.), *Control in the police organisation* (pp. 251–274). Cambridge, MA: MIT Press.

Rew, M., Gangoli, G., & Gill, A. (2013). Violence between female in-laws in India. *Journal of International Women's Studies, 14*(1), 147–160.

Roberts, K. (2014). Towards a psychologically oriented motivational model of honour-based violence. In A. Gill, C. Strange, & K. Roberts (Eds.), *Honour killing and violence: Theory, policy and practice* (pp. 69–88). Hampshire: Palgrave Macmillan.

Roberts, K., Campbell, G., & Lloyd, G. (2014). *Honor-based violence: Policing and prevention* (Advances in Police Theory and Practice Series). London: CRC Press; Taylor and Francis Group.

Rowe, M. (2014). *Introduction to policing* (2nd ed.). London: Sage Publications.

Sackmann, S. (1991). *Cultural knowledge in organisations: Exploring the collective mind*. London: Sage Publications.

Schein, E. (1997 [1985]). *Organisational culture and leadership* (2nd ed.). San Francisco, CA: Jossey-Bass.

Schein, E. (1999). *The corporate culture survival guide: Sense and nonsense about culture change*. San Francisco, CA: Jossey-Bass.

Sen, P. (2005). Crimes of honour, value and meaning. In L. Welchman & S. Hossain (Eds.), *Honour: Crimes, paradigms, and violence against women* (pp. 42–63). London: Zed Books.

Sewell, W. (1992). A theory of structure: Duality, agency, and transformation. *American Journal of Sociology, 98*, 1–29.

Shahid, M., & Hyder, A. (2008). Deliberate self-harm and suicide: A review from Pakistan. *International Journal of Injury Control & Safety Promotion, 15*(4), 233–241.

Shearing, C. (1981). *Organisational police deviance: Its structure and control*. London: Butterworth and Co Ltd.

Shearing, C., & Ericson, R. (1991). Culture as figurative action. *British Journal of Sociology, 42*(4), 481–506.

Siddiqui, H. (2003). It was written in her kismet: Forced marriage. In R. Gupta (Ed.), *From homebreakers to jailbreakers: The work of Southall Black Sisters* (pp. 67–91). London: Zed books.

Siddiqui, H. (2005). There is no honour in domestic violence, only shame! Women's struggles against honour violence crimes in the UK. In L. Welchman & S. Hossain (Eds.), *Honour crimes, paradigms, and violence against women* (pp. 263–281). London: Zed Books.

Siddiqui, H., & Patel, M. (2003). Sad, mad or angry? Mental illness and domestic violence. In *From homebreakers to jailbreakers: The work of Southall Black Sisters* (pp. 109–131). London: Zed Books.

Silvestri, M., & Crowther-Dowey, C. (2008). *Gender and crime.* London: Sage Publications.

Sklansky, D. (2007). Seeing blue: Police reform, occupational culture and cognitive burn-in. In M. O'Neill, M. Marks, & A. Singh (Eds.), *Police occupational culture: New debates and directions* (pp. 19–45). Bingley: Emerald.

Skolnick, J. (1994). *Justice without trial: Law enforcement in democratic society* (3rd ed.). London: Wiley.

Smircich, L. (1983). Concepts of culture and organisational analysis. *Administrative Science Quarterly, 28*(3), 339–358.

Smith, D., & Gray, J. (1985). *Police and people in London: The PSI report* (p. 4). Aldershot, UK: PSI.

Southall Black Sisters Trust. (2001). *Forced marriage: An abuse of human rights one year after 'a choice by right': An interim report.* Southall, UK: Southall Black Sisters Trust.

Strauss, A., & Corbin, J. (1998). *Basics of qualitative research: Techniques and procedures for producing grounded theory* (2nd ed.). London: Sage Publishing.

The Muslim Council of Great Britain. (n.d.). [Online]. Retrieved October 2013, from http://www.mcb.org.uk.

Thiara, R. (2013). It's all about stopping you from getting on with your life: Post-separation violence in the lives of Asian & African-Caribbean women. In Y. Rehman, L. Kelly, & H. Siddiqui (Eds.), *Moving in the shadows: Violence in the lives of minority women and children* (pp. 113–126). Farnham: Routledge. [Electronic resource].

Thiara, R., & Gill, A. (Eds.). (2010). *Violence against women in South Asian communities: Issues for policy and practice.* London: Jessica Kingsley.

Thomas, T. (1988, June). The police and social workers: Creativity or conflict? *Practice, 2*(2), 120–129.

Van Maanen, J. (1978a). Kinsmen in repose: Occupational perspectives of patrolmen. In P. Manning & J. Van Maanen (Eds.), *Policing: A view from the street* (pp. 115–128). Santa Monica, CA: Goodyear Publishing Company Inc.
Van Maanen, J. (1978b). Observations on the making of policemen. In P. Manning & J. Van Maanen (Eds.), *Policing: A view from the street* (pp. 292–307). Santa Monica, CA: Goodyear Publishing Company Inc.
Van Maanen, J. (1978c). The asshole. In P. Manning & J. Van Maanen (Eds.), *Policing: A view from the street* (pp. 221–238). Santa Monica, CA: Goodyear Publishing Company Inc.
Waddington, P. (1999a). Police (canteen) sub-culture: An appreciation. *British Journal of Criminology, 39*(2), 287–309.
Waddington, P. (1999b). *Policing citizens*. London: Routledge.
Welchman, L. (2014). Forward. In A. Gill, C. Strange, & K. Roberts (Eds.), *Honour killing and violence: Theory, policy and practice* (pp. ix–xv). Hampshire: Palgrave Macmillan.
Welden, B. (2010). Restoring lost 'honor': Retrieving face and identity, removing shame, and controlling the familial cultural environment through 'honor' murder. *Journal of Alternative Perspectives in the Social Sciences, 2*(1), 380–398.
Westmarland, L. (2001). *Gender and policing: Sex, power and police*. Devon: Willan.
Wilford, R. (1998). Surveying the ground. In R. Wilford & R. Miller (Eds.), *Women, ethnicity and nationalism* (pp. 1–22). London: Routledge.
Yarrow, S. (2005). The experiences of young Black men as victims of crime. *Criminal Justice System Race Unit and Victims and Confidence Unit*. London: Home Office.
Young, M. (1991). *An inside job: Policing and police culture in Britain*. Oxford: Clarendon Press.
Yuval-Davis, N. (1998). Gender and nation. In R. Wilford & R. Miller (Eds.), *Women, ethnicity and nationalism* (pp. 23–35). London: Routledge.

2

Methodology

The chapter opens by outlining the philosophical approach taken in this research, which is pragmatically oriented and focuses on symbolic interactionism. The application of mixed methods is explored, which involved examining 100 police classified HBA electronic case records (and associated data) authenticated against 15 semi-structured interviews with predominantly detective specialist officers. Mid-sections outline the qualifying criteria and broad demographic of the expert purposive sample of participants. The benefits and limitations of both methods are explored, as is the rationale for examining incident records rather than crime reports. Later sections reflect on the key ethical considerations, the use of grounded theory as a means of analysis and the positionality of the researcher as an ex-detective sergeant of 20 years.

Philosophical Approach

HBA predominantly impacts Asian women and thus the crime is undeniably shaped by the intersections of race, class, culture and gender. Intersectionality theory is central to the interpersonal experiences of

R. Aplin, *Policing UK Honour-Based Abuse Crime*,
https://doi.org/10.1007/978-3-030-18430-8_2

victims (Sokoloff and Dupont 2005; Mulvihill et al. 2018), which may assist in explaining issues of underreporting and victim reluctance to engage with professionals. However, the perceptions of victims were not the primary focus, nor was examining the power hierarchies between police, victims and perpetrators, or even *why* this crime phenomenon occurred. This study represents a micro analysis of police investigatory processes and discretionary practices, based on what officers do and the decisions they make at and post-incident attendance. The study also examined the impact of those decisions on victims, perpetrators and the justice system itself.

Some may suggest that a focus on the criminal event renders this study administrative in nature. Yet the term "administrative criminology," coined by Jock Young in 1986, unflatteringly depicts any research conducted on behalf of government (or in this case with the researcher formerly affiliated to a criminal justice agency, the police) as tainting the academic integrity of the findings (Westmarland 2008; Hough 2014). As Hough tends to imply, this is a harsh and unwarranted critique. A fairer analysis is that this empirical study is real-world research, intended to benefit practitioners (Gray 2018) and driven by technical and interpretive interest (Habermas 1972; also, Ericson 2003). It is pragmatically oriented and less preoccupied with theoretical frameworks, simply wanting to focus on the research "problem" (Creswell 2014; Feilzer 2010: 8; Ritzer 2008). It does not and cannot alter the fundamental structural causes of HBA crime (Habermas 1972). The philosophy of symbolic interactionism underpins this research and its intellectual roots lie in the philosophy of pragmatism, in which reality does not exist "out there" but is actively created as we act in and towards the world (Ritzer 2008). In understanding why people act a certain way, interactionists focus on understanding what people "do" rather than *who* they are (Ritzer 2008; Charon 2010). The researcher was keen to consider a problem-solving and evidence-based "what works" (Lilly et al. 2011: 331) approach to improving police practices in this arena and better safeguard victims of HBA.

Symbolic interactionism complements the basic principles of organisational police culture, because through previous action groups acquire common understandings or "definitions" about how to act in situations

(Blumer 1969: 86). Credence is placed on Shibutani's reference group theory in which the "reference group" adopted acts as a psychological "frame of reference" or anchor point and therefore influences the way in which the individual makes sense of their world (Shibutani 1955: 565). This is likened to psychological studies, where individuals working within one department (e.g. the Criminal Investigation Department (CID)) have an automatic "partisanship" towards their own group, to the detriment of other departments (e.g. traffic unit) (Milne and Bull 1999). The interactionist approach involves reconstructing the reality of police officer experiences to "glimpse that world" from the inside, rather than interpreting the situation from an "outsiders" perspective (Charon 2010: 210).

Mixed Method Research Design

The study was confined to one large UK urban police force. The primary research design comprised a dual-phase methodology. Archived case data from 100 HBA incident (2012–2014) reports to that police force were obtained directly from police computer systems. Quantitative and qualitative data was obtained in this first phase. Second, 15 qualitative semi-structured interviews (2016) took place, largely with specialist Public Protection Investigation Unit (PPIU) officers that routinely investigate HBA cases, including detective constables, sergeants and inspectors (14); and a uniformed NPT (Neighbourhood Policing Team) officer (1).

The research relied on mixed methods, which is considered highly appropriate within one study (Miles and Huberman 1994; Easterby-Smith et al. 2008; Saunders et al. 2009). Quantitative data was used with the intention of providing generalisable conclusions (Hagan 2006; Punch 2014). Qualitative research treats the context of the social world being studied as all important (Caulfield and Hill 2014; Braun and Clarke 2013: 19). The study placed a stronger emphasis on qualitative methods, with quantitative methods as subsidiary in nature. Using mixed methods aids in providing greater validity, as both data sets were relied on to confirm and corroborate ideas via triangulation (Miles and Huberman 1994: 41; Bryman 2012). This also minimises the weaknesses of using qualitative or quantitative research in isolation (Miles and Huberman 1994;

Denscombe 2007; Creswell 2014), which is termed "offsetting" and draws on the strength of both disciplines (Bryman 2012: 633). Qualitative findings aid in amplifying and "put the meat on the bones" of what could be deemed as "dry" quantitative findings (Bryman 2012: 633). A mixed method design, particularly focusing on case comparison, allows one to obtain a stronger more "complete" and holistic understanding of the research problem (Denscombe 2007; Perri 6 and Bellamy 2012; Creswell 2014).

Inductive and Abductive Reasoning

The research approach, particularly the first phase, was inductive in nature with general questions on organisational culture forming the theoretical framework. Theory generated from such data is considered to have more credibility as it explains the behaviour within a situational context and is considered to more cohesively "fit" or "work" (Glaser and Strauss 1967: 32). The abductive approach, known as the third type of logic, was also applied more so in the second phase of interviews. Abduction lies between the polarities of inductive and deductive reasoning. Through abductive logic, the researcher worked backwards generating insights and locating inferences as to the best explanations for decisions made by professionals, victims and perpetrators at HBA incidents. This element of the study related to internal validity and whether a conclusion that incorporates a causal relationship between two or more variables exists or "holds water" (Bryman 2012). The use of abductive logic provides tacit acknowledgment that the researcher did not arrive at the proposed study with an "empty head" (Charmaz 2014: 117).

Phase 1: Documentary Case Studies

The first phase of the research constituted two-thirds of the analysis and was the most time-consuming. All HBA incident reports were obtained by a force intelligence analyst from one police force over a four-year period (2011–2014). The sampling frame totalled 671 incidents (679 including duplicate entries). To reduce sampling bias as far as possible and assure representativeness of the characteristics in the selected sample (Hagan 2006; Bryman 2016; Gray 2018), the researcher applied a proportionate stratified sampling method (Hagan 2006). In terms of time horizons, the study was cross sectional, but because some child cases involved repeat victimisation with a wider examination of action taken by the authorities, there was also a longitudinal element to the study. 2011 data was intentionally excluded from the sample to ensure only up to date cases were sampled. All airport reports were also omitted from the sample because they contained skeleton detail of cases and were either alerts as to breaches in Forced Marriage Protection Orders (FMPOs) or concerns about teenagers being taken abroad. Other than this, the 100 cases were all randomly selected. Each case was subjected to rigorous analysis by accessing all the electronic records on police systems linked to each case. These electronically accessed confidential records comprised the initial incident report (or incident log), secondary investigation documents, DASH[1] risk assessments, police "journal" notes, related crime reports (where applicable) and intelligence items. Each case was holistically evaluated and compared to develop an explanatory model for police practices, seeking to unearth iterative themes.

Case-based research is ideal for assessing the effects that emerge, often in complex ways, from interactions and context. Case study comparison was also useful for teasing out how such causal processes work (Miles and Huberman 1994), termed "causal process tracing" (Perri 6 and Bellamy 2012: 103). This is appropriate for identifying reasons for professional decision-making. Collecting a research sample of sufficient size enabled the researcher to make inferences to a larger population (Hagan 2006; Punch 2014), thereby de-emphasising individual judgements and producing generalisable conclusions (Easterby-Smith et al. 2008).

Incident Reports and Crime Reports

The prime focus for the researcher was examining HBA incidents reported to the police rather than crime reports, as it is considered that the two serve different purposes. Home Office Counting Rules require that "all reports of incidents, whether from victims, witnesses or third parties and whether crime related or not, will result in the registration of an incident report by the police" (HOCR 2018: 5). A police incident log (sometimes referred to as a command and control log) provides a "live time" audit trail of events from a "call to service" report through to a crime submission or until the reported incident is filed away as "no crime." Although incidents must be recorded on an auditable system and subject to the National Standard of Incident Recording (HMICFRS 2018; Home Office 2011), such data does not form part of national statistics. Consequently, it is argued that incident data is much less exposed to management scrutiny than police crime reports.

By contrast, under section 44 of the Police Act 1996, Chief Constables are obliged to provide the Home Secretary with data on the crimes they record, and therefore only crime reports form part of the National Statistics for Police Recorded Crime (HMICFRS 2018). Crime reports are crucial to intelligence analysts in informing local and strategic police force threat assessments. These are subjected to divisional crime evaluation by trained officers, scrutinised by the force crime audit team, all of which is overseen by the Force Crime Registrar, who ensures National Crime Recording Standard (NCRS) compliance. Crime reports are also inspected by senior police management and the Home Office. Individuals are often attentive in improving data quality (such as crime reports) particularly where such artefacts are used as a means of routinely informing senior management decision-making (Maxfield and Babbie 2012). Therefore, from the perspective of the researcher, crime reports are the glossy presentational face (Reiner 2010; 117) of policing, and conversely incidents constitute the "dirty laundry" (Gandy 1979 as cited in Lee 1981: 71; Brown 1996: 182) that is rarely exposed to force audit, infrequently vetted by senior ranks and certainly not viewed by the public. This was the rationale for prioritising the examination of 100 incident reports rather than 100 crime reports.

The Benefits and Limitations of Analysing Documentary Records

Many academics overlook written documents as a research method worthy of analysis and yet many professionals, civil servants and managers in the public and private sectors routinely produce such reports; therefore, this method should be recognised as valuable in its own right (Atkinson and Coffey 2011). In considering the value of official records, Scott suggests that the researcher should meet four criteria: The documents must be authentic in terms of their origin; credible in terms of being free from error and distortion; representative in that the data is typical of its kind; and finally, whether the meaning within the documents is clear and comprehensible (1990). Certainly, in respect of authenticity, representativeness and clear meaning, these are satisfied.

The key benefit of accessing these electronic records is that classified police records are ordinarily difficult, if not impossible, for academic outsiders to access (Brown 1996: 182). Such records proved extremely fruitful in obtaining recorded interactions/correspondence between professionals (police, children's social care (CSC), health, housing, education, the Crown Prosecution Service (CPS)), as there is limited research in existence which explores how these services interact (Cross et al. 2005). Obtaining these candid realities "live" may not have captured such insights.

Second, the volume of cases analysed added both confidence and robustness to the findings, strengthening the precision, validity and stability of findings (Miles and Huberman 1994: 29). Though the official documents produced predominantly qualitative data, the sample was large enough to produce statistical data (Bryman 2012) which was beneficial in highlighting iterative themes. The aim was to achieve external validity, concerned with whether the results could be generalised beyond the cases sampled, to the wider population of similar cases (Perri 6 and Bellamy 2012: 19; Bryman 2012).

Third, some suggest that documents are open to alteration or manipulation (Prior 2011) which may be the case with paper records. However, police electronic records cannot be altered and can only be hidden from view in extreme circumstances—for instance, in a major incident where access from other officers to the content is requested at senior level and blocked by the duty officer.

Fourth, the documents were already "out there" waiting to be found (Bryman 2016) and thus were obtained at a convenient time to the researcher, without the time and expense of undertaking transcription (Creswell 2014).

A fifth benefit is the way that the researcher remained an unobtrusive figure, removed from those being studied. This avoided the problem of reactivity, which might alter participants' behaviours and responses, and thereby impact on the construction of the records (Webb et al. 1966, Denzin 1989; Charmaz 2014), known as the Hawthorne effect. However, this aspect could be deemed a limitation, in that those individuals who helped create such records did not provide informed consent (Bryman 2016), which could be considered deception and has ethical implications. A sixth benefit of documentary analysis was that the researcher did not interpret one document but cross checked and explored the intertextual relationships between all linked official records that related to that one case (the incident, PPI, DASH, crime reports, intelligence). This ensured that the meaning and interpretation was fair and accurate, certifying that Scott's "meaning" criteria were satisfied (1990). In addition, the intertextual relationships between these official records was also used to identify continuities and discrepancies between the different electronic reports, particularly apparent in Chap. 5. Equally, such documents did not reflect one officer's perspective, but many, with police officers, civilian staff and supervisors co-constructing the documentary records (Charmaz 2014). This constitutes a dense network of cross referencing which creates a powerful version of social reality (Atkinson and Coffey 2011: 90).

Finally, the positionality of the researcher was beneficial to the process of documentary analysis. The accessed documents reflected the language or "script" of the particular group, in this case the police (Prior 2011). First, the researcher understands the distinctive linguistic register of police occupational subculture; and second, she can subjectively apply a "common stock of knowledge" and "prior background assumptions" (Atkinson and Coffey 2011: 85–86) that come with having been engulfed within the organisation under investigation. In this sense the researcher is a culturally competent reader, not only able to practically navigate force systems, but able to make sense of case records. This counteracts some of the inherent weaknesses of the method, but inevitably makes replication difficult.

The documentary method is not without its limitations. First, due to the inductive nature of the study, there were difficulties in designing an appropriate instrument for the quantitative data, as it was difficult to pre-empt what might arise. Therefore, more data was gathered than was utilised. Second, due to the volume of the qualitative data and multiple cases being collected and organised, this was the most time-consuming aspect of the research, taking over 14 months. A third limitation was that the researcher had not interviewed the co-constructed authors of these official electronic documents, which meant that the perspectives gleaned could not be validated (Bryman 2016). Nor did the researcher seek the perspectives of the other professionals whose practices may have been critically challenged by police officers in those documents (or interviews) such as children's social care social workers, particularly apparent in Chaps. 3 and 7. The greatest limitation with documentary records is that they cannot be treated as factual, accurate or objective accounts, in the same way that official crime statistics are not firm evidence of what they report (Atkinson and Coffey 2011). Too often researchers focus on documents as "containers of data" (factual content), rather than on a report performing a function (Prior 2011: 95; Atkinson and Coffey 2011). Like police, school and many public service documents, the written text is "recipient designed" with a purpose in mind (Atkinson and Coffey 2011). If we accept this, then we must concede that in terms of credibility, one cannot wholly discount bias and distortion, one of Scott's four criteria (1990).

Goldstein considered that attempting to evaluate non-enforcement decisions from official police records may be too incomplete (1960: 553). In a similar vein, Manning suggests that such data is "intellectually impoverished" as it is hard to discern the "dissembling" of officers through official documents (1978: 253). Bolstering documentary records by conducting semi-structured interviews with specialist officers therefore reduced these limitations.

Phase 2: Semi-Structured Interviews

Target Sample Population: Specialist PPIU Officers

Because HBA is a specialist area of crime, random sampling would not have yielded a reliable or valuable sample. Consequently, the researcher employed non-probability purposive sampling where individuals were sought out where the processes studied were most likely to occur (Denzin and Lincoln 1994 as cited in Silverman 2006; Bryman 2016). The only qualifying criteria for participation was that officers must have some investigative involvement in an HBA or forced marriage incident. Fourteen of the 15 participants worked presently or previously in a Public Protection Investigation Unit (PPIU) and were detective specialist police officers. As experts in actively investigating HBA, they were in a prime position both to understand the nuances of this crime type and to elucidate frontline officers' actions at these incidents. Specialist public protection sergeants not only understand the operational intricacies of cases, but they possess a strategic overview of incidents occurring across their division and advise their staff as to the investigative lines of enquiry to pursue. Sergeants prepare updates at the monthly MARAC[2] meetings and PPIU inspectors often chair these meetings. PPIU detective constables routinely investigate all high-risk (and some medium) DA cases, including HBA. Whilst investigating they often seek FMPOs, safeguard victims and prosecute perpetrators. All participants were obtained through sending an initial e-mail, asking officers to volunteer to take part.

Participants were geographically located from seven of the 11 divisions of one police force. All had specialist operational knowledge in the investigation of HBA, forced marriage and domestic abuse more broadly. These included six detective sergeants from specialist PPIU offices, four of which specialised as domestic abuse leads in HBA and forced marriage. The other two sergeants worked at a strategic level, designing training and writing force guidance on HBA. One of these officers had previously worked in the PPIU as a constable. Two detective inspectors were interviewed, one of which was the force lead for HBA and delivered training on HBA, having also worked as PPIU divisional inspector. The other was employed in a sexual offences unit, having previously worked as a detective sergeant in the PPIU. Six detective constables from the specialist PPIU were interviewed, who actively investigated cases of honour-based abuse and forced marriage. The remaining officer was a uniformed police constable from the Neighbourhood Policing Team (NPT) who had attended numerous HBA and forced marriage incidents.

Eleven of the 15 participants were female. Twelve participants were white British, with three of the participants of Pakistani, Bangladeshi and Indian heritage. The length of service for these officers ranged from 8 to 29 years, with the mean average of those interviewed being 15 years of service. Officers had a combined 228 years of policing experience. The interviews ranged in length from a duration of 33 minutes to 1 hour 35 minutes, with the average interview taking an hour. A schedule of 13 interview questions were devised based on the thematic findings from phase one. All participants agreed to the recording of interviews using a dictaphone as "we cannot rely on our recollections of conversations" (Sacks 1984, as cited in Silverman 2005: 183).

The Benefits and Limitations of Semi-Structured Interviews

The researcher conducted 15 interviews, which is deemed as enough to identify patterns across data (Braun and Clarke 2013: 55). Beneficially, interviews are flexible in their ability to reduce superfluous data by presenting targeted questions that incisively strike at the heart of the matter. Furthermore, in-depth interviews provide a "richer picture" (Easterby-Smith et al. 2008: 72), with data exuding "thick description" (Geertz 1993: 10). The interviews were useful in gleaning valuable insights and current preoccupations that police officers have about blockages to professional practice. Conflicts became evident through the topic of partnership working, compared with the documentary analysis which tended to suppress such issues (Prior 2011). Conducting interviews with officers across a wide geographical area aided in improving external validity (Bryman 2012). Interviews provide a rewarding and therapeutic effect for participants, offering a chance to talk and for their perspectives to be valued, especially when compared to the detached nature of questionnaires or observations. Several officers communicated afterwards how much they enjoyed the interview experience (police officers m, p, i, k).

Limitations include being unable to generalise the results as representative across all police forces. Having 43 relatively autonomous police forces, all with different systems, departments and procedures, indeed complicates analysis (Brogden and Ellison 2013). Interviews provide non-standard unique responses that are difficult to replicate in other contexts, which in turn affects reliability. There were also practical problems negotiating security access to sites or the logistics of fixing times for appointments with busy officers. Due to officers working in extremely pressured and uncertain environments, a handful of participants had to cancel interviews several hours earlier, or the night before, due to unforeseen exigencies of the service. It took approximately four months to complete the interviews, and 20 hours per interview to transcribe and code the data fully. What participants "say" is not necessarily a reflection of what people "do" or "think," which was why it was useful to assess the data against the electronic documents. Using mixed methods therefore minimises the inherent weaknesses (such as validity, replicability and generalisability) of individual approaches (Miles and Huberman 1994; Denscombe 2007; Creswell 2014).

Ethical Considerations

There was no ethics committee and therefore ethical approval to access and interview police officers was formally granted in writing by the Chief Constable as authorising gatekeeper in January 2013. Consent for the study was also obtained through the university ethics committee. The primary goal of ethics is to ensure no one is harmed or suffers adverse consequences because of the research, including embarrassment or invasion of privacy (Cooper and Schindler 2006; Caulfield and Hill 2014). Any indication as to organisational culture influencing positively or negatively on the way crime is investigated and managed has the potential to impact police reputation. Due to this the researcher decided to anonymise the police force. All officers provided signed informed consent for interview participation and were provided with a briefing sheet and opportunities to ask questions. They were assured of their privacy and anonymity (Creswell 2014), ensuring that no link could be made between the data and the research participants. Names, collar numbers of officers, interview participant details, crime numbers, addresses, divisions, victim or perpetrator details were stringently edited out in both phases. The 100 incidents examined were referred to by number (case 1–100) and the interview participants were attributed a letter (interview a to o).

Analysis and Grounded Theory

Grounded theory is a rigorous approach rather than a theory (Bryman 2016) and assists in verifying data (Charmaz 2014). The essence of grounded theory is that the researcher remains close and "grounded" to the data, verifying or refuting theories as details are extracted, at the production stage (Denscombe 2007: 99). The process used was the constant comparative method, which compares data against data. Like grounded theory, case comparison is suitable for developing rather than testing theories. It involves the researcher constantly comparing details within and across cases, checking and refining and interacting with data, thus improving the explanatory power of the concepts generated from it.

Data collection and analysis took place simultaneously (Strauss and Corbin 1998; Charmaz 2014), whereby data was not "fit" into preconceived codes. Open coding took place in which information was "sorted" by means of providing labels to help interpret the data. Categorising did not "end" until well after the second phase of interviews had been completed, with codes or themes under constant revision, which is appropriate for qualitative research (Bryman 2016). My own interpretation is that these higher-order core categories act as "light bulb" moments, in which relationships between these themes suddenly become apparent, resulting in a revision of thought, a synthesis of ideas and a new understanding. In the development of such ideas, a rough diagram was sometimes drawn as a means of establishing the "logic" between concepts (e.g. the core or central category of child reconciliation and how it fits with other concepts, e.g. the wishes of the child; working agreements and section 20 orders). Unbeknown to the researcher, this approach is advocated by grounded theorists to encourage theory building (Strauss and Corbin 1998: 153). Such diagrams helped the researcher maintain distance from the detail (thereby not getting caught in the reeds), but to focus on theorising.

There are numerous benefits to using grounded theory, such as the ability to highlight similarities and differences in the data and the opportunity to reduce complex phenomena to simpler elements (Charmaz 2014). I liken this to reducing the information down into a thick soup, so the key "components" of similar cases remain. This process worked well to help the researcher devise codes and overarching themes for determining interview questions. This research process more closely aligns to Strauss and Corbin's approach rather than that of Glaser, on the basis that reality is constructed through interaction. However, grounded theory methods were not systematically adhered to (in the sense of following a recipe or scientific experiment) and evolved in a free-flowing manner (Strauss and Corbin 1998). The researcher departed from the grounded theory tradition in two respects. Pragmatically, the uncertainties about continued access to the field meant that examining 100 cases was always the set goal rather than being dictated to by reaching "theoretical saturation." Second, unlike the Glaser and Strauss' method (1967), the researcher conducted a literature review prior to the research. There is no prohibition on doing so for fear of "contaminating" the researcher, as there is an acceptance that researchers do not arrive at subjects with a "blank mind" (Denscombe 2007: 90) or without preconceptions (Miles and Huberman 1994). The purpose of grounded theory is to treat any previous research as provisional and open to question (Denscombe 2007). In presenting the research, both the qualitative (text) and quantitative elements (charts) in the study were compared "side by side." As each theme was analysed, these corresponding codes or categories were integrated within the same discussion. This is advocated by Bryman who is critical of researchers who retain these as separate domains (2012: 700; Teddlie and Tashakkori 2012).

Positionality

The researcher represents an "outside insider" (Brown 1996: 181) having served 20 years in the police force. However, there are, understandably, some reservations around positionality, with Brown suggesting "insiders" cannot be objective on the grounds they have a vested interest in the organisation that employs them (1996). However, the researcher distinguishes herself from this perspective, seeing herself as having straddled both reference groups (Shibutani 1955), having undertaken research whilst on a career break and simultaneously teaching within academia during that period. It is argued that there is too much onus on the subjective position of "insider" researcher as being some kind of bias or infliction (Glesne and Peshkin 1992). Ultimately, any view is from a perspective and will inevitably be shaped by the location and lens of the observer. Officers often have a strong ethical "sense of a mission" in trying to protect the weak against the predatory (Reiner 1978 as cited in Reiner 2010), and the desire to influence change for policing improvement, rather than maintain the status quo, is pivotal to the researcher's own personal journey. Insiders can contribute valuable knowledge (Maxwell 2005: 37) and enrich the research process by providing illuminating insights into culture and police practices (Brogden 1995 as cited in Brown 1996; Maxwell 2005: 38). Having already completed a master's degree on police organisational culture, the researcher felt equipped to explore this within the context of HBA. Being a detective sergeant domestic abuse lead (PPIU) and having previously worked in child protection proved beneficial to this research, as the researcher was well versed in policies, procedures, legislation and the operational duties of PPIU staff and response officers. The researcher's previous experience as a crime trainer, particularly in writing and delivering the force crime evaluator course, was advantageous. Knowledge and understanding of National Crime Recording Standards (NCRS), Home Office Counting Rules (HOCR) and the National Standard of Incident Recording (NSIR) proved invaluable. The researcher had a fluent understanding of police powers, criminal legislation and what constitutes officers making "reasonable enquiries." The researcher was also able to recognise the mechanisms officers use to "cut corners" (Holdaway 1983: 8; Punch 2009: 226) in terms of expediting lines of enquiry. Such experiences of policing inevitably contribute to the shaping, directing and interpreting of data (Creswell 2014: 186). Being an insider can act as "a built-in truth check" (Riemer 1977: 474), which can also be considered a form of triangulation.

There was some initial trepidation in re-entering police stations in that participants may see the researcher as a spy (Miles and Huberman 1994:

265) or act "differently" (Brown 1996: 182) because she might not be perceived as part of the group (Shibutani 1955). However, these fears were groundless, and participants were affable and open. The interviews were highly enjoyable for both the researcher and participants. On balance, it felt easier to build rapport with officers due to our identifiable shared histories in the field. Academics often criticise police researchers for possessing little research or methodological expertise, providing pragmatic yet implementable outcomes that lack theoretical grounding. Despite this, several former police officer turned academic "insider(s) turned out" have made considerable contributions to police research, notably Holdaway, McKenzie, Young, Burke and Waddington (Brown 1996: 180).

Notes

1. This is a risk identification, assessment and management model adopted by UK police forces and partner agencies in March 2009 and accredited by the Association of Chief Police Officers (ACPO) council. It is intended to cover cases of Domestic Abuse, Stalking, Harassment and Honour-based violence (DASH 2009). The DASH risk assessment comprises of 27 questions with an additional 10 questions specific to HBA. Seeking answers to the questions enables officers and staff to identify high-risk cases and decide on the appropriate interventions for victims.
2. The Multi Agency Risk Assessment Conference (MARAC) is a problem-solving monthly forum aimed at implementing interventions and reducing risks to high-risk domestic abuse (DA) victims, which includes HBA victims.

References

Atkinson, P., & Coffey, A. (2011). Analyzing documentary realities. In D. Silverman (Ed.), *Qualitative research: Issues of theory, method and practice* (3rd ed., pp. 77–92). London: Sage Publications.

Blumer, H. (1969). *Symbolic interactionism: Perspective and method.* Englewood Cliffs, NJ: Prentice Hall.

Braun, V., & Clarke, V. (2013). *Successful qualitative research: A practical guide for beginners.* London: Sage Publications.

Brogden, M., & Ellison, G. (2013). *Policing in an age of austerity: A post colonial perspective*. Oxon: Routledge.

Brown, J. (1996). Police research: Some critical issues. In F. Leishman, B. Loveday, & S. Savage (Eds.), *Core issues in policing* (pp. 177–190). London: Longman Group Limited.

Bryman, A. (2012). *Social research methods* (4th ed.). Oxford: Oxford University Press.

Bryman, A. (2016). *Social research methods* (5th ed.). Oxford: Oxford University Press.

Caulfield, L., & Hill, J. (2014). *Criminological research for beginners: A student's guide*. London: Routledge; Taylor and Francis Group.

Charmaz, K. (2014). *Constructing grounded theory* (2nd ed.). London: Sage Publications.

Charon, J. (2010). *Symbolic interactionism: An introduction, an interpretation, an integration* (10th ed.). Boston, MA: Prentice Hall.

Cooper, R., & Schindler, P. (2006). *Business research methods* (9th ed.). Boston, MA: McGraw-Hill Series.

Creswell, J. (2014). *Research design: International student edition. Qualitative, quantitative, and mixed methods approaches* (4th ed.). London: Sage Publications.

Cross, T. P., Finkelhor, D., & Ormrod, R. (2005). Police involvement in child protective services investigations: Literature review and secondary data analysis. *Child Maltreatment, 10*(3), 224–244.

Denscombe, M. (2007). *The good research guide for small-scale social research projects* (3rd ed.). Maidenhead: Open University Press.

Denzin, N. (1989). *The research act: A theoretical introduction to sociological methods* (3rd ed.). Englewood Cliffs, NJ: Prentice Hall.

Domestic Abuse, Stalking and Harassment and Honour Based Violence (DASH). (2009). Risk identification and Assessment and Management Model. [Online]. Retrieved May 1, 2019, from http://www.dashriskchecklist.co.uk.

Easterby-Smith, M., Thorpe, R., & Jackson, P. (2008). *Management research* (3rd ed.). London: Sage Publications.

Ericson, R. (2003). The culture and power of criminological research. In L. Zedner & A. Ashworth (Eds.), *The criminological foundations of penal policy* (Essays in Honour of Roger Hood) (pp. 31–78). Oxford: Oxford University Press.

Feilzer, M. (2010). Doing mixed methods research pragmatically: Implications for the rediscovery of pragmatism as a research paradigm. *Journal of Mixed Methods Research, 4*(1), 6–16.

Geertz, C. (1993). *The interpretation of cultures: Selected essays*. London: Fontana press.

Glaser, B., & Strauss, A. (1967). *The discovery of grounded theory: Strategies for qualitative research*. Mill Valley, CA: Sociology Press.

Glesne, C., & Peshkin, A. (1992). *Becoming qualitative researchers: An introduction*. White Plains, NY: Longman.

Goldstein, J. (1960). Police discretion not to invoke the criminal process: Low-visibility decisions in the administration of justice. *The Yale Law Journal, 69*(4), 543–594.

Gray, D. (2018). *Doing research in the real world* (4th ed.). London: Sage Publications.

Habermas, J. (1972). *Knowledge and human interests*. Cambridge: Polity Press.

Hagan, F. (2006). *Research methods in criminal justice and criminology* (7th ed.). Boston, MA: Pearson Education Limited.

Her Majesty's Inspectorate of Constabulary and Fire and Rescue Services (HMICFRS). (2018). [Online]. Retrieved July 11, 2018, from www.justice-inspectorates.gov.uk.

Holdaway, S. (1983). *Inside the British police*. Oxford: Basil Blackwell Publisher Limited.

Home Office. (2011). *The National Standard for Incident Recording (NSIR): Instructions for police forces in England and Wales*. London: TSO.

Home Office. (2018). *Home Office counting rules for recorded crime*. London: TSO.

Hough, M. (2014). Confessions of a recovering 'administrative criminologist': Jock Young, quantitative research and policy research. *Crime Media Culture, 10*(3), 215–226.

Lee, J. (1981). Some structural aspects of police deviance in relations with minority groups. In C. Shearing (Ed.), *Organisational police deviance: Its structure and control* (pp. 49–82). London: Butterworth and Co Ltd.

Lilly, J., Cullen, F., & Ball, R. (2011). *Criminological theory: Context and consequences*. Thousand Oaks, CA: Sage Publications.

Manning, P. (1978). Lying, secrecy and social control. In P. Manning & J. Van Maanen (Eds.), *Policing: A view from the street* (pp. 238–255). Santa Monica, CA: Goodyear Publishing Company Inc.

Maxfield, M., & Babbie, E. (2012). *Basics of research methods for criminal justice and criminology*. International ed. 3rd ed. Andover: Cengage Learning.

Maxwell, J. (2005). *Qualitative research design: An interactive approach* (2nd ed.). London: Sage Publications.

Miles, M., & Huberman, A. (1994). *Qualitative data analysis: An expanded sourcebook* (2nd ed.). London: Sage Publications.

Milne, R., & Bull, R. (1999). *Investigative interviewing: Psychology and practice.* New York, NY: Wiley.
Mulvihill, N., Gangoli, G., Gill, A., & Hester, M. (2018). The experience of interactional justice for victims of 'honour'-based violence and abuse reporting to the police in England and Wales. *Policing and Society*, 1–17. https://doi.org/10.1080/10439463.2018.1427745.
Perri 6, & Bellamy, C. (2012). *Principles of methodology: Research design in social science.* London: Sage Publications.
Prior, L. (2011). Using documents in social research. In D. Silverman (Ed.), *Qualitative research: Issues of theory, method and practice* (3rd ed., pp. 94–110). London: Sage Publications.
Punch, M. (2009). *Police corruption: Deviance, accountability and reform in policing.* Devon: Willan.
Punch, M. (2014). *Introduction to social research: Qualitative and quantitative approaches* (3rd ed.). London: Sage Publications.
Reiner, R. (2010). *The politics of the police* (4th ed.). Oxford: Oxford University Press.
Riemer, J. (1977). Varieties of opportunistic research. *Journal of Contemporary Ethnography, 5*(4), 467–477.
Ritzer, G. (2008). *Modern sociological theory* (7th ed.). New York, NY: McGraw-Hill Higher Education.
Saunders, M., Lewis, P., & Thornhill, A. (2009). *Research methods for business students* (5th ed.). Harlow: Financial Times; Prentice Hall.
Scott, J. (1990). *A matter of record.* Cambridge: Polity Press.
Shibutani, T. (1955). Reference groups as perspectives. *American Journal of Sociology, 60*, 562–569.
Silverman, D. (2005). *Doing qualitative research: A practical handbook* (2nd ed.). London: Sage Publications.
Silverman, D. (2006). *Interpreting qualitative data: Methods for analyzing talk, text and interaction* (3rd ed.). London: Sage Publications.
Sokoloff, N., & Dupont, I. (2005). Domestic violence at the intersections of race, class, and gender. *Violence Against Women, 11*(1), 38–64.
Strauss, A., & Corbin, J. (1998). *Basics of qualitative research: Techniques and procedures for producing grounded theory* (2nd ed.). London: Sage Publishing.
Teddlie, C., & Tashakkori, A. (2012). Common core characteristics of mixed methods research: A review of critical issues and call for greater convergence. *American Behavioral Scientist, 56*(6), 774–788.
Webb, E., Campbell, D., Schwartz, R., & Sechrest, L. (1966). *Unobstructive measures: Nonreactive measures in the social sciences.* Chicago, IL: Rand Mcnally.
Westmarland, L. (2008). Police cultures. In T. Newburn (Ed.), *Handbook of policing* (2nd ed., pp. 253–280). Devon: Willan.

3

Distinguishing Truth from Lies: Victims Are Mad, Bad or Consenting

This chapter introduces the subject of honour-based abuse, delineating the age, gender and family origins of victims/perpetrators. It outlines the key triggers that precipitate this crime and the interventions and outcomes by professionals towards adult victims. It distillates the extent to which professionals are influenced by perpetrator narratives and the subsequent effect this has on victims and ensuing police investigations.

It explores the obscure arena of vulnerable adult abuse and how those with learning difficulties are exploited and forced into marriage by relatives. Professionals sometimes attribute "freewill" to those lacking the capacity to consent. Akin to traditional domestic abuse, perpetrators embellish the poor mental health of victims, which has the effect of undermining the reliability of victim testimony from a professional perspective. Findings expose goal displacement and the problematising and/or medicalising of victims. The trading of labels is evident, with some professionals depicting perpetrators as reasonable and acting in the "best interests" of victims. Conversely, teenage girls are problematised and portrayed as precipitating problems with family members due to their perceived "wayward" behaviour. Final sections evaluate police perceptions of "genuine" and "non-genuine" victims and critically assess the extent to

R. Aplin, *Policing UK Honour-Based Abuse Crime*,
https://doi.org/10.1007/978-3-030-18430-8_3

which police officers are able to distinguish "truth" from "lies" when investigating HBA incidents.

HBA Victim and Perpetrator Profiles

Women represent 96 of the 100 victims in this study (Chart 3.1), reinforcing the view that HBA is a gendered crime. This resonates entirely with Kazimirski et al.'s (2009) research on forced marriages in which 96% were female and 4% male. Equally, Bates's contemporary study provides almost identical figures, in which a statistical analysis of 1474 police incident cases found 94% of victims to be female, with only 4% male (2% unknown) (2018).

As the histogram shows (Chart 3.2), the mean age of HBA victims across the sample of 100 cases was 22.6 years, with a peak of offending against girls aged between 18 and 22 years. Such findings are consistent with international research on the average age of *honour killing* victims across a spread of 300 cases, which was 22 years (Chesler and Bloom 2012) and 23 years (Chesler 2010) (average 22.5 years). These findings also support UK Forced Marriage Unit statistics, where 35% of cases involved 18–25-year-olds (Home Office, FMU 2016: 7).

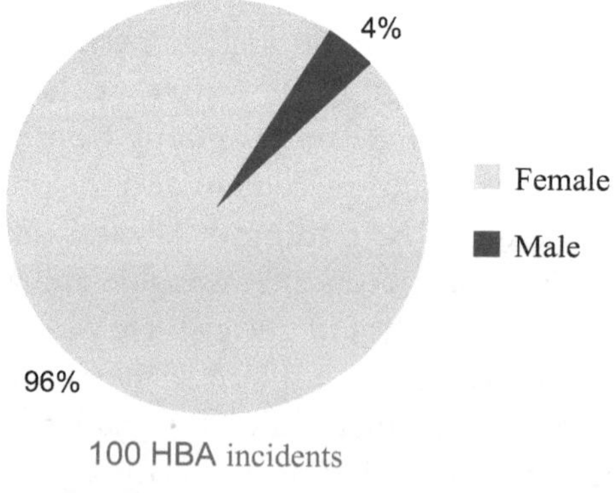

Chart 3.1 Gender of HBA victims

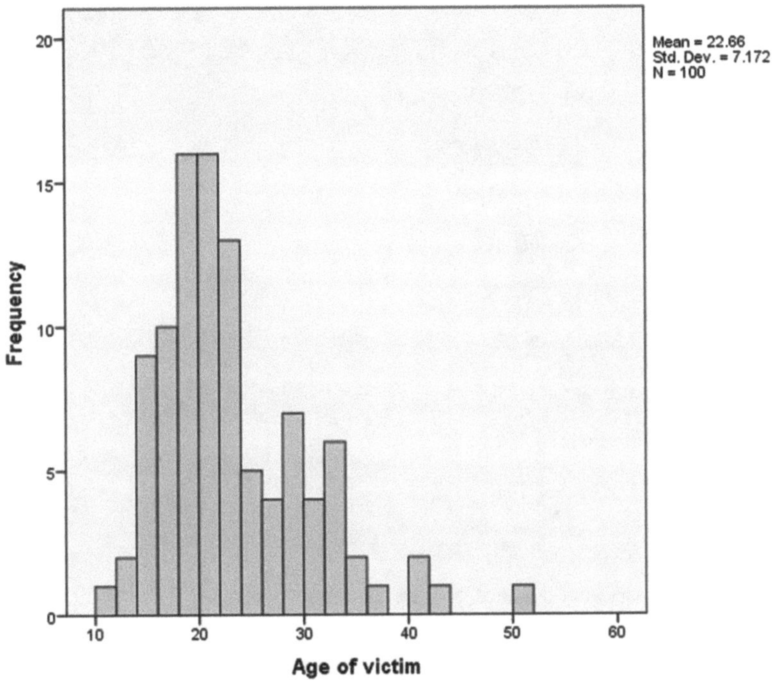

Chart 3.2 Age of HBA victims

Overwhelmingly, the diasporic origin of victims and their perpetrators was largely the same. The only exception was a case in which a white male victim was threatened with death by his Asian girlfriend's Pakistani uncle (case 31). Of the other three male victim cases all were of Pakistani origin, as were the perpetrators (cases 3, 5 and 77). Chart 3.3 outlines the geographical descent of victims and perpetrators in the incident data.

Multiple perpetration of HBA was rife in the incident findings, with 83% of cases involving two or more perpetrators that were predominantly closely related to victims. The key triggers for the perpetration of HBA were varied (see Chart 3.4) but the main trigger was the victim being perceived as becoming sexually active with someone not approved of. The second key trigger, largely prevalent amongst child victims, was of victims being considered as acting too "westernised."

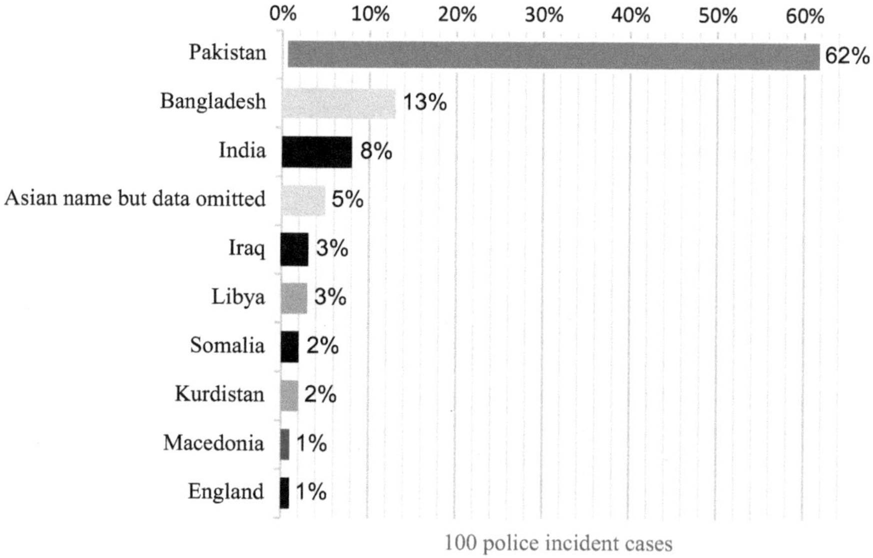

Chart 3.3 Geographical descent of victims/perpetrators

Summary of Outcomes and Interventions for Adult Victims

The most prevalent outcome was that almost a third of victims (31%, 24/78)[1] left refuges, hotels and friends, and returned to risk predicaments of their own volition (see Chart 3.5). Equally, in 73% (16/22)[2] of cases (Chart 7.1) child victims were largely reconciled back with family members by children's social care (CSC) and some police officers. Cumulatively victims returned or were retained in risk predicaments in 40% of all cases (40/100). Findings plotted a familiar trajectory, a well-trodden path of victims being abused (e.g. assault, kidnap, false imprisonment), perpetrators being arrested, or no action taken and victims within days and weeks returning back to the risk of their own volition. Post-marriage victims returned to "work things out" (case 9). Pre-marriage victims returned, often hoping to persuade parents into their way of thinking (case 11, 18).

Some victims stayed due to being financially reliant on perpetrators paying university fees.[3] Some, having been unexpectedly taken abroad, were psychologically worn down by abuse and acquiesced to family demands,

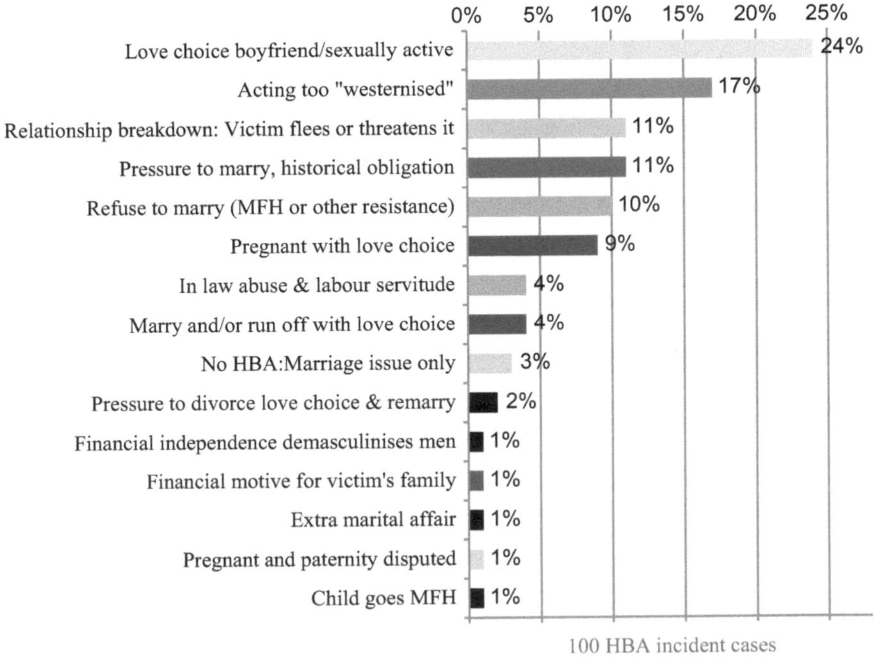

Chart 3.4 Key triggers for honour-based abuse

no longer wanting to be "rescued."[4] Victims were often pressurised into retracting Forced Marriage Protection Orders (FMPOs) after promises from the family that the situation would change.[5] Victims often returned home due to an engineered strategy by the family, designed to make daughters feel guilty and responsible that their resistance and "trouble causing" had seemingly brought on—for example, a parent's "angina" or illness,[6] threats by parents to kill themselves,[7] or deceived into flying abroad on the pretext of ill or dead family members.[8] However, victims often realised after fluctuating uncertainly between prosecution, retraction and rescinded FMPOs, that they had to leave the threat only to be ostracised from the community. Of those 13% (10/78)[9] who fled with love choice boyfriends, some married but were constantly hounded to divorce, some were discredited as mentally ill and others lived in continual fear of further HBA. In 8% of cases (6/78)[10] there was evidence of incoherent strategies applied by professionals (see Chap. 7). Equally, there was evidence of proactive safeguarding in

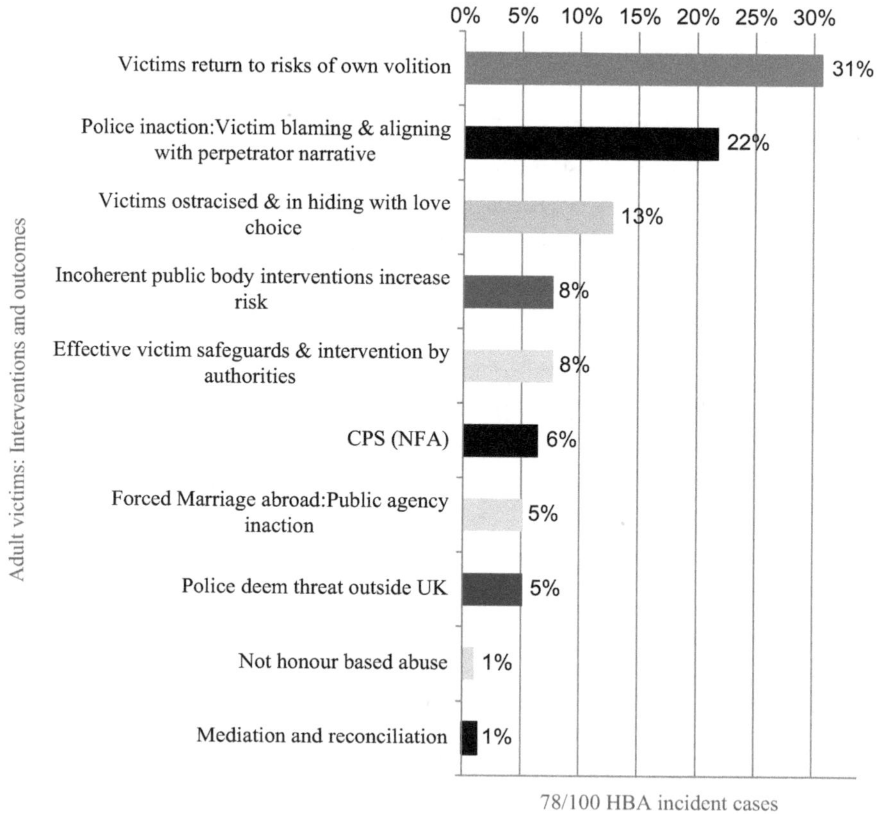

Chart 3.5 Adult HBA cases: interventions and outcomes by professionals

8% of cases[11] with HBA procedures adhered to; FMPOs were implemented, victims were removed to refuges with safety checks apparent, schools appraised, cases referred to high risk MARAC conferences and offenders dealt with in terms of prosecution. Additionally, in some of the cases where victims returned back to the risk predicaments there was also evidence of effective safeguarding (cases 34, 41, 58). Several outcomes involved CPS not prosecuting cases.[12] Some cases were not actioned by officers, on the basis that the threat and potential crimes occurred outside the UK.[13] Some crimes occurring abroad were reported to UK officials, yet not acted upon to prevent forced marriages[14] even when some of those victims were "vulnerable" under the law (cases 12 and 46).

The focus of this chapter is the way that professionals appear to align with perpetrator narratives and how this generates a victim blaming discourse. Equally, embedded along with those themes was evidence of police inaction concerning investigations. This theme was evident in 69% of child cases (9/13) (see Chart 7.1) and over a fifth of adult case outcomes (22%, 17/78)[15] (see Chart 3.5).

Vulnerable Victims

Under section 16 of the Youth Justice and Criminal Evidence Act (1999), those legally defined as "vulnerable" are children under the age of 18 years,[16] those with a mental disorder (defined under the Mental Health Act 1983), those with impaired social functioning (such as a learning difficulty or Asperger's syndrome), and those with a physical disability (i.e. blindness, diabetes or multiple sclerosis). Only 9% of the incident sample (9/100) were categorised by the researcher as vulnerable due to a mental disorder, learning difficulty or physical disability (Aplin 2018) (Chart 3.6).

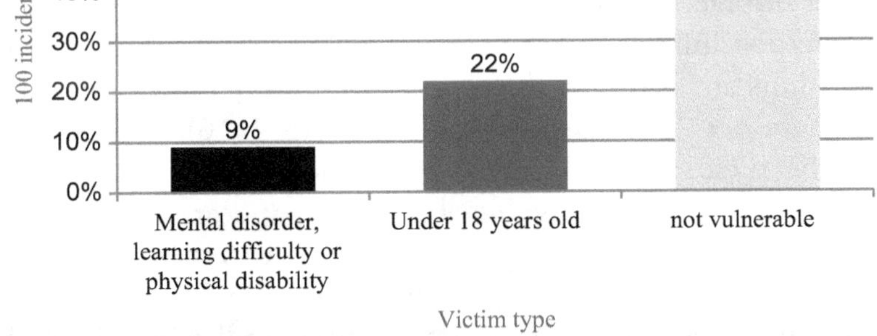

Chart 3.6 The degree of victim vulnerability (Aplin 2018, Copyright Emerald Insight)

Of these, only 3% (3/100) had a recognised and long-standing medical condition that had been diagnosed which pre-existed separately from the long-term effects of HBA, such as a learning difficulty (case 12), mental and physical disability of blindness (case 46) and a combined mental disorder and learning difficulty (case 61). Despite this, only one case (1/100) was categorised by the police as a vulnerable adult (case 46). The other 6%[17] of victims were identified as "vulnerable" (by the researcher) because of the long-term mental trauma of HBA, which precipitated depression, self-injury and suicidal ideation; topics fully explored in a related journal article (Aplin 2018). These low numbers serve to emphasise that HBA involving vulnerable adults is a highly specialist and relatively obscure area of criminality. It is therefore perhaps understandable that over half the specialist officers interviewed (8/15) (53%) had no experience in investigating HBA vulnerable victims with physical disabilities, learning difficulties or mental health issues[18]:

> I've never dealt with any and I don't know of anybody in our office who has dealt with any (police officer p) (Aplin 2018)

Despite the low figures, extant research portends that vulnerable mentally ill and/or disabled people are particularly at risk of being forced into a marriage (Lakhani 2008; Valios 2008; Home Office, FMU 2016; HMIC 2015). National UK figures for forced marriages of vulnerable adults in 2015 stood at 12% (141 cases) (Home Office, FMU 2016). When a person lacks capacity, decisions such as marriage and consent to sexual relations cannot be made on behalf of the victim (Mental Capacity Act codes of practice 2013: 17; Valios 2008). Furthermore, legislation imposes responsibilities on local authorities to make enquiries when vulnerable adults are at risk of abuse or neglect, preventing harm before it occurs (Care Act 2014; Department of Health 2016). Yet the findings indicate that these safeguarding precepts fall short in practice (Aplin 2018).

The practice of marrying vulnerable victims appears to be effected to ensure that vulnerable offspring are cared for, due to their perceived limited options and also because their parents are ageing (Aplin 2018). This abuse also provides a visa for foreigners wanting to live in the UK (Shaw 2001; Lakhani 2008). This was evident in a case of proactive safeguarding when a 19-year-old female on a mental health ward showed hospital staff photos of a "party" on her mobile phone, which transpired to be her own wedding. She had been married without her consent or understanding. Due to the husband receiving visa rejections the parents told staff on the ward:

> We are going to take our daughter back to Pakistan so she can get pregnant by her husband so then he can get a visa because he's got a dependent (police officer j) (Aplin 2018)

Officers sought to annul the marriage and police were proactive in ensuring her and other siblings were protected with FMPOs, despite her protesting that she was "happy to be married" (police officer j). Rather than assume this is a reciprocal arrangement, findings show that deception is often employed with relatives hiding the vulnerability from a potential suitor or bride, often because vulnerable victims are perceived by kin to be "damaged goods" (police officer h) (Aplin 2018). This is evident in wider academic discourse and is termed a "double" forced marriage (Sanghera, as cited in Valios 2008; Shaw 2001). This was apparent when a female bride was brought over from Pakistan and she, along with her family, was unwittingly duped by the suitor's family into marrying a UK male with learning difficulties. It was only after the marriage and realising that her husband attended a special day care centre that the female began to fathom that her husband had learning difficulties (case 30) (Aplin 2018).

Counter-intuitively, vulnerable adults appear less protected by professionals than other adult victims, and in many cases appear to be retained in the care of perpetrators. To illustrate, one 14-year-old had severe learning difficulties and physical disabilities. The family was concerned that she did not constitute good marriage material, deeming her to be "damaged goods" (police officer h). Parents facilitated her sexual abuse to an older male living with them and she became pregnant. Such was her disability that the police were unable to interview her. Although an abortion was formally arranged by the authorities, she was not removed from the family home by any agency despite her having no capacity to consent to the abuse. The mysterious male was "spirited" away and the family denied their involvement in facilitating the pregnancy, both factors scuppering any potential police investigation (police officer h). In a similar case one Sikh girl was violently attacked and left permanently disabled by perpetrators due to her becoming pregnant by her Muslim boyfriend. Yet post-incident, social services left the victim in the care of relatives who police suspected were the perpetrators (police officer h).

The "Freewill" Argument: Protection and Vulnerability Denied

Sometimes when victims appear to have a learning difficulty or physical disability, police apply the "freewill" argument. They proffer that vulnerable victims have the capacity and freewill to make their own decisions to stop a forced marriage, thus downplaying or entirely denying victim vulnerability (Aplin 2018). Only three victims in the incident sample (3/100) had a defined and pre-existing health condition (cases 12, 46 and 61). In all three cases, no officer compiled a DASH risk assessment, and none were formally interviewed to obtain their account, which is concerning given that lack of capacity to consent under the Youth Justice and Criminal Evidence Act (YJCEA 1999) (special measures procedures) constitutes grounds for enhanced safeguarding (Aplin 2018). All three victims were retained in risk predicaments. In two cases, vulnerable victims were forced into marriage (cases 12 and 46) with professionals forewarned of this prior to the marriages taking place. In one case, a father reports to police that his wife is sending their daughter with learning difficulties abroad to be married. The attendant officer suggests the victim consents to the treatment meted out by relatives and abrogates the case, via e-mail, to a PPIU specialist Sergeant, suggesting the victim is in:

> Good spirits. There was no evidence of coercion and she could walk away from this if she wanted to. Regardless if her father suspects the future husband to be a drug dealer, she is an adult and able to make her own decisions (case 12) (Aplin 2018)

Unfortunately, that supervisor was on leave for two days and consequently the victim was taken to Pakistan and forced to marry, with no action taken and no safeguarding or rescue (case 12). What is notable within the "freewill" argument is the way that professionals overlook protestations made by the victim and unquestioningly, arguably too readily, accept explanations proffered by perpetrating relatives. In a different case a mentally disabled and blind victim had, according to the victim's sister, threatened to harm herself unless she was permitted to marry her first cousin (case 46). This explanation was accepted and consequently neither police nor Adult Social Care took any action to rescue the vulnerable victim from Pakistan.[19] The social worker updated the police, who consequently documented the "result" on their records:

> (Victim) made threats to harm herself if she was not allowed to marry her first cousin. Victim is expected back in UK by end of June, however there are concerns that she could be pregnant by then. We are still unsure about her level of capacity to consent to marriage. A FMPO may be difficult to obtain[20] due to the marriage already taken place and unable to prove capacity at the time. However, if (victim) states in any way that she was coerced or pressured unduly (which does not appear to be the case at present), then we should apply for an FMPO immediately. We are still working on hearsay and we do not want to alienate the family or appear heavy handed at all. If (victim) does not return to UK by end of June—we need to arrange a meeting ..//.. It is worth noting that the victim at this stage seems to have persuaded her parents to allow her to marry, which would actually be the polar opposite to a forced marriage. Hopefully this will become clear at the end of the month (case 46) (Aplin 2018)

There are several key points to be gleaned from this extract. First, by accepting the contention that victims' "consent" negates the need for police action and also functions as a means of police self-preservation, should anything subsequently "happen" and officers be held accountable. Problematically, although it is a crime to ill-treat or neglect someone who lacks capacity, the law also states that it must be assumed a person has capacity, unless it is established they lack capacity (MCA 2005 section 1 (2), as cited in Mantell and Clark 2011). It is argued that this caveat is being utilised by some professionals to attribute capacity to those who simply do not have it, rather than its intention, which is to provide patients with choices. Its application under-protects and denies vulnerability, leading to victims being married with the awareness of professionals. Legally, the freewill argument must not be applied to vulnerable victims who lack the capacity to consent. For professionals to admit and record victim vulnerability would inevitably make inaction by the authorities untenable which, it is suggested, is precisely why such vulnerability is denied (Aplin 2018). Principle 4 of the Mental Capacity Act legally obliges authorities to make decisions which are in the best interests of individuals who lack capacity (Mental Capacity Act 2005, section 1 (5); Mental Capacity Act codes of practice 2013: 65) and this takes precedence over victims' "wishes" and views (Mantell and Clark 2011: 60–61). Second, a lack of detailed investigation is apparent. Under HBA force policy, police officers should alert specialist officers who are obligated to make enquiries with the High Commission and Forced Marriage Unit to precipitate a rescue. Neither did officers obtain the details of the suitor she is forced to marry. The fact that the spouse could seek residency to come to the UK is also not considered.[21] As argued by Roberts et al. (2014), the police must take primacy in such situations, but instead they abrogated responsibility to Adult Social Care to manage. Third, the case highlights how professionals latched onto the sister's account as bona fide rather than listening and acting on the victim's testimony. On her return to the UK, the newly married vulnerable adult felt "cheated and tricked" into a forced marriage and was "distressed, angry and hostile" at the "control" and "bullying" she was subjected to by family members. Consequently she:

> Stopped taking her own medication..//.. [and was]..//. refusing treatment and all medical appointments (case 46) (Aplin 2018)

Professionals accept perpetrator explanations that the victim stopped taking her medication by choice, without considering whether this could be her way of protesting to the marriage, as explored by Rasool and Payton (2014). Alternatively, Erwin's US study suggests that caregivers coercively use medication both in order to sedate and to withhold from vulnerable adults as a form of punishment (2000). Denying medical services is specifically alluded to in the new offence of controlling or coercive behaviour (Serious Crime Act 2015). Fourth, although there is scant evidence of race anxiety[22] within the incident findings (4/100), the suggestion that Adult Social Care did not want to appear "heavy handed" implies that social workers are more concerned with maintaining the status quo and/or avoiding accusations of racism being levelled rather than prioritising the needs of vulnerable victims. Race anxiety by practitioners results in a failure to proactively tackle the abuse (Burman et al. 2004; Siddiqui 2003; Gill 2013). Fifth, the extract reflects an inertia by public bodies, with the only actionable item being to have a future "meeting" should the victim not return home. Such inertia is evident in a different vulnerable adult case where police were informed that a group of siblings with profound learning difficulties were being financially exploited by their family as well as being prepared for marriages. A sister disclosed to professionals that her vulnerable siblings are:

> All going to get married off to their cousins. None of them are going to object (police officer d)

Yet, because the sister was unwilling to give a formal statement, Adult Social Care simply "waited" for the vulnerable adults to disclose the abuse personally, with the full knowledge that they lacked capacity and were at risk of forced marriages. Finally, discrediting the victim is evident, a topic that shall be fully explored in a forthcoming section.

It is significant to note that the "freewill" argument is also apparent within child cases and non-vulnerable adult cases. For example, the case of a pregnant victim who miscarried according to police officers "made her own decisions to go back into the house" and return to perpetrating family members of her "own freewill" (cases 65 and 67 linked). In asserting that the victim makes her "own choices" (case 67) this absolves officers of responsibility should any harm come to the victim. Given that this freewill argument is evident across all victim types (vulnerable victims and adults) suggests this is a patterned discretionary police practice which has the effect of placing the onus for a course of action squarely on victims, thereby justifying any lack of action taken by professionals (Aplin 2018).

The Problematising and Medicalising of Victims

Perpetrators Ascribe a "Mental" Label to Victims

Pathologising and problematising women due to alcohol, drugs or mental health (Harne and Radford 2008; Brown 1981) appears to be a relatively common ploy amongst perpetrators of domestic abuse. Victims are often portrayed as precipitating problems due to their own poor mental health, and this is evident in vulnerable adult, child and non-vulnerable adult HBA cases. In 9% (9/100)[23] of the HBA incidents analysed, perpetrators exaggerate the victims' poor mental health in order to unduly stigmatise and discredit them as mentally unstable. Yet such victims suffer the long-term effects of honour-based abuse and there is no evidence of any diagnosed condition, with victims having the capacity to make sound decisions. For example, the controlling mother-in-law and father-in-law opened a daughter-in-law's mail without informing her of the letters. One letter referred to prescription medication for depression. As a consequence, the victim complained of being stigmatised as "mental" during arguments (DASH report, case 9). Such demonising is often inflicted by the wider collective rather than direct perpetrators, and the intention is often to influence the authorities as to the unreliability of victim testimony (Aplin 2018):

> A male cousin, told police "he believes she doesn't really know what she is doing" that "she is not all there" and "may not tell officers the truth if other people are present" (case 14)
>
> A brother stated he had "no idea what (the victim) was going on about" and that she was in an "emotionally distressed state" (case 82)
>
> An 18-year-old victim was "not all there" and had been 'kidnapped' by her brother-in-law. Despite the family claiming she had a learning difficulty, none was evident. It was ascertained the victim willingly eloped with her brother-in-law lover (case 1)
>
> Parents tried to persuade the authorities the victim was "In a bad way with depression..//..was under the care of a psychiatrist and had threatened suicide but has not been known to self-harm" (case 2) (Aplin 2018)

In the latter case, the mental health nurse confirmed to officers that despite being depressed the victim had no pre-existing psychiatric disorder and did have the capacity to make sound decisions (case 2). The more astute officers recognised that perpetrators were trying to discredit victims and thereby influence outcomes:

> (Mother) was also saying that (victim) had mental health problems; but there was no sign of this whatsoever (case 86)

In a similar vein, one father tried to influence authorities that he was overprotective with his 19-year-old daughter because she had the mental capacity of a 10- to 13-year-old and had an alleged physical incapacity to her right leg. The victim apparently:

> Cannot think for herself and has been protected by him and his wife all of her life..//.. he worries about her crossing the road never mind running away from home ..//..He said (victim) cannot care for herself and she is very protected by the family, she needs to be (case 33) (Aplin 2018)

Despite the family claiming the victim was vulnerable and sisters discrediting her as a "nutcase," research across all police systems (DASH, PPI, crimes, intelligence) and documentary inputs from social workers and mental health experts revealed *no* formal diagnosis of any condition (case 33). Such mental health labels are also used to convince professionals that women represent a physical danger to their own children (case 23); that they are unable to financially support their children (case 40) or that mothers are negligent and that children should be immediately removed (case 92):

> Female has left the house on foot and hasn't taken her mobile and any baby food and informant is worried for the welfare of these children. Husband claiming that (wife) has assaulted him tonight and that he says she is mentally unstable and claims she cannot cope with the children on her own (case 92) (Aplin 2018)

Perpetrators threatening to report bad parenting practices to the authorities (Harne and Radford 2008) and consequently CSC threatening to remove children from mothers (Grace 1995) is evident both in HBA and traditional domestic abuse cases.

In stark contrast to the findings regarding vulnerable victims with defined learning and physical disabilities, the poor mental health of victims is often amplified and, in some instances, *entirely fabricated* during interactions with professionals. It seems that such ploys are effective in undermining the competency, credibility and reliability of victims. Moreover, such ploys appear designed to deflect blame and informally resolve the allegation, with perpetrators using professionals to ensure that fleeing victims are returned to the "protective" home in order to avoid further interference by the authorities and justify increased control over victims (Aplin 2018). The findings support extant research that women are "deliberately labelled" by partners and extended family as mentally ill in order to exert control and delegitimise the woman's claim to freedom when seeking help from agencies (Siddiqui and Patel 2003: 109).

Traumatised Victims Are Problematised and Under-policed

There is evidence of the real *or perceived* vulnerability of the victim becoming the central focus for professionals, which deflects attention away from criminal behaviours and results in problematising and "medicalising" victims, under-policing and under-protection. Despite overdosing on three separate occasions and going missing from home, the officer's write-up reflects an acceptance of the family's assessment that the 16-year-old victim was "attention seeking":

> Honour-based issues (are) causing a seemingly normal, very clever young lady to try and kill herself rather than stay at home with what appears at first to be a very happy, clean household. The other children at (address) all spoke freely to me and did not show the same unhappiness and reluctance to be there as (victim) did..//..the family were all spoken to and seem to be of the opinion she was attention seeking (case 45) (Aplin 2018)

Because the house was "clean" and the other siblings did not report similar abuse, there seems, from the officer's perceptions, no logical coherence to the allegation. This extract not only problematises the victim, but shows how officers in trying to predict HBA erroneously use traditional indicators of child abuse to negate neglect, that is, a clean home, with other siblings not showing signs of abuse. In a further case, the family and her estranged husband portray the female victim as mentally ill, resulting in officers aligning with this perspective:

> She may be suffering a breakdown, (therefore they need to determine)..//.. what her mental state is..//..she needs to be spoken to, to establish why she is making these allegations (case 82) (Aplin 2018)

Implicit within the subtext is that the victim is mentally unstable and has fabricated the allegations. It is clear from all related police documentation that the victim did possess mental capacity. In another case a victim is so traumatised by her husband's abuse that, like any other victim of serious crime, she is "a bit haphazard in jumping from topic to topic" (case 2). Yet the write-up reflects signs of a rationale being constructed to justify no action taken by officers:

> When officers spoke to (victim) she was struggling to provide a coherent account and was erratic in the information provided. She was clearly upset and also defensive about certain situations. (Victim) openly admitted she was very tired as she had not slept properly for 3–4 weeks and was struggling remembering things due to her medication (case 2)

These reactions appear consistent with some unsympathetic policing responses to traditional domestic abuse. For example, victims having suffered long-term intimate terrorism (Johnson 2006) exhibit disjointed descriptions of abuse and are deemed by professionals as irrational for returning to abusive situations, compared to perpetrators who portray themselves as the charming, reasonable and functional party (Garrity 1998; Anderson and Umberson 2001; Horley 2002). In this case, the perpetrator husband was permitted to retain the children, a poor decision by officers given that he had threatened to "kill her and kill himself" if she abandoned the arranged marriage. The victim waited patiently for the perpetrator's arrest and for her to undertake a police video interview. Fourteen days later there was no crime report, video interview or arrest.

Worry over the children, combined with perpetrator refusals to leave the family home, led the victim to return home. The victim complained to high-ranking officers that the police were "very slow to take any actions or make any progress." She expressed feelings of being let down as a "tax payer" and by "the system" (case 2). In another case, rather than deal with the crime allegation, the authorities sectioned one gay male victim under the Mental Health Act (1983) due to his depression in trying to resist a forced marriage (police officer a).

In a further case, an adult victim reports having been raped by her uncle in Pakistan and raped by her brother in the UK and yet her alleged *impairment* rather than these crimes became the overriding focus. The victim's perceived vulnerabilities "which had not been defined" by investigating officers, were used as rationale to drop the prosecution case (police officer o) rather than as used as grounds to investigate and provide an enhanced service. This is also evident in the case of the blind and mentally ill victim who had been sent abroad for marriage (case 46). Instead of safeguarding, Adult Social Care used the condition of the victim as a means to doubt her account, negating the control and bullying she experienced as a figment of her own "delusional beliefs" (case 46). Aligning with perpetrators and discrediting those suffering from poor mental health is evident in Cockram's research, where a husband told officers "she's crazy-look at the medication she takes, and they [police] left" (2003: 25; see also HMIC 2015). These findings reinforce the view that police, social workers and other professionals often collude with perpetrators in *accepting* their interpretation of a situation (Siddiqui and Patel 2003, HMIC 2014: 52). Reminiscent of USA traditional domestic abuse research, perpetrators minimised their own role as primary aggressors and shifted the blame onto victims (Anderson and Umberson 2001). Rather than address offending behaviour, the construction of the *victim* as the central problem is also evident in a vulnerable adult case. Instead of protecting the siblings who had profound learning difficulties, Adult Social Care identified some health matters that the victims had which transpired to be "the bigger portion of that enquiry." The forced marriage concerns remained unaddressed and the health matters took primacy (police officer d) (Aplin 2018). All these cases illustrate how, rather than address the honour abuse as a causal factor, professional attention is deflected instead towards the problematising of victims, focusing their gaze on the alleged or real "impairment"; whether that be the unpredictability of mental illness, medicalising victims or dealing with minor ancillary health issues.

The Trading of Labels and Neutralisation of the Crime

Perpetrators Demonise Protective Influences

Findings expose how perpetrators often demonise the boyfriend, or indeed any friend or relative who attempts to harbour the HBA victim, suggesting that they are the "real" transgressors. The intention appears to be to influence the decision-making of police officers and other professionals. Such ploys appear extremely effective. In one case, an uncle was protecting his 15-year-old niece and the father suggests the victim is being kept at his home "by force," that this was "illegal" and that the uncle "had a history of violence" (case 74). Such communication can affect the police assessment of the situation. Officers placed the perpetrating father as "other" on the PPI report, which suggests that they *accept* the argument about him acting for the victim's "own good" (cases 74 and 1). This is also evident in a further case where a perpetrator is categorised as "other" on police reports and yet conversely the police threaten the victim's *boyfriend* with an abduction order (case 64). Particularly where an alleged "criminal" boyfriend is concerned, police officers almost always side with perpetrating parents rather than the victim, as illustrated:

> He had criminality, honestly drugs, violence, you wouldn't want your daughter, take culture away, to touch him with a barge pole. She came in here saying "my mum and dad aren't happy, they're aware of his background and they don't want me to be with him". Well, actually is that honour-based violence, or is that parents genuinely worried about their daughter choosing somebody with a criminal history the length of his arm (police officer j)

In one instance, a 19-year-old Pakistani victim had been betrothed to her cousin for several years. Discovering she had a boyfriend, the family intensified the urgency to take her to Pakistan for marriage. In an effort to discredit the case, the family demonised the victim's boyfriend, who was on remand for possession of class 'A' drugs. The police write-up reflects how officers become convinced by the good intentions of perpetrators, who are:

> Quite happy for (victim) to date who she wants, but as upstanding citizens of the community they do not want trouble on their doorstep (case 53)

Consequently, there is a lengthy exploration by the police on the PPI report about the criminality of the love choice boyfriend, with PPIU officers describing him as "no shrinking violet" (case 53). Some police officers conform to racial stereotypes by being persuaded that the love choice is an "extremist," a "drug dealer" or an exploitative economic migrant. In a linked case (cases 65 and 67), it was indeed the boyfriend who warned police about fears for the safety of his pregnant girlfriend, stating the family may "either throw [her] down the stairs or force her to have an abortion and say that she consented" (case 65). Yet it is the boyfriend who is labelled by parents to the police as:

> A bit of an extremist having recently returned from Pakistan. They are intimidated by him and don't want him at the address..//..They feel that the boyfriend is controlling everything that victim does (case 67)

Supporting police documentation shows no grounds to support this allegation, but nevertheless it prompted consternation from a detective inspector who input intelligence to the counter terrorist unit around potential radicalisation. The discourse originating from perpetrating family members had achieved the aim, which was to doubt the veracity and reliability of the victim and her partner. Consequently, the issue of HBA became entirely side tracked, with the alleged *harassment* of the parents being prioritised (case 65). Despite the victim telling officers that the concerns about her boyfriend are "unwarranted and we (police) shouldn't believe what they are telling us," the police mistake the relationship with her boyfriend as resembling domestic abuse, specifically coercive control (case 67) (Stark 2007). Indeed, at the instigation of the perpetrating family, the boyfriend is advised about harassing the family under the harassment act. Police fail to recognise that the victim moving in with the boyfriend is a *reaction* to the coercive controls exerted by the family collective. In a further case, perpetrating relatives convince officers that a Somalian victim is being exploited into marrying her Tunisian lover in order to "gain citizenship" into the UK:

> Parents are not happy with her choice of husband and believe that his intention is purely to secure his status here in the country. (Victim) refutes this saying they love each other. It could be that her mother has a genuine concern about this male and his intentions to her daughter (case 21)

Sometimes the mistrust of the love choice partner is apparent in police actions even when perpetrators play *no* part in influencing officers (case 79). Despite findings that indicate that love choice boyfriends/husbands alert the authorities[24] to pre-marriage HBA, they themselves become, largely unjustifiably so, objects of mistrust by the police. Officers often side with the perpetrators and fail to listen to victims. In summary, boyfriends, associates and relatives harbouring victims are labelled and demonised by perpetrators as abductors, kidnappers, criminals, terrorists and drug users who allegedly cause harassment to parents and try to control victims. Such labels problematise both victims and protectors and wrongly neutralise the risks posed by parents and relatives.

Professionals Neutralise the Crime

As demonstrated, demonising the victim or those attempting to protect her is often combined with professionals presenting the perpetrators as reasonable, respectable and law abiding. There is evidence in both data sets of police officers defending parents on the grounds that they act in victims' best interests. Particularly with children, parents are considered by professionals as asserting discipline and lawfully chastising them rather than committing a criminal act:

> It's not a forced marriage issue, it is more lack of communication between victim and her parents and the simple matter victim does not like her parent's rules (case 53)
>
> They just want to leave home and "shack up" with the person they're going out with (the victim) It might be just a guidance..//..they (parents) just want to give good advice to the child (police officer g)
>
> It's parents trying to instil a bit of discipline into the house-things like they (victims) want to go out with their friends. Parents are saying "no, because it is dark-or it is late" (police officer c)
>
> Maybe a parent has acted at the end of their tether you've got to be aware of the difficulties at home..//.. but what we hear from the child who's been hit "they're always hitting me" (police officer m)
>
> [Parents] Seemed reasonable people who just wanted the best for their daughter..//..in fact said that they had in effect given their blessing to them marrying (case 83)
>
> The family could be a nice family. Sometimes they want the child to go to further education and not mess about and concentrate on that and go out with someone later (police officer g)

In the case of a vulnerable adult with a mental disorder and a language barrier, despite a catalogue of abuse by perpetrating parents, including financial exploitation and an impending forced marriage abroad, parents managed to convince officers that they were protecting rather than controlling the victim. Parents objected to her love choice, on the basis he was exploiting her naivety due to his immigrant status. The victim was persuaded by him to undress on "Skype" so that he could see her naked (case 61). Taken at face value, these are convincing explanations advanced by perpetrators. Such extracts illustrate the difficulties professionals have in drawing a distinction between those who control and exploit and those who genuinely protect victims. In another illustration of this point, one interviewee recounted a situation where a 15-year-old met her 30-year-old boyfriend on the internet and they ran off to be together. He was from Pakistan living in the UK on a soon to expire student visa. The victim was placed in police protection (PPP) but she kept "failing to see the risks" as "she just wanted her romance." The victim was unaware that the boyfriend had been married before and already had a child. Under false pretences, her father gave his "blessing" of their wedding plans and agreed to take his daughter to Dubai for "wedding material" then onto Pakistan. Once in Pakistan she was beaten and falsely imprisoned to dissuade her from her choice of marriage. With the support of the police and embassy she was brought back to the UK and her parents were arrested, although no prosecution occurred due to victim reluctance. The victim is now unhappily married to the 30-year-old, ostracised from her family and she reflects how she made a "big mistake." Ultimately, the dad was deemed to be acting in her "best interests" (police officer d). In a further case one victim reflected to officers about her poor choice of partner:

> We ended up getting her into a refuge. She was not happy about it at all, but within a week she was back with her parents..//.. (when police visited) she actually said "I wish I'd listened to you-it wasn't love". Even she quoted "I acted like a child didn't I, I realise now he wasn't the person for me" (police officer j)

These extracts illustrate that attempting to draw distinctions between parents who "control" and those who "protect" becomes highly problematic for the police and other professionals, making the justification that parents act in the "best interests" of daughters a highly effective tactic.

Police Fathom the Perpetrators' Agenda

One could suggest that officers are deceived by perpetrator presentations and become unwittingly "side tracked" from addressing HBA issues. This assumption is difficult to entirely accept when there is evidence that police officers are highly astute and alert to the manipulative tactics of perpetrators (cases 4, 14, 34, 60, 72, 86):

> I probably wouldn't trust any parents—I'd say that they're probably aligned together (police officer i)
>
> Whilst police were at the address mother became very upset and was saying that if (victim) left she would kill herself because she would be cast out of the community. She was also saying that (victim) had mental health problems but there was no sign of this whatsoever. She was possibly saying this in an attempt to influence officers and upset daughter (case 86)

> You will not get the truth [from parents and other family members]. You look at some of the cases we've had, you know. If they're of the mind-set to put that child in that situation—they're not going to tell you the truth (police officer f)

Officers do appear attuned to the savvy tactics of perpetrators in trying to influence particular outcomes. In a case involving an assault by step mother officers were not fooled, and on speaking to the other siblings the police felt the children had been primed "not to tell the full story about what has gone on with (victim)" (case 34). Findings also confirm prior research, that people contact the police to manipulate them for their own purposes (Ahern 1972: 16) even if that means telling elaborate lies (Bayley and Bittner 1984: 50). For example, there were several cases where perpetrators attempted to "use" the police to locate victims or to pass on messages to victims. One PPIU sergeant observed that one informant and his wife "appear to be giving slightly conflicting information" as regards the alleged death of the victim's grandfather in India, information which they were anxious that the police disclose to the fleeing female victim. Crucially, the police recognise the ulterior agenda of "pushy" family members, as one write-up indicates:

> I strongly believe that this [incident log] is further attempts by the family to utilise police to trace (female victim) or use us as a means to place emotional pressure on her to return home by informing her of the apparent death of her grandfather and I am not prepared for the police to be used in this way..//..I feel confident that if her grandfather had died, then the victim would be in a position to establish this from trusted sources. The informant would be advised again (as he already has) that (victim) is safe and well..//..we will not pass messages back and forth (case 14)

In a further case of forced marriage, the victim fled the house but returned when her mother deceived her into returning and convinced her that the spouse had left the address. The victim returned but found her husband "waiting upstairs" (case 72). After leaving the home a second time, her mother tried to persuade her that she would support the divorce of her daughter. Despite the naivety of the victim, the attendant officers doubted the sincerity of the mother:

> She thinks that her mum is on her side but clearly last time she lied to get her to return to the address (case 72)

These and other extracts (cases 60 and 40) illustrate that the complicated dynamic and agendas involved in HBA are fathomable by some police officers.

Children Make False Allegations and "Use" the System

Authorities Accept Perpetrator Narratives and Mistrust Victims

Some extracts blatantly highlight a mistrust of victims, with professionals appearing to latch onto perpetrators explanations that problematise child victims in suggesting that they "lie" or make false allegations. In one such case, activities indicative of preparation for marriage were evident; such as renewing family passports, stopping the victim from attending school, overhearing snippets of conversations about taking her on a "holiday." Consequently, the 15-year-old victim went missing, sleeping at her Pakistani boyfriend's house. On disclosing the concern to school about plans for marriage with an older cousin, the police took the child into police protection[25] placing her in foster care. Police fail to recognise that the trigger for the forced marriage was the victim being in a sexual relationship, which could bring shame:

> (Victim) initially reported that her family had threatened to marry a cousin in Bangladesh, however, parents were spoken to by the police and social services. They denied forcing their daughter into marriage, however, they did state that they were having problems with (victim) as she was not coming home at night. It now transpires that she has been meeting a 17-yr male in (area) named (xxxx). She has been staying overnight at his house and not turning up at school. (Victim) denies that she is in a sexual relationship with her boyfriend (case 64)

The authorities appear to become side tracked by perpetrator discourses that blame her behaviour and she was soon reconciled back with family members. In a further example, an 11-year-old Iraqi HBA victim went to live with her aunt out of the force area after divulging physical abuse from her mother. It was 5 days later, after a strategy meeting between social services and the police, that the child was subjected to a PPP. Despite it taking several occasions for the reluctant victim to disclose the abuse, the portrayal from the police officer is that the *mother* is the 'victim' and the child is lying:

> I do not believe there is anything further at this point for police. (Victim) has given various disclosures she has been assaulted by her mother. These accounts are very inconsistent and she has told the school she has lied. She refuses to provide a video interview or have a medical. I do not believe that police should be pursuing any type of investigation with her mother, as on the balance of probabilities her mother hasn't assaulted her and even if she had (victim) won't assist, she describes (victim) as the aggressive one (case 13)

In another case a 14-year-old Pakistani girl is being "beaten," punched and kicked by her strict authoritarian family; she is criticised for being too westernised, wearing make-up ("having a slapped-up face") and using social media. The latest allegation is of her mother banging her head against the metal frame of a bed and of the victim biting her in an effort to defend herself and stop the attack. Despite injuries to the female victim being noted on the incident, the officer negates any crime and refutes the marks:

> Female victim states that she had marks on her back but I have fully checked this and can see no visible injuries (case 93)

Akin to other cases, instead of focusing on the behaviour of perpetrating parents, professionals portray and discredit the victim as the "offender" within the joint visit:

> (Mother) who was clearly upset, she looked tired and stated that she hadn't slept a wink because she didn't know where (female victim) was and didn't know what to do… (mother) is clearly at her wit's end with female victim's

> behaviour and she looked like a broken woman. (Mother) stated that (female victim's) behaviour has only started to go downhill in the last few months. School have sent letters and contacted (mother) stating that female victim has been being unpleasant to other pupils (case 93)

Parental suggestions that the 14-year-old had maltreated her brother was enough justification to entirely side track the issue of HBA and problematise the victim:

> We challenged (victim) about the injuries to her baby brother, she denied she had caused these (case 93)

Despite protestations from the victim, social services assert the victim "would be returning home at some point and she would assist the family in making this happen" (case 93). It is hard not to conclude that Social Care intervention increases rather than reduces the risk to the victim. Social services report:

> I have visited several times, (victim) continues to be rude but mum reports that life at home has improved somewhat (case 93)

These examples illustrate how child victims out of love and loyalty are reluctant to implicate family members. Perpetrator explanations go unchallenged and victim retractions [or alternatively perceived false allegations] represent a "case closed" resolution to the problem. This is aptly enunciated by one police interviewee:

> Sometimes we [police] are a bit quick to go—"Oh, job done, boof"—there you go back again. And there's not enough done around the safeguarding at that point ..//..we [police] could be criticised for how quick we withdraw from them once they [victims] don't support [a prosecution]—and maybe we don't ask enough questions about why they are withdrawing that support (police officer m)

These extracts reflect an interrelationship between victim blaming, victim reluctance (explored in Chap. 4) and professionals reunifying child victims with perpetrating family members (a prominent theme in Chap. 7).

The following linked cases (32, 94 and 96) provide a longitudinal perspective, highlighting the prolonged exposure of children to such risks. These cases involve the same 15-year-old Pakistani victim and perpetrator brother(s). Two of the reports occurred within the space of a week and all three occurred in the same year. Extrapolating police systems assists in providing a more detailed holistic exploration of this particular child victim. Between 20 May 2011 and 13 April 2013 there were a total of eight incidents reported to the police, largely by the victim. Each violent episode involved one key perpetrating brother, and sometimes the abuse was witnessed by parents. The HBA occurred because of the victim's perceived "westernised attitudes" whereby she was staying out late and was sexually active, thus shaming the family. On several occasions the child was abducted in the street by her brothers, bundled into a car and "hit loads of times" (case 32) after being located at late-night bars (cases 32, 96); she was verbally abused—called a "slag and a ho" (case 32), slapped, punched and kicked on the face and body (cases 32, 94, 96), given a bloody nose (case 96) and bruised ribs (case 94). One of the brothers banged her head against the wall and the following morning kicked her in the head in the presence of the mother (case 96). A prior assault shows that the victim was hit with a metal broom handle. It is considered that the labelling assessment by a police officer contributes to the professional response in succeeding years, as a reliable "script" that other professionals relied on:

> It is my belief that the (victim) likes to "flower up" the story for her own advantage and she simply will not do as she is asked by her parents or family, and that she simply wants to do what she wants, when she wants and stamps her feet when she doesn't get her own way. I have no concerns at all for her safety and I believe that she is well cared for and looked after and that she fantasises about incidents that have taken place (linked to 32, 94, 96)

This child was already under a child protection plan for physical abuse by one brother, and yet the following comments made by the child's social worker were documented on police systems by the investigating officer:

> (named social worker) was quite sceptical to (victim) about her account and allegations, saying "if they're true" and stated that (victim) was not at

> risk in the family home. (Named social worker) also accused (victim) of pushing her parents around, which (victim) denied ..//.. (social worker) was quite defensive and said she was 100% that (victim) was not in any danger at home. She reiterated that (victim) had no injuries (case 32)

Medical evidence was sought regarding the assaults on the victim and the injuries were wholly consistent with the victim's account (case 94, case 96). Despite the victim conveying she was scared and did not want to be at home due to the violence and that parents were "allowing this to continue" (case 94), the social worker accepted the brother's denials of assault and "tearful" explanations given by the parents that the victim was "pushing them around." The social worker was deceived by the parents into believing the girl was "lying and doing this as she wants to go out and spend time with boys" (case 94). Such extracts are remarkably reminiscent of the Banaz Mahmod case, in which the investigating officer characterised the victim's death threat allegations as "melodramatic and manipulative" (Payton 2011: 71). However, after her gang rape and murder the officer realises that she has made a terrible mistake (Gill 2011). Findings suggest that professionals misread victims and too readily accept perpetrator explanations, which grossly miscalculate the risks to victims. The child's foster carers at the emergency placement logged a formal complaint about the social worker's "appalling..//..unprofessional" behaviour (case 94). This may help to explain why there is a great deal of distrust of child protection services (Featherstone et al. 2018). In this case specialist officers recognised the risk posed to the HBA child and were proactive in criming, investigating and safeguarding the victim and arresting the perpetrator (section 39 and 47 assaults) despite a reluctance to prosecute by the victim. However, against the views of specialists, a decision was taken by the social service manager to return the child home, even before a victim statement was obtained. She "made it very clear that victim will not be allowed to remain in the foster care and must go home" (case 32). Despite taking the child into police protection on two occasions (cases 32, 94) (in this sample) on three occasions the victim was returned back to the risk situation by children's social care (cases 32, 94, 96). Although the most recent case (case 96) highlights an escalation in violence, the police did not take the child into police protection (PPP). Knowing the case was already "open" to social services, the police accepted and conceded to the views of CSC. It was two years after the first HBA complaint, and ten case conferences later (4 July 2011–6 March 2014) that the victim was retained in long-term local authority care in 2013. This illustrates that social services do not have the resources to target early intervention but deal with those who have already suffered prolonged abuse. Longfield is critical of a situation in which social services attempt to "contain a crisis in children's lives after *allowing it* to escalate" (2018 as cited in Cromarty et al. 2018: 15).

There were only two cases in the incident data where victims admit to exaggerating their accounts. In one case the 22-year old admitted to a refuge worker that she had "embellished the report," suggesting that rather than being struck, her father had stopped short of this (case 41). In another case, embellishing one aspect of the account caused professionals to abandon the case entirely. The police write-up of the victim's video interview stated:

> From the age of 11 things changed, she reached puberty and her father said when this was the case she is now a woman and needs to get married. ..//.. they have brought her in to the world-they decide. Victim has stated that her father is very controlling with her, she attends (name) college and he will drop her off ..//..Victim states that her father knows the security officer and he also keeps an eye on her for her father. Victim stated her attendance has dropped to 85%..//.. her father beat her with a metal towel rail following an incident where he found a cigarette in her bag. Since then he has regularly beat her by slapping her face and punching her body. He has also threatened to kill her on 2 or 3 occasions and on the latest incident he asked her sister to get a knife so he could kill her on the spot. She has been told he is arranging for her to marry her 16-year-old cousin in Pakistan against her wishes (case 44)

As a consequence of these allegations, officers implement an FMPO and PPP and take the child into the care of social services. On arrest and interview the father denies all the allegations. After the father was released from custody, the victim discloses that she "exaggerated" her account, and although she maintains all the allegations, she stated her father had never used a metal bar. As a consequence, officers file the crime as no further action (NFA), the perpetrator's bail is cancelled and CSC returns the child to the risk situation. Police officers consider prosecuting the victim for "wasting police time" (fixed penalty notice). After 12 months the next correspondence is from the girl's social worker. The father had contacted her from abroad to query whether the FMPO had expired, which it had, and the father was then able to force the daughter into marriage without fear of prosecution (case 44). Such victim ambivalence contributes towards professionals doubting the veracity of the original account. One interviewee explained that when victims sometimes make irrational decisions and put themselves back into a dangerous predicament, termed as going "bandit" (police officer m), this adversely influences the way officers deal with future cases:

> People can put themselves back in danger and it does happen and that's why some people [officers] then think "what's the point," wrongly but yeah—what then can detract from the quality of investigation the next time. It's very difficult if that happens to you, to wipe the slate clean and to go into the next one. And I think that can be a danger (police officer m)

This indicates that precedent is vital in officer decision-making, with officers reliant on a predictable script upon which to form the basis of future decisions and actions. Therefore, seemingly irrational decisions made by victims adversely impact on both them and future victims. The same officer suggests that victims often avoid implicating family when they realise the ramifications of the disclosure on their family life and the criminalisation of parents:

> Once you explain the procedure to them about prosecution, they say—"I don't want to see my mum or my dad get into trouble"—so that isn't usually an issue. But yes, if it hasn't been explained correctly—if we've taken it as a handover prisoner maybe and we get further down the line then that comes ahead—they have thought [the victim] "how can I get out of this, how can I get out of this"—"I've made it all up" (police officer m)

Even in cases where victims exaggerate the allegation, little consideration appears to be accorded to the view that children do *tell the truth* but later on "backtrack" due to the incumbent pressure of criminalising their parents or relatives.

Children "Use" the System

Although incident data illustrates the problematising of victims and professionals aligning with perpetrators, it is difficult to find underpinning reasons for this. However, explanations were starkly apparent within police interview data. Some officers suggest that victims "use" the system and the police in order to get their own way in the household:

> Maybe she just wanted her family to take her seriously and go "she is in that relationship" and she's used the police perhaps..//..to like sort of say to her family that she's not messing around, she's being serious about it, she's in this relationship and she's making this decision for herself (police officer p)
>
> The individual, who will ring up saying they want to get me married off.... they are kind of...using the system sometimes.... Just because they want to go out with the bloke they're seeing (police officer g)
>
> We don't maybe treat kids as seriously as we should do. Don't get me wrong there's a lot [victims] who "cry wolf" that does affect how we deal with other people..//.. I think a lot of the Asian kids hear the more westernised life that they could be living with more lax home conditions, provision of things like mobile phones, social networking—and I think some *are* daft enough to think "I'll give that a try"(police officer m)
>
> Young females ..//..between sort of 14 and 18, are using HBV as a way of getting out of the household. In actual fact, when you look deeper into it, it's parents trying to instil a bit of discipline into the house..//..And they'll go to school and say "I'm being controlled. My parents are going to take me out of the country. They're suffocating me. They're not letting me do anything." And you speak to the parents..//.. "we're just trying to instil a bit discipline"..//..the person who is making the report is potentially trying to use the system in order to get what they want—rather than the genuine HBV situation (police officer c)

Officers also attest to children having expectations that going into care is a better life than the stifling control at home, which then becomes motive to fabricate a complaint:

> "Well 'so and so' got removed and they had an iPad"..//..they realise that maybe they [those placements] are as strict as their parents, and it's not as attractive and then they want to go back—and then that's when we get the—"oh I've made it up", or—you know other reasons for not wanting—"oh I don't want my mum and dad prosecuting" (police officer m)

In 69% (9/13) of cases where child victims were reconciled home by CSC (see Chap. 7), professionals exhibit victim blaming attitudes. Both data sets show strong evidence of HBA cases being simplified and decriminalised on the grounds that the problem lay with "unruly teenager(s)" going against the culture by "choosing the wrong boyfriend" (police officer j). If one assesses the triggers for HBA in the incident sample (Chart 3.4), a female having a boyfriend and becoming sexually active is the most prominent trigger (24%) that precipitates abuse by family members. It is proffered that professionals do not necessarily recognise this as the underlying "reason" for the abuse being inflicted on victims. Instead professionals are convinced by perpetrators that a teenager's problematising behaviour is the *cause* of family discord.

Can Officers Distinguish Truth from Lies?

The cynical and mistrustful attitude of police officers towards the public appears to be an iterative feature of policing research (Waddington 1999; Reiner 2010). In Charman's study of new recruits she reinforces extant research by illustrating cynicism as a core characteristic of the police identity (2017). Because police officers experience the darker side of human nature, this in turn "colours the way you see people" (Graef 1989: 498). However, such cynicism adversely impacts on officers' attitudes towards victims of crime, resulting in subjective judgements or 'hunches' that some victims are not "genuine" (police officer c, j and p). At least a third of officers interviewed suggest they were capable of distinguishing between truth and lies, between "genuine" and "non-genuine" victims, suggesting they were highly capable of making moral judgements and "on the spot decisions of guilt or innocence" (Manning 1978: 24; Van Maanen 1978b):

> She upped sticks with a young child. This sounds awful-but they're the genuine cases, if you're going to leave your family, your culture, and are more than prepared to go into refuge with your child who's under 1—there's some fear there isn't there? (police officer j)
>
> You've got to filter it down to what's a genuine case and what's not a genuine case (police officer p)
>
> It's not always a genuine case, it's quite often unruly teenagers going out drinking, smoking, against the culture choosing the wrong boyfriend ..//.. it's not very much you know bringing shame on the family, it's very much, 'you aren't going out with him' (police officer j)

Categorising victims as "genuine" or blameworthy was equally apparent in Charman's research (2017: 283). In seeking certainty in a situation, professionals (i.e. police and social services in these findings) are too quick to come to judgements, using information to attribute characteristics to individuals based on ascribed social categories (Taylor and White 2006; Thompson 2016). However, faulty logic in decision-making is evident, with officers appearing to misread victims or situations. For instance, it took months for a 15-year old to confide in her forced marriage advisor that her mother had sent her to Pakistan for a forced marriage 12 months earlier. As the research interview progressed, it emerged that the officer believed the victim was "using" the police to blackmail her mother into buying her expensive items. Part of this involved the officer sending the victim from temporary foster care back home to live with mother, who was on bail awaiting a CPS charging decision for the crime:

> It was me that set the [bail] conditions..//.. it would be up to a family court, so it would be up to a judge. If a judge deemed it fit that she could return home, knowing full well she was on bail, then I would have been happy with that (police officer c)

Because the victim was not initially forthright in admitting the marriage, it becomes clear that the officer's faith in the integrity of the victim has been severely shaken:

> Researcher: But aren't we putting that kid in a difficult position by putting her back with her mum at this stage while criminal investigations going on, do you not think because she loves her mum she's got torn loyalties?
>
> (c) I don't think she does love her mum.
>
> Researcher: Why does she want to be at home then?
>
> (c) Because she's well looked after..//.. the house is quite cramped, very messy with things all over the place. It wasn't dirty, just messy, and her room was immaculate. She had a big apple computer in there that was worth over £1000, which is completely not in keeping with the rest of the belongings in the house. She had her own room, whereas nobody else did. So, what mum was saying on interview was "She kind of blackmails us, she uses us," and the fact that the police have been involved, and she'll say "If you don't get me this, I'll go back to the police and tell them that you forced me to get married," so mum says, "I've got no choice but to get her this thing because I don't want the police round at the house again"..//.. There's no doubt she got married, but like I say, it's under the circumstances in which she did get married. Mum lied initially, so that's a big cross in her box. But [victim] also lied. She told us initially she wasn't married when she was. So, it's a difficult one, I'm glad I'm not making the decision, to be honest (police officer c)

In these extracts, the truthfulness of the victim appears to be on trial, based on the perpetrator influencing the officer. Mistrust by the officer was based on the delay in reporting the forced marriage and the incongruence of her tidy room and Apple computer, compared to the messy conditions within the rest of the house (police officer c). The officer relied on "gut" subjective judgement, *morally* objecting to the victim apparently "blackmailing" her mother into purchasing an expensive Apple computer. The officer at no time considered the computer may have been an inducement to persuade the victim into marriage. Despite clear evidence of a forced marriage, the officer aligned with the perpetrator and blamed the victim:

> The victim could have been setting those, almost planting those roots, or planting little seeds in the forced marriage worker's mind from an early

stage, being quite devious. It is very devious that, and I know, and we might be over thinking it, but it's still a possibility (police officer c)

This response to victims validates prior research which indicates that if victims are seen to provoke the incident they are deemed as getting their "just deserts" (Brown 1981: 198) because they "brought it on" themselves (Hanmer 2013 [1989]: 107). The attitude of the victim towards police officers can also adversely impact on subsequent professional decision-making. To exemplify, one girl, who had been forced into marriage and had a child abroad,[26] was very mistrusting of police, having already been failed by UK police and CSC professionals. When she ran off with her cousin, who was also being forced into marriage, the officers considered her as "petulant" and anti-police because, in their view, she made unreasonable demands. Any challenge towards professionals is labelled as problematic behaviour, resulting in services punitively pulling together to exclude those victims (Featherstone et al. 2018). Victims must be respectful and if they question, challenge or fail to show deference to professionals, this causes officers to question the credibility of the complainant (Crank 2016). This is evident in the following extracts, where professionals move to a victim blaming discourse when they perceive the victims are having a "laugh" at their expense:

"I want a refuge with other South Asian girls. I want a refuge far away from (place). I want a refuge where we are put together"..//..our officers getting irate. These girls are having all these demands..//..[Officers were saying] "Why are they doing this? Why are they behaving … do they not know what we're doing for them? Do they not know what risks there are? Ungrateful. They've got this little girl [her child from the forced marriage]. Couldn't she think about her little girl?"..//..a couple of officers were saying "What a load of shat [shit] that job was. Yeah, you know, they were just doing it for a laugh. They were just doing it for a bit of a jolly" (police officer d)

They're "laughing along" and it's a bit of a joke and you'll speak to them and say "What do you hope to get out of this?" And they say, "I just want to leave, I don't want to live at home any more. I want to go and live with my friends." And actually it's like "Well, that's not going to happen here"..//..When it's not so obvious you've got to go along with the HB aspect of it because it might be that on one occasion, your "guts" wrong and something might happen to that person-and it's on you then. So to "cover your back" in a way and to try and do the best job you can for that person, you've got to go along with the HBV aspect of it rather than challenging them and saying "I think you're lying, I think you're just going out wanting to be with your mates" (police officer c)

Such extracts reflect a sense in which officers appear very sensitive to "saving face" and being made a "fool" of. Past research illustrates that officers "speak bitterly of the times they were conned" into accepting uncritically a story which they then acted on (Bayley and Bittner 1984: 50, also Klockars 1985: 100). There is a sense in which some officers exude a sense of moral superiority and entrepreneurialism in deciding the culpability of an individual (Van Maanen 1978a). Moreover, as these extracts also show, when professionals mistrust that victims are "lying" and therefore "non-genuine," a presentational veneer of back-covering and box ticking is still employed to provide an impression of service, but essentially the case is paid lip service:

They may disbelieve what the child is saying, as *we* may-but in the interim while we are investigating that we have to put the child somewhere safe (police officer m)

Less is done on those ones, in terms of safeguarding afterwards, because you've found it not to be true. So they're returned home (police officer c)

As is reflected in the extracts, a lack of interest in developing a prosecution case ultimately amounts to a non-enforcement decision (Goldstein 1960: 564). Likewise, Van Maanen suggests that officers conduct such cases with "ceremonial dispatch and disinterest" (1978a: 226) so that the case is quickly expedited.

In summary, there is overwhelming evidence of mistrust and hostility towards child HBA victims by professionals, who suggest that victim injuries are fabricated, that victims are "inconsistent," tell lies,[27] are "devious" (police officer c) and "cry wolf" (police officer m).

This is reflective of the highly cynical police group narrative that "everybody lies" (Charman 2017: 323). Such attitudes highlight that officers have a very polarised view in judging citizens to be either a victim or a potential threat (Van Maanen 1978a: 236; Crank 2016: 201–225), with very little in between. Moreover, such cases entirely reconfigure the roles of "victim" and "perpetrator," with a trading of labels apparent. Officers suggest that teenagers use the police as leverage in order for them to re-establish control over strict parents, in terms of attaining increased freedom, choosing a boyfriend to "shack up with" (police officer g) or gaining material possessions. Officers appear to wrongly evaluate that these are non-ideal victims and are wayward, ill-disciplined teenagers exploiting and using the system in order to get what they want. However, such harsh judgements on victims suggest that the ability of police officers to distinguish truth from lies appears overstated. When officers identify an incongruence within a situation or they are unable to relate to victim behaviours and attitudes, this fosters mistrust as to the integrity and truth of victim accounts. Evidence of faulty logic suggests that officers are influenced and deceived by perpetrators in some instances; hence the difficulty in determining who the "bad guy" is (police officer d). Klockars contends that whether a victim achieves justice largely depends on an officer's willingness to empathise with the perpetrator's predicament (1985). This concept is picked up by Hanmer et al. who suggest that rather than officers consider perpetrators as criminal, perpetrators are merely responding to the "frustration" of the situation (2013b [1989]: 195). Professionals (police and social services) empathising and relating to perpetrators is certainly evident in the extracts. Such cynical perspectives of professionals towards teenage victims may help to contextualise why 73% of children (see Chap. 7) were reconciled with perpetrators or sympathising relatives. Contrary to the overriding principle that victims have a fundamental right to be believed (NSPCC 2015: 10), the testimonies of children were not routinely believed.

Concluding Remarks

This chapter reflects an interplay in the discrediting of victims, professionals aligning with perpetrator discourses and the subsequent inaction of professionals. The trading of labels was apparent, whereby professionals neutralised perpetrator behaviours, displacing the focus away from crime and offenders and towards the perceived or real impairment of problematised victims (and their protectors). Findings highlighted that perpetrators used effective ploys to discredit protective influences, convincing the authorities that victims were being coerced into fleeing the family home. Particularly with child victims, perpetrator behaviours were justified by professionals as lawful chastisement, with parents as reasonable people acting in the victims' "best interests" and instilling discipline into the house, which confirms findings in previous child protection research (Farmer 2006: 129). Reminiscent of traditional domestic abuse literature, these cases reflect a clear reluctance by professionals to define perpetrator actions as criminal (Bourlet 1990; Reiner 2000: 76; Hanmer et al. 2013a [1989]: 2). Despite having very fixed views around the ability to distinguish between genuine and non-genuine victims, it was clear that some officers applied faulty logic and misinterpreted situations, using moral rather than legal judgements. Such ineffective decision-making increases risks to victims (NSPCC 2015: 10).

Under the YJCEA (1999) vulnerable victims should be entitled to an enhanced service, yet only one case across both data sets indicated the protection of a mentally ill victim by professionals. The mental health label, whether genuine or contrived, served to disadvantage and stigmatise victims. Paradoxically, professionals sometimes cultivated the mental illness labels advanced by perpetrators, undermining victims as unreliable, irrational, unhinged and in need of protection from perpetrating relatives, as opposed to enhancing the safeguarding provision *because* of the perceived impairment. Perpetrator explanations, however illogical, often remained unchallenged by professionals (Aplin 2018). Indeed 22% (17/78) of all adult cases in the incident data illustrated how officers aligned with perpetrator narratives and advanced a victim blaming discourse. In the case of mental illness, the perceived vulnerability was exaggerated. Findings highlighted that officials utilised this as a prop or device to discredit and doubt victim testimony, thereby justifying subsequent inaction by officials (Aplin 2018). There appears to be sparse academic literature exploring the concept of professionals using a manufactured vulnerability as a means of discrediting victims in order to expedite enquiries (ibid.). However, a government report suggests that officers often justify "no-crime" decisions on the basis of "mental health or similar issues of vulnerability" in order to avoid having undetected offences on the system (House of Commons PASC 2014: 15). It is the subject of crime recording that shall be the central focus of the following chapter.

Conversely, in cases of diagnosed physical and mental disability some professionals *denied* vulnerability, advocating that victims had the capacity and freewill to make their own choices. This under-protects victims, many of which were left in forced marriage situations or retained under the direct "care" and supervision of perpetrators. However, it is also noteworthy that navigating vulnerability is a highly complex arena for professionals. Victims who suffer poor mental health or have learning difficulties often provide credence to family members, suggesting that their controlling actions are justifiable, necessary and effected for the protection and "best interests" of vulnerable victims. As prior social work studies have established, disabled children are often overlooked by professionals, with parents becoming the "proxies for the voice of the child" (Oliver 2010: 16). Furthermore, if a complaint is made professionals, quite absurdly, have to seek consent from perpetrating family members in order to pursue interviews or formal medical examinations with vulnerable people (Aplin 2018). The arena is fraught with danger when it entails determining who the perpetrator is. However, *not all* families exploit vulnerability. Professionals need to better recognise the difference between family members who seek to protect and those who intend to control, yet establishing this with certainty is difficult (Aplin 2018).

What remains unclear is whether police officers were *wholly* deceived by perpetrator presentations or whether they took the path of least resistance by latching onto these illogical explanations because it fitted their self-interested preferences to do so. Evidence of officers being alert to the manipulative tactics of perpetrators makes it difficult to accept that such practices might be attributed to ignorance or lack of training. Overall, it was problematic to disentangle where perpetrator influences might stop and where police discretionary practices began. The implications are that if perpetrator discourses are so readily advanced by professionals, it raises concerns not only about safeguarding practices, but it adversely impacts on crime recording, prosecutions and notions of deterrence (Aplin 2018). It is argued that rather than investigate and resolve the many complexities of HBA, some professionals adopt the bureaucratic practice of "goal displacement." Work conducted by Manning (1978), Lipsky (1980 [2010]) and Knott and Miller (1987) assist in theorising what is occurring. It involves professionals who "lose track of their goals and engage in ritualistic behaviours, substituting means for ends..//..their objective is forgotten" (Manning 1978: 21). Practitioners appear to displace and deflect the HBA problem and instead address more manageable issues such as having a meeting; managing a teenager's perceived problematic behaviours (or as shall be explored in Chap. 7, devising working agreements); focusing on victim "impairments"; "waiting" for disclosures or dealing with ancillary health issues. In doing so, officials become transfixed in inertia, retreating behind the process of rules and regulations as an "avoidance strategy" (Knott and Miller 1987: 110) which allows them to disengage from victims' needs. Goal displacement provides a veneer of service but little efficacy in outcomes, with under-protection and secondary victimisation by the state evident (Aplin 2018). The proceeding chapter shall rationalise why some professionals may be keen to accept perpetrator explanations and readily accept a victim blaming discourse. Problematising victims is one of several practices relied on by some officers to justify no-crime decisions and it is the subject of crime recording practice which is the focal point of the next chapter.

Notes

1. Cases 2, 6, 11, 14, 17, 24, 30, 33, 34, 35, 38, 41, 42, 48, 52, 53, 54, 56, 58, 71, 72, 75, 90 and 92.
2. Cases 10, 18, 20, 22, 26, 32, 39, 43, 44, 45, 50, 64, 74, 93, 94 and 96.
3. Cases 17, 35, 48 and 72.
4. Cases 75, also 15, 33, 38, 42.
5. Cases 8, 37, 38, 57, 51, police officer k, m, n.
6. Cases 55, 90, 93, police officer m and d.
7. Cases 46, 77, 37, 90, 2, 86, police officer p.
8. Cases 5, 8, 55, 14.
9. Cases 1, 3, 25, 36, 49, 76, 77, 82, 87 and 98.
10. Cases 19, 28, 29, 59, 66, 88.
11. Cases 4, 37, 40, 55, 68, 85.

12. Cases 77, 9, 16, 31 and 91.
13. Cases 23, 27, 78 and 100.
14. Cases 5, 12, 15 and 46.
15. Cases 21, 51, 60, 61, 62, 63, 65, 67, 69, 70, 73, 79, 83, 86, 89, 97 and 99.
16. Juveniles under PACE 1984 were previously those under 17 years. Section 42 Criminal Justice and Courts Act 2015 extends this to any child or young person under 18 years, bringing it in line with the UN Convention on the rights of the child (College of Policing 2017).
17. Cases 2, 28, 34, 35, 37 and 56.
18. Police officers b, c, f, g, m, i, p and n.
19. It was the Foreign and Commonwealth office that contacted police to alert them, and at the time the victim was still in the UK, thus a forced marriage could have been avoided.
20. Authorities failed to consider that an FMPO could have precipitated the victim's return to the UK.
21. Officer should have contacted the Forced Marriage Unit as to whether a spousal visa application had been lodged (HM Government 2010: 23).
22. Race anxiety is when professionals fear being accused of being racist and therefore do not proactively manage the case, also referred to as reverse racism and cultural sensitivities.
23. Cases 1, 2, 9, 14, 33, 78, 82, 86 and 92.
24. Cases 5, 31, 38, 64, 65, 67, 79.
25. Police Protection Plans (PPP) are formerly known as Police Protection Orders (PPO), and legislated under the Children Act 1989 s.46.
26. See Chap. 7 for details.
27. For one interviewee, the victim told "lies" because she *delayed* disclosing a forced marriage (police officer c).

References

Ahern, J. (1972). *Police in trouble: Our frightening crisis in law enforcement*. New York, NY: Hawthorne Books.

Anderson, K., & Umberson, D. (2001, June). Gendering violence: Masculinity and power in men's accounts of domestic violence. *Gender and Society, 15*(3), 358–380.

Aplin, R. (2018). Honour-based abuse: The response by professionals to vulnerable adult investigations. *Journal of Aggression, Conflict and Peace Research*:

Emerald Publishing. Special issue of "Honour" based abuse, violence and killings. Guest editor Roxanne Khan, Vol. 10, no. 4, pp. 239–250.

Bates, L. (2018). Females perpetrating honour-based abuse: Controllers, collaborators or coerced? *Journal of Aggression, Conflict and Peace Research*: Emerald Publishing. Special issue of "Honour" based abuse, violence and killings. Guest editor Roxanne Khan, Vol. 10, no. 4, pp. 293–303.

Bayley, D., & Bittner, E. (1984). Learning the skills of policing. *Law and Contemporary Problems, 47*(4), 35–59.

Bourlet, A. (1990). *Police intervention in marital violence*. Milton Keynes, UK: Open University Press.

Brown, M. (1981). *Working the street: Police discretion and the dilemmas of reform*. New York, NY: Russell Sage Foundation.

Burman, N., Smailes, S., & Chandler, K. (2004). Culture as a barrier to service provision and delivery: Domestic violence services for minoritized women. *Critical Social Policy, 24*(3), 332–357.

Care Act 2014 (c.23). [Online]. Retrieved January 13, 2016, from www.gov.uk/government.

Charman, S. (2017). *Police socialisation, identity and culture: Becoming blue*. Cham: Palgrave Macmillan.

Chesler, P. (2010, Spring). Worldwide trends in honor killings. *Middle East Quarterly, 17*(2), 3–11.

Chesler, P., & Bloom, N. (2012, Summer). Hindu vs. Muslim honor killings. *Middle East Quarterly, 19*(3), 43–52.

Children Act 1989 (c.41). [Online]. Retrieved September 1, 2016, from http://www.legislation.gov.uk.

Cockram, J. (2003). *Silent voices: Women with disabilities and family and domestic violence*. Nedlands, WA: People with Disabilities (WA) Inc. [Online]. Retrieved February 1, 2017, from http://wwda.org.au/issues.

College of Policing. (2017). [Online]. Retrieved January 20, 2019, from www.app.college.police.uk.

Crank, J. (2016). *Understanding police culture* (2nd ed.). London: Routledge.

Cromarty, H., Bellis, A., & Harker, R. (2018). *Children's social care in England*. House of Commons Library.

Department of Health. (2016). *Care act 2014: Factsheet 7: Protecting adults from abuse or neglect*. [Online]. Retrieved March 21, 2017, from socialwelfare.bl.uk.

Erwin, E. (2000). *Intimate and caregiver violence against women with disabilities*. Battered Women's Justice Project. [Online]. Retrieved May 4, 2016, from https://www.thl.fi.

Farmer, E. (2006). Using research to develop practice in child protection and childcare. In C. Humphries & N. Stanley (Eds.), *Domestic violence and child protection: Directions for good practice* (pp. 124–136). London: Jessica Kingsley.
Featherstone, B., Gupta, A., Morris, K., & White, S. (2018). *Protecting children: A social model.* Bristol: Policy Press.
Garrity, R. (1998). *Mediation and domestic violence: What domestic violence looks like.* [Online]. Retrieved May 5, 2016, from http://www.biscmi.org.
Gill, A. (2011). Reconfiguring 'honour'-based violence as a form of gendered violence. In M. Idriss & T. Abbas (Eds.), *Honour, violence, women and Islam* (pp. 218–231). Oxfordshire: Routledge.
Gill, A. (2013, October). Feminist reflections on researching so-called 'honour' killings. *Feminist Legal Studies, 21*(3), 241–261.
Goldstein, J. (1960). Police discretion not to invoke the criminal process: Low-visibility decisions in the administration of justice. *The Yale Law Journal, 69*(4), 543–594.
Grace, S. (1995). *Policing domestic violence in the 1990s.* Home Office Research Study No. 139. London: HMSO.
Graef, R. (1989). *Talking blues: The police in their own words.* London: Collins Harvill.
Hanmer, J. (2013 [1989]). Women and policing in Britain. In J. Hanmer, J. Radford, & E. Stanko (Eds.), *Women, policing, and male violence: International perspectives* (pp. 90–124). London: Routledge.
Hanmer, J., Radford, J., & Stanko, E. (2013a [1989]). Policing, men's violence: An introduction. In J. Hanmer, J. Radford, & E. Stanko (Eds.), *Women, policing, and male violence: International perspectives* (pp. 1–12). London: Routledge.
Hanmer, J., Radford, J., & Stanko, E. (2013b [1989]). Improving policing for women: The way forward. In J. Hanmer, J. Radford, & E. Stanko (Eds.), *Women, policing, and male violence: International perspectives* (pp. 185–201). London: Routledge.
Harne, L., & Radford, J. (2008). *Tackling domestic violence: Theories, policies and practice.* Maidenhead: McGraw-Hill Open University Press.
Her Majesty's Inspectorate of Constabulary (HMIC). (2014). *Everyone's business: Improving the police response to domestic abuse.* London: TSO.
Her Majesty's Inspectorate of Constabulary (HMIC). (2015). *The depths of dishonour: Hidden voices and shameful crimes. An inspection of the police response to honour-based violence, forced marriage and female genital mutilation.* London: TSO.
HM Government. (2010). *Forced marriage and learning disabilities: Multi-agency practice guidelines.* [Online]. Retrieved October 10, 2016, from https://www.gov.uk/government.

Home Office: Foreign and Commonwealth Office. (2016). *Forced marriage unit statistics January–December 2015*. London: TSO.

Horley, S. (2002). *Power and control: Why charming men can make dangerous lovers*. London: Vermilion.

House of Commons Public Administration Select Committee (PASC). (2014). *Caught red-handed: Why we can't count on police-recorded crime statistics Thirteenth Report of Session 2013–14, HC 760*.

Johnson, M. (2006). Conflict and control: Gender symmetry and asymmetry in domestic violence. *Violence Against Women, 12*(11), 1003–1018.

Kazimirski, A., Keogh, P., Kumari, V., Smith, R., Gowland, S., Purdon, S., & Khanum, N. (2009). *Forced marriage: Prevalence and service response*. Research Report No. DCSF-RR128. London: National Centre for Social Research.

Klockars, C. (1985). *The idea of police*. Beverly Hills, CA: Sage Publications.

Knott, J., & Miller, G. (1987). *Reforming bureaucracy: The politics of institutional choice*. Englewood Cliffs, NJ: Prentice-Hall.

Lakhani, N. (2008, July 26). Disabled youngsters forced into marriage to provide passports. *Independent*. [Online]. Retrieved November 7, 2016, from http://www.independent.co.uk.

Lipsky, M. (2010 [1980]). *Street-level bureaucracy: Dilemmas of the individual in public services* (Expanded ed.). New York, NY: Russell Sage Foundation.

Manning, P. (1978). The police: Mandate, strategies and appearances. In P. Manning & J. Van Maanen (Eds.), *Policing: A view from the street* (pp. 7–31). Santa Monica, CA: Goodyear Publishing Company Inc.

Mantell, A., & Clark, A. (2011). Making choices: The Mental Capacity Act 2005. In A. Mantell & T. Scragg (Eds.), *Safeguarding adults in social work* (2nd ed., pp. 48–65). London: Sage Publications.

Mental Capacity Act 2005: Codes of practice. (2013, July). UK Department for Constitutional Affairs, pp. 1–301. [Online]. Retrieved January 12, 2016, from https://www.gov.uk.

Mental Health Act 1983 (c.20). Retrieved November 1, 2016, from http://www.legislation.gov.uk.

National Society for the Prevention of Cruelty to Children (NSPCC). (2015). *Achieving positive outcomes for children in relation to return home from care*. [Online]. Retrieved November 3, 2016, from https://www.nspcc.org.uk.

Oliver, C. (2010). *Children's views and experiences of their contact with social workers: A focused review of the evidence* (pp. 1–39). Leeds: Children's Workforce Development Council.

Payton, J. (2011). Collective crimes, collective victims: A case study of the murder of Banaz Mahmod. In M. Idriss & T. Abbas (Eds.), *Honour, violence, women and Islam* (pp. 67–79). Oxfordshire: Routledge.

Rasool, I., & Payton, J. (2014). Tongues of fire: Women's suicide and self-injury by burns in the Kurdistan Region of Iraq. *The Sociological Review, 2*, 237–254.

Reiner, R. (2000). Crime and control in Britain. *Sociology, 34*(1), 71–94.

Reiner, R. (2010). *The politics of the police* (4th ed.). Oxford: Oxford University Press.

Roberts, K., Campbell, G., & Lloyd, G. (2014). *Honor-based violence: Policing and prevention* (Advances in Police Theory and Practice Series). London: CRC Press; Taylor and Francis Group.

Serious Crime Act 2015 (c.9). [Online]. Retrieved March 4, 2016, from https://www.gov.uk/government.

Shaw, A. (2001, June). Kinship, cultural preference and immigration: Consanguineous marriage among British Pakistanis. *The Journal of the Royal Anthropological Institute, 7*(2), 315–334.

Siddiqui, H. (2003). 'It was written in her kismet': Forced marriage. In R. Gupta (Ed.), *From homebreakers to jailbreakers: The work of Southall Black Sisters* (pp. 67–91). London: Zed Books.

Siddiqui, H., & Patel, M. (2003). Sad, mad or angry? Mental illness and domestic violence. In *From homebreakers to jailbreakers: The work of Southall Black Sisters* (pp. 109–131). London: Zed Books.

Stark, E. (2007). *Coercive control: How men entrap women in personal life.* Oxford: Oxford University Press.

Taylor, C., & White, S. (2006). Knowledge and reasoning in social work: Educating for humane judgement. *British Journal of Social Work, 36*(6), 937–954.

Thompson, K. (2016). *Strengthening child protection: Sharing information in multi-agency settings.* Bristol: Policy Press.

Valios, N. (2008, August 22). *Forced marriage of people with learning disabilities. Community care: Adult safeguarding, Asylum and refugees, children, disability, family support.* [Online]. Retrieved September 20, 2016, from http://www.communitycare.co.uk.

Van Maanen, J. (1978a). The asshole. In P. Manning & J. Van Maanen (Eds.), *Policing: A view from the street* (pp. 221–238). Santa Monica, CA: Goodyear Publishing Company Inc.

Van Maanen, J. (1978b). Observations on the making of policemen. In P. Manning & J. Van Maanen (Eds.), *Policing: A view from the street* (pp. 292–307). Santa Monica, CA: Goodyear Publishing Company Inc.

Waddington, P. (1999). *Policing citizens.* London: Routledge.

Youth Justice and Criminal Evidence Act 1999 (c.23). [Online]. Retrieved September 26, 2017, from www.gov.uk/government.

4

The Grey Figure of Crime: If It Isn't Crimed, It Hasn't Happened

The purpose of this chapter is to explore discretionary police practices around crime recording decisions. It opens by asserting the importance of crime recording and examines the under-recording of Police Recorded Crime, which prompted the introduction of National Crime Recording Standards (NCRS) in 2002. An overview of HBA incident to crime conversion rates across a four-year period in one force is provided, followed by an evaluation of crime recording decisions of the 100 incidents analysed. Crime types are examined, in particular the emergent theme of "threats to kill" being under-recorded by officers. Facets facilitating under-recording practices are explored, notably the low visibility of officers and the lack of supervisory oversight when frontline officers are decision-making. Explanations justifying "no-crime" decisions are probed, such as the poor training of officers, the subjective judgements of officers and the use of quasi-legal rules and procedures. Other factors shaping decision-making include officers pre-empting "no-charge" decisions from the CPS and being adversely influenced by a performance target culture. A visible shift is noted in recording practices, notably "record to investigate." Later sections focus on officers being de-incentivised to record crime when victims are reluctant to prosecute,

R. Aplin, *Policing UK Honour-Based Abuse Crime*,
https://doi.org/10.1007/978-3-030-18430-8_4

which transpires to be a prevalent theme. Officers manufacturing victim reluctance and its relationship with officer workload are scrutinised, particularly by applying Lipsky's research on bureaucratic organisations.

The Importance of Crime Recording

Recording a crime is a "highly significant decision" (Kemp et al. 1992: 17), first, because "what gets measured gets done" (O'Byrne 2008: 413, also Berry 2009) and, equally, what is not measured tends to get ignored. Second, from a strategic policing perspective, crime reports are subject to analysis by local and force intelligence units, shaping short- and long-term local and force strategic threat assessments, which in turn prioritise threats and determine the type and number of resources deployed over a geographical area. Emerging threats may warrant additional government funding, which cannot be sought or indeed justified if the problem remains "hidden" within filed incident data. Third, recording practices are important for procedural justice. A crime report is symbolic acknowledgement and validation for the victim that a crime has occurred and that the police are investigating and seek justice (Varano et al. 2009). Fourth, the recording of crime aids in sign-posting or alerting other agencies in supporting and safeguarding victims of crime. Failure to submit a crime report stifles any future investigation, leaves the victim exposed to further risk and leaves the stone unturned as incidents are not subjected to analysis. To summarise, crime recording informs government policy, identifies crime trends, directs police resources, underpins crime pattern analysis and intelligence-led policing and allows crime reduction initiatives to be evaluated (HMIC 2000).

Overall Crime Is Under-recorded

The measurement of crime is based on two main statistical sources: the Crime Survey for England and Wales[1] (CSEW) and Police Recorded Crime (PRC) (House of Commons PASC 2014). Rather than being preoccupied with the "dark figure" (Manning 1978a: 20; Bourlet 1990; Reiner

2000: 75) of *unreported* crime, this chapter is concerned with the "grey figure" of unrecorded crimes. This is because the findings expose a disparity between what the public report to the police (PRC) and what the police, in turn, formally record (Bottomley and Pease 1986). It is in researching this "gap" that discretionary police practices are readily discernible.

National Crime Recording Standards and the Use of Discretion

Crime recording across all crime types has had a tarnished history. National Crime Recording Standards (NCRS) and Home Office Counting Rules (HOCR) were introduced into England and Wales police forces in 2002, after HMIC critically concluded that crime recording rates across 11 police forces varied between 55% and 82% (HMIC 2000: x). The report highlighted that 24% of incidents reported to officers were not recorded as crimes (HMIC 2000: 53). Even when incidents were appropriately recorded, between 15% and 65% of crimes were incorrectly classified under the wrong crime type (ibid.). Consequently, the aim of introducing NCRS was to promote consistency between police forces in the standard of crime reporting across England and Wales (Home Office 2003). According to Home Office rules, an incident shall be recorded as a crime (notifiable offence) if on the balance of probability[2]:

(a) The circumstances of the victim's report amount to a crime as defined by law (the police will determine this, based on their knowledge of the law and counting rules) and
(b) There is no credible evidence to the contrary immediately available

(HOCR 2015: 9)

The effect of "criming" an incident means it becomes the subject of rigorous evaluation by crime evaluators working to the rules of each force crime audit unit (determined by HOCR and NCRS). A crime can only be "filed" when all reasonable lines of enquiry have been pursued by police officers (HOCR 2014: 5). What serves to exacerbate the issue of crime recording is lack of knowledge by the public, who often believe that when an incident is reported face to face with officers this means it has been counted/recorded as a crime (Coleman and Moynihan 1996: 34), which is not the case.

Despite the introduction of NCRS in 2002 doubts about police crime statistics continue to proliferate. A freedom of information request by the Times (2011) suggests that 32% of crimes in England and Wales are filed without investigation (Policy expert, 2011 as cited in Brogden and Ellison 2013: 49). It is worth noting that in the first two years of NCRS implementation there was an immediate structural increase in the number of crimes recorded (2002–2004), yet overall crime levels have fallen every subsequent year since 2002, at a faster rate than the Crime Survey for England and Wales (CSEW) suggest is credible (House of Commons PASC 2014). Given the consistent pattern, the hypothesis is that there has been an erosion of compliance with the NCRS and that incidents reported are not being captured in the crime recording system; in effect "PRC (police recorded crime) under-records crime" (House of Commons PASC 2014: 3). HMIC attests that if all forces recorded all crimes reported to them in line with current counting rules (HOCR), total crime nationally should increase significantly (2000: 53). This confirms the fears for many that police crime recording, like figures pre NCRS, represents a "faulty portrait of the social reality" (Manning 1978a: 22) as the statistics are based on "crime which the police wish to make known" (Reiner 2000: 76) rather than being a reflection of true crime rates.

Academics have long asserted that official crime is a product of police decision-making (Black 1980; Reiner 2000; Maguire 2012). Although discretionary decision-making by police officers has been researched concerning over-policing, that is, the use of force and arrest (Black 1971; Bayley and Bittner 1984), deaths in police custody (Baker 2016) and stop and search (Bowling and Phillips 2007; Quinton 2011), there is much less research on *under-policing* and the discretion around whether or not to formally record a crime (Varano et al. 2009). Critically, not recording a crime and other actions at scenes tend to be low visibility decisions (Shearing 1981; Klockars 1985; Loftus 2009) that often escape middle management and public scrutiny because:

> [d]ecisions that cannot be reviewed provide fertile soil for abuses of discretionary decision-making. (Warner 1997: 632)

When officers inappropriately apply discretion by failing to record a "crime" this is termed "writing off" or "cuffing" an incident; so termed where officers prematurely file rather than crime incidents by "concealing the truth up [their] sleeves or cuffs" (Young 1991: 324). Cuffing is effectively a means by which the crime is eliminated or hidden from public scrutiny (ibid.). By "cuffing" the officer is concluding that the offence did not take place or is not worthy of police intervention (Myhill and Johnson 2016). In the USA, such cuffing practices are termed "load shedding" (Varano et al. 2009: 554), and equally in the UK "unsolvable crimes" were consigned to file 13—a figurative term for the bin (Young 1991: 324). Decisions around whether officers should "cuff" the incident were often attributed to the likelihood of a "comeback" (Young 1991; Coleman and Moynihan 1996: 36) in terms of whether that course of action might prompt a police complaint, which then might deter the officer-making the practice an "inhibiting" rule (Smith and Gray 1985).

Bourlet contends that there is an overemphasis on the use of discretion by officers, particularly in the domestic abuse arena which leads to the considerable under-recording of crimes (1990). Explanations for the shortfall in officers recording crimes were provided in the 1992 British Crime Survey. Key themes included reports being treated as disingenuous, with police not accepting victims accounts; there being insufficient evidence or reports being deemed as too trivial to justify formal action, especially if the complainant refused to prosecute (Mayhew et al. 1993 as cited in Coleman and Moynihan 1996: 34). Alternatively, some have suggested that performance targets are the cause of "cuffing" as they "drive perverse incentives" to mis-record crime (House of Commons PASC 2014: 8). Although performance targets *do* present officers with a conflict between the achievement of targets and core ethical policing values (ibid.), it is argued that "cuffing" has been an active and widespread policing practice since 1939 (Young 1991). The "numbers game" (Bayley and Bittner 1984: 39) and crime detection have always been central to the ideology of the policing institution as this is a primary means of determining practical police effectiveness (Young 1991). Therefore, it is suggested that performance targets in isolation do not fully rationalise under-recording practices.

HBA Crime Is Under-recorded

It is argued that HBA crimes are not fully captured under current Home Office data returns (College of Policing 2015; IKWRO 2014). This is illustrated in the data returns collated by the Iranian and Kurdish Women's Rights Organisation, who submitted a freedom of information request to all UK police forces (including Scotland and N. Ireland), providing the first useful data of its kind for HBA. Findings from 39 of the 52 forces recorded 11,744 HBA incidents across a five-year period (2010–2014), consisting of beatings, abductions and murders, which equates to an average of 2348 HBA incidents per annum (IKWRO 2015). Equally, HMIC data returns from 41 of 43 England and Wales police forces determined that there were 2600 incidents over a 10-month period (to Jan 31st 2015) flagged as HBA, FM or Forced Genital Mutilation (FGM) with 830 associated crime reports (HMIC 2015: 58). However, the disparity arises when one compares these yearly incident figures (2348–2600) to CPS yearly prosecutions, which are small by comparison. Police referrals to CPS are declining across domestic abuse overall (HMICFRS 2017), but specifically regarding HBA which results in less UK prosecutions, from 251 (2014–2015) (CPS 2015: 11) to 171 (2016–2017) currently standing at 127 (2017–2018) (CPS 2018: 13). It is accepted that not all incidents will necessarily amount to a crime; yet even so the figures indicate that there is a significant reduction in number between the stages where victims report incidents to police and their eventual referral to the CPS. The reasons as to this disparity will be fully explored.

The subset of 100 cases analysed were obtained from a large data set comprising of 671 HBA incidents reported to this police force across a four-year period (2011–2014 inclusive). However, it is considered that the HBA incident numbers are underestimated for several reasons. First, the data was pulled from the system by searching for "honour" codes C58 and C59 within the code qualifier and principal closing codes. Therefore, if control room staff relied on other closing or qualifying codes to categorise the incident, not all HBA incidents would have been captured within the current data set. Second, HBA incidents could have been incorrectly coded within the system; for instance, labelled as domestic violence (only), concern for child or child abuse without any specific "honour" coding attached. Third, many HBA cases are referred through to the police from other agencies, such as the multi-agency safeguarding hub (MASH), the Education sector or children's social care (CSC). Such cases are immediately dealt with by specialist PPIU officers and are therefore not logged through the communications branch.

Analysis of the large data set (Chart 4.1) of 671 cases reflects very poor incident to crime conversion rates longitudinally. On average, 13% (85/671) of all HBA incidents reported to police over a four-year period were recorded as "crimes" and were investigated and subjected to scrutiny by crime evaluators and supervisors. The incident to crime conversion rate remained steadily low in 2011(11%), 2012 (10%) and 2013 (11%).

On average 90% of HBA allegations attended by officers over a three-year period were "filed" as no-crime (2011–2013). Year 2014 was a much better year for crime reporting, in which 21% (30/114) of incidents were crimed. Although this indicates an increase in cases being crimed, Chart 4.1 reflects a year-on-year marked decline in victim reporting, representing the dark figure of crime. Interviewees recognise that the practice of no-criming incidents hides substantial numbers of offences and distorts the grey picture of crime:

> I'd say—why are we not criming this, if we're not criming it, crimes not going to go up..//.. And we're shooting ourselves in the foot I've been saying it for years (police officer i)

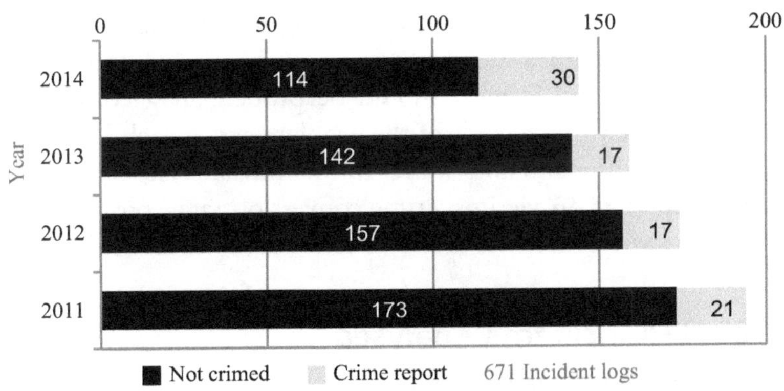

Chart 4.1 HBA incident to crime rate conversion (2011–2014)

These findings reinforce extant research, supporting the view that HBA levels are significantly higher than published data suggests (HMIC 2015: 41), representing the "tip of an iceberg" especially when assessed against victim numbers contacting charitable helplines, which has increased by 47% (2010–2013) (Dyer 2015: 14).

More accurate recording mechanisms are essential in order to identify the scale of honour-based abuse across England and Wales. There are reassuring signs that the crime recording of domestic abuse incidents across England and Wales is improving, with 50% (598,545) of domestic abuse incidents reported to the police being converted into crime reports (ONS 2018: 11), which is an increase from 41% in 2016 (ONS 2016: 29). Yet crucially as a subset of domestic abuse, HBA crime recording data is currently *hidden* amidst ONS statistics. If one compares this information to the present HBA research study, there is a real disparity in crime recording rates, as on average only a tenth of HBA incidents over a three-year period in one police force were formally subjected to a crime report—with 89% of incidents filed as "no-crime" (2011–2013). Yet the discrepancy in incident to crime conversion rates is not visible by examining ONS data. Attempting to disaggregate HBA data from the larger DA data set is neither possible nor practical, because under home office counting rules HBA, like other forms of domestic abuse, encompasses numerous crime categories such as assault, criminal damage, kidnap, false imprisonment, threats to kill, murder. Therefore, it is considered impractical to advocate for an independent crime category as IKWRO suggests (2014). Instead, it is suggested that forces should utilise opening and closing codes for HBA (and related HBA crimes such as FM and FGM) incidents and, second, that all incidents (and crimes) should be properly flagged as HBA, in order to better identify the scale of the problem across each force area and ultimately across England and Wales. In this way analysts could disaggregate and compare HBA victims, crime conversion rates, prosecutions and CPS outcomes with other forms of domestic abuse within the one data set.

The 100 HBA Incidents Analysed

Chart 4.2, illustrating the ratio of 100 incidents analysed (2012–2014), appears healthier when compared with the longitudinal trend, with 31%

(31/100)[3] formally crimed and 69% (69/100) filed as no-crime. However, this means that over two-thirds of the HBA incidents sampled in this study were not subjected to a formal crime report.

Officers were shown Chart 4.2 whilst being interviewed and there were mixed reactions. One officer was "actually surprised that 31% were crimed" (police officer j), whilst another compared these as broadly similar to domestic abuse rates (police officer f). By comparison, half of the specialist officers were surprised at the poor incident to crime conversion rate, not only because of breaches to NCRS and DA recording policy but also because failing to record crimes does not support women and girls in dire need:

> Oh, that should be a lot higher then, yeah, that should be a lot higher then (police officer p)
>
> It doesn't look great, does it?..//..it is staggering, because certainly with the new domestic violence recording policy within (this force) if a third-party person reports it. Based on what they tell us, if a crime has been committed we record it—so how can that only be 69% no-crime? (police officer o)
>
> Officers still don't have a full understanding of the issues—obviously our conversion rate is very poor—because we should have a much higher conversion rate than that—I would say at least 75% should be looking at a 'crimed' incident (police officer a)

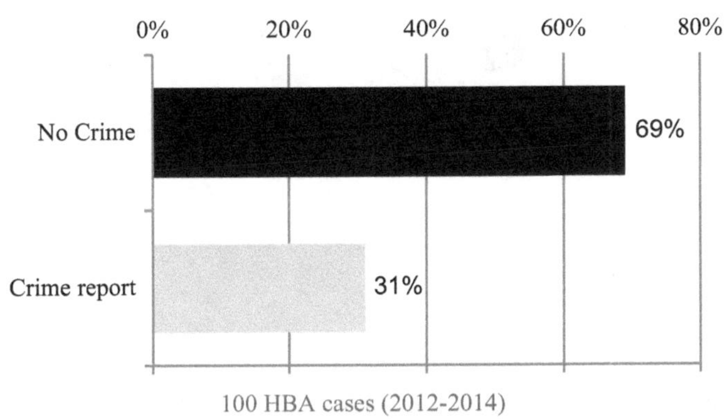

Chart 4.2 HBA incident to crime rate conversion (100 cases)

> I think we're not getting it right ..//.. Those 100 cases—It's got to that scary point of "really now I need help or my friend needs help". I would have thought it should have been the other way about (police officer b)

A summary of the results shows that of the 100 cases analysed 31% (31/100) were formally crimed; a further 25% (25/100)[4] in the view of the researcher[5] breached NCRS and should have been subject of a crime report. Therefore, 56% of the whole sample (rather than 31%) should have been formally recorded as crimes (see Chart 4.3). A further five cases (5/100)[6] were difficult to determine due to insufficient rationale provided by the attendant officers to negate or determine whether a crime had occurred, which in turn breached the National Standard of Incident Recording (Home Office 2011). The remaining 39% of filed cases were,

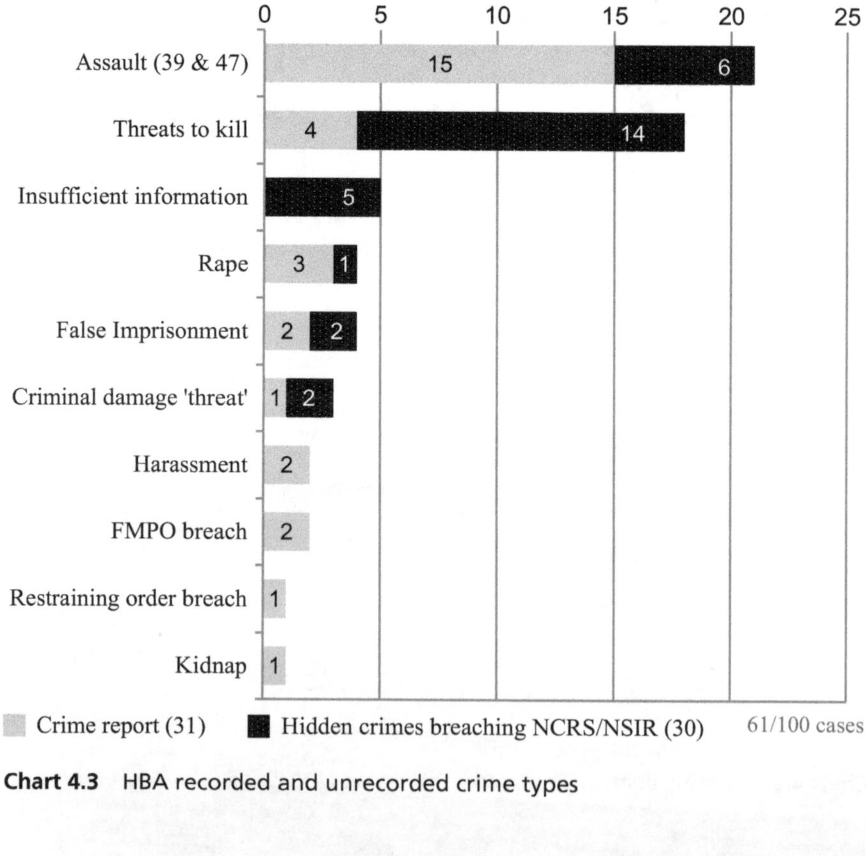

Chart 4.3 HBA recorded and unrecorded crime types

according to the researcher, justifiably deemed as no-crime. It is to be expected that not all incidents reported to the police would necessarily amount to a crime. For instance, they could constitute concerns for welfare or missing from home (MFH) reports. One officer suggested that HBA incidents sometimes amounted to an argument between a brother and sister "about a relationship that they're not happy with" rather than a form of reportable criminality (police officer f). However, the lack of depth in some officer investigations caused concern, as such incidents could expose crimes if the correct questions were posed by officers, an area fully explored in Chap. 5.

Flawed No-Crime Decisions

In attempting to isolate the reasons for no-crime decisions, Chart 4.3 provides the details of which crime types were formally recorded and which crime types should have been formally recorded as crimes.

As illustrated in Chart 4.3, the largest proportion of under-recorded "hidden" crimes were 14 cases of "threats to kill." There were six hidden crimes of assault and a further serious case involving a 13-year-old victim who was brought into the country on a false passport with an older date of birth and forced into marriage, making the crime a historical rape (case 97). There were also several threats to commit criminal damage and false imprisonment cases.

Home Office rules dictate that any incident *not* subsequently recorded as a crime must be supported by the appropriate rationale (HOCR 2014: 39) on the incident log, which should provide "sufficient information to justify actions taken by officers" (Home Office 2011: 1.17). Officers often presented a number of explanations when writing up their rationale, to justify inaction and non-enforcement decisions. Such practices were identified by examining the discrepancies between the officers' summary write-ups compared with witness and victim accounts and demeanours presented within police electronic documentary reports, such as the PPI, DASH risk assessment, intelligence or crime reports. Many officers breached NSIR (Home Office 2011) by failing to rationalise why a crime was *not* being recorded:

> Despite it being documented on the incident that an 11-year-old Iraqi victim alleged mum "keeps hitting her," no crime report is submitted (case 13)
>
> Page one of an incident states victim was "hit by her husband" and yet no crime was input, with the officer's write-up concluding it "does not amount to a notifiable offence" (case 47)
>
> Despite those sheltering the victim being threatened to have their windows "smashed inwards" should they continue to harbour the victim, officers do not crime the threat to commit criminal damage (case 60)
>
> You're getting the officers who are going saying "oh yeah, they've not reported any offences"—well you've got somebody who's saying they were assaulted when they rung up so—you've done nothing to negate that (police officer k)

According to officers, writing off or "cuffing" crimes appears to exist across a range of crime types rather than being specific to HBA:

> I think it would fall into the 'too hard to do' category for some. I think there's a culture if you can 'write it off' then we will (police officer c)
>
> We all know there are FWINs [incidents] out there that should be crimed (police officer f)
>
> In general policing I don't think we meet the NCRS compliance a lot of the time..//.. [victims] say "oh my mum slapped me" and it's been recorded or written off as reasonable chastisement—but you've still got a crime that's occurred. You know you still record it, although it might not be in the public interest and you might not pursue it, you still record it..//.. I think we're missing out on too many (police officer k)
>
> I'll bet in those 90% [of cases which were filed] there were a lot which named offences in the actual body [of] the write-up (police officer m)

Although interviewees broadly acknowledge under-recording practices, some officers attribute these decisions based on lack of knowledge or training of officers in crime recording rules:

> I think it's a training issue rather than officers not wanting to crime it..//..They innocently are failing to identify those signs and symptoms (police officer d)
>
> I don't think it's from officers being lazy or incompetent, I don't think it's generally from that, I just think it's from lack of understanding (police officer i)

> There are times when I've seen a log and a crime *hasn't* been put in and I just think the officers aren't aware sometimes that they are supposed to. So, for example, the incidents in nursing homes, underage children. We've still got to put a crime in even though we write it off, I just don't think they know (police officer b)
>
> I wonder if perhaps officers have been [to the location] and probably not understood the full meaning about it ..//..Perhaps that's been written off when it shouldn't have been (police officer p)

In contrast, other officers (a, g, o and k) suggest there is sufficient knowledge and training of NCRS. Some specialist officers also excuse no-crime decisions made by response officers on the grounds that they are unfamiliar with HBA offences and thus only comfortable with the "bread and butter" (police officer n) "day to day" (police officer b) offences they deal with:

> Maybe they just don't know about the other offences, because their day to day offences are theft, assault and harassment now (police officer b)
>
> It depends on whether front line understands the HBA part of it. But I mean if like you get straight assault, straight 'threats to kill'—then you'd think well they'd put a crime in for that—but whether they understand… I don't know if they understand (police officer g)

However, it is clear from the analysis that the HBA offences constitute the core offences of violence that frontline officers routinely deal with such as assault, rape, threats to kill and false imprisonment. Therefore, the explanation for no-criming cases in this way appears wholly insufficient.

Lack of Supervisory Oversight

In the same vein, officers justify mistakes made by uniformed supervisors on the basis of lack of knowledge of offences, rather than the application of inappropriate discretion:

> It's your response sergeants that will look at whether a FWIN is NCRS compliant—because *they* haven't got a full understanding and awareness of the crimes that are available to them. I think there's a lack of expectation of

> crimes rather than an encouragement *not* to put those crimes in (police officer h)

Findings illustrate that supervisors rarely challenge the disparity between the incident report and the subsequent "write up" by officers. Incident data highlights several occasions whereby incidents are wrongly confirmed by supervision as "NCRS compliant" (cases 39, 62, 86).[7] For instance, in one case a victim was locked inside an address by her mother and uncle. Although the police assisted her in vacating the address, no crime of false imprisonment was logged and the supervisor deemed the case to be "NCRS compliant" (case 86). Furthermore, typing "NCRS compliant" appears to be a 'box ticking' process which has little tangible effect on data quality:

> We're having a lot of sergeants who are saying they are doing the NCRS compliance on the log—But they are not, no (police officer k)

HMIC also detects a lack of supervisory oversight, highlighting that the closure of cases under "no further action" does not routinely have a supervisory review, nor is the rationale for decisions explained. Neither is the long-term safeguarding plan for victims visible (HMIC 2015: 120). Because divisional and force analysts extrapolate information from "crime" reports rather than incidents, the grey figure of crime is not readily recognisable by higher management when information is left languishing on the incident report. It is argued that NCRS rules and the development of information technology can *only* limit the discretionary practices of officers once a crime is already recorded.

It also appears to be the case that the feasibility of supervisors "checking" every incident is an "impossible mandate" (Manning 1978a: 12), particularly given the volume of incoming work and myriad of different computer systems. In a year, this force alone received 2 million calls (Police and Crime plan 2014–2016: 6) responded specifically to 896,912 incidents (2015) and dealt with, on average, 2375[8] incidents in every 24-hour period (2016) (personal communication through accessing force systems, senior force analyst, 2016). On this basis, it is argued that supervisors do not and cannot routinely verify whether incidents are NCRS compliant. Given that since the public spending cuts this force, like many across the country, has had to make estimated savings of £236 million (2011–2018) along with losing 1100 police officers (Police and Crime plan 2014–2016: 27), police forces clearly have to do much more with less. There are rare occasions in the study where supervisors challenge[9] officers about the conflicts between the information provided in the initial call from informants compared to the incident "write up" provided by the attendant officer.

"Threats to Kill" Offences Under-recorded

As a crime of violence, threats to kill falls under the Offences Against the Persons Act 1861 (section 16) and has a ten-year imprisonment term (www.legislation.gov.uk). To prove this offence, the defendant does not have to intend to kill/carry out the threat; and neither does the victim (or officer) have to believe the threat would be carried out. The prosecution must prove that the perpetrator:

1. Made a threat to kill that or a third person (either written, orally or by actions), *and*
2. The perpetrator intended that the victim would fear that the threat would be carried out

(cps.gov.uk)

Courts often consider the victim's situation to determine whether it is reasonable to assume the defendant intended the threat to be taken seriously (cps.gov.uk). CPS guidelines deem that a charge of threats to kill is appropriate when there has been a threat of assault, but an assault was prevented. Therefore, if an assault occurs *in addition* to a threat to kill, an additional charge of threats to kill would be unnecessary (ibid.). Therefore, only the cases in which no crimes whatsoever were submitted were counted as "breaches" within the sample of the 100 cases analysed. Findings showed (Chart 4.3) that despite there being sufficient evidence to crime 18 cases of "threats to kill," only 4 cases were actually crimed. Thus, 78% of all threats to kill allegations within the sample went unrecorded by officers (14/18),[10] representing the largest crime type under-recorded and constituting 47% of all NCRS/NSIR breaches in the data set (14/30). Worryingly, threats to kill offences were particularly prevalent in cases where victims were pregnant.

Akin to other NCRS breaches in the sample, some officers via the incident write-up denied "threats to kill" had occurred, suggesting there was no victim confirmation of crimes. Conversely other tactics involved officers trivialising and diluting the account given by victim(s) and/or wrongly suggesting that the circumstances did not fit the legal definition of a threats to kill (see Chap. 5). However, in these cases the write-up summary by the attendant officers largely conflicted with the initial report taken by the police call handlers. For instance, in one case a father discovered his daughter was in a relationship and forbade it. However, they continued the relationship and she became pregnant. In a phone call, the father threatened to kill the love choice boyfriend on three occasions saying "I'm going find you and murder you" (case 5). He then put his 12-weeks pregnant daughter on a flight to Pakistan to attend a "family wedding," stating "I'll give her what she deserves and you are gonna get the same." The officer intercepted the victim prior to her getting on the plane. However, despite the boyfriend's very "real" belief of the threats to kill, the officer negates the risks to both victims:

> Female victim has been spoken to and has confirmed there has been no assaults, there is no concern over honour-based abuse and she is happy to go to Pakistan..//.. There have been no threats to kill or assaults towards (the named boyfriend) (case 5)

Whether the victims are safe and well is unclear, but the officer took no action and did not input a crime. In a further pregnant victim case (cases 65 and 67 linked), there was a documentary audit trail highlighting that the victim(s) reported "threats to kill" offences to different officers on three separate occasions across a 15-day period. The threats were initially reported to the police station front desk, and then by the concerned boyfriend when he had not seen his girlfriend for four days following the parent's discovery of her pregnancy. Finally, when the female "Facebooked" the boyfriend, the police were alerted so that she could flee the family home. In the first report, the father discovered his daughter had a boyfriend and "made threats to kill" him, which was clearly logged on the incident report. Yet within the PPI report the officer contrastingly documents:

> They did not wish to make any complaint—they only sought advice. No threats of violence were made to any person, neither wish to make any complaint or provide any sort of a statement (cases 65 and 67 linked)

In the second PPI report, a different officer concurs with the previous report suggesting the incident was not a domestic abuse incident but a "concern for welfare" (case 65). In the final report the father was keeping his daughter under "house arrest" and, crucially, by this stage the victim had allegedly had a "miscarriage" at a private clinic. The father threatened:

> If you do decide to leave, then you will have your few months of happiness with him, then I will get you killed as well as (boyfriend) (case 67)

It can be inferred from information supplied by the daughter (explored in Chap. 6) that the parents had encouraged the daughter into having an abortion. Had the police taken a more proactive stance and adequately safeguarded the victim in the initial reports, the child may still be alive.

In some threats to kill allegations, the threat level was high and yet no crime reports were submitted. For instance, an 18-year-old Pakistani victim was at risk of death due to the dishonour brought about by her 7-month pregnancy. The threat came from a third party (the mother) who told police that her husband and son were intent on killing the daughter and had booked flights to flee to Pakistan immediately after her murder. Police took the threat seriously enough to issue a threat to life "Osman"[11] warning and yet paradoxically the Inspector sanctioned that "no notifiable offence" had occurred in terms of a "threats to kill" (case 69, linked to case 70). There was a second "threats to kill" incident reported against the victim's mother by one of her other sons, and neither was this incident crimed. It is posited that if the police were entirely satisfied that the allegation was groundless, they would not have generated a multitude of actions, created an intelligence item about the threat posed to the lives of the females, alerted the national border targeting agency or allocated resources via a green room intelligence cell to manage the investigation. It is hypothesised that the crime report was not submitted by the Inspector because it would remain an undetected crime on the system.

Child cases are managed in a similar way. Despite a 12-year-old Bangladeshi victim contacting the police to report a number of offences by her perpetrator parents, no crimes were recorded and the incident was "written off" as "NCRS compliant." The impetus for calling the police was the victim's behaviour at a strict Islamic school for girls, in which she was found by a teacher trying to dispose of a condom (unused and still in the wrapper) in the bin. She was also questioned by the school about her "Facebook" profile, in which she had worn no headscarf. After arranging an appointment with the headmaster, the father drove his daughter home and made threats to kill her. Believing the threats would be carried out, she dialled 999. On police arrival, the victim disclosed two assaults by both parents and several "threats to kill" offences. Under the "finished incident rule"[12] (HOCR 2016), the historical "threats to kill" and two assaults would not require separate crime reports; however, the suspects could and should have been additionally charged with those offences. The officer should have crimed the recent "threats to kill" against the child, or alternatively, under NCRS guidelines, provided rationale as to why this was not crimed. No crimes were recorded. The incident breached NCRS, but more significantly the child remained at the family home in a high-risk predicament for a further three years (case 39). Hemphill et al. suggest that threats of violence are a good predictor of future violence and hence "threats to kill" is included in the DASH risk assessment tools (1998). From a safeguarding perspective, it is therefore concerning that 78% (14/18) of threats to kill offences in this sample went unrecorded and uninvestigated. However, one interviewee considered that under-recording threats to kill was not limited to HBA but evident across domestic abuse more broadly:

> If you look at any DA incident where there's a threat, you know you'll have the same issue with threats to kill, across the board. I can't visualise any reason why an HBA incident should bring that out, rather than a DA incident (police officer f)

Subjective Judgements and Quasi Legal Rules

Several themes are apparent which appear to facilitate officers under-recording the offence of "threats to kill." First, there is evidence[13] of officers applying a faulty interpretation of the "threats to kill" definition, based on the immediacy of the threat and the timing of the victim reports. Second, officers apply their own highly subjective judgements about the "seriousness" of cases. Both facets were intertwined:

> Threats to kill as a crime probably doesn't always get reported as much as it does because people go "Well, you're not in immediate danger, there's nothing there," they kind of write it off. But they're contacting the police—they're in fear (police officer p)
>
> If they've said "It was over the phone and he's [the perpetrator] not actually turned up," then maybe they're [police] thinking—"Oh, it's not that serious" (police officer b)
>
> '6 months ago he said that if I was to do that he'd kill me' [victim's report]..//.. It could be perceived as—'I don't believe it,' because you know it was so many months ago..//.. the officers might have looked at that and said, Well, it's not a crime because it happened that long ago, she [victim] doesn't believe the threat' (police officer n)
>
> Officers attending have varying views on what threats to kill is and base the need to crime on that, that's what I'm saying. So it is being viewed subjectively (police officer f)

These excerpts illustrate that police decision-making around "threats to kill" subjectively revolves around whose account the officers are most persuaded by, rather than strictly adhering to the legal points to prove in the threats to kill definition. The perceived reliability of victims' hinges on whether officers are convinced by their responses. This illustrates that "all law enforcement is a matter of negotiation" (Manning and Van Maanen 1978: 220) between victims, perpetrators and the police. Third, some officers rely on the presentational validity of quasi legal rules to *justify* no-crime decisions. For instance, officers are loath to crime cases where "threats to kill" were made through a third party. To exemplify, after marrying her love choice against the family's wishes, the "dishonoured" victim and husband fled from the area after being subjected to violence and threats from her brother. When she returned from Pakistan after eight months, the brother communicated a threat through his own wife that "if I see her anywhere, I will get her and her husband killed." Officers did not crime this case on the grounds it was not a "direct threat" (case 29). In a similar case, a male Sunni Muslim and his Shi'a Muslim wife fled to the UK and married against the wishes of their families. Four separate police intelligence items (2011–2012) indicated several "threats to kill" allegations had been made against the couple and yet the attendant officer did not submit a crime report on the grounds:

> No direct person has made a threat, and (the threat is) not immediate (case 99)

Therefore, officers apply quasi legal rules, such as the threat not being "imminent," or based on third-party indirect threats,[14] in order to erroneously justify a "legal" inability to prosecute. However, the legal position is that the threat does not have to be a direct threat and can include a threat communicated via a "third party," and neither does the threat have to be imminent (cps.gov.uk). Extant research reinforces this proposition, evident in Lynn and Lea's research on "wit craft," where officers legitimate a refusal to act based on their apparent knowledge of the law to members of the public. The success of this strategy is highly dependent on the public's lay ignorance of the law. In accepting officers' judgements, this allows selective or "creative" interpretations of the law to pass unchallenged (Lynn and Lea 2012).

As indicated earlier, police officers themselves excuse poor investigations on the basis of lack of knowledge or training, rather than the inappropriate application of discretion. Equally, Myhill and Johnson attribute poor recording practices at domestic incidents to officers failing to identify the risks, rather than this being malicious (2016: 16). However, it is argued that the findings here align with Hobbs's contention that it may be too gracious to suggest that officers pursue "principled non-enforcement" (1991: 604) practices which underrate the self-interested nature of why such offences are not being enforced. This is a worthy of consideration, particularly when some officers apply several "improvised" techniques of "writing off" an incident, that is, case 73 (explored in Chap. 5).

The excerpt below highlights that some officers' rationalisations for no-crime decisions are without foundation:

> There are times when we review a log and a third party's rang it in ..//.. they'll [officers] go "Oh, I spoke to the parties. No crimes", and I have to send it back [the action], saying, "What did the informant say?" And [the reply] "Oh, I didn't speak to them" (police officer b)
>
> Researcher—So they're not investigated properly in order to negate a 'threats to kill'?
>
> No. Nobody ever speaks to the informant (police officer b)

Therefore, whether there is a lack of understanding by officers around the points to prove for threats to kill, or whether this is a device used to "cuff" these crimes is open to interpretation; however, both facets are evident in the findings.

Officers Pre-empt CPS "No-Charge" Decisions

Officers often attribute the under-recording of threats to kill based on anticipated no-charge decisions from the Crown Prosecution Service (CPS). Despite no questions being posed on the CPS, several police officers alluded to being impeded by CPS, who rarely accept a charge of "threats to kill" because of the high threshold test:

> The level they need [CPS] and almost about to kill you before they'll charge on threats to kill, so whether or not they [officers] don't think there's enough to put in a 'threats to kill' (police officer b)
>
> There's always been some resistance to about threats to kill because the [CPS] threshold is deemed to be quite high..//..We all know what CPS wants for threats to kill and it's traditionally a lot more than what we [police] arrest for, and maybe that inhibits officers, but having said that, the CPS want more for every offence that we arrest for (police officer f)
>
> They'll [CPS] say well if it's not immediate, you know the threat's been made but it was an indirect threat that was made 3 months ago, sort of thing, they're not going to charge on it (police officer n)
>
> I think the offence is made out very easily initially, but to actually get a prosecution for it—I think is horrendous. If they [perpetrators]—defi-

> nitely if they have a solicitor—they are told what constitutes the crime of 'threats to kill'. Simple, isn't it—"I didn't mean it to come across as that, I didn't mean when I said that, I was just angry"..//.. We find threats to kill notoriously difficult to 'get home' [to prosecute in court] (police officer m)

Such excerpts first suggest the threshold test applied by the CPS is too high[15] with the offence notoriously difficult to "get home" (police officer m also e), suggesting the legislation is ineffective in protecting victims. Second, there is evidence of officer's decisions being influenced and pre-empted by the likelihood or otherwise of a charging/prosecution decision from CPS, whereby officers act as a "prosecutorial filter" (Lynn and Lea 2012: 363). For instance, the officer documents in the crime report how the victim suffered "slaps across the left cheek." Yet in contrast, the incident report states that "her jaw is sore from the punches, offender has used his fists to punch (her)" (case 16). This certainly shows how, through the constructed "write up" crafted by the officer, a section 47 assault is reduced to a lesser section 39 offence. Rather than rely on the legal points to prove and victim testimony, officers pragmatically submit crime reports based on anticipated CPS charging decisions:

> I think they know [officers] from experience the outcome of what a job would be, and I think some can see "well CPS are never going to run it as attempt section 18, it would be a common assault or 47" (police officer i)

Third, some officers conflate the two different requirements, as crime recording under NCRS and charging decisions have an entirely different standard of proof. The former is based on the "balance of probabilities" and the latter on being satisfied that there is sufficient evidence to provide a realistic prospect of conviction (The Code for Crown Prosecutors 2013). These findings reinforce the House of Commons PASC report, in which officers erroneously "set the evidential bar too high when making a recording decision, based on their perception of the likelihood of a Crown Prosecution Service charge, rather than using the victim-focussed standard prescribed by the NCRS" (House of Commons PASC 2014: 13). However, despite the poor recording practices by some officers, inputting threats to kill was recognised by some specialists as necessary:

> I'm assuming that most of the domestic homicide reviews that we get, there will be a threat at some point..//..So threats to kill..//..It needs to be crimed, there needs to be a safeguarding plan in place because it is one of the most riskiest crimes ..//.. I think if they are thinking of it evidentially, it's very hard to prove without the victim (police officer o)

There was only one other instance in which an officer alluded to CPS being loathe to prosecute "threats to kill" on the basis of victim reluctance:

> But often CPS say it's not in the public interest because the female victim..//.. doesn't want to be involved. They won't support the prosecution (police officer a)

This illustrates that despite CPS advocating good practice and training on "victimless prosecutions" (CPS 2015) for high-risk domestic abuse cases, the practical reality may lie adrift from policy.

There is also evidence of officers possessing the free rein to "satisfice" (Simon 1976) by simplifying or reducing crimes to less serious offences[16]; or choosing one crime (or no crime) or one charge, which is evidentially and legally the "easiest" to prove in court (cases 16, 57, 79 and 62). In another instance, multiple charges should have been laid (e.g. threats to commit criminal damage, assault and threats to kill) (case 62) but no crime was input and no perpetrator arrested. Such simplifications may be pragmatic, and may pre-empt CPS charging decisions, yet this could be perceived as officers aiming for the low hanging fruit whereby other crimes and multiple perpetrators, including female perpetrators (see Chap. 6), could easily be overlooked, resulting in the under-protection of victims.

Police Preoccupation with Performance Targets

Investigate to Record

The findings strongly support extant research which indicates that officers (between 2005 and 2014) were encouraged to "trawl the margins" for detections (not recording, misclassifying crimes, encouraging criminals to admit to other crimes they had not committed, solving minor, or easier, "volume crime") in order to improve figures instead of actively investigating more serious crime (HMIC 1999). Indeed, what better way is there to "convince the politicians they have used their allocated resources efficiently" (Manning 1978a: 10) by reducing *undetectable* crimes, rather than investigating all the crimes reported to them?

Officers spoke candidly of a pervasive performance culture or RAG culture (red, amber, green) (police officer o, m) when some officers "were putting more effort into 'getting rid' of crimes rather than investigating the ones that we knew happened" (police officer f), particularly when "detections" were unlikely. This practice was prevalent where victims were unwilling or "reluctant" to prosecute. The pressure to reduce non-detectable crimes was achieved by some officers endeavouring to disprove the victim's report before a decision was made to record the crime; a discretionary unethical practice termed "investigate to record" (HMIC 2014: 86–87; HOCR 2016). The majority of officers denied such a pressure,[17] whilst conversely several officers suggested that management put pressure on officers to reduce non-detectable offences (police officers i, f, m and o):

> Just that the figures were now red, not necessarily anyone—and I suppose what *you* would do then I suppose—shit rolls downhill, if you were a supervisor you'd probably get a grip of the member of staff "Is there a way we can detect this, is there a way we can write this off, no-crime it—go back [to the victim]—has this really happened—if they waver I want that crime getting rid of" you know that kind of culture (police officer m)
>
> Researcher: So did it come from senior officers' then—this pressure?
>
> I think the words were said in the meeting as such—"you'll be getting rid of this one, won't you"..//.. It just doesn't sit right. Thankfully we are coming away from that now (police officer m)

Acquisitive crimes in particular were discussed, whereby robbery, burglary and volume crime squads were established (2002 onwards) with a particular remit, seemingly to question the validity of some crimes in order to no-crime:

> Certainly, not honour crime specifically, but I think going back six/seven years—everything was about detection, detection rates. There seemed this willingness to get anything crimed that could be detected. For instance, if you look at robbery, the investment that the divisions were putting in to get people to be able to say that a robbery hadn't happened. So a crime could be no-crimed and they could get it written off the books (police officer f)
>
> Historically the culture in [this force] was—if we have less crime, then it means it's not happened—and we look better. Whereas it's just had the knock on effect that we don't have the right staffing levels because you don't realise the crime levels ..//.. It's almost I suppose, 'playing, playing with figures', the crime is still going to happen regardless..//.. so I'd say before that, going back ten years, I'd say there was a problem with crime reporting—certainly (police officer o)
>
> To actually not record it—or to fudge the figures, no. It must have happened ..//..I know, a lot of officers got moved, I think that was about 2005/2006, were I think whole offices got disbanded based on that (police officer o)
>
> It wasn't just this force, you'd go to meetings, national meetings and everybody talked about the culture at that time was to drive down, well to 'increase detections'. So in order to increase detections the pressure was there to reduce the non-detectable crimes..//.. It's viewed by a lot of people, senior leaders now, that it was unethical (police officer f)

Such findings reinforce the PASC report by illustrating that a dysfunctional and target driven mentality created "perverse incentives and sacrificed core policing values" (House of Commons PASC 2014: 48). Although police officers referred to a performance pressure in the area of volume/acquisitive crime, this also existed in other serious crime areas such as rape allegations:

> Certainly rapes weren't recorded historically—they ran on a FWIN..//..[an incident record], so there was almost reluctance to crime, as opposed to an order not to crime (police officer o)

Several police officers conceded that the pressure came from police managers, such as bosses in the CID, volume crime teams and superintendents in the morning performance meetings, due to the prevalent performance "target driven" culture (police officers m, i, o, n). There was only one interviewee who felt the government were to blame for the performance culture, stating "but that wasn't just something that a division or a force came up with, that was national" (police officer f).

The research reflects the historical pressure rank and file officers were put under to avoid criming cases that would remain "undetected" in the system (House of Commons PASC report 2014). The over focus on government targets appears to have spawned such dysfunctional outcomes. Performance culture and preoccupation with detections appear to reflect a collective organisational pressure to "clear up crime" and present a favourable image. As the findings suggest, reducing non-detectable crimes is not limited to acquisitive crime but potentially all non-detectable cases, including serious and violent crime. It is noteworthy that of the 30 incidents breaching NCRS/NSIR in this sample, 77% constituted violent crime[18] (threats to kill, assault, false imprisonment and rape). Therefore, this refutes the notion that "cuffing" by officers is limited to crimes of a "low level" (Roberts et al. 2014: 79) or less serious nature (HMIC 2014: 86). Crucially, HMIC finds that violence against the person offences have the highest under-recording rates across England and Wales police forces, with an estimated 1 in 3 (33%) violent offences being under-recorded (HMIC 2014: 65). This HMIC report supports the current findings which allude to a culture embedded within the crime recording process (ibid.).

Record to Investigate

The dramatic shift in police crime recording practices occurred as a consequence of the directive given by the then Home Secretary Theresa May (2010) at the ACPO annual conference to "cut crime" (Curtis 2015: 20), along with the HMIC recommendation (11) to discontinue "investigate to record" practices (HMIC 2014; HOCR 2016). There appears to be a visible shift in attitudes when one compares HBA incident data with officer interview data. Officers were consistent in expressing that a dramatic shift and change of ethos in recording practices had occurred over the previous two years (2014–2016) (police officer f and c) with officers being directed to submit crimes now that "targets have gone" (police officer j). When asked whether officers were put under pressure "not" to record crimes, over half the officers interviewed[19] denied such a pressure existed. Indeed, several suggested the opposite, that they get directed to put crimes in:

> No. It's completely opposite. We get told to crime things that we don't actually think should be crimed (police officer c)
>
> Targets have gone now. I have never known an officer to be pressurised not to put a crime in for DV, it's 100% the other way (police officer j)
>
> They've never said to me don't record that, don't record a crime or don't record any of these crimes (police officer p)
>
> Asking me 'not' to record—I've never experienced that..//.. I would be saying "no it's going in", but I mean there's many a time I've come across something and an officer hasn't crimed it and I've discussed it with my supervision and they've said—"yeah you're right we need to put that crime in" (police officer k)

A number of officers commented favourably on the positive push in crime recording, which intended to eliminate the ethos of artificially keeping crime figures down:

> Since we got a nice kicking [from HMIC]..//..everything gets crimed..// When Theresa May got rid of that I thought that was actually a good thing..//. That has a negative impact on victims and dealing with cases, so hopefully now is the time we can turn that around (police officer i)
>
> [The ethos] has changed completely I must say—the last two years, that focus on detections has gone, which would mean—with the focus on 'record to investigate'. It's completely switched round everything gets crimed now (police officer f)

One interviewee erroneously perceived that a "72-hour window" (police officer c) was available to investigate these reports:

> We 'record to investigate', rather than 'investigate to record'. That's the buzz phrase, so what used to happen was, we had a 72-hour window, was when a report was made to us, we could investigate that report and determine whether it was a false report or not, whereas, now we're not allowed

> to do that..//..You get pulled up on it—"Why did it take so long to do this"? You record it immediately (police officer c)

This observation illustrates how some officers used NCRS rules themselves to disprove a report rather than the timeframe being used for its intended purpose in order to trace victims/witnesses. Officers recognise that previous non-recording practices not only failed to reflect the "true picture" of crime (police officer m) but were unethical (police officer f) and had a "negative impact on victims" (police officer i). Yet equally, the pragmatism of officers is evident in that accurate crime recording could create a long-term demand that was difficult for officers to sustain:

> That could also come back to bite us ..//..because if we're putting more crimes in and we can't deal with them all then they're going to start..//.. Trying to privatise the police ..//..Let's get another agency in to take on board other aspects of policing (police officer n)

It is also worth acknowledging that the current political climate of budget cuts and reduced resources might incentivise officers to record more crimes, which was observed by one officer:

> I think they want crime figures to go up. They want more and more crime to be recorded so that they can say "actually we have got less officers, we've got less money, but crime's going up" (police officer c)

This has come to fruition as the statistics reflect recent rises in violent crime reporting (ONS 2016) despite a downward trend in previous years. Lipsky's research aids in explaining this phenomenon by arguing that where bureaucratic organisations, like the police, "perceive themselves under attack" (2010 [1980]: 92), they work harder to demonstrate that the service they provide is essential. This suggests that crime recording is politically driven rather than a reflection of reality. The shift towards ethical recording should be because officers "genuinely feel empowered to do the right thing" (Curtis 2015: 52; also Berry 2009) for victims of crime, and not because it advances the cause and continued existence of the policing organisation itself.

The 'Reluctant' Victim

Victims Unwilling to Prosecute

Victim reluctance is highly relevant to crime recording, particularly because of its impact on the *process* of crime construction. Key reasons for officers not criming cases revolve around victim unwillingness to prosecute, victims not confirming a crime has occurred or not providing perpetrator details, all essentially on the grounds of victim reluctance. Such findings not only replicate Coleman and Moynihan's study (1996) but they reinforce UK statistics[20] showing a rise in unsuccessful HBA prosecution outcomes based on "victim issues," where victims either retracted cases or refused to attend court (from 35% in 2013–2014 to 46% in 2014–2015) (CPS 2015: 73; HMIC 2015: 62). However, these statistics only encompass "crimed" cases and do not factor in incidents that never led to arrest or charge (the grey figure of crime).

As explored in Chap. 1, culture issues create additional barriers that inhibit victims from prosecuting relatives. The key issues revolve around fear of racist attitudes by the authorities, concern around family honour and personal honour, along with fearing the social ostracism associated with bringing "shame" on the family. Yet central to the theme of victim reluctance is the ambivalence of victims in prosecuting family members. Despite being betrayed by those closest to them (HMIC 2015: 8), few HBA victims are prepared to prosecute family members (Phillips and Dustin 2004: 542):

> A lot of them are obviously quite unwilling, they don't want to give statements, they don't want to go through the process (police officer e)
>
> I think the reluctance can be the risk—the risk posed to the victim, that they're scared, very scared (police officer f)
>
> Sometimes forced marriages we just do the protection side of it if they don't want to have anything else to do with a prosecution (police officer g)

Loyalty amongst kin is central to notions of honour (Jafri 2009: 20) and a crucial barrier preventing victims from reporting abuse (Hanmer 2013[1989]: 119):

> They'll say "Well, I didn't want to tell the police because I was frightened about what would happen to my family, I don't want my family to get into trouble," so I do think it is the loyalties (police officer k)

Such loyalty also increases risks to victims. One Sikh family had a "funeral" for their daughter when she ran off with a Muslim. When that relationship broke down, she and her children returned to live on the same street, but her relatives continued to ostracise her:

> They're still my family, and I'm hoping one day they will acknowledge me or my children (police officer h)

The added dimension and considerable emotional trauma associated with being asked to prosecute parents and relatives, rather than an intimate partner, should not be underestimated:

> A lot of victims say—no I don't want to go ahead with this. I don't want to criminalise my parents, I will not go to court (police officer a)
>
> They're [victims] not seeking to criminalise parents (police officer h)
>
> They just want to live safely..//..if you're looking at prosecuting your own family members..//..it will upset everyone in the family or alternatively you can pick up your stuff, move on and start a new life somewhere, the vast majority of people will start a new life (police officer o)
>
> We can do all the prints and investigate and arrest people and do Forced Marriage Protection Orders but a lot of the time, by the time we've got to that stage they have retracted or they don't want to do any more—and they want to go home (police officer b)
>
> I'm talking 99% of the cases it seems to be that the victim withdraws support or at some point has to go back to the family (police officer m)

Victims minimise the severity of perpetrator offending and/or retract complaints out of loyalty to family members, including rape retractions[21] or retracting FMPOs.[22] Unheeded pressure to retract complaints can result in victims being socially ostracised by kin and community (Pease and Flood 2008; Siddiqui 2005) and demonised as perpetrators. Continuing a prosecution can inhibit "bridges to be rebuilt [with relatives] thereafter" (Mr Justice Peter Singer cited in Phillips and Dustin

2004: 542). Consequently, adult victims of HBA often return back to the risky home predicament of their own volition[23] due to fearing the ramifications of going against the collective (police officer f), with abuse often being reinstated. Equally, there were significant numbers of child victims "reconciled" with perpetrating family members (explored in Chap. 7).

Victim Reluctance, "Relational" Distance and No-Criming

Although the prior section emphasises the cultural elements of HBA, victims refusing to make statements or withdrawing support to prosecute even before offenders are charged (Hoyle 1998) shows a considerable overlap between HBA and traditional domestic abuse victimology. Policing domestic disputes are seen as the most problematic for officers, due to the close relationship between victims and perpetrators (Bayley and Bittner 1984; Edwards 1986a; Grace 1995). Black argues that in "relational" encounters, sublegal controls operate; in that the closer the relationship between victim and perpetrator, the less likelihood of the police pursuing arrests because parties were more likely to "repair" their differences. Conversely, there is a higher likelihood of arrests if the perpetrator is a stranger (1971). Complainant preference is a powerful situational factor in the police and victim interaction, and where domestic abuse victims did not want police to arrest, despite a legal right to, they did not in all but 10% of cases (ibid.). Research suggests that an officers' decision to arrest or take any action is heavily influenced by the victims' willingness, or otherwise, to prosecute or testify (Berk and Loseke 1980; Edwards 1986a, b; Grace 1995; Hoyle 1998; HMIC 2014, 2015).

Police officers interviewed overwhelmingly concur that a lack of crime recording is based on the victim's reticence[24] in pursuing prosecutions. In Edwards' research, 96% of retracted cases were subsequently no-crimed by officers (1986a: 236). Equally, in a HMIC (2000: 203) focus group with 81 officers, the top reasons for not recording crimes included lack of evidence (238), the complainant not being present (84) ascertaining whether a victim will make a complaint (65) and "no" complaint by the victim (59). The centrality of victim testimony as "evidence" in HBA/domestic abuse cases remains crucial:

> A lot of them are obviously quite unwilling, they don't want to give statements, they don't want to go through the process, so then when you're looking for other evidence, and obviously your other evidence can then be in short supply because generally speaking they [victims] *are* your evidence (police officer e)

Victims do have a choice as to whether they wish to pursue prosecutions. Yet crucially a victims' willingness or otherwise to prosecute should not feature in an officers' decision-making as to whether to submit a crime report. When a victim confirms a crime has taken place to officers, a crime must be recorded (HOCR 2015) regardless of any prosecution. Findings illustrate that officers do have a comprehensive grounding in NCRS compliance, understanding that being "reluctant" does not preclude inputting a crime report:

> But then we're told and trained to put a crime in if a crime's been confirmed. So even if it's a simplest of a section 39..//..then we still have to put a crime in (police officer g)
>
> It should be recorded—unless we find something that says that what they are saying isn't right..//.. We should crime it to investigate it, we shouldn't investigate it, to crime it..//.. However, for that to be a no-crime without investigation seems really, really high (police officer o)

Manufactured Victim Reluctance

An iterative theme is of officers suggesting that victims are reluctant to disclose abuse (inherently different to pursuing a prosecution) by refusing to provide "victim confirmation" of a crime,[25] therefore providing "insufficient evidence" to record offences. These findings challenge the contention that such incidents "fall short of notifiable offences and are therefore not recorded as crimes" (ONS 2018: 6). The conviction that problem lies in lack of victim cooperation (and creates evidential difficulties in prosecuting cases) (HMICFRS 2017; ONS 2018: 18) is evident in HBA and domestic abuse more broadly. However, corresponding electronic documents evidence that victims are willing and disclose sufficient information to call handlers to warrant a crime report. By the time the attendant officer concludes the write-up, a clear juxtaposition and bizarre "U turn" in behaviour is evident, with victims presented as uncooperative and uncommunicative:

> She was very reticent with myself on the phone and has not told me what her address is down there..//..Has been very vague and has not been very forthcoming with information (case 88)
>
> A 14-year-old child divulged instances of physical abuse by her father and stated that if she was "taken home she would kill herself." Despite this candour, the officer suggests in the write-up that the young victim "would not expand on this" (case 81)
>
> Page 1 of the incident report states the victim has been "forced into an arranged marriage". Yet by the time an officer obtains the information she is "very reluctant to give too much information to front desk.... she did not elaborate further or wish to disclose anything to me at all" (case 17)
>
> Despite a mother currently being imprisoned in Pakistan by her siblings until she concedes to her daughter being married, the report states "she was not held against her will" and "did not want to go into detail about this" (case 78)

In one case the officer claims the victim "refuses" to provide a statement or complete a DASH questionnaire, she is "reluctant to go into detail" and it is "sorted":

> Victim appeared very cagey as though she did not want to speak to me at all. She appeared very defensive also (case 16)

Such alleged victim reluctance is not limited to adults. A previous incident highlights that a 15-year-old victim is "refusing to go home in fear of her father beating her again." The present incident communicates "she was still scared to go home" and if "taken home she would kill herself" (case 74). There was evidence of previous bruising under the child's eye and yet no action was taken in terms of arresting the father, no crime report was input and no effort was made to video interview the child. Indeed, there was a real risk of the victim being taken out of the country for marriage, yet the police report states:

> There is nothing to corroborate this fear..//..It would seem from all write-ups that the child will not disclose fully what has gone on (case 74)

In a similar case, a 16-year-old Pakistani victim outlines to her college tutor several incidents of being kicked, hit with vacuum cleaner attachments and having her hair pulled. She fears being sent abroad for a forced marriage. The rationale that officers provide for not criming the case was that:

> Victim does not wish to speak to the police to make a criminal allegation against her parents at this moment in time..//..Did not want to discuss the comments she made in her hand written note regarding her parents assaulting her. The note confirms violence, but it does not give any dates or times (case 57)

The fact that the victim confides in her college tutor and produces a handwritten note of the allegations shows cooperation rather than an unwillingness to disclose abuse (case 57).

Examination of these excerpts first shows that all cases breach NCRS rules, as no rationale is provided to negate the original allegations. Second, throughout the narrative, victim reluctance is used as a means by which officers justify police inaction. Ironically, some officers rely on the formal NCRS rule requiring "victim confirmation of a crime"[26] in order to subvert the policy itself and justify non-enforcement decisions, akin to the police use of quasi legal rules to mislead the public. Third, this indicates that "front work" or the manipulation of appearances (Manning 1978b) is being employed through the officers' summary write-ups (half-truths, omission of information, discrediting of the victim) in order to portray an alternative version of events. Such crafted "write-ups" appear reminiscent of the verbal inventions or alleged "admissions" of guilt that were historically attributed to suspects on arrest, with officers appearing adept at "putting words in people's mouths" (Holdaway 1983: 112). Therefore, it is argued that the genuine reluctance of these victims is open to dispute, as numerous excerpts provide direct evidence that victims are willing to disclose criminal offences to the police. Previous research shows how the attitudes of some officers *influence* the victims' withdrawal

(Harne and Radford 2008) with pressure placed on victims by professionals not to prosecute, to withdraw or downgrade the report (Bourlet 1990; House of Commons PASC 2014: 11). Moreover, Waddington suggests that the alleged wishes of the complainant can be manipulated by some officers, exploiting the vulnerability of women to convince them not to press charges (Waddington 1999: 58). In a similar vein Patel argues that police "fuel the myth" that women do not want to press charges, when in fact they allegedly dissuade women from pursuing complaints (2003: 180). These findings align with those of Brown's (1981) and Holdaway's (1983) research, which suggest that victim reluctance, in some instances, is manufactured by some officers as a "pretext to avoid taking any action at all" (Brown 1981: 205). In effect this leads one back to the social construction of crime, with low numbers of crimes recorded and few prosecutions reflective of the response by professionals, rather than indicative of reluctant victims. Replicating this research, Myhill and Johnson show that although victim assaults were disclosed in the initial call, these were negated when victims allegedly retracted the allegation to officers (2016). It is argued that victims being labelled as reluctant, non-compliant, "silent" or uncooperative is a patterned policing practice (Lipsky 2010 [1980]). Fourth, it must be noted that the distinction between genuine and "embellished" victim reluctance is incredibly difficult to delineate, yet both facets were prevalent in the findings. This point shall be revisited.

Reluctant Victims and Rationing Workload

Rather than accept the position that there is insufficient evidence to prosecute these cases, the findings instead indicate that some officers do not "crime" cases, do not "dig deeper" and "don't probe further *because* of victim reluctance" (police officer h). Victim reluctance de-incentivises officers from formally recording crimes and pursuing rigorous initial investigations, particularly when there is little prospect of them being "cleared up" (Coleman and Moynihan 1996: 35) or "detected." Reminiscent of the performance targets discussion, officers cuff crimes because there is no potential detection to be had and no incentive to take on workload, particularly when victims "waver" (police officer m) in showing an inkling of reluctance to prosecute:

> You could look at it two ways, can't you? They're being cuffed by the officer and no crimes going in—or actually they're ringing for help but [victims] don't want to go down the criminal routes (police officer j)
>
> I used to get quite a bit of flack off my old shift years ago when I first joined..//.. I wasn't bothered—I'd put a crime in, even go to domestics. I think it like was the 'old sort of way of thinking'—"oh, if they don't want to prosecute, we'll just write no crime's [has] occurred" (police officer i)
>
> They would be written off at source through some form of DNFP—doesn't want to prosecute—and then we didn't record the crime. I think that's the kind of things that's would be going on. "I've turned up, she [victim] said this—but she won't support—so who are we to believe?" And it just gets closed and left as that (police officer m)

Cuffing serves to distort the picture of crime (Mcabe and Sutcliffe 1978, as cited in Waddington 1999). These attitudes are reflective of 1980s/90s domestic abuse research, with officers getting frustrated and manifesting cynicism, particularly if a reconciliation with perpetrators is anticipated (Stanko 2013 [1989]; Grace 1995). Such reluctance reinforces an officer's grounds not to pursue the case, as Brown suggests, officers consider "if they [victims] won't take it seriously, why should we?" (1981: 205). Many officers also pragmatically lean towards conflict resolution in domestic disputes (Stanko 2013 [1989]) because prosecution in itself will not solve the problem (Brown 1981; Hoyle and Sanders 2000), especially if victims intend to reconcile. Patrol officers continually make judicial decisions in deciding whether the law will achieve what the spirit of the law seems to call for (Bayley and Bittner 1984). Consequently, this reluctance results in under-enforcement by some officers:

> The complexity of the law and the difficulty in obtaining a complainant (statement) tend to combine to make the police man (sic) under-enforce the law to overlook, ignore, dismiss, or otherwise erase the existence of many enforceable breaches of the law. (Manning 1978a: 17)

Several officers suggest that whether officers crime cases is based on their individual motivation, along with the type and complexity of the incident:

> I think they're encouraged "you should be recording" and I think if they're not doing, it's down to the individual officer not recording for potentially various reasons (police officer e)
>
> You could have all the training in the world but if you've got somebody who can't be bothered or you know is just too lazy, you'll still get the same response even *after* they've had the training (police officer k)
>
> Researcher: When officers don't crime crimes why do you think they don't do it?
>
> I think it's to keep the 'stats' down or because they genuinely don't want to investigate (police officer k)
>
> Researcher: And if they don't want to investigate what do you think the reason for that is, particularly in this context of honour abuse?
>
> You get a lot of lazy cops, you get cops who are quite happy turning up in to your public order kind of situation, and you've got cops who don't have enough experience to actually investigate (police officer k)

Officers also base enforcement and discretionary decisions (arrest or otherwise) on their own workload or whether another department would take responsibility for prisoner processing[27]:

> They are [response] only pushing to get that person in at the beginning of the shift[28]..//.. they would [when the case was handed to a different department] go "let go and see if we can get 'so and so' [wanted person] he's supposed to be back now—he's supposed to be at the job centre"—There will be none of that [after the changes] because it's their number [collar number] next to it. You will also get the phone call as well "is it high risk this one, are PPIU picking it up, is there a pack there, are you good to go, have you got someone in there who can deal?" "Vvoooom"—they will go out and get [the prisoner] (police officer m)
>
> Just before someone is due to finish maybe, or someone who seems to, you know, be a bit immune to this [work] "full stop". Same collar numbers are next to the jobs—'no offences' 'no offences' 'no offences' (police officer m)

To summarise, interviewees provide many explanations for officers no-criming cases (in all crime categories): because of the complexity and lack of experience in investigation (police officer k); because it fell in the "too hard to do category" (police officer c) as opposed to a "straightforward" offence, such as a public order matter; lack of interest in investigating due to being "too lazy"; and to "keep the stats down" (police officer k). Particularly when officers want to finish "on time," they "control" their own workload in avoiding arrests or cuff incidents as "no offences" (police officer m). Whether it would be that officer's personal responsibility to process that prisoner would affect whether, when, and *if* the officer decides to arrest, delay the process or alternatively apply discretion. Officers might also under-enforce if they were imminently due to finish work. Klockars suggests that the wishes of the complainant are the single most important influence on police selective enforcement practices (1985). However, these findings contradict this contention and highlight how some officers prematurely file cases on the basis of self-interested motives, working "consistent with their own preferences" (Lipsky 2010[1980]: 19). When managing personal workload, officers pragmatically appear to begin with the end in mind. The fact that officers interviewed can rationalise what others do, whilst not subscribing to those dysfunctional practices, illustrates a degree of rational choice in decision-making.

"Wasted" Workload

The research illustrates that officers are acutely mindful, as they were historically, that recording a "crime" generates increased workload and process for them, which is deemed as "wasteful" (Brown 1981: 205) and a "drain on resources" (Edwards 1986a: 235) particularly when victims are reluctant to prosecute:

> Researcher: But if they don't want to prosecute it's different, if they don't want to prosecute we are still *obliged* to put a crime in
>
> But then, they still have to go through all the paperwork, the admin and everything else, that's what people knew you have to go through that pro-

> cess and it becomes an NFA[29] at the end *because* of the victim, and the support you're doing—and all that extra work—effectively people think it's for nothing. And I tell you what—I do understand that, but at the same time I'm like—I'm not going to be the one that has MIT [Major Incident Team] ringing them on my day off and say "this person's murdered, what did you do at that job?" I've had that, and luckily the person wasn't murdered..//..I thought 'thank god I actually did a proper job on it' (police officer i)

The same officer recalled an argument she had with CID officers for inputting an attempt section 18 assault, which resulted in generating more work:

> So I was like, "yeah, it's an attempt"—
>
> "no, don't be criming that as attempt section 18".
>
> So you put it in and I think well "sod you"..//.. Then you get criticised later on, someone writes up saying "Well, that's not attempt section 18." And you get made to feel bad that you've created work for someone—but at the end of the day, it is our job (police officer i)

This indicates that central to crime recording is the issue of managing personal workload. Unquestionably, some victims are reluctant to prosecute relatives, which makes the practice of "cuffing" inherently difficult to identify. It is argued that both facets of genuine and manufactured reluctance exist, and this is precisely why some officers utilise the "reluctant victim" theme to stifle further investigative lines of enquiry, because it is a highly plausible explanation. As Goffman identified, the more closely the "impostors" performance approximates the real thing, the more intensely we may be threatened (Goffman 1990[1959]: 59) as it becomes difficult to decipher the competent performance of legitimate police authority from that of the "shirker." Even HMIC appears to be unable to establish with certainty how much victim retractions reflect "the victim's perspective" as opposed to being reflective of "policing activity" (HMIC 2015: 129). It is inferred, therefore, that embellishing victim reluctance is a shortcut practice used by some unscrupulous officers to limit demand and reduce workload in order to "make tasks more manageable" (Lipsky 2010 [1980]: 83). Such findings in this section show, particularly for the "work shy" officer (Manning 1977), that avoiding inputting a crime report is an opportunistic way of keeping the workload light (Lynn and Lea 2012).

Practical Issues: Improving HBA Crime Recording

There are other practical issues which cumulatively impact on the accurate recording of HBA across England and Wales and these centre on poor information management systems (HMIC 2015: 128). First, certain police forces link crimes of HBA with forced marriage or alternatively record these two issues separately (IKWRO 2014). A distinctive feature of this research is that 64% of the HBA cases analysed (64/100) directly link to a forced or imminent forced marriage (see Chart 6.6). Parents faced with what they consider to be a child "off the rails" (Ballard 2011: 5) are keen to arrange a marriage in order to "halt the corrupting influence of the West" (Siddiqui 2003: 76; Phillips and Dustin 2004) with assaults, threats to kill and other HBA incidents often preceding a marriage. Therefore, "counting" cases can indeed prove problematic if these two seemingly interrelated concepts of forced marriage and HBA are separated. To avoid obtaining a "partial" picture of reports, it is advisable for forces to capture information management data from *both* HBA and FM incidents, whilst ensuring these incidents are not double counted. Second, as much of this chapter illustrates, whether a case is crimed is less about adhering to law and procedure and more dependent on the individual motives and integrity of the attendant officer. Third, system issues create a lack of standardisation between UK forces, making HBA rates across the country difficult, if not impossible, to compare. This is because there are wide variations between forces in terms of the flagging, categorising or criming of HBA (HMIC 2015). Current system issues create a "post code lottery" of service provision for victims (IKWRO 2014). Some forces only "flag" HBA cases that are formally crimed and do not include incident reports, thus obscuring a large proportion of cases, which is highly relevant against the present findings. Some forces are only able to identify HBA cases by conducting a time-consuming "manual search" of each case (ibid.). Other system issues include forces holding information on several systems rather than one, which makes identifying an effective policing response difficult to determine (HMIC 2015: 69–70).

Despite former ACPO recommendations for forces to implement effective mechanisms for recording HBA incidents (2008: 27), an IKWRO report identifies that 20% of forces fail to flag HBA cases reported to them (IKWRO 2014: 16). HMIC recommendation 10, in part propelled by the work of IKWRO, places an obligation on forces to have information management systems in place by June 2016 (HMIC 2015). Although the recommendation to collect annual data returns from all forces (HMIC 2015: 132) is welcomed, this will not address how to manage the inappropriate discretion applied by some officers through the circumvention of crime recording rules.

It is encouraging to report that the Home Office will begin collecting HBA figures from April 2019 which will be published by the ONS in the near future (personal e-mail communication from analyst, violent crime statistics, crime and policing analysis, Home Office, 20 February 2019).

Concluding Remarks

The importance of recording crime should not be underestimated. Extant research confirms that victims get a "better service" once a crime has been recorded (HMIC 2014: 56). Crime report creation is pivotal in placing victim needs on the radar and for placing the actions of officers under direct supervisory scrutiny. Once an incident is "filed," there is no onus on officers to safeguard, pursue lines of enquiry and no consequence for failure to follow procedures outlined in force policy. Officers evading the formal crime process means that investigative outcomes are not visible. Crucially, if it is not crimed it has "technically" not happened.

The findings dispel the notion of a decline in police officers "cuffing" crimes (Coleman and Moynihan 1996: 34), establishing that "writing off" crime remains an enduring police discretionary practice. Of the 100 cases analysed, 69% (and 89% of incidents between 2011 and 2013) constitute cases filed and not subject of further investigation. Thirty per cent of the 100 incidents analysed breached NCRS and NSIR. Whilst attrition rates are of strategic concern, it is argued that the "grey" figure of under-recorded crime constitutes the greatest volume of missed opportunities. The poor incident to crime ratio replicates HMIC findings on data integrity which calculates that 19% of all crimes (1 in 5) are not recorded (800,000 crimes per annum) which is "inexcusably poor" (2014: 50). Some of the most harmful cases of HBA show prolonged and repeat victimisation of children (explored in Chaps. 3 and 7). HBA certainly appears to be the poor relation when compared to its traditional domestic abuse counterpart, as only a tenth of HBA incidents are crimed in this study, compared to the crime conversion rate for domestic abuse, which currently stands at 50% (ONS 2018: 11).

The findings support the institutionalist perspective that official crime statistics are a product of police decision-making (Black 1980), with Police Recorded Crime representing the "tip of the iceberg" and "actual" crime largely hidden from view (Carrabine et al. 2014: 33; also Coleman and Moynihan 1996). In attempting to reconcile disparities between incident and crime figures, HMIC suggests that HBA may have been reported before a substantive "offence" has actually been committed (2015: 58). However, the current findings do not reflect such pre-crime preparatory behaviours, showing evidence of the offences having already taken place. Moreover, the problem appears to be systemic rather than isolated to HBA, with one officer suggesting that failing to crime incidents is generic across many crime types. Certainly, Myhill and Johnson's domestic abuse research identifies the same disparities between initial logs and attending officers' accounts, indicative of cases having been cuffed (2016: 11).

The reluctant victim theme was the most prevalent reason supporting a no-crime decision. Officers suggested that it was victim refusals to *confirm* crimes which led to insufficient evidence and prevented officers from recording of crimes. Depicting victims as uncooperative, "cagey," who do not want to "elaborate," "discuss the comments" or "refuse" to "disclose" details is a means by which some officers can justify no-crime decisions. Such lack of victim cooperation is difficult if, not wholly impossible, to reconcile with the archived records that evidence willing and detailed disclosure of offences. Supervisors routinely attest to checking all incidents; however, the reality, exacerbated by public spending cuts to services, makes checking all incidents an "impossible mandate" (Manning

1978a: 12). Compounding this is the low visibility of officers (Shearing 1981; Holdaway 1983: 165; Reiner and Newburn 2008: 363) and the latitude officers have in wielding broad powers of discretion (Brown 1981; Holdaway 1983), which means that few, other than attendant officers themselves, can attest to victims manifesting such reluctant behaviours. Thus, no-criming cases are not wholly reflective of a genuine unwillingness of victims to prosecute. It concerns the time and effort officers need to invest in that endeavour, which "because of the victim" may constitute "extra work..//..for nothing" (police officer I) if the victim decides not to support a prosecution. Frontline officers pragmatically begin with the end in mind. Officers appear to internally conduct a cost/benefit analysis as to whether a case is worthy of time investment, given the close relational distance of victims to perpetrators, a likelihood of reluctance, the complexity of the case, the likelihood of CPS prosecuting, or even whether officers have to physically "process" the prisoner. All these factors influence whether an officer is likely to "act."

In a similar vein, the exploration of performance targets highlights a relationship between victims who waver in pursuing prosecutions and officers filing incidents as no-crime, particularly when there is little chance of a "detection." It is argued that the target driven culture merely exacerbates the problem of a few "bad apples" that apply corner cutting (Punch 2009) practices, because victim blaming, the shredding of crime reports and other "cuffing" practices existed prior to the era of performance targets. Manufacturing victim reluctance provides the unethical "lazy" (police officer k) officers with grounds to validate their own inaction, and thus legitimately circumvent what they perceive to be "wasted" workload.

No-criming cases results in many lost opportunities to safeguard vulnerable victims, as 78% (14/18) of threats to kill offences reported to police in this sample went unrecorded and uninvestigated. Whilst there is some evidence of officers wrongly interpreting the threats to kill definition, there is stronger evidence of officers using incorrect but convincing quasi legal rules, such as the "imminent" nature of the threat and third-party reporting, to justify to victims the *legitimacy* of the decision through a legal "inability" to prosecute. As the findings show, the law does not dictate action (Brown 1981; Bittner 1978; Reiner 2010) and perceived legalities as well as formal rules, such as NCRS requiring "victim confirmation" of crimes, are used as a shield behind which some officers apply discretionary practices such as no-criming. Such creative rule bending by officers has resulted in changes to NCRS, which now demand that crimes must be recorded even for "unwilling victims" (HOCR 2016: 4). Consequently, the data shows a discernible relationship between no-crime decisions, victim reluctance and officer workload. Many researchers have analysed these facets separately, including exploring the unsympathetic attitudes of officers, without recognising the subtle interplay between these features. Lipsky's work on "street bureaucrats" in public sector organisations helps to speculate on what these findings mean. He argues that due to large caseloads and scarce resources public officials develop "short cuts" and simplifications which limit demand. Officers modify their concept of the job (this could be interpreted as lowering standards) and also modify their client base (Lipsky 2010[1980]: 83). In support of this, HMICFRS suggest that some forces may be suppressing demand due to insufficient officers available to respond (2017).

The findings show that some officers apply bias, judgement and morality in decision-making. In rationing their own workload, some officers pragmatically "simplify" and aim for the "low hanging fruit" and, in doing so, reduce their clientele. Such self-serving needs, goals and behaviours (Brown 1981; Manning 1978a) seem counter-intuitive to the role of public servants and incongruent with the service model of policing (Myhill and Bradford 2013), yet Lipsky asserts that such behaviours are commonplace in bureaucratic organisations (2010 [1980]). The cuffing of crimes appears to be less about the external needs of victims and more concerned with internally managing the workload pressures of police officers. Young suggests that manipulations in counting and recording have been created and are being sustained by officers, so much so that it has become a "structural necessity" (1991: 333).

The impact of cuffing such crimes distorts the picture of crime and fails to deter perpetrators or bring them to justice. Crucially this also portrays victims as embellishing their original accounts either through victim blaming, as explored in Chap. 3, or in the omission/"retraction" of data, explored in this and the proceeding chapter. This has the effect of erroneously exaggerating the extent of false reporting. Some attendant officers often defend and disguise their dubious no-crime decisions in the application of skilfully crafted language within the summary write-up. In doing so, they present an alternative version of reality which contrasts to the victim narrative. These carefully constructed linguistic representations shall be explored in the following chapter.

Notes

1. Formerly British Crime Survey.
2. This is the standard expected when an officer crime's an incident. This is a civil (not criminal) standard of proof and is therefore easier to prove.
3. Those cases which were crimed were 1, 6, 7, 9, 16, 18, 21, 24, 25, 26, 31, 32, 37, 38, 43, 44, 49, 50, 51, 57, 59, 60, 66, 68, 80, 85, 91, 92, 94, 95 and 96.
4. Assaults: cases 13, 34, 39, 47, 74, 93. Threats to kill: cases 2, 5, 29, 41, 59, 64, 65, 67, 69, 70, 77, 78, 87, 99. Rape: case 97. False Imprisonment: cases 79, 86. Criminal damage 'threat': cases 62 and 73.
5. The researcher was formally a CID trainer for several years and, aided by the Force Crime Registrar and crime audit unit, wrote and delivered the force wide crime evaluators course, specialising in training evaluators in NCRS and HOCR.
6. Cases 15, 40, 61, 72 and 84.
7. In other cases, incidents were closed due to communications operators accepting the officers 'write off' which negated the offences (cases 47, 13, 60).
8. The lowest incident counts per day was 1893 with the highest 2913.
9. Case 73 is an excellent illustration of resilient management bucking the trend.
10. Cases 2, 5, 29, 41, 59, 64, 65, 67, 69, 70, 77, 78, 87, and 99.
11. An Osman warning is given by police officers to intended victims to warn them of a threat to their life. This is derived from the case of R v Osman 2000 in which the ECHR ruled that public bodies such as the police are under a positive obligation to take preventative operational measures to protect an individual when there is real and immediate risk to life from the criminal acts of others. The Osman family appealed to the ECHR after one of their family was killed, arguing that the police owed a duty of care to the victim, that police should have taken steps to safeguard the victim and should not hold immunity from prosecution (Donald et al. 2009).

12. The finished incident rule states that an incident comprising of a sequence of crimes between the same offender (or group of offenders) and the same victim should be counted as one crime if reported to the police simultaneously (HOCR 2016: 21).
13. Cases 62, 29, 69 and 70 and police interviews n and f.
14. Evident in cases 62, 29, 69, 70, 99 police officer n, f, b.
15. Police officers m, b, f, n, i, e.
16. This is reminiscent of 'criming down' where officers reduced section 47 assaults to 'common assault' resulting in victims having to seek civil rather than criminal redress (Bourlet 1990). It was the Domestic Violence, Crime and Victims Act 2004 legislation that inhibited this, making section 39 common assault an arrestable offence (www.legislation.gov.uk).
17. Police officer a, b, c, g, h, j, p and k.
18. Violent crime is defined as crimes of violence with or without injury: Wounding and assaults (GBH, ABH); homicide, sexual offences such as rape, manslaughter, threats to kill, harassment, stalking, intimate personal violence (domestic abuse) (Home Office 2011).
19. Police officer a, b, c, g, h, j, p, k.
20. Which include FGM and FM.
21. Cases 7, 9, 18, 20, and 58.
22. Cases 8, 37, 38, and 51.
23. Cases 11, 19, 24, 28, 33, 58, and 72.
24. Police officers a, b, e, m, k, f, o, g and i.
25. Evident in cases 16, 17, 39, 41, 57, 60, 74, 78, 79, 81 and 88.
26. Under old HOCR rules, there was no requirement to 'crime' an incident unless there was a victim who would confirm the crime (HOCR 2014: 3). The new rules specify that officers are obliged to crime record the crimes even in the case of "unwilling victims." This includes recording crimes made by third parties (HOCR 2016: 3).
27. Prisoner processing includes doing fingerprints, photograph, descriptive forms, conducting interviews, preparing initial court prosecution file, conduct secondary investigation (interview other witnesses etc.).
28. Arresting at the beginning of a shift was common practice, as most officers realise that arresting at the end of a shift would result in finishing at least 4 hours late to process the prisoner process, which would impact on an officer's personal life.
29. No further action [NFA].

References

Association of Chief Police Officers (ACPO). (2008). *Honour-based violence strategy*. London: National Policing Improvement Agency (NPIA).

Baker, D. (2016). *Deaths after police contact: Constructing accountability in the 21st century* (Critical Criminological Perspectives). Palgrave Macmillan.

Ballard, R. (2011). Honour killing? Or just plain homicide? (chapter 6). In L. Holden (Ed.), *Cultural expertise and litigation: Patterns, conflicts, narratives* (pp. 124–147). London: Routledge.

Bayley, D., & Bittner, E. (1984). Learning the skills of policing. *Law and Contemporary Problems, 47*(4), 35–59.

Berk, S., & Loseke, D. (1980). Handling family violence: Situational determinants of police arrest in domestic disturbances. *Law & Society Review, 2*, 317–346.

Berry, J. (2009). *Reducing bureaucracy in policing: Full report*. London: Home Office.

Bittner, E. (1978). The functions of the police in modern society. In P. Manning & J. Van Maanen (Eds.), *Policing: A view from the street* (pp. 32–50). Santa Monica, CA: Goodyear Publishing Company Inc.

Black, D. (1971). The social organization of arrest. *Stanford Law Review, 23*, 1087–1111.

Black, D. (1980). Production of crime rates. In D. Black (Ed.), *The manners and customs of the police*. New York, NY: Academic Press.

Bottomley, A., & Pease, K. (1986). *Crime and punishment: Interpreting the data*. Milton Keynes, UK: Open University Press.

Bourlet, A. (1990). *Police intervention in marital violence*. Milton Keynes, UK: Open University Press.

Bowling, B., & Phillips, C. (2007). Disproportionate and discriminatory: Reviewing the evidence on police stop and search. *Modern Law Review, 70*(6), 936–961.

Brogden, M., & Ellison, G. (2013). *Policing in an age of austerity: A post colonial perspective*. Abingdon, Oxon: Routledge.

Brown, M. (1981). *Working the street: Police discretion and the dilemmas of reform*. New York, NY: Russell Sage Foundation.

Carrabine, E., Cox, P., Fussey, P., Hobbs, D., South, N., Thiel, D., & Turton, J. (2014). *Criminology: A sociological introduction* (3rd ed.). Abingdon, Oxon: Routledge.

Coleman, C., & Moynihan, J. (1996). Understanding crime data: Haunted by the dark figure. In M. Maguire (Ed.), *Crime and justice*. Buckingham: Open University Press.

College of Policing. (2015). *Estimating demand on the police service*. London: TSO.

Crown Prosecution Service. (2013). *The code for crown prosecutors* (7th ed.). London.

Crown Prosecution Service. (2015). *Violence Against Women and Girls Crime Report (2014–2015)*. London: CPS. [Online]. Retrieved February 1, 2016, from www.cps.gov.uk.

Crown Prosecution Service: Delivering Justice. (2018). *Violence Against Women and Girls Report (2017–2018)*. London: CPS. [Online]. Retrieved February 5, 2019, from www.cps.gov.uk.

Crown Prosecution Service. [Online]. Retrieved August 2015, from cps.gov.uk/legal.

Curtis, I. (2015). *The use of targets in policing*. London: ACPO.

Domestic Violence, Crime and Victims Act 2004 (c.28). [Online]. Retrieved July 1, 2016, from www.legislation.gov.uk.

Donald, A., Mottershaw, E., Leach, P., & Watson, J. (2009). *Evaluating the impact of selected cases under the Human Rights Act on public services provision*. Equality and Human Rights Commission Research Report Series. Manchester. [Online]. Retrieved August 3, 2015, from https://www.equalityhumanrights.com.

Dyer, E. (2015). *Honour killings in the UK*. London: The Henry Jackson Society.

Edwards, S. (1986a). Police attitudes and dispositions in domestic disputes: The London study. *Police Journal, 59*(3), 230–241.

Edwards, S. (1986b). *Policing domestic violence in London*. London: Central London Polytechnic.

Goffman, E. (1990 [1959]). *The presentation of the self in everyday life*. Harmondsworth: Penguin.

Grace, S. (1995). *Policing domestic violence in the 1990s*. Home Office Research Study No. 139. London: HMSO.

Hanmer, J. (2013 [1989]). Women and policing in Britain (chapter 5). In J. Hanmer, J. Radford, & E. Stanko (Eds.), *Women, policing, and male violence: International perspectives* (pp. 90–124). London: Routledge.

Harne, L., & Radford, J. (2008). *Tackling domestic violence: Theories, policies and practice*. Maidenhead: McGraw-Hill; Open University Press.

Hemphill, J., Hare, R., & Wong, S. (1998). Psychopathy and recidivism: A review. *Legal and Criminological Psychology, 3*, 139–170.

Her Majesty's Inspectorate of Constabulary (HMIC). (1999). *Police integrity England, Wales and Northern Ireland. Securing and maintaining public confidence*. Swindon: Swindon Press.

Her Majesty's Inspectorate of Constabulary (HMIC). (2000). *On the record: Thematic inspection report on police crime recording, the police national computer and phoenix intelligence*. London: TSO.

Her Majesty's Inspectorate of Constabulary (HMIC). (2014). *Crime-recording: Making the victim count. The final report of an inspection of crime data integrity in police forces in England and Wales*. London: TSO.

Her Majesty's Inspectorate of Constabulary (HMIC). (2015). *The depths of dishonour: Hidden voices and shameful crimes. An inspection of the police response to honour-based violence, forced marriage and female genital mutilation*. London: TSO.

Her Majesty's Inspectorate of Constabulary and Fire & Rescue Services (HMICFRS). (2017). *A progress report on the police response to domestic abuse*. [Online]. Retrieved February 4, 2019, from www.justiceinspectorates.gov.uk.

Hobbs, D. (1991). A piece of business: The moral economy of detective work in the east-end of London. *British Journal of Sociology, 42*(4), 595–608.

Holdaway, S. (1983). *Inside the British police*. Oxford: Basil Blackwell Publisher Limited.

Home Office. (2003). *National Crime Recording Standard (NCRS): An analysis of the impact on recorded crime*. Companion volume to crime in England and Wales 2002/2003. Part One: The National Picture.

Home Office. (2011). *The National Standard for Incident Recording (NSIR): Instructions for police forces in England and Wales*. London: TSO.

Home Office. (2014). *Home Office counting rules for recorded crime*. London: TSO.

Home Office. (2015). *Home Office counting rules for recorded crime*. London: TSO.

Home Office. (2016). *Home Office counting rules for recorded crime*. London: TSO.

House of Commons Public Administration Select Committee (PASC). (2014). *Caught red-handed: Why we can't count on police-recorded crime statistics*. Thirteenth Report of Session 2013–14, HC 760.

Hoyle, C. (1998). *Negotiating domestic violence: Police, criminal justice and victims*. Oxford: Oxford University Press.

Hoyle, C., & Sanders, A. (2000). Police response to domestic violence: From victim choice to victim empowerment? *British Journal of Criminology, 40*(1), 14–36.

Iranian and Kurdish Women's Rights Organisation (IKWRO). (2014). *Postcode lottery: Police recording of reported 'honour' based violence*. [Online]. Retrieved September 4, 2015, from http://ikwro.org.uk.

Iranian and Kurdish Women's Rights Organisation (IKWRO). (2015). *New research reveals: In only five years, police record more than 11,000 'honour' based violence cases*. [Online]. Retrieved July 2, 2016, from http://ikwro.org.uk.

Jafri, A. (2009). *Honour killing: Dilemma, ritual, understanding* (2nd ed.). Oxford: Oxford University Press.

Kemp, C., Norris, C., & Fielding, N. (1992). *Negotiating nothing: Police decision-making in disputes*. Aldershot: Avebury.

Klockars, C. (1985). *The idea of police*. Beverly Hills, CA: Sage Publications.

Lipsky, M. (2010 [1980]). *Street-level bureaucracy: Dilemmas of the individual in public services* (Expanded ed.). New York, NY: Russell Sage Foundation.

Loftus, B. (2009). *Policing culture in a changing world*. Oxford: Oxford University Press.

Lynn, N., & Lea, S. (2012, March). Civil disputes and crime recording refusals, disinterest and power in police witcraft. *British Journal of Criminology, 52*(2), 361–380.

Maguire, M. (2012). Criminal statistics and the construction of crime. In M. Maguire, R. Morgan, & R. Reiner (Eds.), *The Oxford handbook of criminology* (5th ed., pp. 206–244). Oxford: Oxford University Press.

Manning, P. (1977). *The social organisation of policing*. Cambridge, MA: MIT Press.

Manning, P. (1978a). The police: Mandate, strategies and appearances. In P. Manning & J. Van Maanen (Eds.), *Policing: A view from the street* (pp. 7–31). Santa Monica, CA: Goodyear Publishing Company Inc.

Manning, P. (1978b). Lying, secrecy and social control. In P. Manning & J. Van Maanen (Eds.), *Policing: A view from the street* (pp. 238–255). Santa Monica, CA: Goodyear Publishing Company Inc.

Manning, P., & Van Maanen, J. (1978). *Policing: A view from the street*. Santa Monica, CA: Goodyear Publishing Company Inc.

Myhill, A., & Bradford, B. (2013). Overcoming cop culture? Organizational justice and police officers' attitudes toward the public. *Policing: An International Journal of Police Strategies & Management, 36*(2), 338–356.

Myhill, A., & Johnson, K. (2016). Police use of discretion in response to domestic violence. *Criminology and Criminal Justice: An International Journal, 16*(1), 3–20.

O'Byrne, M. (2008). Can Macpherson succeed where Scarman failed? In B. Spalek (Ed.), *Ethnicity and crime: A reader*. Maidenhead: McGraw-Hill; Open University Press.

Offences Against the Person Act 1861. s.16 (c.100). [Online]. Retrieved July 5, 2016, from www.legislation.gov.uk.

Office for National Statistics (ONS). (2016). *Statistical bulletin: Domestic abuse in England and Wales, year ending March 2016*.
Office for National Statistics (ONS). (2018). *Statistical bulletin: Domestic abuse in England and Wales, year ending March 2018*.
Patel, P. (2003). The tricky blue line: Black women and policing (chapter 8). In R. Gupta (Ed.), *From homebreakers to jailbreakers: The work of Southall Black Sisters* (pp. 160–187). London: Zed Books.
Pease, B., & Flood, M. (2008, Summer). Rethinking the significance of attitudes in preventing men's violence against women. *Australian Journal of Social Issues, 43*(4), 547–561.
Phillips, A., & Dustin, M. (2004). UK initiatives on forced marriage: Regulation, dialogue and exit. *Political Studies, 52*(3), 531–551.
Police and Crime Commissioner. (2014–2016). *Police and crime plan* [This police force, anonymised].
Punch, M. (2009). *Police corruption: Deviance, accountability and reform in policing*. Oxon and Cullompton: Willan.
Quinton, P. (2011). The formation of suspicions: Police stop and search practices in England and Wales. *Policing and Society, 21*(4), 357–368.
Reiner, R. (2000). Crime and control in Britain. *Sociology, 34*(1), 71–94.
Reiner, R. (2010). *The politics of the police* (4th ed.). Oxford: Oxford University Press.
Reiner, R., & Newburn, T. (2008). Police research (chapter 7). In R. King & E. Wincup (Eds.), *Doing research on crime and justice* (2nd ed., pp. 340–364). Oxford: Oxford University Press.
Roberts, K., Campbell, G., & Lloyd, G. (2014). *Honor-based violence: Policing and prevention* (Advances in Police Theory and Practice Series). London: CRC Press; Taylor and Francis Group.
Shearing, C. (1981). *Organisational police deviance: Its structure and control*. London: Butterworth and Co Ltd.
Siddiqui, H. (2003). 'It was written in her kismet': Forced marriage (chapter 4). In R. Gupta (Ed.), *From homebreakers to jailbreakers: The work of Southall Black Sisters* (pp. 67–91). London: Zed Books.
Siddiqui, H. (2005). There is no honour in domestic violence, only shame! Women's struggles against honour violence crimes in the UK (chapter 13). In L. Welchman & S. Hossain (Eds.), *Honour crimes, paradigms, and violence against women* (pp. 263–281). London: Zed Books.
Simon, H. (1976). *Administrative behavior: A study of decision-making processes in administrative organisations* (3rd ed.). London: The Free Press; Collier Macmillan Publishers.

Smith, D., & Gray, J. (1985). *Police and people in London: The PSI report.* Aldershot, UK: PSI. 4.

Stanko, E. (2013). Missing the mark? Policing battering (chapter 3). In J. Hanmer, J. Radford, & E. Stanko (Eds.), *Women, policing, and male violence: International perspectives* (pp. 46–69). London: Routledge.

Varano, S., Schafer, J., Cancino, J., & Swatt, M. (2009). Constructing crime: Neighborhood characteristics and police recording behavior. *Journal of Criminal Justice, 37*(6), 553–563.

Waddington, P. (1999). *Policing citizens.* London: Routledge.

Warner, B. (1997). Community characteristics and the recording of crime: Police recording of citizens' complaints of burglary assault. *Justice Quarterly, 14*(4), 631–650.

Young, M. (1991). *An inside job: Policing and police culture in Britain.* Oxford: Clarendon Press.

5

Deconstructing Crime Through Language

Oh, what a tangled web we weave, when first we practice to deceive
—Sir Walter Scott, *Marmion Canto vi. Stanza 17*

This chapter explores the power of language exhibited through semantics within HBA incident write-ups. Police practices are exposed by examining the contradictions and/or omissions in detail between allegations in the initial incident report and the subsequent secondary investigative documents (PPI, DASH, crime reports). Such discretionary practices appear to be used as a means of *deconstructing* crime.

The chapter opens by examining the completion of DASH risk assessments by officers and whether these are effective in managing risks to victims. The prevalence of data omission is explored, particularly the detrimental impact of this on child and vulnerable adult victims. This is followed by a focus on the extent to which interpreter services and language line are used. Middle sections assess how victim narratives are altered and trivialised by some officers through language employed in the summary write-up which dilutes the seriousness of cases, stifles legitimate lines of crime enquiry and decriminalises the reported event. Several themes such as "family dispute" and the unwillingness of victim to divulge

R. Aplin, *Policing UK Honour-Based Abuse Crime*,
https://doi.org/10.1007/978-3-030-18430-8_5

abuse, exhibited through compressed closed answer summaries, appear to replicate traditional domestic abuse stratagems. Later sections explore recategorising domestic incidents as "concern for welfare" and whether supervisors are complicit in frontline officer decision-making. The final section provides examples of good practice on detailed DASH risk assessments.

DASH Risk Assessments

The accredited Domestic Abuse, Stalking and Harassment and Honour Based Violence (DASH 2009) Risk Identification and Assessment and Management Model was implemented across all UK police forces in March 2009 (www.dashriskchecklist.co.uk). Its purpose is to assist practitioners in identifying and responding to risks. Therefore, at the scene of a domestic incident frontline officers are required to ask victims 28 questions and an additional ten HBA screening questions (Richards 2009), which officers refer to as a "DASH." Of the hundred cases analysed in this research, officers submitted DASH reports in 73% (73/100) of cases. Chart 5.1 identifies the weighting of incidents evaluated as high, medium or standard and the quality of those reports.

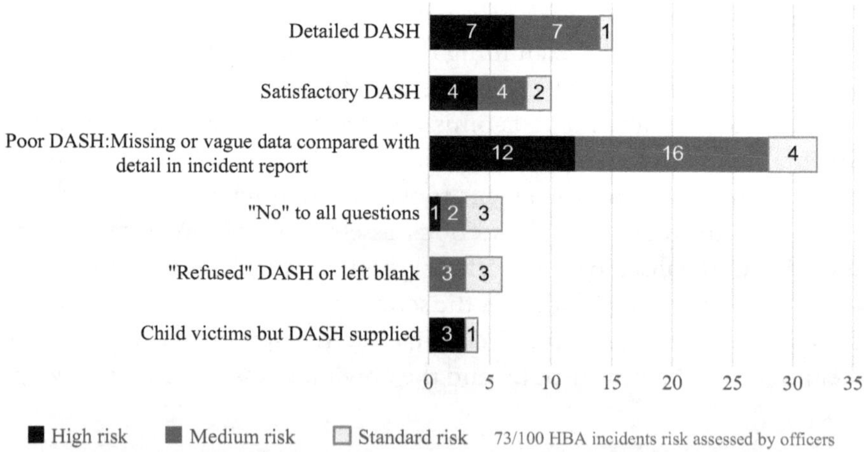

Chart 5.1 HBA DASH reporting: Risk level set as high, medium or standard

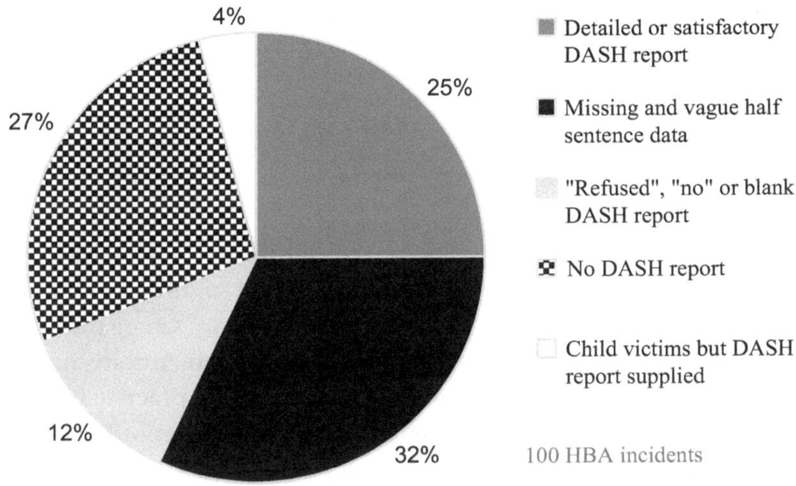

Chart 5.2 The quality of HBA DASH risk assessments

Chart 5.2 assesses the quality of HBA DASH risk assessments. Of the 100 incidents over a quarter of cases evidenced detailed (15%)[1] or satisfactory quality (10%)[2] information on the DASH risk assessment for professionals to be able to sufficiently assess risk. A further 4% constituted cases in which DASH risk assessments on children were supplied (cases 20, 32, 39, 95). However, the remaining 71% (71/100) of HBA DASH risk assessments appeared inadequate in their ability to reflect and gauge the risks posed to victims. These consisted of almost a third of cases (32%)[3] where the information provided was poor, identifying missing data or providing vague half sentence information. Twelve per cent of cases contained the word "no,"[4] in which the DASH was, according to officers, "refused" or data sets were left blank.[5] Finally, in 27% (27/100) of the sample, no DASH risk level (high, medium and standard) was set because no DASH risk assessments were conducted by officers. The largest proportion of these constituted child cases (19%), as policy in the police force studied dictates that police officers are not required to conduct DASH risk assessments for children. A further 6% were recategorised by officers as "concern for welfare" rather than being a domestic-related incident; and in a further 2% of cases victims were trapped abroad, with officers physically unable to establish the details, but officers were no longer required to complete a DASH due to this recoding (cases 38 and 42).

Detailed DASH Risk Assessments

Cases evaluated as high-risk require a referral to the monthly MARAC[6] (Safe Lives 2015: 3) where professionals discuss high-risk cases in the local area and implement practical interventions to safeguard victims. Two illustrations of high-risk rated DASH risk assessments are appended to the end of this chapter. These are examples of good practice by officers (cases 7 and 68) as such comprehensive risk assessments fully reflect the fears, pressures and risks faced by the victim(s). What is clear from the latter extract is that the discourse is documented in the first person, giving a strong sense that the victim was present when the officer posed those questions, which contrasts sharply with some poorer-quality DASH findings.

Deconstructing Crime: Sin by Omission

In 32% of cases many fields in each DASH report were left blank and data consisted of brief, half sentence information. A large proportion of the DASH questions (80–90%) remained unanswered or were responded to with a "no," which included cases where officers evaluated the risks as "high." In many poorer-quality cases, much valuable information was created by police communications operators but was left languishing on the "incident" report, which was eventually electronically filed away without the data being placed on the DASH report. Below are two complete illustrations of medium risk assessment answers. Answers to all other questions were left blank:

> Q5. Ans: She has taken overdose because of exam pressure and not wanting to get married
> Q6. Ans: She has tried telling her parents she does not want to get married and forced marriage unit involved, 6–7 times

Q8. Ans: They harass her, talking about the marriage
Q13. Ans: Parents threaten to prevent her from seeing her siblings if she does not marry. Dad might "force her" into marriage but no threats have been made, mostly just guilt and shame
Q14. Ans: She is starting to panic as the date to the wedding nears
Q25. Ans: Overdose today as per FWIN (incident report)(case 35)

Q2. Ans: Frightened that her family will force her to go back to Pakistan and live with her husband
Q3. Ans: Frightened that they will take her to Pakistan
Q4. Ans: Victim said her family do not like her going out and she doesn't see many friends
Q5. Ans: Took an overdose of tablets which resulted in her in hospital(case 28)

In 12% of cases, frontline officers justified data omissions by relying on the alleged reluctance of the victim (as explored in Chap. 4), suggesting that the DASH questions were "refused," entries were left blank or the word "no" was placed in the entry:

Victim has not been able to be specific with what has actually been said to herself (case 23)

The AP has answered 'no' to most of the questions and it is a possibility so she's not been very forthcoming with information (case 1)

However, there was sufficient information from the victim in the corresponding documentation (incident, PPI, intelligence, crime) to doubt the alleged "reluctance" of the victims. Yet, officers in such circumstances were still able to evaluate the risks as standard, medium or high-risk. There are several scenarios that may help to explain this. It is possible that officers obtained details but did not log these in the DASH risk assessment; that victims did "refuse" or that officers did not obtain the information required to evaluate the risk level that was set.

There appears to be a frustration in officers having to replicate information across varying electronic documents, resulting in some officers pursuing "short cut" practices such as cutting and pasting identical entries[7] into several fields of the DASH report, evident in the following high-risk case:

> Q9. Ans: (victim) is currently 7 months pregnant.
> Q17. Ans: (Victim) perceived the threats against her life to be viable, but did not appear to take them seriously, even when spoken to alone, away from her friends.
> Q28. Ans: (Victim) perceived the threats against her life to be viable, but did not appear to take them seriously, even when spoken to alone, away from her friends (case 69)

A similar time-saving practice was apparent in a DASH evaluation by HMIC where officers populated data from old DASH risk assessments into new cases, undertaking a new assessment only if officers considered a prosecution to be likely (Robinson et al. 2016: 3). There appears to be a process-driven approach to officers completing DASH reports, with officers providing succinct, yet vague half sentence information:

> Q10. Are there any children, step-children that aren't (perpetrators) in the household? Or are there other dependants in the household (e.g. older relative)?
> Ans: He has 3 children but I do not know their names (case 1)
> Q14. Is the abuse getting worse?
> Ans: Regularly (case 41)
> Q17. Has (perpetrator) ever threatened to kill you?
> Ans: Daily (case 41)
> Q11. Has (the perpetrator) ever hurt the children/dependants?
> Ans: Lawful chastisement (case 34)
> Q16. Has (the perpetrator) ever used weapons or objects to hurt you?
> Ans: A small stick (case 34)

In the last example, rather than the DASH adequately evaluating the risks to the child, the child being hit with a small stick is explained as "lawful chastisement" (case 34) which serves to defend the officer's non-enforcement decision. First, such cryptic half sentence write-ups prompt more questions than provide answers, as alluded to by one interviewee:

You'll always know someone who doesn't tie it off right and it leaves *more questions..//..* I read through some [write-ups] and I think—I can see questions appearing from this as I'm reading through—why can't you? And it's left to you then, isn't it? And that depends then, who reads it a second time [the individual officer] whether it's somebody who will go "I'm going to sort this out" or whether they go "but they've put their name to it now"—and it gets filed again (police officer m)

Second, the above extract identifies the subjectivity and inconsistencies between professionals as to whether an officer would pursue a full investigation or whether another would abrogate responsibility to specialist officers. Third, such short form answers illustrate how high-risk cases are, through the power of language, counter-intuitively reductionist in nature. Some could argue that this is simply pragmatic policing; however, it is unclear whether this practice is effected in order to dilute the risks to victims or reduce officer workload, but both outcomes are apparent. In a similar vein, there is evidence of officers pragmatically avoiding duplication in workload and saving time by logging sparse[8] information on the DASH, yet referring to extant information on other corresponding reports in order to "answer the question":

Q25. Has (…) ever threatened or attempted suicide?
Ans: Overdose today as per FWIN (incident report) (case 35)
Q17. Has (perpetrator) ever threatened to kill you or someone else and you believed them?
Ans: As per PPI write-up (case 5)
Q10. Are there any children, step-children that aren't (perpetrators) in the household? Or are there other dependants in the household (e.g. older relative)?
Ans: All details on DASH write-up[9] (case 34)
Q20. Is there any other person that has threatened you or that you are afraid of?
Ans: As per FWIN / crime (case 37)
Q28. Other relevant information (from victim or officer) which may alter risk levels.
Ans: Info is all written on log (case 62)

Such simplifications and data omissions have the impact of diluting the perceived threat level to victims and affect the perceptions of supervisory officers monitoring these investigations. To illustrate, in one case a 16-year-old HBA victim is presented on the incident log as having a "history of threatening suicide" but crucially this information is not logged on the DASH and the "risk" is thus categorised as "standard" (case 20). In another similar omission, a 6–8 weeks pregnant female divulges fears to officers of being forced to marry abroad. She explained that a number of her friends had been sent to Pakistan for defying the family and that the Muslim community "internalised these issues and families would liaise between each other to make sure that the 'desired result was achieved'" (case 83). Yet this contextual information, which better conveys the risks to her and the unborn child, is not placed on the PPI for supervisors to react to, consequently she is not categorised as "high" risk by the frontline officer. She remained at home with her parents (case 83). The adverse impact is that with blanks in risk assessments and sparse information, victims will not be referred and/or signposted to appropriate professionals, for example, CAAMHS, Women's Aid, IDAA, housing, immigration (Robinson 2006). Even if these cases *are* referred, agencies require quality information in order to implement effective interventions.

Although Robinson et al deem that there is widespread police and partner support for implementing the DASH model (2016) specialist officers were sceptical, evaluating that DASH was not "sold to response officers very well" (police officer h), in terms of providing the rationale as to what the information would be used for:

> We need to utilise the risk assessment for HBA more effectively (police officer a)
>
> There's a whole wider discussion about the relevance of the DASH at the moment (police officer f)
>
> I don't think there's enough done with DASH risk assessments—so I'm not sure there's a point to them (police officer h)

This first suggests officers are not motivated to undertake workload if no outcomes are visible. Second, these responses aid in rationalising why DASH are poorly completed, in that when officers have no idea what the information is used for (Ericson and Haggerty 1997), this is a "disincentive" to thorough collection (Robinson et al. 2016: 14). Finally, there is a sense in which officers are process driven to complete the DASH, rather than out of a need to identify and manage risk in order to safeguard victims. One interviewee alludes to the way officers are mechanistically "just focussing on the questions and the answers" (police officers f) rather than using these as grounds for strategic action. This perception of DASH as a "tick box" (Roberts et al. 2014: 123; HMIC 2014: 69) administrative burden (Ericson and Haggerty 1997) is replicated in wider research but it is concerning that the threat is "recorded" and "filed" away by some officers (Robinson et al. 2016: 14) rather than being acted upon. There is a lack of cognisance from some frontline officers that they need to do more than log the risk, with an assumption that others are responsible for *managing* the risk.

No Risk Assessment for Vulnerable People

Findings across this research, particularly within Chap. 7, suggest there is a need to risk assess child cases. In 19 of the 23[10] child cases, no DASH risk assessment was completed, nor under force policy is there any obligation to complete. Findings identify that some officers acquire inadequate information to assess risk levels to child victims. Akin to no-crime reports, what is not written does not exist. The poor mental health of children is apparent in corresponding documents, but they are not routinely referred to support agencies. As explored in Chap. 3, children represent 27.5% (8/29) of victims that self-injure, and equally of the 39% of victims suffering from depression 26% (10/29) are children. Although the DASH tool is not designed for children but adults (Safe Lives 2015), it appears counter-intuitive to exclude teenagers from risk assessment, as changes incorporating 16-year-olds and over within the domestic abuse framework (Home Office 2013)[11] reflect the reality that many domestic abuse victims are children. This is arguably more so in the case of honour-based abuse due to the collective nature of offending and also given that 63% of victims in this sample are *pre-marriage* victims (see Chart 6.6). Even the first question within the HBA screening questions relates to victims under 18 that "play truant" (DASH risk identification model 2009: 6); therefore, not applying the DASH risk tool runs contrary to the logic of the question.

Equally, none of the formally diagnosed vulnerable adults in the sample had had a DASH risk assessment conducted. All cases, according to officers, were allegedly "refused" or with "no" information provided in the DASH. Yet all of these cases involved imminent forced marriages abroad and were therefore high-risk situations. There was no rationale attached to explain why officers did not compile a DASH in these instances. One possible explanation is that vulnerable persons, like children, require an appropriate adult if being questioned by police, even in an informal situation. This can be particularly difficult if relatives are suspected of abuse. Officers avoided questioning children for this reason, but as Chap. 7 indicates this tends to mask the risks to children. The level of omissions in the DASH process, particularly pertaining to vulnerable (child and vulnerable adult) victims, raises serious questions around the efficacy of DASH as a tool to gauge and manage risk. This is not a criticism of the DASH risk identification model (2009), but rather of some officers circumventing its application in the pursuit of saving time and reducing workload. These findings reflect a recent report, suggesting that the DASH risk tool is not applied consistently, that specific detail is altered or omitted and that information is recorded in an inconsistent or incomplete way (Robinson et al. 2016). That research was specific to domestic abuse and excluded an examination of HBA cases. However, given the overlap in both sets of findings, this supports the contention that such discretionary police practices are not specific to HBA.

Lost in Translation: The Use of Interpreters

Continuing with the omissions theme, 12 HBA victims (12/100)[12] specifically required interpreters. HBA policy specifically encourages the use of language line and accredited interpreters and conversely guards against the practice of using family members and friends as interpreters (FM and HBV Policy and Procedure 2013: 7). Yet the findings illustrate that officers' breached force policy in 67% (8/12) of cases by employing either no

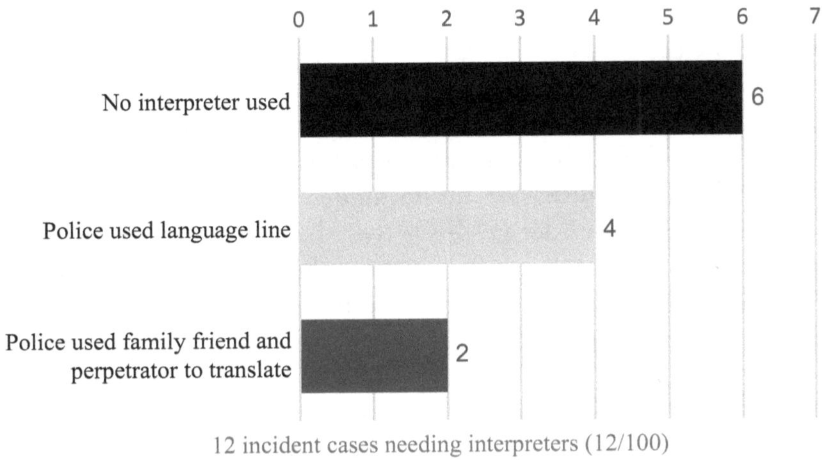

Chart 5.3 The use of interpreters by police officers

interpreters (6/12)[13] or inappropriate persons to translate (2/12) (Chart 5.3).[14]

In several cases, officers used the language barrier as grounds to argue that there was lack of evidence to substantiate a crime report, complete a DASH risk assessment and effectively "get to the heart" of the matter. The officer said of a Kurdistan victim:

> I could not confirm a great deal with (victim) as her English was limited..//..No offences have been disclosed (case 73)

Ironically the victim's account was unintelligible, which was why interpreter services were required. Cases presented to CPS for a charging decision also indicate that the language barrier inhibits prosecuting suspects. CPS suggested in one case that the verbal exchange between the victim and perpetrator could not be corroborated because the key witness did not understand Punjabi. In effect the language barrier appears to "doubly" disadvantage victims:

> The victim has given an account and her partner has also done so, but it is hard to draw corroboration for the alleged threats to kill, as the conversa-

tion between [female victim] and her uncle took place in Punjabi/Urdu which [love choice] did not understand (case 31)

Perpetrators themselves utilise language barriers as a tool to evade prosecution. In one case, the perpetrating parents argued that due to their own poor English ability they did not understand the terms of a Forced Marriage Protection Order (FMPO) that their daughter had instigated with the help of the police a year earlier. The court judge accepted the explanation and it absolved the parents from being convicted of a "breach" when they went on to marry their daughter in Pakistan several months' earlier (case 38).

Despite victims being unable to communicate their abuse, policies were breached by professionals. For instance, despite the fact that a communications operator attested "I couldn't understand what the informant was saying as her accent was very strong too" (case 25), an officer took a written statement from the victim regarding a harassment crime. This appears to be a discretionary police practice employed to save time, but moreover is evidentially unsound from an "achieving best evidence" perspective. Witnesses should always be interviewed in the language of their choice unless exceptional circumstances apply (Ministry of Justice 2011: 57). For legal and evidential reasons, victims requiring interpreters should not provide a written statement (case 25), nor sign an account (case 40) that is not in their native language, as they cannot comprehend what they are signing.

Conversely, a further practice is of officers attesting to the competency of the victim in understanding English, despite clear evidence to the contrary. Through this device officers argued that victims communicated a reluctance to prosecute. In both instances this circumvents any requirement for interpreter services[15]:

She is a Somali speaker; she is able to communicate reasonably in English. She informed me what had happened but stated that she did not want to give a statement or go to court. She said that this was because she just did not want any trouble (case 51)

A 22-year-old Libyan victim attended the police station and passed a note to the clerk which read "my life is in danger please help me, my family

> have threatened to kill me." The victim spoke limited English. Yet despite the initial allegation, according to officers she did not want to "take the matter any further" police merely acted as transport, collecting items for the victim (laptop, phone, and passport) and arranged for her to be placed in a refuge. She left the refuge 4 days later (case 41)

By officers suggesting that the victims had a reasonable grasp of the English language, victims were able to elucidate their refusal to prosecute. Therefore, officer narratives were often interwoven with victim reluctance and breaches to NCRS crime recording, themes fully explored in Chap. 4.

In 17% of cases (2/12) officers inappropriately used a family friend and even a perpetrating husband to translate for the victim (cases 47 and 85). In a joint meeting orchestrated by social services and attended by police, a pregnant victim relied on her perpetrator husband to translate (case 47) as professionals did not appoint a translator. The incident report clearly states that the husband was the assailant. There were also allegations of cruelty and forced servitude at the hands of the mother-in-law, yet despite this the case was informally resolved. The PPIU detective observed:

> I was advised by my colleague that mother [victim] has a good comprehension of spoken English. However, when I asked her simple questions she continuously looked to her husband as if she needed him to translate (case 47)

On another occasion a random member of the public was used by officers to assist with translation due to the "telephony reception being unavailable" (case 61). It is evident in all these cases that professionals pursue a number of strategies to avoid enlisting interpreter services. It is argued that this is workload related—a means by which some officers can circumvent a long winded, complex and time-consuming (Belur 2008: 430) process of obtaining an accredited interpreter,[16] arranging the payment to the interpreter and enlisting a different interpreter for the suspect interview. Academics also suggest that police officers feel both "ill equipped" and "frustrated" communicating through interpreters (Morant and Edwards 2011: 290). The inability to utilise interpreter services appears tacitly related to the issue of "sin by omission." If victims with limited English ability cannot explain their fears and the circumstances of the offence through approved interpreters, victims remain unheard and HBA allegations remain hidden. Albeit unwittingly, failure by professionals to follow policies renders perpetrators rights as prioritised above that of victims.

Interpreters, Omissions and DASH Risk Assessments

It is uncertain how officers can adequately gauge risks when HBA victims are unable to explain those risks in their native tongue. In just over half (58%) (7/12) of the cases needing an interpreter, officers completed the DASH risk assessment form (Table 5.1). Of the 12 cases requiring interpreters, 33% (4/12) of those victims were categorised as high-risk,[17] 50% (6/12) medium risk,[18] and the remaining two cases as standard risk.[19]

Officers assessed that 83% (10/12) of victims were deemed as having elevated risks (high and medium risk) and yet in 42% (5/12) of these cases the DASH risk assessment was either blank or allegedly "refused" (17%),[20] or the word "no" was placed in the risk assessment (25%).[21] "No" suggests either there were "no risks" to victims, or that the informa-

Table 5.1 DASH risk levels for HBA victims needing interpreters

Interpreters: Assessing risks using DASH	
Level of risk	**DASH content**
Standard (2/12) 17%	blank or 'refused' (1)
	no (1)
Medium (6/12) 50%	completed (5)
	no (1)
High (4/12) 33%	completed (2)
	blank or 'refused' (1)
	no (1)
	Total (12)

tion could not be gleaned from the victim. Yet as explored, language barriers clearly impede a full understanding of the risks, so it is difficult to rationalise why in 42% of these cases there was no information present on the DASH to justify that risk level set. This suggests that officers appear to "guesstimate" the risk. The poor rate of DASH completion supports the qualitative data, suggesting that frontline officers did not ask the victims the questions to gauge the risk, simply because an interpreter was needed to facilitate this.

In half of the apparently high-risk cases (2/4), the risk assessment had no information within it. Therefore, it is misleading to suggest that omitting information is used solely to justify a standard risk. Research shows that for cases classified as medium or high-risk these are referred direct to specialist domestic abuse units for intervention (Myhill and Johnson 2016). Similarly, in the force sampled the policy dictates that all "high" risk cases are immediately investigated by specialist PPIU officers without involvement by frontline officers. It is therefore posited that some frontline officers pay lip service to DASH and base the risk level less on the risks presented by victims and more on officer personal preference and workload. The findings here suggest that some officers suggest the risks are high and yet are not necessarily prepared to undertake the work in employing an interpreter to establish this, thus abrogating work to the specialist department immediately resolves this dilemma.

Language Line

Although it is encouraging that Language Line are used in 33% (4/12)[22] of cases to obtain initial victim accounts, two issues are worthy of note. First, across the whole data set of 100 HBA cases there is no evidence of an approved interpreter being enlisted to obtain a statement from victims. Second, in two of the language line cases (61 and 63) there are strong indications that officers did not ask language line staff to pose the DASH risk assessment questions to victims. This is because in one extract, the officer attests to using language line to speak to a vulnerable victim with learning difficulties (case 61). Yet on surveying the DASH, all the answers are "no" and the risk level is set as "high." Similarly, in a further case, despite language line allegedly having been used, the DASH risk assessment had the word "no" against each question (case 63). In both cases, this suggests that officers used Language Line to speak direct to the victims, but not necessarily to pose the risk assessment questions. Had these cases not been placed at "high" risk, specialist officers would not have reviewed the case and the victim would have remained in the risk predicament.

Deconstructing Crime: Distorting, Altering and Trivialising Language

Individuals often underestimate that the "primary tool of the police is language" (Manning 2008: 286). It is a negotiation tool when in a volatile situation; essential for grasping "what happened" at an incident; crucial for interviewing suspects and victims, and necessary for drafting and collating evidence for a prosecution file. Part of an officer becoming accomplished and learning their trade is their ability to write off an incident. They are taught how to write it proficiently, "cover every base" (police officer m), consider every eventuality and execute it well. Officer write-ups require "special collaborative writing skills" (Hobbs 1989: 176) to ensure the story is coherent and above all plausible.

Stifling Crime Enquiries

An iterative theme is the way officers withhold and limit the presentation of data capture through a closed line of questioning, even if the information may have been captured at the scene. Such responses, on paper, stifle the opportunity for further enquiries. For example, there were multiple concerns regarding a victim who was vulnerable due to a combined mental disorder and learning difficulty and was also isolated by the language barrier. Yet the officer did not obtain an interpreter or place information in a DASH report, though he attested to having done so:

> DASH by myself, via language line. No offences, no alcohol, No children. Log closed. She answered all dash questions [these were all "no"] and gauging from her responses, it did not appear that she was in distress. She also stated that her parents were arranging for her to be married to a male that currently lived in the UK and that if she didn't want to marry him then she would be sent back to Pakistan. She re-confirmed that she was safe and well at her home address and repeated that she wanted to go back there (case 61)

The PPIU conducted remedial work by contacting language line to obtain the necessary detail in order for the case to be risk assessed and referred to MARAC. By comparison, PPI specialists catalogued a history of abuse in which the family removed the victim's bankcards, preventing her from accessing her benefits; she was assaulted by her younger brother, as well as subjected to intensive surveillance; mother and brother both physically "slap her for not listening"; a threat of forced marriage was also apparent (case 61). Therefore, the information presented by the frontline officer is rife with contradiction and conflicts with the details ascertained by PPIU specialists. This was indicative of diluting the threat level posed by family members. In a further similar case, one female victim was falsely imprisoned by her family and she fled the force area only to return back into the risk area with her love choice husband in order to make a formal complaint to police. The victim waited four days for police to speak with her. The frontline officer appeared eager to negate lines of enquiry and the write-up was brusque, reflecting a compressed summary with limited open questions:

> I asked each person if they had been assaulted, they both replied "no." I asked if any person had made any sort of threats towards them both or separately, they replied "no". I asked (female victim) if she had been imprisoned or kidnapped, she replied "no" (case 79)

Such a "closed" line of questioning avoids capturing essential detail but moreover fails to elucidate what was expressed in the initial police incident report, that the victim had been pushed, slapped, had her phone removed during a four-day imprisonment by family members. She received multiple threats from her family on voicemail. No crimes of assault and false imprisonment were input on the basis that the victim, according to the officer's write-up, "refused to confirm or deny this" (case 79) using the justification of "no victim confirmation of a crime" (as explored in Chap. 4). Perpetrators were never questioned about the incident. In short, it becomes difficult to reconcile the proactivity of victims with their alleged "reluctance" to support police action. Why report a case, wait four days for police attendance, then subsequently refuse to cooperate?

In a further extract, an officer's documentary write-up appeared to be used as a mechanism to wholly expedite, rather than develop, investigative lines of enquiry. The officer explained, in a perfunctory fashion, how the victim did not want to go in a refuge; refused to be video interviewed; did not want a replacement phone; was not at risk from family members; does not believe she is at risk of forced marriage; does not want to cut ties with her family; does not want any family members arresting (case 65 and 67). Again, a similar write-up reported by the brother of a victim involved an allegation where his new brother-in-law was "trying to get into her room to rape" his sister in order to consummate a recent forced marriage. The phone call to the brother captures the victim "screaming" and sounds of a disturbance. Yet, paralleling the above discourses, there followed a thorough negation of all potential crime avenues by the officer:

> There have been no offences disclosed, (man and wife) have had an argument over this as the (victim) has not wanted to have sex with him. At no point has her husband even touched her or tried to attempt to have sex with her, it has been verbal only. (Victim) has been directly asked 'have you been assaulted' to which she replied "no," and I asked her if she had been sexually assaulted to which she replied "no," or raped or attempt rape, to which she replied "no," and she went onto say he hasn't physically touched her at all (case 88)

The findings indicate that there is something very formulaic in these officer write-ups/write-offs,[23] akin to a "family resemblance," even if there are nuances to particular situations (Shearing and Ericson 1991: 491). Moreover, these cases expose a disjoint between the constructed presentation and the original version portrayed through the incident report and other documentary data, evidencing the victims' fears, allegations, violence and psychological abuse. This reflects Hobbs discourse on the subject, in which a situational encounter becomes a "reality filtered through paperwork" (1989: 175). Several interviewees allude to these stilted and non-committal accounts, which often fail to capture the essence of the situation and appear to be artificially constructed to justify officer decision-making:

> What officers are seeing at the properties doesn't reflect what's going on the logs. Because they're (officers) turning up, they're seeing all the shouting, the screaming, how people's demeanour is at the property—so they can say actually there's something not right here..//..then when you come to a log, nothing. You'll get a comment such as 'non ACPO DV 1-8 to follow' and then it's just the very brief no risk assessments, no 'how everybody was', no factual information from the events (police officer k)
>
> You'll have half of the write-up about 'they are a mess, they are alcoholics, they got mental health— or whatever. But they told me this, so I'm happy with that and we're closing it' [the incident]. And I just think there is too much variation—are we believing them or are we not? (police officer m)

A different officer suggests that the problem is precipitated by uncooperative victims combined with a shallow approach by frontline officers, which inhibits effective case investigation:

> They [victims] won't give us enough disclosure to put a crime in—but actually with a bit more probing we could very effectively realise that there is an investigation there..//..They [officers] don't probe, they sort of think… sometimes it's quite apparent that there's more going on—but if we don't ask the question, then we won't get the answer (police officer h)

It is argued that writing up detailed qualitative responses generates an account which then necessitates many investigative actions for officers; hence the reason why some officers present compressed summaries. However, one interviewee suggests that officers are universally comprehensive in documenting everything on the PPI, out of deference and safety to victims:

> Everything is absolutely documented on the PPI and a lot of it's back-covering. I know that sounds awful, absolutely you're safeguarding the victim but a lot of it's back-covering because you know in the back of your mind the worse-case scenario could happen and she could end up dead (police officer j)

Albeit some officers are diligent and hardworking, omissions in data do not support this view. The findings support the contention that some officers employ "back-covering" (police officer j and c) tactics to ensure that "what is written expresses the best possible picture of the actions of the officer" (Manning 2009: 459). Moreover, as is evident, by some officers "withholding information" in the form of selective editing and compressed summaries, this not only avoids allegations of neglect of duty but crucially "depresses service demand" (Lipsky 2010 [1980]: 91) by stifling investigative lines of enquiry and reducing personal workload.

Altering Language in the Crime Deconstruction Process

Words and language more broadly hold legal significance for law enforcement officers, particularly in establishing whether an incident "fits" a particular crime definition. This concept links particularly well with NCRS and crime recording, explored in Chap. 4. The findings show several cases of officers omitting or altering important words which would otherwise warrant crime report submission, particularly that of threats to kill, with "kill" or "death" removed:

> A 14-year-old from Kurdistan resists marrying a suitor and is told by parents "if she does not [marry] then she will bring shame on the family and she will be killed. She has repeated this concern to social workers" (case 81, incident)
>
> By the time the PPI report was constructed, the threat that "she will be killed" was removed from the PPI document, rendering the incident as no longer fitting a 'threats to kill' definition (case 81, PPI).

This was evident in other corresponding reports:

If you go (to aunties) I'll do something to you when we go to Bangladesh in July. I'll kill you and make it look like an accident (case 39, incident)

[Victim] is very scared that he will kill her when they go away to Bangladesh (case 39, DASH risk assessment)

In the above extract, although the threat was from the same source (father), the changed emphasis first removes the threat to occurring abroad, outside the UK jurisdiction. Second, instead of presenting this as a threat to kill (incident) the altered emphasis presents this as an inherent "fear" of the victim, rather than a direct threat made by a perpetrator, negating both a crime and any intervention from police and social services. Crucially, the altered wording negates the need to act. Similarly, in another case a male Sunni Muslim and his Shi'a Muslim wife fled to the UK and married against the wishes of their families. They have been pursued ever since. Four separate police intelligence items (2011–2012) indicate several threats to kill allegations were made against them. When details of their plight were journalised in a magazine, an alleged female "friend" wrote to the editors requesting details of the couple's location. Included in the information was a letter written in Urdu outlining that the family were "thirsty for her blood" and that "the village elders have decided that they should both be stoned to death" (case 99, incident). Crucially, by the time the attendant officer creates the PPI, the threat they will be "stoned to death" has been altered to "they are to be stoned" (case 99, PPI) with the crucial word "death" omitted. The same altered emphasis is revised in the DASH risk assessment, rendering it no longer a threat to kill crime. In a further case, siblings of a victim make "threats to break his legs" [love choice Indian boyfriend] if he contacts their sister ../ /..(and also) "to kill him" (case 49, incident). These detailed threats to kill were omitted from the PPI report, hidden from the supervisory gaze of a reviewing sergeant or Inspector. When officers in a different force area were tasked with checking on the welfare of the boyfriend, police failed to communicate the "threat to kill" allegation to the force concerned (case 49, PPI). Should the boyfriend have been murdered, the force omitting this data did not convey the threat to life and neglected their "duty of care" as outlined in the stated case of *R v. Osman*.[24]

These cases reflect the selective discretionary practices of officers, carefully crafting a particular presentational reality, omitting language that not only circumvents the inputting of crimes and reduces workload; it increases victim risks and allows perpetrators to continue unabated. Manning referred to this manipulation of appearances as "front work," with officers using evasion, half-truths, responding only to some aspects of questions, leaving unsaid implied or unpleasant truths (1978).

Language That Trivialises: Victims Not "Fazed" or "Concerned"

A further practice evident was of language used by professions which served to downplay and trivialise risks to victims and/or partners. Officers portrayed victims as reluctant to prosecute, wishing and choosing to stay with perpetrators. In particular, officers suggest that victims themselves decline safeguarding interventions due to them being "not fazed" (case 29), "not bothered" (case 5), "not concerned" (cases 69 and 78) or generally not distressed (cases 87 and 61) about returning to the risk, information which conflicts with extant electronic data. In one case an 8-week pregnant victim discusses her feelings of isolation in the DASH risk assessment (completed by a different officer). Yet the uniformed officer's write-up conflicts with the initial account, and this is evident in other cases:

> The victim did not seem too fazed at the thought of returning to [the force area where the offenders live] (case 29, PPI)
>
> He states that he is not bothered and is only concerned about the safety of his girlfriend (case 5)
>
> Gauging from her responses, it did not appear that she [the victim] was in distress (case 61)

A seven-month pregnant victim was told that her father and brother intended to kill her and then flee to Pakistan. Yet according to the frontline officer the victim:

> Does not appear to be too concerned at all this..//..she is not willing to fully engage with police ..//..Nothing happened in the end so now she can't be bothered with the hassle. [She] perceived the threats against her life to be viable but did not appear to take them seriously. [Victim] ..//..Is not engaging or wishing to move address to keep her safe [but conversely] ..//..She is frightened of baby getting harmed (case 69)

This particular case depicts the victim as reluctant, blasé and not fully cognisant of the risks posed to her. Unless supervisors challenge officers about the accuracy of such information, these remain the bona fide accounts provided by victims. Such findings replicate Myhill and Johnson's domestic abuse research, in which an officer downgraded or "squared away" an incident, suggesting "no one at the address was distressed, and the woman subject to the threats appeared unfazed," which negated a "threats to kill" offence as she "did not take his threat seriously" (2016: 11).

Echoing some features of the last case, a mother had flown to Pakistan from the UK and was falsely imprisoned by her two siblings, who tried to coerce her into agreeing a marriage between her daughter and one of their sons. Across two paragraphs and on three occasions the officer's write-up stresses that the daughter was "not concerned" (case 78) about her mother's safety, nor about the serious threat to kill her if she did not comply with a forced marriage arrangement. Again, in a third pregnancy case, the ultimatum provided by the mother to her 18-year-old daughter was to terminate the child or marry the love choice boyfriend in order to remove the shame. The first page of the incident report alerts officers that the victim was "due to have an abortion" the following day, even supplying the exact time of the appointment. Despite this the write-up confirms the victim was:

> Satisfied the threat level was not as initially suspected. It is felt that the family have reacted poorly to the news as they're concerned about their daughter being a mother at such a young age..//..she understood the family would be caused significant embarrassment but did not feel the comment had been made with a view to being carried out and stressed her father was not a violent man (case 87, incident)

The discourse presented by the officer contrasts sharply with the initial victim's report which describes her as being "very afraid" and the mother as "very agitated" (case 87, incident). The police do recognise the extant threat from family members because they warn the victim that "she should still be wary and cautious and not put too much trust in even her parents." Yet despite this, the presentation does not reflect the risk and the officers leave the 11-week pregnant female in the same predicament and log the risk as "standard." This resulted in a situation where the mother tried to hit the victim in the stomach the following day in order to cause harm to the unborn baby (case 87).

In some cases, more direct deception and misrepresentation of the facts by frontline officers was employed through the use of language. A Somalian aunt had called the police, specifically to assist in ejecting her own niece, as she had been threatened by the brother-in-law that if she continued to shelter her he would "burn the house down" (case 51). An Inspector enquired:

> Do we know why she has moved out of her aunt's house? If her father has caused her to move, it appears he has breached the order. Can we confirm any of this?

The write-up by response officers' conflicts with the initial incident report by suggesting the victim was:

> Sofa surfing..//..The family there did not know why she has left. This was not un-ordinary as she has been staying on their couch on and off and staying at friend's houses…she has declined all other safeguarding (case 51)

Such wording trivialises and decriminalises the reason for the niece leaving, suggesting she left by consent rather than "fleeing" due to extant threats made by the perpetrator. Instead, it was specialist PPIU officers who undertook remedial work and began "criming" and investigating the case, acknowledging that "night group officers previously spoke with aunty and took no action" (case 51).[25] The niece was at risk, as a recent crime report reflects the severity of the father's offending when he threatened to kill his wife earlier that year and stamped on her between the legs shouting: "You can't take the children, I will kill you…I'll kill you, that way I'll have the children" (case 51, related crime report). At the time of the present threats, the perpetrator was living with his wife in clear breach of existing bail conditions (case 51), which response officers may have realised had the case been fully investigated.

Using language to trivialise is also reflected in an MG 3 summary by a Crown Prosecution Service (CPS) case worker, in one of the few cases involving a male victim (4/100). The white male was in a relationship with a Muslim female and she had left the family home to be with him. The male had planned a Muslim conversion and the female was under the misapprehension that her parents consented to the relationship. Her uncle attended their place of work and used emotional blackmail to try and lure the Muslim female home by suggesting her "mother was crying every night." He then offered to pay her to come home and said he would buy her a house. Continuing to refuse, the uncle increased the pressure saying "what are you doing with this white boy. He will not make you happy" (case 31). Finally, he presented the ultimatum, if she chooses not to return with him, he will snatch her. When she refused, he threatened them both suggesting he would "get a knife, kill him and show (the victim) his heart before killing her." Whilst on the phone to police, the perpetrator threatened to kill them both a second time. Although the perpetrator was arrested, the CPS case worker refused to prosecute the case, providing the following documented (MG 3) rationale:

> The suspect denies making any threats, though he agrees they had a heated discussion and that he made it clear that he was unhappy about her choice of partner and her decision to ignore her parents..//..Personally I think the circumstances favour (female victim) version of events, but it is not beyond the bounds of possibility that she has overstated the level of threat or pressure applied to her to conform to her family's wishes. I do not think we can prove a threat to kill (case 31)

In a different case a similar dilution was evident. The police officer downplayed a threat to "kill your family and burn your house down" suggesting to a supervisor that:

> The text [written to family members after the threatening phone call] was not a direct threat, it simply stated that he [the perpetrator] was sorry for a previous conversation and that he was just angry about the situation but meant no harm (case 73)

Both cases illustrate how through the power of language, professionals reduce and deconstruct a serious threat to kill allegation from a crime into a "heated discussion" or a "previous conversation" that could be informally resolved and thus decriminalised.

HBA as a "Family Dispute" or "Feud"

Police categorising HBA as a "family dispute" or "family feud" is particularly apparent within the data findings. Despite a victim having intensified controls placed on her, having her phone, bankcard and keys removed with an impending threat to take her to Pakistan for a forced marriage, officers expedite the incident as:

> Really a fall out between the family members that has ended up blown out of proportion (case 90)

Several other cases were expedited using the same family dispute[26] theme:

> No offences that have been disclosed. There is a long-standing dispute between the AP and the rest of her family, all of whom are pressuring the AP into marrying her first cousin (case 19)
>
> I don't feel there are any risks of harm at this moment in time from anyone involved in this family dispute. I'm not convinced she will be killed or there's any honour issues but will keep this PPI as a high and make (another division) aware (case 67)
>
> We are unable to distinguish if any offences have taken place as it appears to be a dispute within a large family where several people are getting involved (case 73)

Officers decriminalising HBA incidents as "family disputes" or "long-standing family feuds" immediately ascribes these cases as non-police matters that fall outside the remit of criminal law. This resonates with the way officers historically normalised domestic disputes, deeming them as non-legitimate aspects of police work (Edwards 1986: 235; Hanmer et al. 2013 [1989]). Moreover, downgrading incidents through the family dispute device remains prevalent in contemporary domestic abuse research (Myhill and Johnson 2016). However, for these strategies to be effective, officers rely on the public being ignorant of legal knowledge (Lynn and Lea 2012).

Police discretionary practices explored in this and preceding chapters can significantly overlap and this is evident in the following extract. On discovering her husband was a bigamist leading a double life, the 22-year-old Bangladeshi victim left him, and before fleeing to her aunt and uncle's house, she took several thousand pounds from their joint savings account. Despite the very serious threat by the husband to "rob" them (to reclaim money his wife took), "burn the house down and kill everyone" (case 73), the frontline female officer abrogates the responsibility to the specialist PPIU by writing an e-mail[27] (recounted below) to the sergeant. In this, she trivialises the case and attempts a formal handover to the specialist unit:

> I could not confirm a great deal with (victim) as her English was limited. She stated that the reason she left her husband was because she was treated like a slave and she found out that her husband had another wife and children. She stated that he (husband) had never been violent towards her but I got the impression that he was very controlling..//..The text [written to family members after the threatening phone call] was not a direct threat, it simply stated that he [the perpetrator] was sorry for a previous conversation and that he was just angry about the situation but meant no harm. It seems that there is a long-standing feud between the family and it was clear that any threats were telephone calls between several different family members and the (victim) would not confirm that she had been threatened in any way. She (female victim) did not seem intimidated ..//..I have concerns regarding (victim). There was no DASH to complete because of the circs detailed above, however I think a follow up by a member of your team would be beneficial. (Victim) is safe and well at her uncles ..//..No offences

> have been disclosed but if you could review both (incidents) she is receptive to a call from your team (case 73)

A cacophony of discretionary practices is evident here. First, the officer uses the poor English skills of the victim to justify no evidence of complaint. Second, the officer dilutes the seriousness of the case by suggesting the incident was a "long-standing family feud" and "dispute" within a large family. Third, the officer reduces the threat to kill and "burn your house down" to a "previous conversation." There appeared to be a careful withholding and omission of information evident, as too much detail may have prompted a requirement for enforcement and inputting crimes of "threats to commit criminal damage" and "threats to kill." Fourth, the officer reinforces the non-enforcement decision as legitimate, on the basis that the victim apparently "did not seem intimidated".//.."did not take the threats seriously and had had an apology off the male" (case 73). Therefore, through the skills of articulate wording, omissions and the alleged non-confirmation of crimes by the victim, the officer circumvents formal crime recording and a protracted investigation. Despite thwarting every line of enquiry, the officer abrogates responsibility to the specialist unit for an anticipated "follow up by a member of your team" (case 73), making the case someone else's responsibility to resolve. It was only through effective supervisory intervention that the officer was required to undertake actions to improve primary investigative standards.[28] Despite the officer attempting to plead ignorance by suggesting there was "confusion" due to lots of relatives saying different things at the address, with one phone call the PPIU sergeant was able to establish the full situation. Even when challenged by the sergeant, the officer still avoids investigating the matter and changes her approach, as the previous strategy had been ineffective. She refers to the perpetrators as a "well-meaning family," thereby neutralising the offending behaviour, a theme explored in Chap. 3. Like previous extracts involving non-English speakers,[29] the victim was apparently now able to successfully elucidate the circumstances of the case, resulting in the officer negating the requirement for a crime report(s):

> I spoke to the wife who has fled her husband and she had enough of an understanding of English to understand what I was asking regarding abuse. She categorically denied any abuse in any way shape or form (case 73)

In summary, the "family dispute" theme is often combined with "no-criming" and the alleged reluctance of victims, therefore it appears to be a discretionary practice used to justify non-enforcement decisions by officers. These numerous and indeed conflicting explanations constitute "improvisations" (Shearing and Ericson 1991) in the officer's effort to perfect her "script." When the "family dispute" and "limited English" tactic proved ineffectual, the officer changed approach. In summary, it is argued that there are too many competing explanations presented by one officer in one case for these to have been authentic. As the findings illustrate, it is less about whether the write-ups are necessarily truthful, and more about whether the methods used by the officer to expedite some cases as no further action actually "work" (Crank 2016: 213–214). Such extracts reflect the way in which an officer's discourse, whether verbal or written, is "thick with stratagems" (Bayley and Bittner 1984: 41).

"Concern for Welfare" and Victim "Refusals"

The findings show that in 6% of incidents officers sought to recode domestic abuse incidents as "concern for welfare." One interviewee alludes to this practice when discussing a perpetrating brother "kicking off" with a sister who allegedly had mental health issues (explored in Chap. 3). The attendant officer asked communications to recode the HBA incident as a "vulnerable person" (concern for welfare) rather than domestic abuse incident, but the specialist was sceptical as to the underlying motives for this:

> It saves them doing a DASH..//.. It's lazy. But we're getting 'DASH' where they're ticking 'refuse, refuse, refuse', and you ring them [victims—and they say] "no, nobody's asked me any questions"..//..And I know why and I appreciate that officers have a lot to do..//.. but you can't fully risk assess unless those questions have been asked (police officer k)

This extract suggests that some officers erroneously ask for incidents to be recoded as a concern for welfare, rather than domestic abuse, which then eliminates the requirement for officers to complete a lengthy DASH report. The suggestion is that this is effected to ease personal workload rather than because it is an appropriate course of action, even if that means manufacturing victim refusals or negating a domestic abuse incident. The above extract almost identically replicates a HMIC report compiled the same year, which reinforces the view that these are patterned policing practices rather than outlier anomalies:

> Some of the time I think some of them [officers] actually make it up without even asking them, because sometimes we ring up and [victims] say nobody has asked us that (Robinson et al. 2016: 17)

Are Supervisors Complicit in the Presentation?

Such findings lead one to consider to what extent police supervisors might be aware of, or complicit in, the discretionary decisions made by some officers. Extant research informs us that the relationship between the frontline and supervision is one of mutual dependence. Aware that frontline officers work in high-volume understaffed situations, they can, on occasion, hold supervision to ransom by withholding cooperation using a number of devices such as "not in my job description," absenteeism, apathy or doing the "bare minimum" (Lipsky 2010 [1980]). It is therefore easy to envisage a situation where the busy sergeant, reliant on officers to "get through the queues," could "look the other way" (Lipsky 2010 [1980]: 19), becoming complicit in the culture by "turn(ing) a blind eye to rule bending" whilst simultaneously "retreating behind the formal paradigm as a cover your ass[30] shield" (Punch 2009: 35; Crank 2016: 274), particularly when a transgression might be too blatant to be concealed (Bittner 1978). This is a particularly militaristic tactic (ibid.) in which supervisors protect their own reputation when an officer's conduct is under scrutiny (Lipsky 2010 [1980]). The supervisory distance between frontline and management aids in providing a "shield" protecting supervisors from criticism (Kappeler et al. 1998).

Punch suggests that the higher echelons of the policing organisation are weak, negligent and even collusive with other officers in the poor handling of investigations (2009). However, in agreement with Lipsky, it is proffered that due to the relatively low visibility and autonomy of frontline officers (Brown 1981), some of these discretionary practices are often unsanctioned by managers (Lipsky 2010 [1980]: 18). Moreover, frontline officers "resent" the interference by uniform supervision, often because they are deemed as having less specialised knowledge and also because they have not attended the incident personally (Tifft 1978: 98). By comparison, specialist sergeants are seen as having more expert and legitimate power (ibid.). The findings in this research, however, indicate that frontline officers very much control the "presentation" both to the victim (externally) and of the victim to the *internal* organisation. Through the presentational write-up officers are able to control the flow of their own workload by withholding, distorting, trivialising and altering language. As suggested in Chap. 4, there is scant evidence of supervisors checking and challenging poor DASH risk assessments or incident details, reflecting HMICs assessment that the existing approach is "unsatisfactory" (HMIC 2015: 92). Unless police supervisors query the content and re-contact victims personally, there is often no way of verifying victim explanations as these lie under the "sacred canopy" (Manning 1977: 5).

Furthermore, there is some credence to the argument that as a frontline officer you "have to be there" to appreciate what is going on within a particular encounter, and as a consequence, supervisors are heavily reliant on officers accurately relaying the circumstances of the incident (Tifft 1978; Holdaway 1983). Extracts support extant research that supervisors ultimately "accept and trust the goodwill" of the report writer (Manning 2009: 453), which is the current advice given to crime evaluators when assessing NCRS compliance. This was evident in Chap. 4, whereby even if a case "isn't as it seems" the sergeant often accepts at face value an officer's write-up (police officer f). These findings attest that some frontline officers as knowledge producers provide "inconsistent data to secondary risk assessors" (Robinson et al. 2016: 35). Therefore, there is limited evidence of supervisors being complicit in condoning discretionary practices, and consequently supervisors may instead be recipients of these distorted realities. However, there clearly are inconsistencies apparent between the incident data and corresponding data sets, as these findings attest. Overwhelmingly, the volume of data makes identification of such practices difficult for supervisors to detect, requiring time that they do not possess and ultimately making micromanagement too difficult to envisage. Yet where these conflicts *are* recognised, it is the responsibility of supervisors to challenge these accounts.

Concluding Remarks

The central feature of this chapter illustrates how through the power of language some police officers are highly adept at inappropriately crafting "no-crime" decisions in the incident summary write-up. Documents (electronic or otherwise) should not be considered as containers representing a collection of "facts," but instead are used by professionals as discursive devices in order to *persuade* an audience (Prior 2011; Atkinson and Coffey 2011) (namely, supervisors and scrutinising senior officers) of a particular world view, in this case that no further action is warranted.

In summary, numerous patterned practices (Lipsky 2010 [1980]) are identified which reflect the craft of language and the propensity for some officers to present a distinctly *different* "reality" through the presentational write-up—for example, omissions and withholding information from a variety of electronic documents (such as DASH), trivialisations, altering language by removing key words (kill or death); non-committal formulaic write-ups which dilute the risks by presenting information in a compressed closed question format, thereby suppressing the opportunity for supervisors to generate investigative lines of enquiry. These write-ups provide sound "back-covering" justifications for officers to dilute or entirely negate extant risks to victims, rendering situations as no longer constituting a crime with the sole purpose of "no-criming" an incident. Some victims are attributed a reluctance by officers that they did not appear to routinely "possess" on corresponding electronic documents.

Such discretionary practices are indicative of some lazy officers pursuing courses of action based on personal preference and self-interested motives, rather than on what policy dictates should be the preferable option. This is termed the "Rational Choice Model of Ignorance and Bias" (Knott and Miller 1987). This advocates that professionals in bureaucratic organisations act on biased information which rewards them and supports their own incentives, in which they often "ignore" or "screen out" information that would lead them to make decisions that they do not want to make (ibid.). It is suggested that in this research context the incident report acts as a "knowledge shield" (Messick 1999) in which access and scrutiny are inhibited by the outside world. Some officers' accounts, evident in the write-up and through inclusions and omissions in DASH and other electronic reports, represent the "smokescreen" (ibid.).

Rather than showing how the application of DASH makes it "less prone to personal bias" (Roberts et al. 2014: 121), the extracts conversely illustrate how officers' write-ups are carefully crafted and biased selective constructions. Even when good information exists on incident and PPIs to make better decisions in respect of proactive HBA investigations, as is evident in the findings, the information appears to be "distorted to fit the incentives" (Knott and Miller 1987: 186). Consequently, individuals' manifest behaviours of selective attention, relying on (and conveying) biased information to make decisions and then convincing others within the organisation (ibid.) through their presentational writing or verbal write-ups of the correctness of that course of action.

Interestingly, policing and prevention advice for HBA alludes to the importance of officers documenting actions in order to "provide a paper trail of law enforcement attempts to protect victims" (Roberts et al. 2014: 72). However, the findings suggest that this advice is redundant, as some officers already place central primacy on the presentational account, on their workload and crime queue. What in some cases begins as a serious allegation becomes eroded until the final write-up no longer resembles the initial report. Some officers use selective bias in constructing and carving an alternative documentary version of reality, one which appeared to serve self-interested motives in the cuffing or easing of workload. Such constructed versions decriminalise the actions of perpetrators, stifle further enquiries, justify inaction and deconstruct the crime process. Crucially, by officers negating crimes, not documenting or withholding data, this serves "on paper" to severely downgrade risks to victims. Such practices are compounded by the manufacturing of victim reluctance, or at the very least suggestions that victims voluntarily wish or choose to return to abusers. The alleged blasé responses of victims as "not fazed" and "not concerned" and needing no protection concerning extant threats, particularly when victims are pregnant, serves to validate police action as unnecessary. In essence, Chaps. 3, 4 and 5 are inextricably linked. Victims are problematised and presented as perpetrators; and through omissions and the crafting of an alternative version of reality "on paper," language is effective in deconstructing the crime process and thus validating "no-crime" decisions.

These discretionary practices appear to be new ways of managing the same old crime problems. For instance, in the 1980s there was talk of detectives shredding crime reports in order to ration workload. Young discusses how a crime recording register was previously a carbonated book and this was locked away in order to prevent "silly undetectable crimes" from being entered (Young 1991: 306). Indeed, the police have always suffered from volume overload and as such "demand is open ended and must be rationed" (Manning 2009: 453). The development of electronic crime recording scuppers some of these discretionary tactics, and as is evident, some officers spend considerable time "writing around" the crime through the use of language, avoiding formal paradigms by denying the crime.

Chapter 6 is an excursus, temporarily disrupting the examination of police discretionary practices, which focuses on unexpected, yet prevalent, data findings concerning the involvement of female perpetrators in honour-based abuse. Final sections return to police culture in delineating how gender role expectations and lack of recognition of female perpetration adversely impacts on safeguarding practices by professional bodies.

Examples of Good Practice: Detailed High-Risk DASH Responses[31]

Case 7

Q1. Has the current incident resulted in injury? (Please state what and whether this is the first injury.)

Ans: The victim is reporting many incidents of domestic violence over a period of 7 years. Many of these incidents have resulted in injury. Such as the offender hitting the victim in the mouth, causing her mouth to bleed. Hitting victim in the head with a fan, causing lumps and bumps to her head as well as bruising to various parts of body and swelling to the face that has been sustained from differing incidents over the 7-year period.

Q2. Are you very frightened?

Ans: The victim is terrified of the offender and what he might do to her and her children. Especially now that the police are involved and believes that he would kill her and her children as he has made threats to do this.

Q3. What are you afraid of? Is it further injury or violence? (Please give an indication of what you think (name of abuser(s)…) might do and to whom.)

Ans: As above, the victim is frightened that the offender will kill her and her children as he has made threats to her to do this. He has also made threats to the victim's friend (ref to a different incident) that he will slit the victim's throat.

Q4. Do you feel isolated from family/ friends, that is, does (name of abuser(s)…..) try to stop you from seeing friends/family/Dr or others?

Ans: There are issues with the family in that there are cultural issues as she has ran away from India as she married outside of her religion so she states that her or his family would kill her and the children. Victim states that both the victims and offenders' family live in India. States offender stopped her from seeing her friends and he was very controlling, checking her phone and always keeping an eye on what she was doing. The offender is also actively trying to locate where the victim is now she has fled from the house, contacting her friend on several occasions asking where she is and threatening her and the victim states that she is very frightened that now she has gone to the police her and her children will be killed. Therefore, at risk of HBV.

Q5. Are you feeling depressed or having suicidal thoughts?

Ans: Victim states that she is depressed from what has been happening, although is not under any treatment for this as states was afraid to go to GP. Also states that has thought about suicide on more than one occasion.

Q6. Have you separated or tried to separate from (name of abuser(s)….) within the past year?

Ans: The victim has now separated from the offender and is currently in emergency accommodation.

Q7. Is there conflict over child contact? (please state what).

Ans: Has threatened to take and kill the children.

Q9. Are you currently pregnant or have you recently had a baby in the past 18 months?

Ans: The victim does state that she had a miscarriage 6/7 months ago and did not know that she was pregnant.

Q11. Has (…) ever hurt the children/dependants?

Ans: Victim has stated that the offender has hit the children on more than one occasion, slapping them across the face and has even put their youngest child in a dark cupboard for over 15 minutes and he was crying.

Q12. Has (…) ever threatened to hurt or kill the children/dependants?

Ans: He has threatened to take and kill the children.

Q13. Is the abuse happening more often?

Ans: States that it is getting worse in the past four months and that it has been like torture.

Q14. Is the abuse getting worse?

Ans: The victim states that more recently she has been beaten by the offender badly.

Q15. Does (…) try to control everything you do and/or are they excessively jealous? (In terms of relationships, who you see, being "policed at home," telling you what to wear, for example. Consider honour-based violence and stalking and specify the behaviour).

Ans: The victim states that the offender has control of everything in relation to her, all her paperwork, her mobile phone in that he owns the contract and is always checking her phone. Also states that he always states that she is seeing someone else and calls her a slag and a prostitute. Also, as stated above the offender is actively trying to locate the victim and has threatened to kill her and the victim is scared of being in public places though fear of her husband trying to locate her.

Q16. Has (…) ever used weapons or objects to hurt you?

Ans: Victim states offender has used objects to assault her—such as a fan, shoes, perfume bottles, creams. Victim states that he uses anything close to hand and that he has also put a shawl over her face and nose.

Q17. Has (…) ever threatened to kill you or someone else and you believed them?

Ans: offender has threatened to kill the victim and the children and has threatened to kill the victim to the victim's friend.

Q18. Has (…) ever attempted to strangle/choke/suffocate/drown you?

Ans: Attempted to strangle victim by putting hands round her neck and has also tried to suffocate her by putting a shawl over her face.

Q19. Does (…) do or say things of a sexual nature that makes you feel bad or that physically hurt you or someone else? (Please specify who and what).

Ans: The victim is called a prostitute and a slag and has been subject to being raped by the offender.

Q20. Is there any other person that has threatened you or that you are afraid of? (If yes, consider extended family if honour-based violence. Please specify who. Ask 10 additional HBV questions*).

Ans: Victim states that two women whom she thinks her husband is seeing once came round to her house and started arguing with her and slapped her.

Q21. Do you know if (…) has hurt anyone else? (children/siblings/elderly relative/stranger, for example. Consider HBV. Please specify who and what).

Ans: Offender has hurt both the victim and the children as detailed above.

Q27. Do you know if (…) has ever been in trouble with the police or has a criminal history? (If yes, please specify).

No further known. Ongoing for seven years.

Q28. Other relevant information (from victim or officer) which may alter risk levels. Describe: (consider, e.g. victim's vulnerability—disability, mental health, alcohol/substance misuse and/or the abuser's occupation/interests—does this give unique access to weapons, i.e. ex-military, police, pest control) or is there serial offending?

Ans: Victim states that she cannot find any of her personal documents, cannot find them at home and does not know where they are. Victim also had no money.

Case 68

Q1. Has the current incident resulted in injury? (Please state what and whether this is the first injury.)

Ans: Yes, although you can't see any marks on my neck at the moment I am finding hard to speak from being strangled.

Q2. Are you very frightened?

Ans: Yes, I am. My brother has made it clear that he has connections. That he can do anything. Even arrange for (my ex-husband) to continue to evade police arrest and assist (ex) in taking my children out of the country.

Q3. What are you afraid of? Is it further injury or violence? (Please give an indication of what you think (name of abuser(s)…) might do and to whom.)

Ans: Yes, where will this stop. I fear it will only get worse and worse until I give in to their demands.

Q4. Do you feel isolated from family/friends, i.e. does (name of abuser(s)…..) try to stop you from seeing friends/family/Dr or others?

Ans: Yes, only my older sister (name) is in a similar situation to me being divorced herself. However, this has only polarised the rest of the family into believing that there is too much dishonour in the family already, putting increased pressure on myself. The rest of the family have all sided with (ex). We all live really close too and its constant pressure.

Q5. Are you feeling depressed or having suicidal thoughts?

Ans: No I have two children.

Q6. Have you separated or tried to separate from (name of abuser(s)….) within the past year?

Ans: Yes, we split up most recently in (date 2013). After a long history of domestic abuse which I have reported to yourselves.

Q13. Is the abuse happening more often?

Ans: I fear this is the beginning of a long road of abuse from my family.

Q15. Does (…….) try to control everything you do and/or are they excessively jealous? (In terms of relationships, who you see, being "policed at home," telling you what to wear, for example. Consider honour-based violence and stalking and specify the behaviour).

Ans: Yes, he is attempting to force me back into a violent relationship with my husband for the sake of avoiding dishonour to our family.

Q20. Is there any other person that has threatened you or that you are afraid of? (If yes, consider extended family if honour-based violence. Please specify who. Ask 10 additional HBV questions∗).

Ans: Yes, he has threatened to break my legs if I do not comply with him and get back together with my husband for the family's honour.

Q28. Other relevant information (from victim or officer) which may alter risk levels. Describe: (consider, e.g. victim's vulnerability—disability, mental health, alcohol/substance misuse and/or the abuser's occupation/ interests—does this give unique access to weapons, e.g. ex-military, police, pest control) or is there serial offending?

Ans: I am so scared as my brother and all my family live close by. I just want this to stop, I need my family to understand that my relationship with (ex) was so bad that I cannot even begin to describe to them what it was like. I haven't even told my mother all the things he did to me. I have tried to tell my brother but he is so focused on the honour of our family he doesn't listen.

Notes

1. Cases 6, 7, 9, 37, 47, 48, 67, 68, 76, 85, 86, 87, 90, 91 and 99.
2. Cases 17, 29, 31, 40, 52, 59, 62, 70, 80 and 98.
3. Cases 1, 2, 3, 4, 5, 11, 19, 21, 23, 24, 28, 30, 34, 35, 36, 41, 49, 51, 53, 54, 55, 60, 69, 71, 72, 78, 83, 88, 92, 58, 66, 89.
4. Cases 12, 15, 25, 61, 63 and 75.
5. Cases 16, 46, 56, 65, 73 and 100.
6. Multi Agency Risk Assessment Conferences (MARACs) are where statutory and voluntary agency representatives share information and problem-solve around high-risk victims of domestic abuse in order to produce a coordinated action plan to increase victim safety. Meetings usually take place monthly. At the heart of a MARAC is the working assumption that no single agency or individual can see the complete picture, but all may have insights that are crucial to their safety. The MARAC is not an agency and does not have a case management function. The responsibility to take appropriate actions rests with individual agencies (Safe Lives 2015). In most MARACs the police chair the meeting and take a lead role.
7. Cases 21, 34, 58, 66, 69 and 89.
8. Cases 5, 34, 35, 37, 60 and 62.
9. However, this info was not on the DASH.
10. Case 97 was an adult reporting rape as a child. This is excluded from the 22 child cases.
11. The Domestic Violence, Crime and Victims (Amendment) Act 2012 was introduced to include 16- and 17-year-olds within the definition of domestic abuse. This definition came into effect on 31 March 2013 (Home Office 2013).
12. Cases 25, 30, 34, 40, 41, 51, 61, 63, 72, 73, 47 and 85.
13. Cases 25, 34, 41, 51, 72 and 73.
14. Cases 47 and 85.
15. Cases 34, 40, 41, 51, 69 and 73.

16. Often difficult if the language is rarely spoken in the UK, e.g. Somalian.
17. Cases 34, 61, 72, 85.
18. Cases 30, 40, 41, 47, 51, 63.
19. Cases 25 and 73.
20. Cases 34 and 73.
21. Cases 25, 61, 63.
22. Cases 30, 40, 61, 63.
23. A "write-off" means to expedite the case, usually by closing it as no further action (NFA). A "write-up" is a condensed summary of events. Many cases in this study allude to inappropriate write-ups that constitute "write-offs."
24. This is derived from the case of *R v. Osman* 2000, in which the ECHR ruled that public bodies, such as the police, are under a positive obligation to take preventative operational measures to protect an individual when there is real and immediate risk to life from the criminal acts of others.
25. Van Maanen contends that it is "demanded that one [officer] covers for the mistake of another" (1978: 126), yet several cases show that diligent officers resent having to rectify other officers' investigations and either do it begrudgingly (case 51) or refuse to do it by inaction (case 65/67).
26. Cases 73, 19, 67, 24, 77, police officer a.
27. Cut and pasted onto the PPI.
28. E.g. submit a crime report, DASH risk assessment, obtain interpreter and witness statement, refer case to the fire service for a fire safety risk assessment, code the incident as C59 honour violence crime.
29. Cases 34, 40, 41, 51.
30. Back-cover is an informal UK term, referred to in the USA as to "cover your ass". To cover oneself is to foresee and avoid the possibility of criticism. Therefore, back-covering is a precautionary measure to protect oneself against future blame or liability.
31. Note: Any missing questions had blank entry responses.

References

Atkinson, P., & Coffey, A. (2011). Analyzing documentary realities. In D. Silverman (Ed.), *Qualitative research: Issues of theory, method and practice* (3rd ed., pp. 77–92). London: Sage Publications.

Bayley, D., & Bittner, E. (1984). Learning the skills of policing. *Law and Contemporary Problems, 47*(4), 35–59.
Belur, J. (2008). Is policing domestic violence institutionally racist? A case study of South Asian women. *Policing and Society, 18*(4), 426–444.
Bittner, E. (1978). The functions of the police in modern society. In P. Manning & J. Van Maanen (Eds.), *Policing: A view from the street* (pp. 32–50). Santa Monica, CA: Goodyear Publishing Company Inc.
Brown, M. (1981). *Working the street: Police discretion and the dilemmas of reform.* New York, NY: Russell Sage Foundation.
Crank, J. (2016). *Understanding police culture* (2nd ed.). London: Routledge.
DASH risk model: Saving lives and changing lives through early identification, intervention and prevention. (2009). [Online]. Retrieved June 30, 2016, from www.dashriskchecklist.co.uk.
Edwards, S. (1986). Police attitudes and dispositions in domestic disputes: The London study. *Police Journal, 59*(3), 230–241.
Ericson, R., & Haggerty, K. (1997). *Policing the risk society.* Oxford: Clarendon Press.
Forced marriage and honour-based violence policy and procedure. (2013). [This police force].
Hanmer, J., Radford, J., & Stanko, E. (2013 [1989]). Improving policing for women: The way forward. In J. Hanmer, J. Radford, & E. Stanko (Eds.), *Women, policing, and male violence: International perspectives* (pp. 185–201). London: Routledge.
Her Majesty's Inspectorate of Constabulary (HMIC). (2014). *Everyone's business: Improving the police response to domestic abuse.* London: TSO.
Her Majesty's Inspectorate of Constabulary (HMIC). (2015). *The depths of dishonour: Hidden voices and shameful crimes. An inspection of the police response to honour-based violence, forced marriage and female genital mutilation.* London: TSO.
Hobbs, D. (1989). Policing in the vernacular. In D. E. Downes (Ed.), *Crime and the city* (pp. 154–181). London: Macmillan.
Holdaway, S. (1983). *Inside the British police.* Oxford: Basil Blackwell Publisher Limited.
Home Office. (2013). *Information for local areas on the change to the definition of domestic violence and abuse.* Produced in partnership with AVA, Against Violence & Abuse.
Kappeler, V., Sluder, R., & Alpert, G. (1998). *Forces of deviance: Understanding the dark side of policing* (2nd ed.). Prospect Heights, IL: Waveland Press.

Knott, J., & Miller, G. (1987). *Reforming bureaucracy: The politics of institutional choice*. Englewood Cliffs, NJ: Prentice Hall.

Lipsky, M. (2010 [1980]). *Street-level bureaucracy: Dilemmas of the individual in public services* (Expanded ed.). New York, NY: Russell Sage Foundation.

Lynn, N., & Lea, S. (2012, March). Civil disputes and crime recording refusals, disinterest and power in police witcraft. *British Journal of Criminology, 52*(2), 361–380.

Manning, P. (1977). *The social organisation of policing*. Cambridge, MA: MIT Press.

Manning, P. (1978). Lying, secrecy and social control. In P. Manning & J. Van Maanen (Eds.), *Policing: A view from the street* (pp. 238–255). Santa Monica, CA: Goodyear Publishing Company Inc.

Manning, P. (2008). Performance rituals. *Policing: A Journal of Policy & Practice, 2*(3), 284–293.

Manning, P. (2009). Policing as self-audited practice. *Police Practice & Research: An International Journal, 10*(5–6), 451–464.

Messick, D. (1999). Dirty secrets: Strategic uses of ignorance and uncertainty. In L. Thompson, J. Levine, & D. Messick (Eds.), *Shared cognition in organisations: The management of knowledge*. Mahwah, NJ: Lawrence Erlbaum Associates.

Ministry of Justice. (2011). *Achieving best evidence in criminal proceedings. Guidance on interviewing victims and witnesses, and guidance on using special measures*. London: Ministry of Justice.

Morant, N., & Edwards, E. (2011, July–August). Police responses to diversity: A social representational study of rural British policing in a changing representational context. *Journal of Community & Applied Social Psychology, 21*(4), 281–296.

Myhill, A., & Johnson, K. (2016). Police use of discretion in response to domestic violence. *Criminology and Criminal Justice: An International Journal, 16*(1), 3–20.

Prior, L. (2011). Using documents in social research. In D. Silverman (Ed.), *Qualitative research: Issues of theory, method and practice* (3rd ed., pp. 94–110). London: Sage Publications.

Punch, M. (2009). *Police corruption: Deviance, accountability and reform in policing*. Oxon and Cullompton: Willan.

Richards, L. (2009). *Domestic Abuse, Stalking and Harassment and Honour Based Violence (DASH, 2009): Risk identification and assessment and management model.* [Online]. Retrieved March 1, 2016, from www.dashriskcheck-list.co.uk.

Roberts, K., Campbell, G., & Lloyd, G. (2014). *Honor-based violence: Policing and prevention* (Advances in Police Theory and Practice Series). London: CRC Press; Taylor and Francis Group.

Robinson, A. (2006). Reducing repeat victimization among high-risk victims of domestic violence. *Violence Against Women, 12*(8), 761–788.

Robinson, A., Myhill, A., Roberts, J., & Tilley, N. (2016). *Risk-led policing of domestic abuse and the DASH risk model* (pp. 1–46). [Online]. Retrieved November, 23 2016, from http://www.college.police.uk.

Safe Lives. (2015). *Safe Lives dash risk checklist: Frequently asked questions.* [Online]. Retrieved March 2, 2017, from http://www.safelives.org.uk.

Shearing, C., & Ericson, R. (1991). Culture as figurative action. *British Journal of Sociology, 42*(4), 481–506.

Tifft, L. (1978). Control systems, social bases of power and power exercise in police organisations. In P. Manning & J. Van Maanen (Eds.), *Policing: A view from the street* (pp. 90–105). Santa Monica, CA: Goodyear Publishing Company Inc.

Van Maanen, J. (1978). Kinsmen in repose: Occupational perspectives of patrolmen. In P. Manning & J. Van Maanen (Eds.), *Policing: A view from the street* (pp. 115–128). Santa Monica, CA: Goodyear Publishing Company Inc.

Young, M. (1991). *An inside job: Policing and police culture in Britain.* Oxford: Clarendon Press.

6

Female Perpetration of Honour-Based Abuse

The role of female perpetration transpires to be a prevalent theme in this study. The purpose of this chapter is to explore the nature and extent of abuse effected by women, more specifically mothers, mothers-in-law and sisters. The study categorises the dimensions of abuse into six broad themes which explore the use of violence; violence used due to pregnancy; the application of "hard" psychological abuse (e.g. surveillance, threats and false imprisonment); the use of "soft" psychological abuse (e.g. manipulating victims through emotion and feigned friendship, thereby facilitating the abuse); women who ostracise victims; and finally, women who condone offending by turning a "blind eye" to the infliction of violence. Middle sections briefly explore factors which adversely impact child victims, notably the relationship between HBA and forced marriage and the key trigger precipitating the abuse which is "westernisation". This chapter evaluates the contrasting positions as to whether women represent peripheral figures acting against other women due to duress and patriarchal oppression, or whether women are complicit and willing perpetrators of abuse. Extracts highlight that the perspective adopted influences police decision-making around crime recording and further investigation. The bond between mothers and daughters is explored in

R. Aplin, *Policing UK Honour-Based Abuse Crime*,
https://doi.org/10.1007/978-3-030-18430-8_6

later sections, in terms of how love and loyalty by daughters can impede law enforcement's recognition of female perpetration. Final sections rationalise why officers under-record cases of female perpetration. The chapter concludes by considering the wider public protection implications as to whether women, particularly mothers, are capable of safeguarding child victims of HBA.

Exploring Female Perpetration

Until relatively recently (Aplin 2017; Bates 2018), there has been a distinct absence of research around the functions and manifest behaviours exhibited by female perpetrators of HBA. The notion of women being involved in policing the behaviours of other women and their participation in physical violence or murder are not an iterative theme in traditional domestic abuse settings (Sen 2005; Rew et al. 2013; Roberts 2014). Yet, interestingly as Bates identifies, women are statistically more involved in HBA perpetration (14%) in comparison to traditional forms of domestic abuse (8%) (CPS 2017 as cited in Bates 2018). Moreover, a substantial body of academic literature argues that HBA perpetrators are predominantly male (Chesler 2010; Welden 2010; Belfrage et al. 2012; Eisner and Ghuneim 2013), involving fathers, brothers and uncles (Jafri 2009; Gill 2013; Gill and Brah 2014). Such research implicitly, but arguably erroneously, accepts it is "usually men who carry out the violence" (Gill and Brah 2014: 75) despite evidence of the willing involvement of mothers in high-profile UK honour killings (Rukhsana Naz 1999; Shafilea Ahmed 2003), with the latter fully explored by Gill (2014).

Which Females Perpetrate Honour Abuse?

Of the 100 HBA investigations, 76% (76/100) illustrate varying levels of involvement by women in honour abuse, which is unexpected (Chart 6.1). This empirical finding is supported by Bates, who also analysed police data and found that 50% (81/162) of cases involved female perpetrators in either a primary or a secondary role (2018).

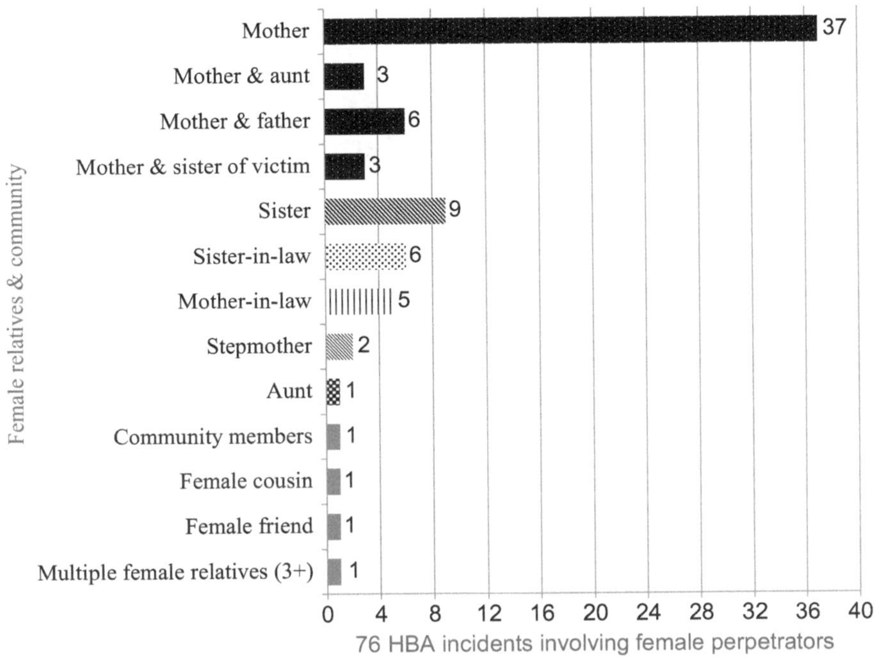

Chart 6.1 Which females perpetrate honour abuse?

Overwhelmingly, the largest proportion of female perpetrators in these findings are mothers, who act either independently or in concert with male perpetrators (largely with sons and brothers) in 48% (37/76) of all cases involving women. Mothers perpetrate with husbands in 8% (6/76) of cases and aunts (3/76) and daughters (3/76) in 4% of cases (Aplin 2017). Therefore, mothers cumulatively offend against daughters across the range of behaviours in 64% (49/76) of all female perpetration incidents, appearing to play a fundamental role in female perpetration. The highest proportion of female offenders after mothers is sisters, representing 9 of the 76 cases (12%). However, sisters also act in concert with mothers and thus cumulatively offend in 16% of cases (12/76). Other female perpetrators are sisters-in-law (6/76) (8%), mothers-in-law (5/76) (6.5%) and stepmothers (2/76) (2%). To a lesser extent, there are negligible levels of abuse from multiple women, a female friend, a community member, a female cousin and an aunt, all offending once, which aggregates to 6.5% (5/76) (Aplin 2017).

Officer Perspectives of Female Perpetration

The only question posed to officers within this topic was "what role, if any, do women play in the perpetration of honour violence?" Their responses provide a variable picture concerning abuse by women. In line with the incident findings, several police officers centralise the role played by *mothers*, rather than discuss roles played by other women. Almost half of the officers (7/15) (47%)[1] acknowledge that women play a "large" (police officer g), indeed "massive" (police officers a, c, d), role in HBA perpetration (Chart 6.2).

Two police officers go further in suggesting that women are the "driving force" behind HBA (police officers f and h), with another officer stating that the abuse is "just as bad from the women" (police officer b):

> Females can be quite domineering as well in incidents of that type of nature—maybe rare but they are there (police officer g)
>
> I think they're just as bad [women], yes, because I suppose if that's how they've lived and they've never really had any problems, then they just expect you to do the same (police officer b)

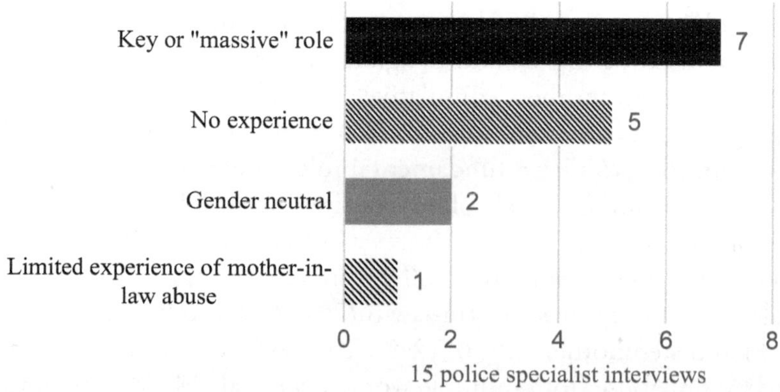

Chart 6.2 Police perspectives: the role of women in HBA

> I think mums have a very, very big part to play in it and I think—much as there are issues around strength and isolation with Asian females—I think that they do still have quite control, a matriarchal control on households. And I do think they're the key to ending any form of honour-based violence (police officer h)
>
> You've got the ones where they can be the main perpetrator and have a lot more control in the family—because it's all to do with reputation, isn't it? (police officer g)

Yet paradoxically, despite being specialist experts in HBA, a third of officers (5/15) (33%) had never investigated a female perpetrator (police officers e, i, p, n and o). However, there is some acceptance that female perpetration exists:

> The victims that I have dealt with have mainly been women, and the offenders have been men, but I would hate to say that—that's it—because there must be cases contrary to that—there must be (police officer o)
>
> I've never dealt with any [cases] where the female has been highlighted as being a perpetrator of it, but I suppose there's been massive news cases, Shafilea Ahmed ..//..mum was quite heavily involved in that (police officer p)

Despite having had no experience of dealing with female perpetrators, one officer opined that women play a "peripheral" function, condoning offending behaviour rather than perpetrating abuse directly (police officer e). Another officer had only experienced abuse by mothers-in-law (police officer j) (1/15) (7%). Two officers concur there is an element of "wilful blindness" (police officer f) with mothers "turning a blind eye" (police officer e) to behaviours, yet still possessing a full awareness of the abuse. Conversely, one officer explores emotional blackmail in women luring female victims back to the family home (police officer m). Therefore, there is a very mixed picture concerning abuse by women, with officers fluctuating in perspectives as to whether women were peripheral or integral to HBA.

No Involvement by Females

A quarter of all incidents (24/100) highlight no involvement by women (Chart 6.3). Of these, 50% (12/24) indicate clear evidence of no involvement.[2] However, a further 29% of cases (7/24)[3] show evidence of offending behaviour but insufficient investigation by police officers to ascertain who the perpetrators were.

In 3% (3/100) of incident cases there is evidence that mothers who do not keep daughters in line are equally placed at risk (cases 54, 69 and 70), and the latter two cases involve pregnant victims. In one of these cases, the brother threatened to kill his sister because he perceived her as "too westernised." The father had suffered a stroke leaving him severely disabled and thus the son took on the mantle as head of the family. Intelligence showed that several years earlier the male perpetrator had cut chunks of his sister's hair off with scissors whilst she slept in her bed. He was arrested and given a restraining order. He was now making threats to kill his own mother due to his ideological beliefs that women are beneath him, stating "If I see you; I am going to slash your throat good and proper—did you hear that? Good and proper" (case 54).

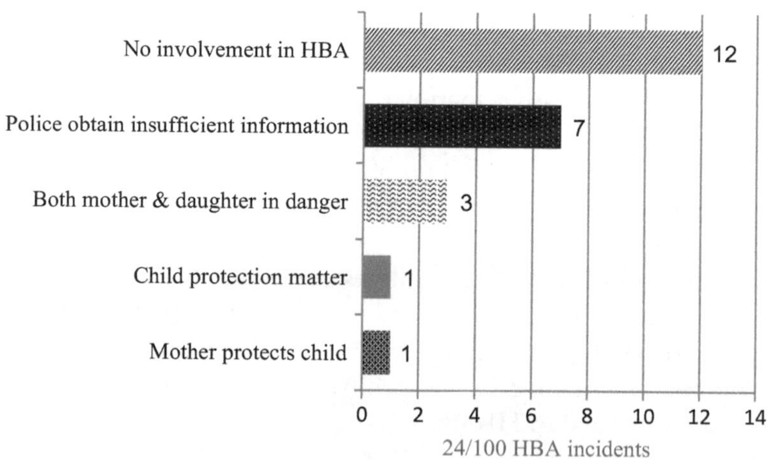

Chart 6.3 No involvement by females in HBA

There is scant evidence showing genuine support and protection by female relatives towards victims. Support is apparent in only one interview, with a mother exhibiting "relief" when an FMPO was implemented so her daughter could be more effectively protected (police officer f). Similarly, there is only one case in the incident data (1/24) (4%) of a mother protecting her child (Chart 6.3). The mother ousted her Bangladeshi husband from the family home when she discovered he had tried to obtain a dowry by selling his daughter into marriage for $10,000. The father had initially reported his daughter had been "kidnapped" by several males, one an alleged "illegal immigrant." However, it transpired that maternal uncles had protectively rescued the victim from her own father (case 63). The only outlier (1/24) (4%) involved a mother who, against the wishes of her immediate family, had gone to Pakistan to pursue a relationship with a new lover and in doing so abandoned her four children, an issue of child neglect (case 80).

Dimensions of Female Abuse

Categorising the specific roles performed by women proved to be problematic, since 83% (83/100) of HBA incidents in this study are inflicted by multiple perpetrators, each performing varying and overlapping functions; highlighting the collective nature of the crime as a group activity. Equally, quantitatively "counting" behaviours is a crude tool, failing to capture the complexities of each situation. For example, although case 24 is categorised under "soft" deceptive psychological abuse by the aunt, it also includes "hard" elements of threats and false imprisonment. Each themed category is explored qualitatively. Bates too recognises limitations in researching HBA, notably in the 162 police data cases she examined they did not routinely expose *which* of the parents inflicted the abuse. It was only in 19 cases that the functions women performed were clearly delineated (2018). The quantitative charts in this study aid in providing an overview and supplement the qualitative data. Yet moreover "counting" is beneficial in highlighting the centrality of *mothers* in perpetrating HBA. Similarly, the greatest volumes of perpetrating females in Bates'

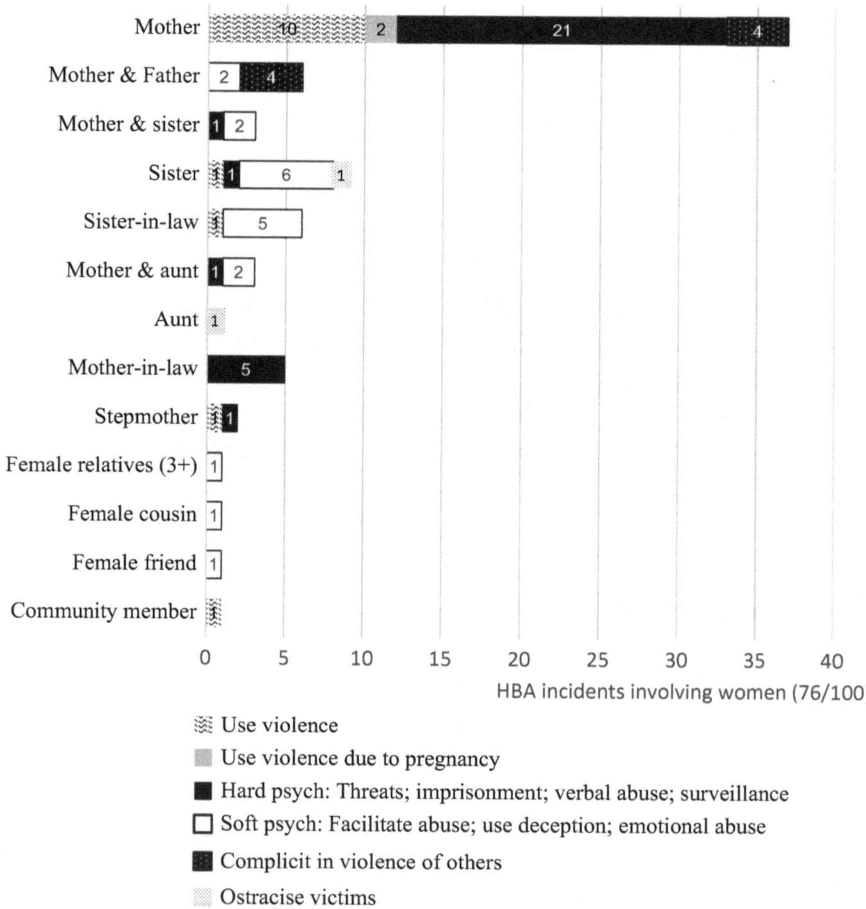

Chart 6.4 Dimensions of female abuse: types of behaviours (Aplin 2017, Copyright Elsevier)

study transpired to be mothers (42/81) accounting for 52% of cases, nearly double that of mothers-in-law (28%) (2018).

Findings from both data sets highlight a clustering of behaviours that are delineated into six key classifications (Chart 6.4): physical violence; mothers induce daughters to abort babies or assault victims whilst pregnant in order to forcibly terminate a pregnancy; "hard" psychological abuse consists of intrusive surveillance, dark threats, verbal derision, false imprisonment and emotional blackmail; "soft" psychological abuse involves women who "manipulate the situation" (police officer m) in order to gently persuade victims back home using emotive language, tears and/or deception; women also offer support but then ostracise victims due to the pressure placed on them by patriarchs; finally, women passively and complicitly condone the violence inflicted by others, mainly by sons.

Mothers Use Violence

Direct violence by women is uncommon across the whole findings, representing 18.5% (14/76) of all female behaviours. This resonates with Bates's contemporary study, which proffers that physical violence is significantly less likely in cases involving female perpetrators (2018). However, crucially in this study, it is *mothers* who inflict 71.5% (10/14)[4] of the direct acts of violence against daughters (Aplin 2017). Daughters were attacked by mothers (and other females) in a variety of ways, consisting of having their hair pulled (cases 39, 93) or in some cases cut off (police officer m, case 54); being slapped (61, 72, 20); being "hit" and punched (cases 26, 13, 39 and 93) and kicked (case 93). Mothers also used household objects to assault daughters with, such as a hoover pipe (case 20), the metal frame of a bed (case 93), mothers threw "chairs and shoes" (case 17) or slapped children on the head with slippers (case 84) (Aplin 2017):

> Her mum has thrown shoes and chairs at the victim in the past, in the family home (DASH[5] case 17)
>
> Mums who have dished out, in their eyes, chastisement over [for instance]—the daughters walked home from school with a lad and they've been seen in public; they've been assaulted as a result of that by mum; the type of clothes they've worn; being found with a mobile phone—assaults for [that]; to actually being removed—they are at the airport with Mum and not Dad—Dad may already be abroad (police officer m)

In another case a 14-year-old child was tied to a chair and systematically assaulted, having her hair cut off by both mother and grandmother because she had been missing from home (MFH) and was found in the park. The intention was to:

> [s]top her becoming wayward, they thought that she was going to get a boyfriend, she was going to drop out of further education; she was generally becoming more westernised, shall we say, than they wanted her to be..//..She had been the victim of assaults and false imprisonments, shackled to chairs, and things like that—having her hair cut off—to make her less attractive and less likely to go out (police officer m) (Aplin 2017)

Sometimes, there is no real "justification" for the infliction of violence by mothers. A 12-year-old Bangladeshi child divulged to officers that her mother punched her five times and pulled her hair because she "wouldn't pick something up off the bedroom floor because she [the victim] was tired" (case 39). In another case a vulnerable victim with learning difficulties was "slapped" by her mother "for not listening" (case 61). Mothers not only use violence but condone the cruelty and ill-treatment of the "perceived" transgressor by bullying and encouraging others to injure the victim. One officer recounted a case where the child was chatting to a boy on Facebook: her sister found out and assaulted her, then her mum assaulted her, and then her brother hit her (police officer k). Similarly, a mother not only slapped her 16-year-old daughter in the face but hit her on the arm with a hoover pipe. She then encouraged her son to hit her with a ruler, which he did. This occurred because the victim left the house without permission. Consequently, she was forcibly locked in the house pending a report back to the child's father (case 20) (Aplin 2017). In another extract, a 14-year-old victim attested that the mother had locked herself in a bedroom in order to monitor her daughter's Facebook pages. A fight ensued whereby the mother jumped on top of the child and started to bang the victim's head against the metal frame of the bed. In an attempt to stop the violence, the child "bit" her mother on the hand. During the attack, the younger sister contributed by pulling the victim's hair. Later that day the younger sibling came into the kitchen and began to tease her sister with food, to which the mother said "let her starve" (case 93).

These extracts illustrate isolated acts of violence, but moreover expose evidence of relentless bullying by the wider collective, with relatives colluding and encouraging each other to perform violent acts on perceived transgressors (Aplin 2017). Such relentless bullying appears reminiscent of Gill's evaluation of the Shafilea Ahmed case, in which the mother physically attacked the daughter "countless times" for "the most trifling reasons" (Gill 2014: 185). The mother psychologically tormented her about an intended forced marriage in Pakistan; she locked her daughter in a bedroom for two days without food, only letting her out to use the toilet. Both parents financially abused the victim, stealing £1000 from her part-time work account. On the night of the murder, it was the mother who searched the victim's bags, accusing her of "hiding" her earnings and pushed her on the settee, encouraging her husband to kill by saying in Punjabi "just finish it here" (Gill 2014: 186). Testimony of the daughter, Alesha Ahmed, exposes the mother as a willing participant and co-conspirator. Yet, despite this the defence team unsuccessfully sought to present the mother, Farzana Ahmed, as a secondary victim, unable to defend and protect her children due to the violence she feared from her husband. Whether women are willing agents or secondary victims acting under duress is worthy of consideration and shall be fully evaluated towards the close of this chapter.

Violence by Other Women

Isolated episodes of violence by other women were apparent; for instance, sisters-in-law "joined in" with husbands in trying to "rag [the victim] round with her head scarf and tried to strangle her with it." Having lent her brothers £7000 for their start-up business, in the eyes of the family, the female victim had emasculated the brothers, who had "lost face" because of the sister's financial independence (case 59). Violence from stepmothers largely replicates behaviours by mothers-in-law towards daughters in terms of exhibiting stifling and over-controlling behaviours, false imprisonment and assault. One teenage victim heard the stepmother on the phone planning her own marriage, as the police incident report states:

> (Victim) came to England when she was 11-years-old after her mother died in Bangladesh. Since she was around 15 years her father and stepmother have been very strict with her and she is often punished for wearing western clothes and being disobedient. This punishment consists of being hit with a stick which has on occasions left marks on her. Also she is locked in her bedroom. Her bedroom [door] has a thick bolt lock on the inside and outside. She states her brothers have also been hit, but that this is lawful chastisement and not as often or to the extent as she receives. She states that this is the case as she is female and not the biological daughter of her step mum. She also states her brothers are only locked out of their bedroom, not in it like her, in order to stop them messing their room up (case 34)

It is interesting that the victim attributes the behaviour of the stepmother to her non-biological status rather than to her gender.

Mothers Use Violence Due to Pregnancy

Of the 100 cases of honour abuse 10% revealed that pregnancy outside marriage[6] was a key trigger precipitating HBA, which was an unexpected finding. The cases predominantly revolve around mainly young Asian females "defying" families by having illicit relationships with disapproved-of men and becoming pregnant. The perceived remedy for dishonouring the family is that victims are "forced to have an abortion," involving close liaison with community and family to ensure "the desired result was achieved" (case 83). The role of women, and in particular mothers, in precipitating this course of action should not be underestimated. Findings showed that in the five pregnancy cases where violence was used, two cases illustrated the violence was from mothers (cases 95, 87). In the third case, it was unclear which relative perpetrated the crime (case 100). In a further two linked cases, there appeared to be significant levels of psychological abuse from women precipitating an abortion (linked cases 65, 67) (Aplin 2017). In the first case, unveiling the pregnancy was entirely engineered by the sister-in-law, who transported the unaware victim and her boyfriend to the parents' address. On realising the deception, the boyfriend took the first train back home, leaving his girlfriend at the mercy of her mother, who, on hearing the news of the five-month pregnancy, hit and kicked her to the stomach "knowing full well she was pregnant." The mother set about verbally demeaning her as:

> Dirty, no longer part of the family, they all wished she was dead, they hope she dies, they hope her child is born disabled and that she is going to be kicked out of the family home with only the clothes she was wearing (case 95)

In a second almost identical case, a mother slapped her pregnant daughter twice in the hip, rather than the stomach, because the victim had taken evasive action by moving out of the way. The victim firmly believed the "mother was trying to hit her in the stomach to cause harm to her unborn baby" (case 87). Mothers in these two cases appear to act with an almost unnatural abhorrence towards their daughters, inflicting violence that constitutes nothing less than an attempt to induce an abortion (Aplin 2017). The third case was entirely extraordinary by comparison, whereby a fast pregnancy after an arranged marriage in Pakistan led family members to doubt the paternity of the unborn child. This resulted in persons (unnamed in the police report) whilst in Pakistan trying to "give her medicine to kill the child" (case 100). The victim, still pregnant, fled to the UK only to be treated as a pariah by her own family who were pressured into refusing her sanctuary. The lack of probing or recording by the frontline officer meant that no one was implicated in the crime and it is uncertain whether the perpetrator was her own family or the in-laws (case 100).

The concern around believing that mothers unequivocally protect their offspring has adverse consequences for victims. This is particularly apparent when observing the responses by public bodies, who appear to accept this assumption. In one case (linked cases 65 and 67) the police were warned by the boyfriend that the family may:

> Either throw her [the pregnant victim] down the stairs or force her to have an abortion and say that she consented (case 65)

The victim also confirmed to the attendant officer:

> If she did have an abortion, it would be because her family had made her (case 65) (Aplin 2017)

Yet the attendant officer took no proactive steps to safeguard her. Akin to narratives presented in Chap. 3, the perpetrating family successfully demonised the boyfriend to officers, and conversely suggested that they were acting in the victim's "best interests." Ten days later in a separate police report, the boyfriend again alerts the police that the victim needs help escaping the family home. She is locked in the home by her mother and sister and the property is secured behind an electric gate. Consequently, the police have trouble effecting entry. The victim is no longer pregnant and discloses to the officers that she had a "miscarriage" six days after police attendance and was "taken to a (named) private clinic." This is not further probed by the police officers. Although foul play and assault regarding the victim cannot be confirmed, it is suggested this is indicative of a victim having been psychologically "worn down" into aborting a baby. This tends to be corroborated by the victim's account in the officer write-up:

> She will get married without her friends or family present if that's the way it has to be. I've asked what the rush is and she told me it's because in Islam you're not supposed to have sexual relations with anyone and aren't really meant to live or be together. By them having sex and being together they commit sins every day. By being pregnant it was a sin and she doesn't want to sin anymore (case 67) (Aplin 2017)

There may be a clear rationale behind women, and mothers in particular, putting a stop to unplanned pregnancies. In one case a seven-month pregnant 16-year-old was pre-warned by her mother of a plan that she would be killed by a third party at the instigation of her father and brother. The younger brother alerted his mother that the father was on route to Pakistan to kill her (his wife) too, and as a result "Osman warnings"[7] were issued by the police, reflecting a threat to life for both the mother and the pregnant daughter (linked cases 69, 70). Extant literature supports the view that the woman's family of origin (as well as the victim) can be blamed or tainted by the perceived dishonourable behaviour of the victim (Elden 2011; Haj-Yahia 2011; Chesler and Bloom 2012). In a collectivist society, women who fail to keep others "in line" can end up being "tarred with the same brush" (Van Eck 2003 as cited in Cooney 2014: 417).

In summary, of the five cases of violence/drugging and pressure towards pregnant women, there was direct violence by mothers in two cases. Conversely, there was no evidence across both data sets of any intentional violence by men towards pregnant women with intent to kill the foetus.[8] In the five remaining pregnancy cases one girl gave birth and the child was immediately placed in local authority care. She became pregnant again soon after and, like her sister, remains at risk of sexual exploitation (cases 69 and 70); one pregnant female was sent to Pakistan after being given a veiled threat that her father will "give her what she deserves" (case 5). In a further two cases, pregnant victims returned to the risk situation, hoping to be supported by their mother (cases 83 and 89). The pregnancy theme was only alluded to by two officers within the interviews. However, narratives were equally poignant and centralised on the role of mothers:

> You get pregnant, if you get pregnant in those communities—we talked about that example where Mum's 'kicked the shit' out of her daughter—excuse my language—that's how it is. I am 52 now and I do not know one Asian girl in my whole surroundings, cousins, families, friends, who has got pregnant [out of marriage] because that would be the worst thing you could do—even worse than having a cig (cigarette) or going out with a boy from the wrong culture (police officer a) (Aplin 2017)

Another officer dealt with a particularly harrowing case in which a Sikh girl became pregnant by her Muslim boyfriend:

> She were lay in the road, she was unconscious and she had— it was quite horrific actually, I remember it now, she had quite a lot of injuries. She had the imprint of a ceremonial sword on her back that had been *burnt* onto her back...//... But mum seemed to be very much the driving force behind

> that—and I think mums have a very, very big part to play in it and I think, much as there are issues around strength and isolation with Asian females, I think that they do still have—quite control—a matriarchal control on households (police officer h)

As a result of the attack, the victim lost her unborn child and was so badly injured that she was left permanently physically disabled. The police were unable to prove that relatives inflicted the extensive injuries. Despite this, the investigating officer believes in her "heart of hearts" that the family who ironically still "care" for her are the perpetrators. Consequently, she considers that women are "the key to ending any form of honour-based violence" (police officer h) (Aplin 2017).

These pregnancy cases illustrate that, first, like "traditional" domestic abuse, there is an increased risk of harm to women during pregnancy. Second, such "miscarriages" need to be examined through a new lens, as discussion and action around forced abortions appeared to be largely instigated through women. Third, although undoubtedly men play a key role in HBA perpetration, findings revealed that there was no evidence of violence by men towards daughters due to pregnancy, only by mothers. Such findings challenge the stereotypical notion that men are perpetrators and mothers are secondary "victims" who are nurturing and supportive of daughters. The reality is much more complex.

"Hard" Psychological Abuse

Analysis and comparison of the incident data illustrates that victims are often exposed to many of the six dimensions of abuse. However, psychological abuse is overwhelmingly the cogent thread interwoven throughout a significant proportion of narratives, with "hard" and "soft" psychological abuse inflicted by women across 66% (50/76) of the sample.

As Chart 6.4 indicates, the largest proportion of "hard" psychological abuse is overwhelmingly inflicted by *mothers* (70%, 21/30, of cases); mothers in conjunction with aunts and sisters were involved in 6.5% (2/30) of cases; mothers-in-law in 16.5% (5/30) of cases; and a stepmother and sister in one case each (7%, 2/30). Psychological abuse is extremely debilitating for victims (Aplin 2017). "Hard" psychological control is categorised here as direct threats, verbal abuse, false imprisonment (albeit this is a "crime" in itself), intrusive surveillance, and labour servitude/forms of slavery. It predominantly involves "policing" and surveillance behaviours (n = 41), imprisoning victims so they feel like "prisoner(s) in her own home" (case 28); prohibiting and punishing victims for wearing make-up or wearing westernised clothes; searching victims' bags; predominantly confiscating items such as bank cards, bus passes, passports, mobile phones, or alternatively "monitoring" iPads and phone calls; and prohibiting access to social media sites, such as Facebook. Such measures result in children hiding their phone or sometimes possessing two phones (cases 84, 89 and 94). Several honour incidents in the research were "discovered" and "reported back on" due to intensified "spying" by women, for example, finding abortion leaflets in the daughter's bag (case 89) or the sister-in-law finding folic acid tablets (cases 65 and 67). These policing behaviours intensify considerably when a daughter or son (case 77) is found to be in an "inappropriate" relationship (n = 43).

Westernisation: A Key Trigger for Child Victims of HBA

Although the main trigger in the incident data is parents discovering the daughter may be sexually active (24%), victims being perceived as too "westernised" (17/100) is the second highest trigger (see Chart 3.4). Yet compared with adult victims, "westernisation" is the *most* dominant trigger for child cases, constituting 50% (11/22)[9] of all child cases (see Chart 6.5). Behaving as "too westernised" constitutes girls behaving in a supposedly un-Islamic manner which dishonours the family. It includes behaviours such as wearing make-up and "western" clothing; using social media (e.g. Facebook) in order to contact boys; having a secret mobile phone; being "disobedient" and unruly; failing to wear a headscarf; associating with people "outside" the culture; staying out late; drinking alcohol; going missing from home (MFH).

The westernisation theme is apparent across both data sets. The extracts illustrate stifling and "extreme levels" (case 17) of control by women on a routine and daily basis, involving false imprisonment of juveniles by

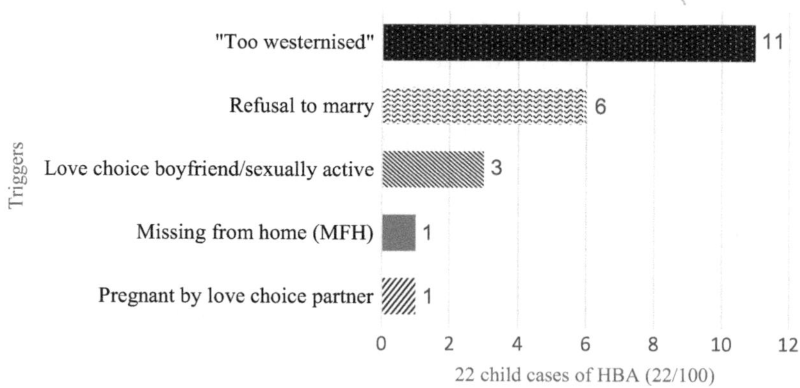

Chart 6.5 Triggers for HBA in child cases

mothers, and to a lesser extent siblings and aunts. It is important for professionals to recognise that the theme of westernisation is related to the suspicion that girls, through their behaviours, are not adhering to culture norms, are getting boyfriends and might become sexually active. Indeed, this finding is apparent in Bates' study, where the key triggers for abuse were rejecting a marriage, choosing a love choice boyfriend over the family's choice or for leading a "westernised lifestyle." In that study three Asian girls were subject of HBA because they were dating white boys (2018: 8). This research supports the view that forced marriage is deemed as the family remedy for wayward and non-compliant girls and young adults. Furthermore, this fear of westernisation tends to support Cantle's (Institute of Community Cohesion 2001) assessment that such communities self-segregate in order to resist unwholesome polluting western influences. Over-controlling behaviours and westernisation were key interlinked themes:

> Mother and brother considered her "unruly and that they cannot control her or the outward influences affecting her"..//.. she needs to be married off soon as preferably before college due to her unholiness..//.. Unhappy with her being educated and to minimise her outside influences and reduce her time at school they request that she comes home for lunch. Mother has also taken her mobile phone off her..//.. Her Mother has stated that (relatives)

will break her legs, making it look like she has fallen down the stairs[10] and this will reduce the amount of time she spends out of the address (case 22)

They won't allow her to become westernised. She said that it is one rule for her and one rule for the rest of her family..//.. Her mum checks up on her to an abnormal level whenever she leaves the house..//..to extreme levels. She is being over-controlled by her overbearing mother so just stays in her bedroom when she is at home (case 17)

In another case an Indian mother, described as "quite controlling of late, doing more snooping," had found an abortion leaflet whilst rifling her daughter's bag (case 89) (Aplin 2017)

It is particularly concerning that professionals did not identify the cues that children were at risk, arguably because statutory services perceived these as trivial issues (girls possessing cigarettes, condoms, mobile phones, talking to boys, being late home etc.).

The role of mothers as the central intelligence repository, policing such behaviours within the family, should not be overlooked. In one case the siblings discovered that their sister had sneaked her boyfriend in her room, so they locked her in the house pending their mother's arrival (case 10). Mothers sometimes use the power of the patriarch as a means of wielding control over child victims, threatening them with "just wait and see what he (father) thinks about it" (case 20). Mothers communicate father's threats to the victim, possibly as a means of influencing daughters into making particular decisions, with one father allegedly saying through the communication of the mother, "If she's at the home when I get back and still pregnant—I'll kill her" (case 87). In another case it was only after spending 18 months in care that one victim disclosed that it was her mother who generated and sustained the "psychological warfare" (police officer d) she had suffered:

Mum is the biggest offender in this victim's eyes..//..Dad is saying "Look, whatever the girl wants. If she wants to come home, if she wants to go to college. We want her to do well"..//.."Yes, my mum just basically controlled everything I did, everywhere I went, what I wore, what my room looked like. She suspected I had a boyfriend, so—my restriction to freedom. There were arguments at home. My dad wasn't really that bothered..//.. but it was *mum* (police officer d) (Aplin 2017)

Children are often threatened with harsh ultimatums that daughters will be "dead to them" (cases 53, 95, 96), that they will be "thrown out" (case 11) or "cut off" (cases 33, 77, 93) if they fail to comply with a marriage or refuse to stop a relationship with a boyfriend. Findings suggest that mothers can be equally as pecuniary as men in considering the financial implications of marriage. One mother wanted to send her daughter to Libya for a forced marriage, as she was unhappy about her being in a relationship with a black man. The mother bartered with the love choice boyfriend, telling him he would "need to pay $10,000 (sic) for the wedding to go ahead" (case 27). In other cases, denying children the funds to attend university (case 48) or "medical school" (case 66) is used as leverage to ensure that victims comply with family wishes. Pre-marriage victims are also denied access to their siblings if they do not return home (case 33) or marry (case 35). Mothers are particularly effective in communicating particularly harsh commentary, with several stating that if they did not marry they would "be killed":[11]

> Mother told victim: "I'll just get you married to one of your cousins. If anything happens I'll just hope you die and if you don't die I will just kill you myself and there will be a funeral for you" (case 64)
>
> My mum said a long time ago women used to have babies, find out it's a girl and kill them after being born. She said that's what should have happened to me. She said she didn't care about me and she wanted me dead because of all the stress I gave her (case 96) (Aplin 2017)

Such narratives wrought on children by mothers lead one to reconsider portrayals of mothers as passive secondary victims within the family dynamic.

HBA and Its Relationship to Marriage

Although this study concerns HBA and not forced marriage, the interrelationship between these two facets is self-evident across the qualitative findings. A quantitative examination was undertaken across the 100 cases of HBA and marriage was a feature within 64% of cases (64/100) (includ-

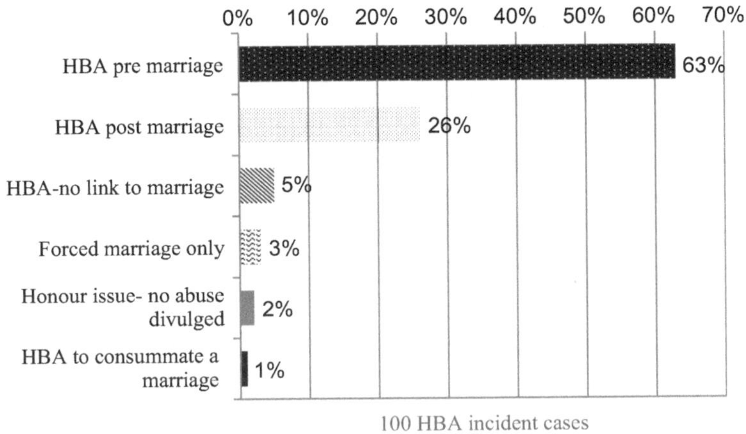

Chart 6.6 HBA and its relationship to marriage

ing consummation of marriage). What is notable in Chart 6.6 is that victimisation against pre-marriage juveniles and young adults is far more widespread than *post*-marriage abuse. Moreover, the qualitative data illustrates that pre-marriage offending also appears to be more high risk compared to post-marriage abuse. This supports Swedish research by Belfrage et al. (2012), in that, of the eight cases classed as being of lethally high risk, 75% of victims were daughters rather than estranged wives.

The Wrath of the Mother-in-Law

Abusive behaviours by mothers-in-law predominantly involve the policing of the daughter-in-law, domestic servitude and false imprisonment in "post" marriage abuse (also Bates 2018). The nature of offending is essentially hard psychological abuse, manifested in verbal belittling and personal insults that the daughter-in-law "cannot cook, she can't walk, she smells" (case 30), to derision about her "poor background." In the eyes of the victim, nothing is "good enough" (case 47), she will "never have a future and is a 'nobody' " (case 9). Such bullying and derision are reminiscent of Ballard's view that women are resourceful in their use of language to belittle and mock, creating spaces in order to construct "internal hierarchies" (Ballard 2002: 3). In stark contrast to the abuse by mothers, mothers-in-law are keen to progress pregnancy and deride the victim for *failing* to get pregnant, giving iron and folic acid to the daughter-in-law in order to increase the chances of conception (case 30). Mothers-in-law also resort to tactics of emotional blackmail in order to more effectively control and force compliance from daughters-in-law. A threat to post-marriage victims is that of "sending her back to Pakistan" (cases 47, 30, police officer j), arranging a replacement wife and removing her children (cases 47, 40 and 92). Women constantly live under the threat that they will be "sent back" to the shame of their families. Such tactics are wholly consistent with Thiara's domestic abuse research (2013).

Certainly, the findings around the violence of the mother in prior sections lie in stark contrast to Bates' analysis of 19 cases, in which it was instead *mothers-in-law* who applied direct violence such as slapping, pushing and beating (2018). However, direct violence by mothers-in-law (and other women) was barely discernible in this research. In one case a daughter-in-law divulged to police that she had been sexually abused by her Romanian father-in-law. Due to the shame the allegation wrought on the family, the victim was hit in the face by the mother-in-law, who forcibly bundled her into a car to transport her to a local solicitor in order to force her to retract the complaint (police officer b). Controlling and oppressive behaviours by mothers-in-law centre on policing and surveillance activities, such as preventing employment and prohibiting access to finances (case 9). Women are controlled in so far as they are told what to eat and what to wear (case 47) and are often not allowed out of the house unaccompanied (cases 4, 30, 47). Victims feel isolated and possess poor English language skills. Victim language is reflective of confinement and they describe to officers as being "treated like a slave" (cases 47, 40) or a "prisoner in her own home" (cases 28, 40, 4).

Further surveillance behaviours involve mothers-in-law intercepting mail from abroad and they monitor, as well as curtail, phone calls from the mother of daughters-in-law. In one case the victim was only permitted to speak to her mother "publicly" using the speaker phone, and only after the mother had conversed with the mother-in-law (case 91). In one instance a victim agreed to an arranged marriage in order to escape from the controlling sphere of the stepmother, only to be subjected to a similar confinement from her new mother-in-law, experiencing labour servitude, false imprisonment and the confiscation of bank cards (case 4). This is reminiscent of the serial victimisation evident in high risk domestic abuse cases. Marriage, in effect, becomes a tool to suppress female autonomy (Payton 2011) as well as appearing to be a source of cheap labour. The daughter-in-law is derided for poor housekeeping and is made to clean the house daily, cook and even massage the mother-in-law's feet (case 30). In another case because a daughter had fled the address (due to HBA), the son was obligated to take on a wife so that she could "do the housework" for his mother (case 96).

It is worthy of note that such vigilant surveillance and chaperoning is perceived by the family as supportive protection and guardianship (Payton 2011) and, in turn, is successfully advanced to professionals as such. Yet Payton reminds us that this is essentially about self-interest in protecting the market value of family assets. Women are treated as commodities and part of a "transaction" with the daughter-in-law a symbolic representation of the "family brand" (2011: 69). The family must protect their investment. The current research confirms the relative power that older matriarchs have over the "weak" daughter-in-law, who lies at the bottom of the pecking order and is constantly at the beck and call of mothers-in-law (Ballard 1982: 19). Older women play an important role in controlling younger women (Yuval-Davis 1998; Rew et al. 2013) and it is only after the birth of children, particularly sons, that the social capital of the daughter-in-law is increased (Ballard 1982; Rew et al. 2013; Durbas 2015). Having suffered the trials and tribulations of first being a daughter and then being a daughter-in-law, it appears that mothers-in-law are loath to sacrifice their now dominant position. They therefore have a "vested interest" in perpetuating coercive and controlling practices over the daughters-in-law (Rew et al. 2013: 147).

As explored, multiple perpetration is rife within the findings (83%) and husbands often condone the abuse inflicted by their own mothers, who also encourage sons to keep their wives "in line" (cases 2, 47, 30). Ironically, in Gill's (2004) UK HBA study the husband was identified as the main perpetrator. Yet, in half of the 18 cases sampled, it transpired that mothers-in-law were also involved in perpetrating abuse. This lends weight to the view that female perpetration causes significant "discomfort to feminists" as it erodes ideas of feminist solidarity (Rew et al. 2013: 148), which may explain why such a thorny issue has been scantly documented within academia. Condoning abuse by the husband is evident across both data sets:

> She constantly is reminded of the fact she comes from a poor background in Pakistan and she should thank them for what they give her..//..The family even dictate whether she can go to the shops to buy some milk for her baby. Often the family tell her of sending her back to Pakistan alone, taking her child from her. The only gripe victim has of her husband is that he stands and watches the family abuse her. He does not challenge them (case 47)
>
> "My husband sides with his mum; mother-in-law treats me like a slave, I've got to do everything for the mother-in-law. Husband goes out to work, father-in-law goes out to work, I'm stuck at home all day with mother-in-law"../.. I've not known a sister, I've not known a mother [perpetrator]—it's the mother-in-law. Again, massively under reported though isn't it? (police officer j)
>
> "They won't let me out of their sight"..//..mother-in-law used to beat her..//.. husband used to stand back and watch..//.. Husband had never laid a finger to her. What mother-in-law says 'goes'..//... The mother-in-law has this major status in the family ..//..that was beating, mother-in-law beater. So it was very much mother-in-law who wouldn't let her out of the house (police officer j)

In a further extract the victim was pregnant, financially independent and working full time in a well-paid job and paying for all the family holidays. Yet the daughter-in-law was still openly criticised by the mother-in-law to her son on the grounds that the housework had not been completed to her satisfaction (case 2). Such control exerted by mothers-in-law appears highly reminiscent of the Duluth wheel of power and control (Pence and Paymar 1993)[12] highlighting an overlap with traditional forms of domestic abuse, with the same control mechanisms exerted by mothers to young daughters in pre-marriage abuse. Such extracts illustrate women as central and willing participants in perpetuating oppressive practices against other women (Okin 1999; Gill et al. 2012; Eisner and Ghuneim 2013).

By contrast, distinctly new findings also emerge from the quantitative incident data. As indicated in Chart 6.6, post-marriage abuse accounts for a much smaller proportion of HBA cases (26%) in comparison to pre-marriage abuse. Second, in a departure from previous research (Gill 2004; Rew et al. 2013) the quantitative findings highlight that abuse by mothers-in-law is relatively rare and inflicted in only 6.5% of cases (5/76).[13] However, it must be highlighted that Bates' study conflicts with these findings in identifying a greater volume of cases involving mothers-in-law (23/81) (28%) (2018). Third, although psychological abuse is debilitating, humiliating and stifling in its replication of over-controlling surveillance behaviours, there is scant evidence of the severe bullying and multiple perpetration that is so evident in the mother against daughter extracts. Fourth, there is significantly less evidence of direct violence by mothers-in-law, with no evidence of violence in the incident data and only two instances of direct violence (police officers b and j) by mothers-in-law across 15 police interviews. Therefore, findings expose that the nature of abuse by mothers-in-law is not as debilitating and is relatively infrequent. However, it is worth acknowledging that many victims brought to the UK for marriage may not possess knowledge around reporting mechanisms, nor have the confidence in language skills to progress any complaint, which may contribute towards these lower reporting rates.

"Soft" Psychological Abuse

Counter-intuitively, there is evidence of female relations attempting to maintain a psychological bond of friendship with victims, almost akin to grooming behaviours. Note the findings of Wiener, who makes a similar link in the coercive control context (2017: 7). Findings highlight how women act as enablers of HBA, heavily engineering situations, communicating and facilitating HBA either through deception or practically "transporting" victims to their punishment. Women use the communication of tears and emotive language prompting other protagonists into "action." However, this behaviour is insidious and includes deceptive tactics to present a duplicitous narrative to both victims and public authorities, all with the aim of luring victims back for punishment and/or reconciliation.

Key perpetrators in the "soft" psychological domain are sisters (6/20), sisters-in-law (5/20) accounting for 55% of cases, and equally mothers with the aid of sisters (2/20), aunts (2/20) and husbands (2/20). More distant relations (cousin, friend and female relatives) play a role in 3/20 cases.

Women as Communicative Messengers

Although many of the behaviours do not constitute criminal "offences," female relatives appear adept at using communication skills to verbally antagonise and create problems for female victims. In a pregnancy case, a female cousin was "stirring things up about the family honour ..//..putting pressure on [the victim's] mum to encourage victim to have a termination" (case 87). Such Machiavellian "stirring" caused the mother to slap her own daughter twice in the hip with the intention of hitting her stomach.

Females also act as "messengers" and in doing so falsely present a veneer of protecting and warning victims. A victim fled her flat with her love choice boyfriend, whom she later married. Her "trusted" female cousin had keys and regularly accessed the flat and acted as "messenger" by passing information between the victim and her ex-lover perpetrator. The female cousin betrayed and exploited the trust by passing the victim's mail to her own husband, who was a close personal friend of the perpetrator. Notably, there was no recognition within the data, either from the police or the victim, as to the cousin's role in facilitating the harassment. The cousin was the conduit communicating the threatening messages, telling the victim and her love choice that the ex was going to "find them, kill them both and chop them up with a knife." Such actions precipitated the poor mental health suffered by man and wife,[14] almost dissolving the marriage (case 85). As such there appears to be a lack of solidarity between some women. In a similar case, a male Sunni Muslim and his Shi'a Muslim wife fled to the UK and married against family wishes and have been pursued ever since. When detail of the plight was journalised in a magazine, a female friend of the female victim wrote to editors requesting details of their location. Included in the information was a letter written in Urdu outlining that the family were "thirsty for her blood" and that "the village elders have decided that they should both be stoned to death" (case 99). The purpose of contacting the magazine appeared to be to locate the victim(s) using the seriousness of the threat as persuasion. In a similar vein, a 26-year-old Iraqi victim of post forced marriage abuse living with her new husband received mail suspected to be from her estranged sister-in-law. It contained a "welcome to your new home" card with approximately 50 photos of her husband's family with cuts through their faces, necks and head, which in the Kurdish culture is deemed to be a serious threat (case 25). These final three cases illustrate how victims, through the involvement of female messengers, are psychologically maintained in an anxious and hyper-vigilant state.

Sisters

In two-thirds of cases involving perpetrating sisters (6/9),[15] they enabled HBA by keeping lines of communication open with fleeing victims, in some instances acting as a close and trusted "confidant." In the honour killing of Aqsa Parvez, it is worth acknowledging that it was sisters who policed and reported back to parents the way the victim dressed at school, in terms of removing her hijab (Welden 2010).

In the current research, victims were duped into believing sisters afforded them genuine love and support. This is evident in the case where the "trusted older sister" persuades the victim "look you need to come home I've managed to iron all this out now things are sorted, come on" (police officer m). One 20-year-old Bangladeshi fleeing from HBA complained she was getting "constant calls and texts" from her sister, yet police officers trivialised this by giving advice (case 66, also evident in 37, 45, 46) without appreciating the role of women in locating victims and persuading them back into the fold. Similarly, in the case of a victim with learning difficulties, it was the *sister* who successfully convinced Adult Social Care that the victim consented to a marriage—which ultimately the victim had been "tricked" and "cheated" into (case 46).

There is also evidence of sisters being openly hostile and "stirring up" trouble, encouraging other "would be" perpetrators into committing offences, particularly in defence of patriarchy. When one victim rejects an arranged marriage, her sister vigorously discredits the victim and concocts an alibi for her father so that he could avoid criminal prosecution. She suggests her "sister is evil..//..*she* had arranged marriage at 17 and she …should do the same" (case 49). In another case a sister made counter-allegations against the victim, erroneously telling the police that the victim had tried to kick her in the stomach (she was pregnant) in the hope this would influence officers into taking no further action against the perpetrator uncle (case 60). There was no evidence across the sample, of genuine support by sisters towards victims. Like mothers, sisters appeared to fluctuate from "supportive" "soft" yet deceptive behaviours to "hard" denigrating behaviours, suggesting these are underhand disingenuous tactics designed to deceive and/or discredit victims.

Women Deceive and Enable

Deception is often used by women to help physically "deliver"[16] victims home to receive their punishment, often to the surprise of unsuspecting victims. In several cases, parents 'string victims along' under the misconception that they accept the relationship (cases 24, 42), but this resembles a deceptive "delaying" tactic. In one case the victim was imminently due to marry her betrothed partner of six years and was under the misapprehension that her parents consented. A situation was engineered by the aunt, who instead of taking her "shopping" as promised, delivered the victim to the uncle's house with the victim's father following in a car close behind, indicating the premeditated nature of the act. The uncle hit her, stating she would not be marrying her love choice and falsely imprisoned her for "about a week." Rather than express regret or guilt at such a betrayal, the aunt threatened her with—"if you want to go to the police, go ahead and see what happens" (case 24). In a similar case, the parents "stopped" the victim dating a male she had met on Facebook and consequently she went MFH. Parents provided hollow promises that she could continue the relationship, but instead they took her to Pakistan to visit "relatives." After a short time, they cancelled her flight home, told her she was marrying her cousin and locked her in a room (case 42). Again, the parents deceived victims and appeared to be "biding their time" to force victims into compliance with the demands of the collective.

The level of planning by women in facilitating HBA, whether that involves transporting victims to their punishment or making wedding arrangements, is often overlooked but it is evident:

> The male party may have been the physical side, but you've got somebody in the background who's make the plans as well who's having those communications you know buying the wedding clothing, wedding jewellery putting it in storage, getting everything together, they're as much culpable as the physical side (police officer k)

In a pregnancy case it was the sister-in-law who was told in confidence of the pregnancy and "convinced" the victim to divulge the information to her parents. Yet, instead of extricating herself from involvement, she engineered the dangerous situation by transporting and "presenting" the unaware victim and her boyfriend at the parent's address, whereupon the victim was kicked in the stomach by her mother. Ironically, despite this betrayal, the sister-in-law rang the police some weeks later trying to elicit information as to the victim's whereabouts, persuading the authorities that she "supported" the victim and was "willing to give a statement against her mother" (case 95). Victims often appear deceived by women who betray them one moment and "support" them the next, highlighting a clear disjoint between words and action. Mothers often use deception, tears and emotional "pulls" and promises to facilitate the recovery of daughters. This is evident when one victim of a forced marriage left her husband and fled with her children to a hotel. Her mother convinced her to return, stating her husband had left the address. Yet when she did the victim found the husband "waiting upstairs" (case 72).

There are numerous other occasions where female relatives erroneously "reassure" victims that the husband has left the address (case 88) or that the "mother had thrown him out" (case 98) merely as a ruse to facilitate the victims' return. For those already within a forced marriage, a second ploy is to convince the victim that the husband is "willing to give her a divorce." This promise led to a victim being fooled a second time in the hope that "mum is supporting her and her mum is going to speak to her dad to see if he will accept her new relationship" (case 72). The police themselves even doubt the sincerity of the mother when they comment on the incident log—"she thinks that her mum is on her side but clearly last time she lied to get her to return to the address" (case 72). Victims are often lulled into a false sense of security, with optimistic yet unrealistic hopes for a family reconciliation. This "softer" approach appears a more effective strategy in playing on the victims' emotions. This was evident when a fleeing victim of HBA was visited by female relatives at her place of work:

> Her mother was very emotional and was crying, (victim) spoke to her grandmother on the phone as she was also crying, her mother assured (victim) that they did not know her home address and they just wanted to have contact with her, if they had wanted to do her harm, (victim) said that they would have kept hidden and followed her home. Her mother told her the estranged husband no longer lived with her she had thrown him out (case 98)

In another case, a mother was extremely volatile to police officers when they arrived, screaming at them to "fuck off" as they escorted the daughter to safety. Yet within 24 hours, she reverted to the softer skills of negotiation, tears and emotional blackmail:

> "Mother called, crying on phone, saying everything would be fine if she returned home." And so, she returned back home (case 89)

Female relatives are particularly effective at "smoothing over" trouble, of convincing victims that more freedom would be forthcoming, that if she left the refuge "everything would be ok if she went home and she could do what she wants" (case 18). Females, often sisters and sisters-in-law, make conciliatory phone calls (cases 66, 37), text messages and pleas to "meet" in order to reconcile, often with the hollow promise that female relatives will negotiate with the father to "accept the relationship" (cases 65, 42, 48, 49) that was initially so reviled. This can involve "delay tactics," for example, persuading victims to "postpone" a planned marriage with a love choice in order to seek the consent of opposing parties (cases 79, 42). Duping victims by suggesting that they are going on "holiday," to "visit relatives" (cases 23, 42, 64) or attend a family wedding abroad (cases 5, 38) usually results in victims finding out later on that it is *their* wedding.

Women also employ euphemistic language to underplay the "finality" of a forced marriage. For instance, the mother may suggest she go to Pakistan "for a holiday only" (case 90), or the aunt may intersperse discussions of marriage with notions of a "holiday" or "long engagement" (case 64). These appear to be negotiation strategies by the collective, in order to make the "offer" more palatable to victims. Feigning a family illness (an ill grandmother) appears to be a common strategy used to ensure victims travel abroad. Indeed Bates' (2018) research shows that mothers commonly use emotional manipulation, such as threatening to kill themselves if daughters did not comply with their demands. Such emotional blackmail has the effect of "pulling on the heartstrings" (police officer m), not only impacting a victim's mental health and overall safety but effectively facilitating the retraction of crimes:

> There seems to be a pattern forming..//.. sister, or maybe even from Mum saying—"the worry you've brought onto the family has caused Dad to have a heart attack"—or "your Mum is now very poorly"—to try and lure them back, to get the withdrawal. So I think—you have the trusted older sister..//..saying "look you need to come home I've managed to iron all this out now things are sorted, come on"—and it's more about that trust element I think, whereas the men are seen as the risk from the physical side; the ones who actually 'do the damage'. I think that it's in some cases the females in the family who get the child back into the family, where then the incidents can take place. I think they do have a part to play definitely—they pull on the heartstrings (police officer m)
>
> Mum sometimes does play that role, but plays it quite 'slyly' really (police officer n)
>
> Women play—"A big role. The unseen role..//..They do, from my experience and knowledge, the 'emotional chipping away' exercises..//..she'll tell you that "My mum, my eldest auntie (it seemed to be like the lieutenants in all of this) and my grandma just chipped away every single day.

> Mum wouldn't talk to me. I felt abandoned. Nobody would talk to me. People would say, you know, your mum is going through all of these health issues because of you. I'd have arguments with my dad." So, yes, what role do they play? A massive role..//.. the minute she strays, or he strays in marrying a different culture, then I think that person would revert to 'psychological warfare' as I call it, to make sure that they don't cause an embarrassment to the family, embarrassment to the community (police officer d)

In several instances, officers appeared unaware of the "feigning illness" tactic and consequently they unwittingly assist in returning the female victims back to perpetrators:

> She needed to go back and help her mum and support her mum that her mum had been ill recently, whether her mum was still ill or how seriously her mum was ill—we never got to the bottom of (police officer p)
>
> (Mother) is clearly at her wit's end with female victim's behaviour and she looked like a broken woman (case 93)

Findings showed insincere and inconsistent support by female relatives. As one victim commented after returning home from a refuge, the family:

> Did not stick by their word and slowly things returned to how they previously were (case 48)

These extracts of soft psychological abuse highlight a dichotomy or clear disjoint between words and deeds. Friendship and support are afforded, but this contrasts with denigration and a "fanning of the flames" behind the scenes by women. Such persuasive strategies appear to be hollow rhetoric and are fundamentally employed to "reel" victims back home in order to exert further, more intensified, pressure and reinstate the abuse. This supports Ballard's contention that women have the capacity to "pursue their own ends on their own terms," hurling insults and satisfying their own agenda in playing "all sorts of dirty tricks" (2002: 3). Women are effective in negotiating women and girls back home, effected through both hard and soft psychological strategies, using the power of language, emotional blackmail, tears, manipulation and deception. These extracts confirm Chesler's proposition that women can be the chief negotiators in luring young victims back to the family home (2010).

Females Ostracise Victims

Women do harbour female victims of HBA. However, such support appears to be short lived and swiftly withdrawn. This was evident when an 18-year-old Somalian victim attained a Forced Marriage Protection Order and fled to her aunts. The brother-in-law threatened that if his sister-in-law "did not set her free he would burn the house down,"[17] so she asked the victim to leave as she "didn't want any trouble" and would not support a police prosecution (case 51). This lack of solidarity is apparent even between sisters. In the case where the pregnant victim had been drugged in Pakistan and fled back to the UK, the sister harboured her for several days, but the father threatened to "disown her" if the support continued (case 100). There are also instances where women who harbour victims also facilitate the abuse. A female cousin witnessed a brother assaulting his 16-year-old sister. He assaulted the victim on numerous other occasions, and the cousin was encouraged by CSC to give her refuge. Given the consistent assaults and the fact that the cousin had been taking the underage victim to late-night bars, this was a poor CSC decision. The female cousin was found to be taking the victim to her brother's address for "visits" in clear breach of police bail conditions (case 96). Therefore, there is undoubtedly pressure placed on women by some men *not* to harbour victims, and the outcomes illustrate that self-preservation rather than female solidarity is the priority.

Turning a "Blind Eye": Mothers as Complicit, "Hapless" Secondary Victims?

In these findings it is mothers who are largely responsible for condoning physical abuse and failing to intervene in any violence meted out (see Chart 6.4). Mothers personally condoned violence inflicted by sons (cases 68, 50) and, in concert with fathers, were complicit in the sons' violence (cases 32, 71, 94, 96). Mothers also condoned their own brother's violence to daughters (cases 21, 43). However, interwoven throughout some police narratives is the sense that mothers acquiesce and turn a "blind eye" (police officer e) to offending but play an "unseen" (police officer d) role:

> They're witness to it ..//.. they know what goes on in that house whether they agree with it or not, you know. But they perhaps don't say anything, you don't do anything about it..//..there is probably an element where they encourage it or whether they acquiesce to it, you know. I don't know—the accepting of it (police officer p)
>
> Not necessarily committing the abuse themselves but knowing about it and saying or doing nothing. Being on the periphery to the point where they're either covering or trying to mediate, or acceptance of it. That's what you have to do. That kind of periphery, rather than the abuser, so to speak…//.. the cases I've had, mum's role has been quite defined in it, but never as the abuser (police officer e)
>
> Researcher: So have mums been condoning activity?
>
> Potentially, yes. Or turning a blind eye (police officer e) (Aplin 2017)

This concept of mothers as "invisible" is absent within the incident data and conflicts sharply with the extracts highlighting violence from mothers. However, it resounds with Welden's assessment of the Aqsa Parvez honour killing, whereby the mother is considered "nearly invisible" and the power relations between man and wife highly asymmetrical (2010: 389). Moreover, detected in these discourses are police judgements that the mother is a "secondary" or "indirect victim" (police officer g), acting under a patriarchal pressure rather than being perceived and defined as a perpetrator:

> Sometimes you [the mother] are doing it because you *have* to do it—and you are doing it because if you don't do it these are the ramifications. But other times I think they actually do it because they feel that that is their *role* to do it..//..I believe that Mums—and they are often told to do it by the father. [Be]cause the father's like—"I go out, I am the breadwinner, you are the mother who looks after the children—you bring her up right. You get her ready for marriage" (police officer a)

They [females] can play quite a big part—you've got the one where they are the wife of the main perpetrator and their children are being HBA or FM..//..even if they wanted to help their child it's very difficult because they themselves can be an HBA victim. It's not direct—it's indirect because, if—for example, a mother was trying to help her daughter not go through an FM—threats of HBA can come from her husband or extended family, not just to the victim, but the mother as well. Sometimes I think they are oppressed—pressured into complying with it (police officer g) (Aplin 2017)

This last extract highlights the difficulty for officers, and possibly other professionals, in differentiating between the "oppressed" mother and the "controlling" female perpetrator; which rationalises why female perpetration is poorly recognised and crimed, and why children are left in risk predicaments. One officer eloquently highlights the complex interplay of factors involved in female perpetration which includes issues of duress, patriarchal culture norms and dutiful obligation:

Because it's usually honour crime against females they [victims] look to the older females in their family, so mum, older sisters, aunties for guidance..//..they [women] have to 'toe the party line' (probably not quite the correct terminology) because they are being made to do it as well, they will be giving the advice that the males want the females to give, rather than the advice that they actually believe in. So, the younger kids are listening to that from the older females thinking "Oh well, it must be right then, so I'll have to go along with it"..//.. So for example, marriages are 'arranged' and that's that. There is no going back from that. But I think women play a massive part in it. And I think it's duress and an element of—sometimes they believe it, they believe it should be happening so they're passing that information to the younger people, because it's their thought process—their belief (police officer c)

Officers appear to fluctuate uncertainly between positions of perceiving mothers as secondary "victims" to that of culpable "villains" who fail to protect their children (Aplin 2017). The view is contingent upon each situation. For instance, one 14-year-old Romanian victim kept running away from home with her boyfriend. Her mother had seven children, who attended four different schools. The mother could not drive, spoke no English, was reliant on her controlling husband and was entirely isolated from her own family as the husband had previously attacked her relations. The husband was trying to marry his daughter off by trying to sell her for £10,000 pounds. He was issued with a DVPN as a policing strategy in order to provide the mother with the "breathing space" to work with the IDVA team (police officer h). The intention of that policing strategy was to empower the mother in order to more effectively protect the children. In this instance the mother was treated as a "victim" under the control of the father, rather than a potential perpetrator. However, achieving empowerment and dismantling cultural norms is far from a simple process.

The stance taken by professionals in given situations is crucial, as it affects the police criminal investigation but also highly influences the safeguarding of victims. Viewing mothers as secondary victims is not universal amongst officers, with one police officer seeing women who failed to protect as equally culpable:

> If you've got a young boy or a young girl who is at risk and you've got family members who are the perpetrators and you've got a mother who is failing to protect, I think they are as much responsible as the people who are actually physically doing that abuse (police officer k)

This is aptly illustrated in a case (fully explored in Chap. 3) of systematic HBA from an older brother for which the victim was on the child protection register. Amidst the instances of physical violence, the victim's mother stood and watched her son kick her daughter in the head and "eventually ..//..told the son to stop, but he didn't" (96 also linked to 94 and 32). Clearly in this instance, the authorities took the stance that this was isolated individual offending and that the parents were not complicit in the abuse. It was a gradual dawning, rather than an immediate realisation from professionals, that parents condoned the abuse. Yet, by this stage the victim had been suffering abuse for a prolonged period. It took nearly two years and many more assaults for CSC to place the victim in long-term foster care (Aplin 2017). Any attempt at motherly intervention in these extracts appears wholly half-hearted and ineffectual. In another case the actions of the mother paint a contradictory picture, failing to protect her child and yet on a superficial level appearing to support and reassure the victim:

> Uncle grabbed her by the hair and dragged her to the top of the stairs. He then continued to rag her about. He then dragged her back down the stairs. At this point the mum intervened and victim was instructed to sit down. Uncle went into kitchen and picked up a knife and threatened to kill her should she go missing again (case 43)

The intervention by the mother consists of her telling the uncle (her brother) to "go." The mother then "hugged" the daughter and "tried to reassure her." However, the uncle was still able to threaten the victim with a knife and told the victim "had his sister not been there he would have done so" [killed her] (case 43). The write-up by the attendant police officer highlights the difficulty in concluding whether the mother is a victim or a colluding perpetrator:

> The mother is either assisting uncle or is in fear of reprisals from other family members (case 43) (Aplin 2017)

Despite clumps of hair being located around the house, the mother and elder sister closed ranks against the police and victim, denying the uncle was even at the address. The mother refused to allow the witnessing children to be video interviewed. The uncle's dramatic threat to kill by using a knife, like many threats to kill within the findings, is a very public display designed to demonstrate moral resolve. However, such examples of passively condoning abuse, rather than signifying a frightened mother acting under duress, seem more consistent with the family developing an orchestrated family strategy or "coalition" (Welden 2010: 389) designed to regain control of a victim's wayward behaviour.

Contradictory Behaviours and a Daughter's Unwavering Loyalty to Mother

Moreover, the way mothers present themselves to victims creates the perception that mothers are "secondary" or indirect victims. Both data set findings indicate that despite evidence of controlling and oppressive behaviours, victims are reluctant to divulge abuse inflicted by the mother, often due to an abiding sense of love and loyalty around getting "mum into trouble" (cases 10, 17, 87 and 67). Against their own best interests, daughters possess unwavering trust in mothers. Victims perceive that mothers will protect them from the wrath of fathers, regarding hiding discreditable or shaming behaviour, such as knowledge around "secret" boyfriends (police officer d), or when caught "sneaking out" of the house at 01:00 a.m., one daughter was convinced the father was "unaware" (case 62) (Aplin 2017). Another mother intercepted a letter from her daughter's lover, but the victim remained adamant "she doesn't believe her mother will tell dad any of this" (case 6). Victims possess a naive and misguided belief that mothers pose no risk and that they will continue to protect their best interests. This implicit trust appears tied to the vain hope that mum will "eventually support her" (case 87) regarding her chosen boyfriend, even when this seems unlikely to an objective outsider. One female presented to officers as if she had mental health issues. She would draw injuries on herself but this was deemed by the officer as a "desperate act":

> This girl presented to officers as almost as though she was barking, as if she was crazy. She wasn't..//.. She never betrayed her mum..//.. [she was saying] "I was doing things that I didn't like just to keep her 'on side', just to see her happy, just to see her smile"—but she was living a life that she did not want to live (police officer d) (Aplin 2017)

In another case an officer recalls the way in which victims are made to feel guilty for prioritising themselves over the family, and it is clear that the "emotional chipping away exercises" (police officer d) had taken effect, reflective of Wiener's "drip, drip" (2017: 9) analogy, where victims are sucked into the perpetrator's world view:

> All these female adults, the male adults, the patriarch, the matriarch system is kicking in and she feels very guilty, "mum's depressed, etc, to bring her out of that I'll agree to this, I feel guilty myself"..//..So, she gets on a plane and then slowly, that thing I said to you about victims coiling back thinking "You know what, this is just a load of fuss. The less fuss I make, the easier it is" (police officer d)

As evident in a prior example (case 43), there are inherent contradictions in the behaviours of mothers towards daughters. For instance, one victim spoke tearfully to the police of her father beating her mother in Macedonia when they were children (Aplin 2017). Yet it was the *mother* who demanded that her daughter marry a suitor in Macedonia to reduce the embarrassment of the family (case 58). Despite conflicting behaviours of mothers, daughters tend to view them in a favourable light:

> Her mum is on her side but she slapped her the other week (case 72)
>
> Her mum told her that 'she had to marry this male' but recently she has gone back on this with mother stating 'she only wants (victim) to do whatever makes her happy' (case 61) (Aplin 2017)

Despite one victim being twice being duped by her mother into returning home, the victim *still* had faith in her. When she returned home a third time the victim was in fear of further violence from her overbearing father, husband and two brothers. The mother reacts differently, supporting her escape from the address and exhibiting what could be deemed as guilt and regret:

> Her mother gave her a phone and told her to run away, which she did, and apologised for allowing the marriage (case 72) (Aplin 2017)

Such behaviours might reflect the inner turmoil mothers face in securing daughters in a life of misery. Yet conversely, when analysed alongside the deceptions within the soft psychological abuse narratives, these could be considered as ploys to ensnare victims in order to resume the cycle of abuse. Unwavering loyalty is also apparent but to a much lesser extent, in victims' attitudes towards sisters, sisters-in-law and cousins (cases 37, 65, 87 and 95). As explored previously, it was the verbal "stirring" of a cousin (case 87) and a sister-in-law (case 95) which precipitated serious levels of violence against daughters by mothers. In another case the same misplaced loyalty was evident, with the police write-up stating:

> (Victim) seems to have a lot of trust in her sister-in-law and seems to think that her presence means her family are much more reserved and understanding than they would usually be (case 65)

Yet in all of these cases victims remain almost oblivious to the sleight of hand and betrayal by female relatives which precipitates the abuse. Victims often fail to recognise the "wolf" lurking in sheep's clothing.

Policing Response to Female Perpetration, Duress and Individual Agency

Police Stereotype and Under-record Female Perpetration

The role of police officers in managing female perpetration is both obscure and complex. An exacerbating feature is the inability by some frontline officers to recognise mothers and women more generally as perpetrators. Despite police incident reports directly implicating mothers in violence (solely or with others), frontline officers did not place mothers as perpetrators on police computer systems (PPI) or within formalised crime reports in 12%[18] of cases (Aplin 2017). Instead, fathers were often logged as perpetrators and/or arrested, sometimes based on little to no evidence. In one case, despite only the *mother* being implicated in the violence by throwing shoes and chairs at the victim, surprisingly only the father is named as key perpetrator in the crime report (case 17). In a different case, despite both parents being implicated in slapping their 15-year-old daughter, only the father is arrested (case 26). Similarly, a mother had argued with her female child and then hit her with a slipper. Despite this, only the father was placed on the police nominal as "perpetrator." Within the incident report it was rationalised by the victim that:

> Mother always obeys her father's instruction and that she [the mother] has fallen out with her family members [abroad] and they do not have any contact (case 84)

Certainly, police responses reflect a typically feminist asymmetrical argument that perpetration is highly gendered and almost exclusively made up of men (Dobash and Dobash 1979; Stark 2007; Johnson 2006).

The author does not dispute this contention, yet this fixed world view impedes recognition of female abuse. The frontline officer's write-up (case 84) in line with the victim's defence of her mother tends to portray the mother as much of a victim as the daughter, oppressed under a patriarchal regime and committing acts of violence out of duress to satisfy the demands of her husband. Interviewees suggest that frontline officers are heavily influenced by gender role expectations, possessing stereotypical views of mothers as non-criminal, nurturing and supportive, with men as offenders and women as victims (Aplin 2017):

> I think Dad is always made out to be the one who's the main person to be concerned about (police officer n)
>
> I think sometimes people forget to look ..//..I think sometimes they [women] are overlooked as being a bigger part of it as they should be (police officer p)
>
> You can tell that by the way that we all speak [police]—because the perpetrator will always be called "he" and the victim will always be "she"..//.. because we're going off numbers, aren't we—you'll deal with 10—[males] to every one [female] and unfortunately it can sway what you say. I think we are getting better, just to be open to the investigation mindset of—'who was responsible for this,' rather than thinking it must be Dad. So just thinking it can be anyone. It can be sister, or an aunt or a mum—yeah (police officer m)
>
> A lot of the focus is on the male relatives whether it be fathers, uncles, brothers etc. (police officer p)
>
> Sometimes we're [police] a bit stereotypical and we see it as the male as being the perpetrator and not just in the honour-based stuff as well..//.. it could be a male victim who's covered in blood..//.. female's the first person who will say "well, he assaulted me" and then they end up locking the male up..//.. I think we are stereotypical in that way where we see it as a male dominant issue but it's not, it's not gender specific it should be anybody's responsible (police officer k)

Such discussions imply that the gender of a parent can lead practitioners to make erroneous assumptions about their level of culpability. It also reflects how uncomfortable professionals may be about conceiving that mothers may be perpetrators or accomplices in systemic physical abuse (Haringey local safeguarding children board 2009 as cited in Broadhurst et al. 2010). This inability to recognise mothers as complicit in abuse is evident in UK homicide cases, where mothers manipulate the authorities by providing misleading narratives which successfully conceal ongoing abuse. In the case of Shafilea Ahmed, the mother acted as key communicator to the authorities in justifying the victim's bleach swallowing incident as "accidental" (Gill and Brah 2014: 77). In the case of "Baby P," murdered at 17 months (2007) by his mother's boyfriend and his brother, mother Tracey Connelly prioritised her relationship with her boyfriend over that of her children. Connelly was highly manipulative, often lying and hiding Peter's horrific injuries from social services and the police. She consistently justified injuries found on her infant son as accidental, even smearing chocolate on his face to hide bruises from the authorities (Jones 2014). Such findings reconfigure the landscape and challenge the professional assumption that mothers, and females more broadly, can and do routinely safeguard.

Moreover, there is recognition from specialist officers that far from being archetypal perpetrators, men can sometimes perform a protective function (Aplin 2017). For instance, one mother sent her 17-year-old daughter off to Pakistan in order to marry her cousin, but because the daughter did not consent it was the uncle rather than the mother who halted the wedding plans (police officer b):

> 'Well I'm not forcing my child to get married to someone who doesn't want to marry him'. So if it wasn't for *him*, she would have probably ended up in a forced marriage from her mother (police officer b)
>
> Sometimes the partners may disagree—the actual father may disagree.... (police officer a) (Aplin 2017)

It was only through observing a DVD during child genital mutilation training that one officer's personal paradigm shifted entirely concerning the role that women play in abuse:

> I heard the children screaming and mum's pinning them down while they're doing it. That's what's opened my eyes really as to any future jobs that I might attend, after seeing that video—is not to always discard mum

..//..Because normally you would think that mum is this nice person who does all the cooking and has the family kind of organised and does everything, but mum I think in a lot of cases probably does play a lot more of an active role than is ever disclosed really (police officer n) (Aplin 2017)

The Duress Argument Versus Individual Agency

It is clear from the narratives that two conflicting positions emerge in terms of the professional response to female perpetration. That is, the notion that women are seemingly obligated and under duress to act against their own kin, or conversely that they possess individual agency in being willing and complicit in that perpetration.

The typically traditional approach to female perpetration, herein referred to as the duress argument (Aplin 2017), suggests that mothers are likely to be held accountable for the "sins" of "wayward" daughters (Wilford 1998; Akpinar 2003; Haj-Yahia 2011; Chesler and Bloom 2012) and are therefore pressured by men into acting against women out of dutiful obligation (Wilford 1998: 17; Akpinar 2003) particularly evident in situations of illegitimate pregnancy. Many feminist academics subscribe to this sympathetic, almost "excusing" approach, notably Durbas (2015), who examined 174 honour killing court cases in Turkey. Whilst accepting that mothers can be sole perpetrators who both instigate and collude in abuse, academics argue that women are obligated to remain loyal to the male-dominated collective rather than being loyal to each other or suffer a high price as a consequence (Elden 2011; Durbas 2015; Bates 2018). Due to the implication that "bad goods belong to their owner" (Durbas 2015), mothers may therefore attempt to mitigate that there is a degree of "necessity" to their actions against daughters.

Although findings show that some officers concur with the traditional feminist perspective that mothers are secondary victims, the quantitative data, along with recognition from other specialist officers (7/15) (47%), challenges the accuracy of this perception. Overwhelming evidence of abhorrent behaviours by women is hard to reconcile with notions of women as "hapless" or "passive victims" (Yuval-Davis 1998: 31). Mothers deceive and denigrate daughters, ostracise them from kin, barter to sell them, wish them dead and threaten to kill them or throw them downstairs. The extracts illustrate how mothers, in the name of "honour," are as capable of serious violence against daughters as men and play a central role in HBA perpetration. Such depictions highlight that feminist explanations of the phenomenon that is violence and abuse against women by other women remain "inadequate" (Rew et al. 2013: 154). This perspective is supported by Ranalvi, Indian founder of the organisation "we speak out" (www.wepeakout.org) against Female Genital Mutilation (FGM) (termed khafz), who argues that women who support prevailing oppressive practices against other women, such as the Dawoodi Bohra Women's Association for Religious Freedom (DBWRF) (n.d.) (dbwrf.org), do so of their own volition rather than out of duress (Ranalvi 2018). Such countervailing female forces supporting FGM are highly intelligent (some possessing postgraduate qualifications) and they level the argument that those condemning FGM practices are merely tutored by a western colonial narrative (ibid.). The notion that mothers represent a grey, indistinct and "nearly invisible" figure within the family dynamic (Welden 2010: 389) is barely recognisable in these findings. Moreover, the prospect of a mother's safety being actually jeopardised due to the behaviours of wayward children is barely discernible in these UK findings, with direct evidence of this in only 3% of incidents (3/100).

There is some evidence which accepts that both propositions (individual agency *and* duress) can coexist. This is evident in the contradictory behaviours by women that are present in the findings, in simultaneously deceiving and then appearing to afford support to victims, which is apparent from mothers and extended female relations, notably sisters and sisters-in-law. Such ambivalent attitudes reflect the "coping mechanisms" referred to by Kandiyoti (1988: 285), with women under an obligation to accommodate and adhere to the "patriarchal bargain" by punishing wayward family members, then "resisting" these obligations out of love and loyalty. This is indeed a ruthless "bargain," with women constantly appearing to strategise within their limited constraints. It may be too simplistic to suggest that the attitudes and behaviours of female perpetrators are wholly independent "rational choices," somehow "separate" from patriarchy. Such subordination to social norms subconsciously permeates the context of a woman's early socialisation (Kandiyoti 1988: 285). Yet equally, an abundance of evidence reflects the conniving way women conspire against other female relatives, which makes *who* to trust extremely challenging for victims. Ultimately, findings show how women, and mothers in particular, appear to sacrifice the victim due to self-preservation and a fear of losing reputation, which could destabilise their own position (see also Elden 2011). A lack of genuine solidarity towards women in the extracts tends to support this sceptical assertion.

Furthermore, rather than view the motivations for the use and support of violence around what female perpetrators functionally aim to *gain* (Rew et al. 2013), it could also hinge on what women *fear to lose* by *not* supporting the collective. Perhaps women perceive that it is not in a woman's best interests to subvert the gender order by behaving otherwise. Conforming to social norms, rather than to personal relationships, affords women greater personal protection, security and stability (Kandiyoti 1988). Lack of evidence of mothers performing a protective function (1/100) reinforces this assertion. Women have become negotiating "experts in maximising their own life chances" (Kandiyoti 1988: 280). However, in the context of these findings, this is interpreted as self-interest in terms of "saving one's own skin" and has adverse ramifications for the safeguarding of children and young adults, as explored in the following chapter.

Despite the data set showing significantly large volumes of multiple perpetration (83%), paradoxically police officers appear to "simplify" and dilute cases by arresting and processing only one "key" offender, very often a male. Operational expediency assists in explaining this, in which officers rationalise their workload, as explored in Chap. 4. This may involve keeping it "simple" and doing what is "satisfactory" (satisficing) in an environment of diminishing resources (Simon 1976). Yet, although this argument has merit, it does not explain why women are not arrested in cases where *only* they are solely implicated (Aplin 2017). This supports the contention that some police officers, like some academics (Wilford 1998; Akpinar 2003; Durbas 2015), perceive of matriarchal perpetrators as indirect victims. Incident data findings suggest that, particularly where there appears to be a blurred distinction between mothers as controlling "perpetrators" and mothers as oppressed "victims," there exists a difficulty in professionals "labelling" (on PPI and crime reports) females as perpetrators. Furthermore, where this blurring is apparent there *also* exists an enduring loyalty by daughters who appear reluctant to blame mothers for the infliction of HBA, again alluding back to the theme of victim reluctance explored in Chap. 4. Victims often underplay the involvement of mothers and constantly mitigate the actions committed by them. Mothers who are viewed in a favourable light by victims, despite evidence of contradicting and controlling behaviours, remain unblemished by the criminal justice system (Aplin 2017). It is therefore argued that the perception of mothers as secondary victims (by officers and communicated by victims themselves) actually influences and impacts police decision-making; with officers unlikely to categorise mothers as perpetrators or pursue formal action, especially when mothers are portrayed as prioritising the best interests of victims, therefore figuratively seen as "more sinned against than sinning." Police interview data supports this contention, as a third of officers (5/15) had never investigated a female offender of HBA, despite being operational specialists in this field. This may signify that frontline officers are not bringing these incidents to specialist attention, because they have not recognised female perpetrators as "criminal" nor logged them on crime reports as such (ibid.).

The fact that victims refuse to prosecute parents, particularly prevalent in the research, may lead officers to apply discretionary practices in circumventing NCRS crime recording rules (see Chap. 4). Even when there is direct evidence that mothers and other female relatives pose a risk to victims, police take no action, highlighting that victim wishes may be utilised by officers to legitimate police inaction. This is evident in several pregnancy cases where victims and boyfriends predict the outcome and clearly outline the threat posed by the family (cases 65 and 87) and yet officers did nothing to mitigate the risk. The unwillingness of victims to take cognisance of the risks posed by mothers should not be "used" by officers to justify non-enforcement practices. It is difficult to ascertain with certainty whether police turn a blind eye to female perpetration as part of a larger set of non-enforcement practices; whether it is through lack of training that officers fail to recognise female perpetration; or whether officers perceive the mother to be an "indirect victim" and therefore not "culpable." However, it is highly probable that all facets play some part in shaping the criminal justice response to female perpetration (Aplin 2017).

Concluding Remarks

Female perpetration of HBA is an unanticipated finding of this research, and also the most controversial amongst feminists studying gendered abuse. Such findings present a challenge to the asymmetrical stereotypical constructs that women are victims and men are perpetrators. Due to socialisation, women enter a "patriarchal bargain" and in order to resist total male control, they become willing participants with a vested interest in a system which perpetuates oppressive practices against other women (Kandiyoti 1988; Okin 1999; Gill et al. 2012; Eisner and Ghuneim 2013). These findings depart from previous research by illustrating that, far from playing a peripheral role, women, and mothers in particular, exert much more control, influence and involvement in HBA than extant research has thus far advocated.

It is erroneous to consider these six categories (use violence, forced abortion, hard and soft psychological abuse, ostracising victims and being complicit in the violence) as existing on a continuum from the "least" to the "most" serious levels of abuse. Indeed, the corrosive and emotional "chipping away" exercises by women appear more psychologically damaging to victims, as these pull on the heartstrings, inhibit victims from pursuing prosecutions and often retain them in risk predicaments. Such psychological warfare adversely impacts the mental health of victims, causing them to be doubly discredited by both perpetrators and then professionals. Long-term, psychological abuse is as damaging as physical violence (Campbell 1995; Stark 2007), and the UK offence of controlling or coercive behaviour in an intimate or family relationship (Serious Crime Act 2015: s.76), which specifically covers HBA and forced marriage, acknowledges this. Degrading victims, isolating them from family and friends, financial abuse and depriving them of a job, all evident within these findings, are all behaviours specifically alluded within this Act of parliament (Home Office 2015). The practicalities of prosecuting psychological abuse remain difficult territory for law enforcement, as implied by Wiener (2017), no physical evidence compounded by an unwillingness to prosecute relatives makes prosecutions difficult to execute.

Women are deemed as integral to ending HBA and it is proffered that governmental policy should focus more on women in order to halt the cycle of abuse. Professionals in the safeguarding arena (police, CSC, health, education) must reconsider the role played by the mother and other women, rather than assume that the natural position of women is to protect. That mothers at the very least turn a blind eye to HBA perpetration should encourage a re-evaluation of law enforcement and social services strategies, to avoid children and young women returning to or remaining in risk predicaments. Equally, it is important for agencies to be more discerning in assessing the attitudes of other female relatives within the family dynamic, such as sisters, sisters-in-law, aunts and cousins. Because, in an environment of dwindling resources, such relatives are requested to "care" for child victims due to difficulties in locating secure foster placements or long-term local authority care. Social workers and police officers must ensure that victims are not returned back to the abuse by relatives who enact and condone equally oppressive practices (Aplin 2017). It is this subject of child reconciliation and the role played by professionals in such interventions which is the focus of the following chapter.

Acknowledgements Sincere gratitude goes to Senior Lecturer Nicola Groves for providing helpful insights regarding an earlier draft of this chapter.

Notes

1. Police officers a, b, c, d, g, f and h.
2. Cases 1, 3, 5, 14, 15, 16, 19, 31, 41, 73, 82 and 92.
3. Cases 8, 48, 52, 76, 81, 88 and 97.
4. Cases 10, 13, 17, 20, 26, 39, 61, 72, 84 and 93.
5. DASH is a risk identification, assessment and management model adopted by United Kingdom police forces and partner agencies in March 2009 and accredited by the Association of Chief Police Officers (ACPO) council (now NPCC). It is intended to cover cases of Domestic Abuse, Stalking, Harassment and Honour-based violence (DASH 2009). The DASH checklist comprises of 27 questions and provides staff with a

practical tool to assist in the early risk identification and decide on the appropriate level of intervention for victims (high, medium, standard risk). There are an additional 10 questions specific to HBA.

6. Cases 5, 65, 67, 69, 70, 83, 87, 89, 95 and 100.
7. An "Osman warning" is given by police officers to intended victims to warn them of a threat to their life. This is derived from the case of *R v. Osman* 2000 in which the ECHR ruled that public bodies, such as the police, are under a positive obligation to take preventative operational measures to protect an individual when there is real and immediate risk to life from the criminal acts of others.
8. There was one case where the husband slapped his pregnant wife across the face, causing swelling and bruising to the eye (case 9). However, the pregnancy itself was not the trigger for the HBA.
9. Cases 13, 20, 22, 32, 39, 44, 45, 57, 74, 93 and 96.
10. Such findings not only show female involvement but support the contention that some honour killings in the UK and abroad may be disguised as accidents or suicides.
11. Cases 81, 96, 64 and 53, police officer c.
12. Originally devised in 1982 due to the Domestic Violence Intervention Project, Minnesota, USA.
13. Cases 2, 9, 30, 47 and 91.
14. Constant harassment by in-laws and husbands can also often push married women to *commit* suicide (Waters 1999 as cited in Rew et al. 2013; Cihangir 2013; House of Commons 2008).
15. Cases 37, 45, 46, 49, 60 and 66.
16. Cases 24, 32, 37, 45, 55, 60, 61, 66, 72, 94, 95 and 96.
17. There is some evidence of perpetrators threatening to burn down the house of those who *harbour* honour victims (cases 51, 37, 73).
18. Cases 12, 13, 17, 26, 27, 44, 58, 62, 64, 84, 87 and 89.

References

Akpinar, A. (2003). The honour/shame complex revisited: Violence against women in the migration context. *Women's Studies International Forum, 26*(5), 425–442.

Aplin, R. (2017). Exploring the role of mothers in 'Honour' based abuse perpetration and the impact on the policing response. *Women's Studies International Forum, 60*, 1–10.

Ballard, R. (1982). South Asian families: Structure and process. In R. Rapaport, M. Fogarty, & R. Rapaport (Eds.), *Families in Britain*. London: Routledge.

Ballard, R. (2002). *Riste and ristedari: The significance of marriage in the dynamics of transnational kinship networks* (pp. 1–27). Unpublished. [Online]. Retrieved January 29, 2016, from http://www.casas.org.uk.

Bates, L. (2018). Females perpetrating honour-based abuse: Controllers, collaborators or coerced? *Journal of Aggression, Conflict and Peace Research*, 1–12.

Belfrage, H., Strand, S., Ekman, L., & Hasselborg, A. (2012, Spring). Assessing risk of patriarchal violence with honour as a motive: Six years experience using the patriarch checklist. *International Journal of Police Science & Management, 14*(1), 20–29.

Broadhurst, K., White, S., Fish, S., Munro, E., Fletcher, K., & Lincoln, H. (2010). *Ten pitfalls and how to avoid them: What research tells us* (pp. 1–41). [Online]. Retrieved January 16, 2017, from www.nspcc.org.uk.

Campbell, J. (1995). *Assessing dangerousness: Violence by sexual offenders, batterers, and child abusers*. Thousand Oaks, CA: Sage Publications.

Chesler, P. (2010). Worldwide trends in honor killings. *Middle East Quarterly, 17*(2), 3–11.

Chesler, P., & Bloom, N. (2012, Summer). Hindu vs. Muslim honor killings. *Middle East Quarterly, 19*(3), 43–52.

Cihangir, S. (2013, May). Gender specific honor codes and cultural change. *Group Processes & Intergroup Relations, 16*(3), 319–333.

Cooney, M. (2014). Death by family: Honor violence as punishment. *Punishment & Society, 16*(4), 406–427.

Crown Prosecution Service (CPS). (2017). *Violence Against Women and Girls Report 2016–2017* (10th ed.). London: Crown Prosecution Service.

Dawoodi Bohra Women's Association for Religious Freedom (DBWRF). (n.d.). [Online]. Retrieved November 13, 2018, from dbwrf.org.

Dobash, R., & Dobash, R. (1979). *Violence against wives*. New York, NY: Free Press.

Durbas, B. (2015). *Perpetrators of domestic violence: Interpretation of the role of women in honour-based violence*. Paper presented at the British Society of Criminology, Plymouth, 2 July 2015.

Eisner, M., & Ghuneim, L. (2013). Honour killing attitudes amongst adolescents in Amman, Jordan. *Aggressive Behaviour, 39*(5), 405–417.

Elden, A. (2011). Men's violence and women's responsibility: Mothers' stories about honour violence. In M. Idriss & T. Abbas (Eds.), *Honour, violence, women and Islam* (pp. 128–141). Oxfordshire: Routledge.

Gill, A. (2004). Voicing the silent fear: South Asian women's experiences of domestic violence. *Howard Journal of Criminal Justice, 43*(5), 465–483.
Gill, A. (2013, October). Feminist reflections on researching so-called 'honour' killings. *Feminist Legal Studies, 21*(3), 241–261.
Gill, A. (2014). All they think about is honour: The murder of Shafilea Ahmed. In A. Gill, C. Strange, & K. Roberts (Eds.), *Honour killing and violence: Theory, policy and practice* (pp. 177–198). Hampshire: Palgrave Macmillan.
Gill, A., Begikhani, N., & Hague, G. (2012). Honour-based violence in Kurdish communities. *Women's Studies International Forum, 35*, 75–85.
Gill, A., & Brah, A. (2014). Interrogating cultural narratives about 'honour'-based violence. *European Journal of Women's Studies, 21*(1), 72–86.
Haj-Yahia, M. (2011, July–August). Contextualizing interventions with battered women in collectivist societies: Issues and controversies. *Aggression & Violent Behavior, 16*(4), 331–339.
Home Office. (2015). *Controlling or coercive behaviour in an intimate or family relationship: Statutory guidance framework*. London: TSO.
House of Commons Home Affairs Committee Report. (2008). *Domestic violence, forced marriage and 'honour'-based violence*. Sixth Report of Session 2007–08, Vols. 1 and 2. London: TSO.
Jafri, A. (2009). *Honour killing: Dilemma, ritual, understanding* (2nd ed.). Oxford: Oxford University Press.
Johnson, M. (2006). Conflict and control: Gender symmetry and asymmetry in domestic violence. *Violence Against Women, 12*(11), 1003–1018.
Jones, R. (2014). *The story of Baby P: Setting the record straight*. Bristol: Policy Press.
Kandiyoti, D. (1988). Bargaining with patriarchy. *Gender & Society, 2*(3), 274–290.
Okin, S. (1999). *Is multiculturalism bad for women?* Princeton, NJ: Princeton University Press.
Payton, J. (2011). Collective crimes, collective victims: A case study of the murder of Banaz Mahmod. In M. Idriss & T. Abbas (Eds.), *Honour, violence, women and Islam* (pp. 67–79). Oxfordshire: Routledge.
Pence, E., & Paymar, M. (1993). *Education groups for men who batter: The duluth model*. New York, NY: Springer Publishing Company.
Ranalvi, M. (2018). *Tackling FGM: A South Asian perspective*. 13 November 2018 presentation within the Festival of Politics & International Relations 2018, Leeds Beckett University, Leeds.

Rew, M., Gangoli, G., & Gill, A. (2013). Violence between female in-laws in India. *Journal of International Women's Studies, 14*(1), 147–160.

Richards, L. (2009). Domestic Abuse, Stalking and Harassment and Honour Based Violence (DASH, 2009): Risk identification and assessment and management model. [Online]. Retrieved March 1, 2016, from http://www.dashriskchecklist.co.uk.

Roberts, K. (2014). Towards a psychologically oriented motivational model of honour-based violence. In A. Gill, C. Strange, & K. Roberts (Eds.), *Honour killing and violence: Theory, policy and practice* (pp. 69–88). Hampshire: Palgrave Macmillan.

Sen, P. (2005). Crimes of honour, value and meaning. In L. Welchman & S. Hossain (Eds.), *Honour: Crimes, paradigms, and violence against women* (pp. 42–63). London: Zed Books.

Serious Crime Act 2015 (c.9). [Online]. Retrieved March 4, 2016, from https://www.gov.uk.

Simon, H. (1976). *Administrative behavior: A study of decision-making processes in administrative organisations* (3rd ed.). London: The Free Press; Collier Macmillan Publishers.

Stark, E. (2007). *Coercive control: The entrapment of women in personal life*. Oxford: Oxford University Press.

The Institute of Community Cohesion. (2001). *Review of community cohesion in Oldham* (T. Cantle, Ed.). Coventry: Coventry University.

Thiara, R. (2013). It's all about stopping you from getting on with your life: Post-separation violence in the lives of Asian & African-Caribbean women. In Y. Rehman, L. Kelly, & H. Siddiqui (Eds.), *Moving in the shadows [electronic resource]: Violence in the lives of minority women and children* (pp. 113–126). Farnham: Routledge.

We Speak Out. [Online]. Retrieved November 13, 2018, from www.wespeakout.org.

Welden, B. (2010). Restoring lost 'honor': Retrieving face and identity, removing shame, and controlling the familial cultural environment through 'honor' murder. *Journal of Alternative Perspectives in the Social Sciences, 2*(1), 380–398.

Wiener, C. (2017). Seeing what is 'invisible in plain sight': Policing coercive control. *The Howard Journal of Crime and Justice, 00*(0), 1–16.

Wilford, R. (1998). Surveying the ground. In R. Wilford & R. Miller (Eds.), *Women, ethnicity and nationalism* (pp. 1–22). London: Routledge.

Yuval-Davis, N. (1998). Gender and nation. In R. Wilford & R. Miller (Eds.), *Women, ethnicity and nationalism* (pp. 23–35). London: Routledge.

7

HBA Child Protection and Partnership Working

Protecting vulnerable people is one of the highest areas of threat, harm and risk currently faced by policing (NPCC 2018). A person is vulnerable if, as a result of their situation or circumstances, they are unable to take care of or protect themselves (or others) from harm or exploitation (College of Policing n.d.). Children are defined as such when they are not yet 18 years old (Children Act 1989; HM Government 2018), and on the basis of their age, they are legally deemed as "vulnerable" in much the same way that vulnerable adults are (Youth Justice and Criminal Evidence Act 1999 s.16). Children under 16 years are unable to consent to sexual relations or medical treatment (excluding Gillick competency) (Mental Capacity Act codes of practice 2013: 17), and there is a requirement for children under 18 years to have an appropriate adult if a child is a witness or arrested as a suspect (PACE 1984 as amended by Criminal Justice and Courts Act 2015 s.42).

This chapter focuses on the nature of professional interventions[1] when children are victims of honour-based abuse (HBA) and assesses this within the context of child protection more broadly. The central practice in this chapter transpires to be mediation and child reconciliation whereby child victims are returned to perpetrators by local authority children's social care

R. Aplin, *Policing UK Honour-Based Abuse Crime*,
https://doi.org/10.1007/978-3-030-18430-8_7

(CSC) social workers. The risks to children are examined, along with the processes used to protect those at risk of significant harm, such as Police Protection Plans (PPP),[2] formerly known as Police Protection Orders (PPO) (Children Act 1989 s.46). The middle sections examine the practices used to justify child reconciliation: these include having mediation meetings; the devising of "working agreements"; the implementation of section 20 arrangements[3]; police and CSC deferring to the "wishes" of the child; and the perception that perpetrators adhere to advice imparted by professionals at the point of mediation. It was only during interviews with police officers that the rationale for premature child reconciliation, in terms of fiscal and workload pressures, became apparent.

The concluding sections explore partnership working in terms of how referrals are managed between agencies, the existence of silo working and the extent to which information sharing is effective. The chapter evaluates which agency should take ownership of child safeguarding and considers the difficulties posed in the police management of domestic abuse cases inflicted against child victims. It explores the significance that CSC place on legal expertise, physical injuries and police prosecutions.

The Background to Child Protection

The Children Act 1989 s.17 places a duty on local authorities to safeguard and prioritise the welfare of children in need that live in their local area. So far as is consistent with that duty, CSC must promote the upbringing of children by their own families (www.legislation.gov.uk). Yet this is a problematic duty to impose, particularly when a criminal allegation is made that children are victims of abuse from their guardians. Historical child protection cases identify the difficulty that social workers have in striking the right balance between protecting children and eroding the rights of parents through unwarrantable state interference in family life (Stevenson 1976: 151; Parton 1991). Louis Blom-Cooper's inquiry into Jasmine Beckford's death was judgemental of the way in which social workers treated the parents as "clients," and he concluded that the child's interests should be paramount even if this conflicts with parental wishes (London Borough of Brent 1985).

Conversely, the 1987 Cleveland enquiry appears to marginalise the voice of the child by focusing on parental rights and moreover challenges the appropriateness of professional interventions. Medical evidence provided by two paediatricians diagnosed sexual abuse in 121 child cases across Cleveland. Yet the diagnoses were disputed, leading to entrenched and disparate views of doctors, social workers and police officers, which resulted in a judicial enquiry (Cleveland Report 1988). The thrust of the Cleveland media coverage was that innocent families had been wrongly accused of sexual abuse by overzealous and incompetent paediatricians and social workers (Parton 1991; Department of Health 1995; Kitzinger 2000; Thompson 2016). The rhetoric of "innocent families being torn apart" obscured any possible conflict of interest between fathers, mothers and children (Kitzinger 2000: 63–64). Paradoxically, the real scandal behind Cleveland was not that the parents had been wrongly accused but that some children were returned home[4] possibly to face ongoing abuse (Channel 4 1997; Kitzinger 2000: 73). The role of professionals in reunifying child victims back home, possibly to face further HBA, is the subject of this chapter. The Children Act 1989 s.47 reinforces the legitimacy of professional "intrusion" into family life by providing local authorities with a duty to investigate and intervene if a child is suffering or likely to suffer significant harm (Children Act 1989 s.47; Parton 1991; Thompson 2016). Statutory guidance under the Children Act 2004 states that police officers are responsible for identifying children in need, taking them into police protection (PPP) and ensuring their welfare (www.legislation.gov.uk; HM Government 2018).

The death of seven-year-old Maria Colwell in 1973 and the enquiry following this allude to "failures in communication" and the central importance of services (schools, education welfare, CSC) in cooperating and working together to share information in order to effectively safeguard children (Colwell report 1974: 61). It precipitated new guidance, the establishment of child protection case conferences and the child protection register (now child protection plans) (Thompson 2016). Despite these reforms, child deaths resulting in serious case reviews and public enquiries (i.e. Jasmine Beckford 1985; Tyra Henry 1987; Victoria Climbie 2000; Peter Connelly 2007; Khyra Ishaq 2008; Hamza Khan

2011; Daniel Pelka 2012) highlight the continued inadequacies of the child protection system (ibid.), particularly regarding poor information sharing between different agencies.

The Practice of Mediation

Mediation is defined as an "intervention in a dispute in order to resolve it" (English Oxford Living Dictionaries 2016). Mediation practices seek to decrease the role of the state in responding to crime and instead increase the role of the community and family in repairing harms, latterly alluded to as restorative justice approaches (Featherstone et al. 2018). It is proffered that the use of mediation by professionals (police and CSC in this HBA context) has adverse consequences which is why police policy deems it a prohibited practice (HBA and FM Policy and Procedure 2013: 20; IKWRO 2014: 8; HMIC 2015). This is because there is often a degree of approval and collusion from community and family members in the abuse (HBA and FM Policy and Procedure 2013), making it difficult to identify those who genuinely aim to protect victims. The majority of specialist officers (60% 9/15) deem mediation to be unacceptable on the grounds it is dangerous, contravenes force policy and gives mixed messages to victims:

> It's a massive thing in the policy, never mediate between family members (police officer j)
>
> I'm not sure if I would ever consider mediation to be an option in HBV because if there was any form of control or coercive behaviour (police officer o)
>
> It is a dangerous thing to do..//..I know cases nationally where that's gone wrong (police officer f)
>
> We should never be seen to be prescribing mediation, no matter how right it might seem (police officer d)

One officer concludes that by mediating and too readily accepting perpetrator explanations, professionals could be seen as "colluding with the drivers" (police officer d) and thus providing authoritative sanction for controlling and criminal behaviours. Several officers presented no view.

Yet some police officers appear divided as to the appropriateness of mediation as a strategy. A few officers consider mediation as a last resort rather than a routine practice (police officers a, h and p), particularly if adult victims are adamant on returning to the risk. To exemplify, one victim wanted a Forced Marriage Protection Order (FMPO)[5] but was not prepared to leave the family home. The patriarch of the family "was under pressure himself from external family to bring his daughter into line" (police officer h). The interviewee explained how the father used the existence of the FMPO as a way of justifying to the community why he could *not* marry his daughter, in that his "hands were tied," whilst also getting to "keep" his daughter (police officer h). This illustrates that there may be some scope, albeit limited, for specialist mediation. Two of these officers also suggest that mediation is a useful tool which serves to educate perpetrating family members:

> You can't have a frontline officer mediating..//.. We've always said—don't do it..//..and I stick by that—but what I think is, we *have* got a place for mediation, somewhere along the line. It's about educating the parents (police officer a)
>
> I think mediation works in a lot of circumstances. Would it change somebody's belief system? Perhaps not. Would it change the way people view the honour in the family? Perhaps not, it might educate them and open their eyes to things (police officer p)

It is highly questionable as to whether authorities can be effective in altering cultural beliefs and norms of perpetrating family members in such a limited timeframe:

> No. I think it's potentially a bad idea..//..Imagine if they went back, saying, "Oh, I got made to sit in a police station and had mediation about how to deal with my own family." I think it's going to upset some people (police officer i)

Other officers highlight the dangers of mediation because of a victim's inability to make sound judgements due to the psychological hold perpetrators have over them, a view which resonates with domestic abuse victimology more broadly:

> If you've been brainwashed you're not going to see it any other way, are you?..//.. it could be 36 times before you ring the police and say "Listen, I'm in trouble", but over that period of time you've been so controlled, you know (police officer n)
>
> Sometimes they [victims] are that controlled and that insecure that they can't make rational decisions and we've got to take it out of their hands (police officer h)
>
> And if they *are* as terrified of that family member as what they're making out—then they [perpetrators] could say anything; they can do anything. Half of the conversations in the office are over—"how could she go back to him after this—how could someone want to go back after they done that to them?": *Because of the 'hold'—because of the 15 to 20 years before you [police] turned up* (interviewee emphasis added) and have gone—"I think I'll lock you up for damage—thank you very much". You know that's nothing—that that's a 'milli second' in their relationship. And we're trying to forget the previous 15 or 20 years and wondering why she hasn't given us a statement—for the 30 odd times before that he's nearly put her in hospital and stopped her from doing this that and the other; so I just think, it's really, really dangerous to be doing that [mediation]—but maybe there is a place for it (police officer m)

Mediation between offenders and victims is rarely instigated by police officers[6] in the findings and is only alluded to by one interviewee (police officer m):

> I've read some horrific cases where they're [officers] speaking to them [victims] *in front of* the parents, who they just alleged to *somebody else* (interviewee emphasis added) that they've [the parents] been taking [them] abroad to get 'married off' or they have been assaulted by them or whatever. I just think—would you do that with your DV victim? Would you have a woman with a black eye stood in front of the guy with the bloody knuckles and say "has he just hit you?" (police officer m)

Yet, mediation is actively employed by social workers and this is reflected in wider social work practice (Timms and Thoburn 2003; Morgan 2006: 17). As the above extracts illustrate, mediation practices can inhibit victims from disclosing abuse. Children not only need to be believed, but they need to be put in a safe and trusting environment to be able to disclose (Breckenridge and Ralfs 2006; Ofsted 2010). Given the use of mediation by CSC and the disparate views of police officers on this topic, it is concerning that the current UK National Policing Strategy for HBA (NPCC 2015) does not evaluate the appropriateness of mediation as a strategy.

Child Reconciliation Home by Children's Social Care (CSC)

One officer had not "heard of any horror stories of children's services putting a child back in an honour-based violence situation" (police officer j) and yet the most prominent theme across the research revolves around children who post complaint are "reconciled" back home to abusive situations predominantly by children's social care (CSC). Almost three-quarters of all child HBA victims (73%) (16/22) were either returned by CSC to perpetrating parents (13/22), placed with sympathising relatives (2/22) or retained at home on police advice (1/22) (Chart 7.1). These were not isolated "one off" incident reports, as in 59% (13/22)[7] of cases HBA formed part of a longitudinal pattern of behaviour, with several agencies (CSC, health, education, police) having ongoing involvement with the victim. A number of victims already had a dedicated social worker. For instance, threats of removing children for marriage abroad involved schools; threats of self-harm and suicide involved health; victims going missing from home and/or previous allegations of physical abuse involved the police.

In 9% of cases (2/22), there were no documented outcomes as to whether children were safe (cases 57 and 81). A further 9% of cases (2/22) involved children being taken into police protection but being placed by CSC with relatives that were found to sympathise with the perpetrators (cases 20 and 22); this also occurred in case 96. In 9% of cases (2/22), there was evidence of proactive safeguarding (cases 8 and 84). In a further 9% of cases (2/22), victims were placed outside the force area or in a refuge (cases 13 and 95). Despite the victim from case 95 being pregnant and aged 17 years, no PPP was considered. In one case (5%) the police officer disbelieved the victim and placed her back home (case 45). Children being discredited by professionals (police and CSC) was the

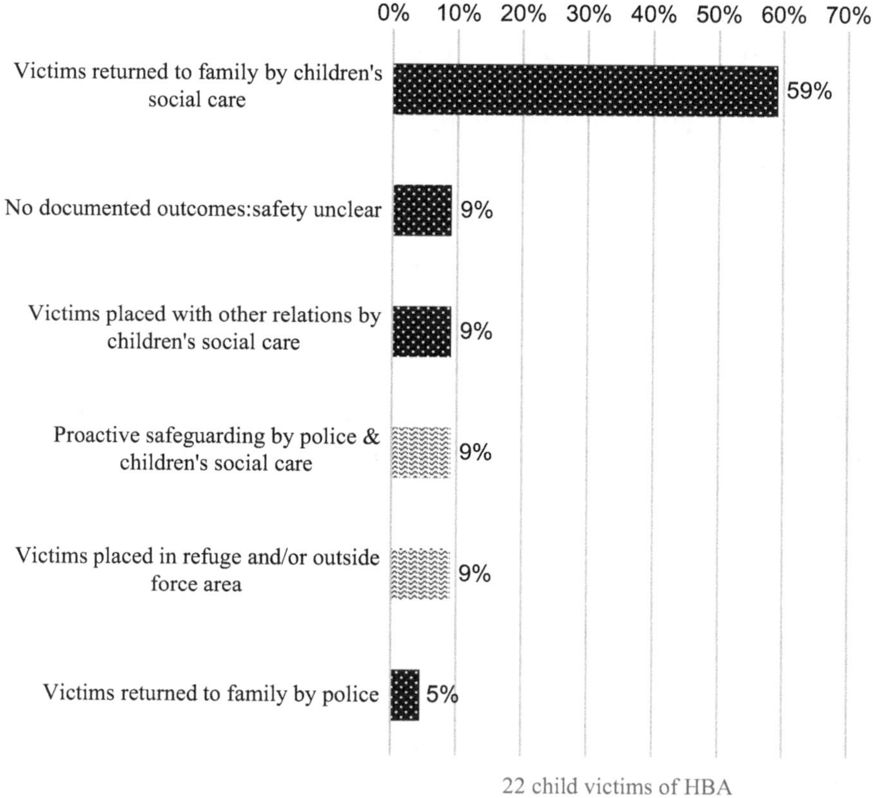

Chart 7.1 Child HBA cases: interventions and outcomes by children's social care and police

most prominent mechanism used to justify child reconciliation back with perpetrating relatives (explored in Chap. 3) and, to a lesser extent, victims presented as being reluctant to prosecute (explored in Chap. 4).

Police Protection Plans, Emergency Protection Orders and Section 20 Voluntary Arrangements

In 64% (14/22)[8] of child HBA cases, victims were put into police protection (PPP) by police officers and were therefore deemed "at risk" and therefore likely to suffer significant harm (Children Act 1989 s.46). Once a PPP is implemented, the local authority is responsible for making an application for an Emergency Protection Order[9] (EPO) within a 72-hour period. Yet the findings align with extant literature in showing how CSC often use care proceedings as a "last resort" (The Blueprint project 2005: 16; Oliver 2010: 17) and "mediate" between victims and perpetrating family members, exploring the child's perceived behaviour and/or discussing parental discipline. Outcomes show that CSC either reconciled victims back home to the abuse (often within 24–72 hours of the complaint) or opted for section 20 arrangements, seeking parental consent for a child to be placed with other family members as an alternative to applying for an EPO.

Police incident data shows how section 20 arrangements facilitate victims being placed with inappropriate relatives that appear to condone as well as inflict honour-based abuse (n=6).[10] In one case police took the child into police protection and she had recently been staying with her boyfriend and his parents. CSC were trying to arrange for her to stay at her aunt's house which, it transpired, was not appropriate as the victim had "not been fed (there) and she has had to sleep on a concrete floor" (case 20). The victim was insistent that if she went to her aunts, her father would come to recover her (ibid.). In another case, having been subjected to HBA by her mother, the child was given into the care of her father under a section 20 arrangement. The father subscribed to the same cultural views expressed by the offending mother, suggesting the child was behaving in an "unholy" way. The victim remained "concerned she may just disappear one day and she is feeling scared" (case 22). In a case explored in Chap. 6 (case 96), it was CSC that encouraged the female cousin as part of a section 20 arrangement to give the victim refuge. Yet, this was an inappropriate placement, as the same cousin took the victim on several visits to see her perpetrator brother in clear breach of police bail conditions (case 96). These extracts illustrate, first, the collective nature of honour abuse, but second, that placing child victims of HBA with other relatives can be fraught with risk, especially when considering the role females play in facilitating that abuse (see Chap. 6). Consequently, trying to safeguard HBA children is far more problematic because of the added complexity of multiple perpetration:

> Would social services put them with their own family or just a different part of it? But they're all still within that. I don't know I think it's a lot more difficult (police officer i)

This section highlights the flaws associated with section 20 voluntary care arrangements. The "misuse and abuse" of section 20 was broached by the chief of the family courts, Sir James Munby. He issued guidelines (November 2015) criticising social workers for misusing their statutory powers and he deemed that section 20 arrangements were not only bad practice but a denial of the fundamental rights of parents and children, which could expose professionals to substantial damage claims. He suggests that section 20 arrangements are being applied "as a prelude to care proceedings for lengthy periods" and that such cases have been steadily increasing since 2013 (Stevenson 2015).

Police officers rationalised CSC decisions to reunify children home in a number of different ways. Two officers suggested that children were returned home after a PPP because CSC had insufficient grounds to pursue an EPO (police officers f, h). Conversely, one officer suggested that some social workers lack the knowledge around trying to seek EPOs through their own legal department, or even because the legal team may "not work on weekends" (police officer o). Reasons were often attributed to lack of knowledge rather than ascribed to discretionary professional working practices. One officer recounted a discussion in which one social worker manager actively dissuaded a senior police officer from using their safeguarding powers because there were "too many children" being put in police protection:

> They've felt [CSC] that too many children were being PPO'd and the numbers had shot up. It's been a problem across the force, but for some reason in (this division) it was the highest..//..So what we do have now is dialogue with social care. It could be that a section 20 agreement is appropriate instead of a PPO..//.. we [police] can't put a section 20 in—it's up to them [CSC] to make the arrangements for it—so that dialogue does reduce the number of PPOs (police officer f)

CSC were critical of police officers being too quick to use their child protection powers when "there were easier options and we'd just gone down that route straight away" (police officer f). It is concerning that the informal agreement *not* to take children into police protection (PPP) appears to constitute the police acceding to the decision-making of social workers, which does not prioritise the needs of the child. Extracts support extant child protection research in that there appears to be a "reluctance on the part of social services to place or retain [child victims] in care" (Ward et al. 2005: 15). Police officers should not be dissuaded by partners from identifying children at risk of significant harm, particularly on the basis of cost and resource limitations.

Working Agreements

Findings show that mediation is largely facilitated by CSC, who devise contractual working agreements between authorities and perpetrating relatives in order to "work with" families, as opposed to placing children in care. Working alongside families, to support rather than disempower, was actively encouraged in the concluding observations of the Department of Health (1995). Yet at a practical level, applying this approach has counterproductive effects when children are victims of crime. As explored in Chap. 3, professionals (police and CSC) appear to support and concede to the controlling agenda of perpetrators rather than protect victims. For instance, a linked case involving the same victim (cases 32, 94, 96) shows how a community occupational therapist was assigned to visit an address on a daily basis. The social worker had devised a "working agreement" with parents that the "(victim) will not be physically chastised or assaulted in the home" (case 32). UK legislation already makes a distinction between chastisement and assault, and therefore this appears to be a written "agreement" in which the social worker negotiates with perpetrators not to break the law. A further control set by the CSC core group, but at the instigation of the parents, was of the child victim having to "relinquish her phones every night and according to her parents she hadn't been doing this" (case 32). The police log explores how the social worker criticised the victim for not conforming to parental boundaries, suggesting the victim "hasn't been willing to compromise as much as her parents have" (case 96). This adolescent victim was in and out of the care system over several years, which reflects CSC aligning to the perpetrators' agenda and under-protecting the victim. Reinforcing these findings, extant literature shows that older children are much less likely to be the subject of a PPP. Especially where there is a long history of involvement from services, teenagers tend to be categorised as resistant and "hard to help" (Brandon et al. 2008: 6). Consequently, professionals can become desensitised and this results in services being inappropriately withdrawn from teenagers (Broadhurst et al. 2010: 25).

In a different case across a two-year period, the only joint action agreed between a police child protection officer and a school teacher was for the teenage HBA victim to "come into school later in the morning and leave earlier, in order to avoid interaction with her friends" (case 74). The data suggests that the parents did not want their daughter mixing with perceived "unwholesome" influences, resonating with the westernisation theme evident in Chap. 6. It could be suggested that this decision is made with the best of intentions, with police and teachers negotiating with parents in order to encourage regular school attendance. Yet, equally these extracts illustrate that working agreements do not "safeguard" but set additional controls for child victims and appear to legitimate and sanction the tight coercive controls already established by perpetrators. Such working agreements replicate "traditional" domestic abuse situations where agencies mediate and form a contract predicated on an abuser's "agreement" not to abuse, provided the victim agrees to certain conditions. The problem is that mediation assumes that both parties will cooperate to make agreements work (Garrity 1998). If the victim fails to adhere to the agreement, then the perpetrator has "permission" to abuse her. This not only decriminalises the perpetrators' actions but shifts the professional focus on to the "problematic" victim, reflecting back on the iterative themes of Chap. 3. Both perpetrators and professionals sometimes promote mediation to the detriment of victims, as alluded to by one interviewee:

> Mediation is what a *family* wants to pursue, "we'll sort it out"..//..restorative justice, we love all that, and that's sometimes what we get sucked into, rather than focusing on the victim..//..we [police] can't be adding weight to that..//.. there's a danger that the victim might see us colluding with the

> drivers, the other agents and certain people from that fraternity yes ..//.. isolate [the victim] if they were seen to be colluding with any of their [perpetrators] mind-set (police officer d)

Extracts here reinforce child protection research by Farmer and Lutman showing that in 38% of cases social workers gave parents far "too many chances" to show they could care for their children (2012). Perhaps social workers find it difficult to strike a balance between being empathetic yet honest with parents without creating hostility (Forrester et al. 2008). This is apparent in the way that working agreements are conciliatory in expecting relatives to do the "right thing" by victims. This "rule of optimism" is already a danger for child protection social workers, where perceived cooperation from the parents leads professionals to believe a situation is improving (Dingwall et al. 1983 as cited in Littlechild 1998; Munro 1999). Eagerness to accept parental explanations at face value to the detriment of children is evident in several serious case reviews (London Borough of Brent 1985; Laming 2003). In the case of Victoria Climbie, social workers made premature judgements about the victim's relationship with her great aunt and were "unquestioningly accepting" of the contradictions provided by the perpetrator (Laming 2003: 205).

In summary, preceding sections have illustrated that a social worker's primary focus is of keeping families together, termed a "family saving" discourse (Cross et al. 2005; Harne and Radford 2008). Whether this is based on compliance with s.17 Children Act 1989 or other factors shall be open to further exploration. However, the impact of this appears to be detrimental to child protection. Social workers, through the use of mediation, promote the view that parents "cooperate" or are "working with" the authorities (police officer b), which gives conflicting messages to victims, shows social workers as acceding to perpetrator demands and leaves victims at risk. Children, understandably, do not want to prosecute parents but they do want to be safe.

Listening to Children: Best Interests and Wishes

In line with "traditional" domestic abuse victimology, incident case data illustrates that almost a third of adult victims (31% 24/78) return to perpetrators of their own volition (see Chart 3.5), representing a major stumbling block to effective HBA investigation management. As explored in Chap. 6, victims return to risks out of love, loyalty and due to being psychologically worn down. Police officers feel powerless when HBA victims return home, because as adults they possess freewill and therefore a right to choose. Victim reluctance not only inhibits any prosecution, but appears to adversely impact effective safeguarding:

> So why are you going back home?
> (Victim)—"You know why? Because I love him—it's my dad..//..he's my family..//..I just want my dad being told he can't send me anywhere." When somebody's 23 and they're saying to you—"Oh, I'm going home", how can we stop that, you know?..//.. It's the last thing we wanted to do..//..But we had no choice, because that's what she wanted (police officer n)
> The victim may not always engage, and I think if you've got the lack of engagement sometimes it's not always easy to be able to safeguard that person if they're saying "I'm going home" (police officer k)

The Children Act 2004 s.53 outlines the need to give due consideration to the wishes and feelings of children in any decision regarding the provision of services (www.legislation.gov.uk). It appears that this legal rule may be used by some police officers and social workers as justification for resolving cases as "no further action," suggesting that a professional's underlying rationale is based on the "freewill," "voice" and "wishes" of the victim. This is more so apparent in child cases and yet ironically, compared to adults, children cannot *choose* to remain in the risk predicament (Hanmer 2013 [1989]: 99). For instance, despite a mother denying the crime on police interview, yet admitting to a social worker that she had sent her 15-year-old daughter to Pakistan for a forced marriage 12 months earlier, the officer recommends that the child be reconciled with the mother, who was at the time still on bail for those criminal offences (police officer c):

> (c) (Victim) was married but she wasn't forced to do it, it was her choice and it was against mum's wishes that she got married..//..[abroad]
> She's 16 [now] so, the voice of a child has to be heard …
> Researcher: And what are her wishes?

(c) She wanted to go back with Mum. She wanted to go back and live at the address, which I think is why, in the end, family court proceedings have said "Yes, go back" (police officer c)

Notice, too, how the officer places the responsibility on the *child* (rather than the parents) for getting married, whilst also "inject(ing) caring narratives" (Taylor and White 2006: 941) into the police decision-making, reconciling the child home on the basis that these are her wishes. In a similar vein, other police write-ups conclude:

[A 15-year-old] returned to her home address of her own free will and with the care of social services (case 50)

[A 14-year-old] was able to "change her mind about this" [a marriage]../.. She agrees that her family were against the proposal as she was too young. She has now regretted her decision and wishes to back out of the engagement (case 81)

Police officers use the wishes, voice and freewill of the child as grounds to decriminalise incidents and justify reconciling children back home to perpetrators. Such discretionary practices prioritise a child's wishes over their best interests. Child victims, specifically those under 16, legally lack the capacity to make decisions such as getting married and consenting to sexual relations. Neither can such decisions be made by others on a victim's behalf (Mental Capacity Act codes of practice 2013: 17). Surely an act taken which contravenes the victim's best interests (including the right to be safe from abuse) is a moral, if not professional, abdication of the responsibilities ascribed to professionals?

Acting in a child's best interests and considering a child's wishes remain impossible to reconcile, as these concepts pull in opposing directions (International Federation of Social Workers 2002). Yet it is clear that acting in a child's best interests should be the primary consideration for professionals (London Borough of Brent 1985; Children Act 1989; The United Nations Convention on the rights of the child 1989 (article 3.1); International Federation of Social Workers 2002: 25). Rather than acquiesce to the victim's "wishes" not to prosecute family members (or to return them to family members) as is evident in the findings, police and social workers should override the victim's wishes (Roberts et al. 2014:

70) and prioritise the victim's best interests. The psychological hold that perpetrators have, impacting detrimentally a victim's ability to make rational decisions, may mean that the decision should be taken out of their hands.

Albeit the "vocabulary of official guidance is embedded in professional talk" (Thompson 2016: 110), there appears to be a clear disconnect between agency words ("the voice of a child has to be heard") and safeguarding interventions, with children's wishes *not* to return home often overridden. Such fears of children are tangible and relate to dark threats of death and serious violence. Some children protest that they want to be placed in care, with others being scared and threatening to kill themselves if they were sent back home. Roberts et al. suggest that fear is a very good predictor of violence (2014: 173) and yet 73% of children in these findings were returned to the abuse. In 59% of all child cases, they were sent home contrary to their own wishes (13/22).[11] Agencies did not accede to the wishes of the victim and neither did they prioritise the child's best interests. Social workers need to elicit children's views both concerning transition into care (Oliver 2010: 18) and on returning home from care (NSPCC 2015). These findings mirror wider child protection research in illustrating that a child's best interests are often paid "lip service," with their needs overshadowed by the interests of adults (International Federation of Social Workers 2002: 26; Ofsted 2010; Munro 2011: 27). The Jasmine Beckford inquiry (London Borough of Brent 1985) was unequivocal in stating that a social worker's primary responsibility is to protect children. Themes in this and Chap. 3, highlight that social workers prioritise and accede to the views of adults rather than listening to children themselves (Timms and Thoburn 2003; Morgan 2006; Forrester et al. 2008; Ofsted 2010; Munro 2011). Such outcomes lie far from the child-centred approach advocated by the UK government, which focuses on listening to children and "take(ing) their views seriously" (HM Government 2018: 10).

Perpetrators "Nod Their Head" in the Right Places

Two officers doubt the effectiveness of mediation in safeguarding children once they are "behind closed doors" (police officer k). They consider that perpetrators placate social workers and other professionals by "nod(ding) their head" in the right places (police officer k). This theme was apparent in police interviews but difficult to isolate in the incident data.[12] In one of the few male cases (4/100), a photograph of a teenage boy was circulated on social media with his legs shackled together as he was stood in the street after he had "escaped" from home:

> That was his chastisement for misbehaving. That they [parents] would shackle his legs so he couldn't run off at night—he was coming in at all times basically (police officer m)

The photo was shown to the teacher and he was immediately placed in foster care. Yet within days the victim would not make a formal complaint, could not be placed with other family members and was returned home by CSC, who were "continuing to work with" the family. Some officers are cynical about the level of genuine cooperation displayed by perpetrators to CSC professionals:

> It's a real risk of—is that still going on; are they [perpetrators] now more aware and hiding it better? (police officer m)
>
> You can try and mediate with them, and as we've already discussed they [perpetrators] can nod their head and say 'Yeah, great, we'll engage with you' and thumbs up to everything, but once that's closed [the case] and it's behind closed doors, who's going to monitor and watch what's going on? So it's difficult (police officer k)
>
> And I'll come back to it again—it's just words, it doesn't matter, anyone can just "put on a show" for 5 minutes in front of someone, can't they? Give the kids a hug and yeah—and everything's going to be fine [and perpetrators say] "When she comes home she should be treated like a princess, don't you worry"—and it's worth nothing, is it? (police officer m)

First, these extracts suggest that perpetrators "perform" and present a semblance of feigned cooperation and assent to authority figures. Parents appear to deceptively cooperate with social workers as part of a strategy to disarm them (Brandon et al. 2008). This was apparent in the Peter Connelly (baby P) case (2007) where the mother, Tracey Connelly, initiated communication with social workers and took the child to health care appointments on eight occasions. Consequently, social workers placed a "high level of trust in" the mother and concluded she was "cooperating with the child protection plan" (Jones 2014: 198–199). In retrospect, this assumption was wrong. In most cases there is an assumption that including parents in decision-making will result in the best interests of the child being served (Littlechild 1998; Munro 2011). When cases of abuse are suspected, departing from this assumption and taking more direct protective measures is necessary (Littlechild 1998). Second, mediation meetings provide a semblance of bureaucratic service provision, but this appears to be a displacement exercise in which a meeting is convened, perpetrators appear to assent to professional advice and CSC file those cases. Third, in contrast to the limited use of mediation by the police, there is significant evidence of CSC professionals mediating with perpetrators as part of a larger process of reconciling children back at home after a brief period in care. Some social workers maintain a working relationship with HBA perpetrators, often to the detriment of child victims.

Increased Demand for Services and the "Cost" of Social Care

Child reconciliation is a prominent theme identified through the incident data. Yet the data fails to shed light on *why* mediation, reconciliation and victim blaming (Chap. 3) occur. By contrast, police specialist interviews suggest that the reasons for child reconciliation revolve around lack of placements in the system and the cost of retaining children in care (police officers a, b, f, o, k, h, m).

Partnership Working: Silo Working and the "Battlefield"

A departmental silo[13] is described as existing when professionals have different philosophies, values and divergent cultures (Cameron et al. 2012). Managers are often unaware of the priorities and goals of other departments and there is little communication, collaboration and teamwork between these business units (Beal n.d.). Consequently, a silo mentality does not incline professionals to think "much outside their immediate operational box" (Moore and Hamilton 2016: 117) and they focus on their remit rather than the priorities of other departments (ibid.). When considering these definitions, there appears to be very little to distinguish "silos" from the concept of organisational culture(s).

The current findings display a divergent and fractious relationship between specialist police officers and CSC, which is often described as a "battle" (police officer k), with police and social workers at "loggerheads" (police officer o), pursuing inherently different agendas (Grace 1995; Harne and Radford 2008) instead of working together as expected (HMIC 2015: 91). Agencies appear to work in isolation under the banner of partnership working, with no cohesive long-term strategy to manage the complexities of HBA:

> I'd go to strategy meetings and it's always gung-ho..//.. none of them have had any experience of forced marriage. Indeed, people are 'googling' on the phone, and they're all looking to me to lead on it because they have heard that I'm a forced marriage expert..//..There's no quality assurance on the decision-making. I'm making all the decisions and people are just going ahead with it (police officer d)
>
> I don't feel there was any partnership with any agencies, I kind of felt like the police were 'on their own' trying to deal with it—unless you want housing you can get a woman into a refuge (police officer i)

Trust and respect between professionals are critical to the success of joint working between agencies (Cameron et al. 2012). Yet, little appears to have changed since Parton's assessment that partnership working is signified by "conflict, different interests and mistrust" (1991: 207; Cameron et al. 2012; Featherstone et al. 2018). Such mistrust and conflict are epitomised in the following extracts:

> [CSC] Where are you going to put them [children]?"
>
> I said "I'm not going to put them anywhere, you are" and we ended up with
>
> [CSC]—"We haven't got anywhere to put them. We've been working with this family a long time"

I said—"I don't care"—and we end up in a row (police officer b)

I think the problems come when we get to loggerheads to say that 'we have PPO'd that child for a reason'—and children's services want to return them to the family (police officer o)

I think children's services..//..I think they still very much deal with things on a—'it's a family issue go back home and sort it out with your Mum'..//..There is still that mentality—'if you go back home we will talk to your parents, we will sort it out' (police officer a)

We PPP the kids and they end up in somebody else's care, or a lot of the time, after those 72 hours, they'll go back home (police officer b)

They [CSC] wanted to put her back in the family and then obviously I objected to that—but they were then approaching the family to say "Look, let's see if we can sort something out, let's get you mediating between yourselves"..//..They told me that's what they were going to do. I wasn't happy about her going back—she needs to stay where she is. But they [CSC] do it quite often, if they've got a child who has been placed in local authority, just because their families are not getting on as such, they will try and mediate between them to try and integrate them back within the family (police officer k)

These extracts appear to be symptomatic of silo mentalities where departments (inside and outside organisations) do not understand the functions and perspectives of professionals in different units and they operate in seemingly contradictory silo-based value systems (Moore and Hamilton 2016). A study of the resettlement of male prisoners in a UK open prison reflects how prisoners felt that they were "just pawns in the middle of" different professionals that undermined each other's efforts (Moore and Hamilton 2016: 122). Detrimentally, it appears that the behaviour of professionals working in isolation serves to alienate the end user that the very "intervention" was intended to consider. In the HBA context, strategic decisions from the professionals who are entrusted to intervene in child safeguarding appear highly contradictory. For instance, social care professionals dissuade specialist officers against implementing PPPs; frontline officers *remove* children perceived at risk (PPP) and within 72 hours social workers mediate to return them. Rationale for such reconciliations appears to revolve around avoiding placing children in the care system. One 16-year-old kept going missing from home but the social worker continually placed the child back home, even though the police officer was insistent that this was inappropriate:

> "There is a reason why this girl keeps going missing and saying why she doesn't feel like she is safe at home." The social worker said "well there's nothing going on, we've assessed it, let's put this child back in the family" (police officer k)
>
> They [CSC] want to try and mediate; parental classes or some other early help or intensive support—to try and get the child back home to prevent them remaining in care (police officer k)

This is disturbing given the collective nature of offending and the sense that there is no clear protective influence for child victims. Officers were cynical of action taken by CSC, with one suggesting, "Once we refer it to social services, we have no idea what they would" [do] (police officer g). Although there is evidence of police and CSC often being at "loggerheads," there was also evidence of *agreement* between the police and CSC about outcomes, notably when victims are deemed as blameworthy and inconsistent, particularly apparent in Chap. 3. This is referred to by Thomas as "implicit camaraderie in a mutually hostile environment," with both police and social workers performing an adversarial function (1988: 126–128). The findings in this chapter and Chap. 3 illustrate that social workers display a "blaming and inquisitorial focus form of child protection practice" (Clapton et al. 2013: 805). Yet, rather than suggest these "confrontational and at times aggressive" communication styles by social workers (Forrester et al. 2008: 23) represent a "blurred" distinction between the police and CSC as "social" policers (Thomas 1988), it is suggested that these show evidence of *both* sets of professionals pursuing discretionary patterned practices.

Unmanageable Workloads and the "Cost" of Social Care

Police officers were unequivocal in the view that CSC decisions to retain or return children home are based on *cost* rather than the risks posed to children:

> But I think they [CSC] do it because of money, and they haven't got anywhere to put them, so they'll leave them at home (police officer b)
>
> You can be cynical, and I was—and still am to a degree—that it's a cost-saving exercise (police officer f)
>
> A lot of it is about finance you know and we've had experiences where we've had people who've fled DV or honour-based matters and they don't have recourse to funds and then it's about arguing with the local authority as to where they put them..//.. It's trying to get across to them like—"we need to make this person safe"—it's not just about the money (police officer k)

Several police officers discuss the practical difficulties of having to donate money, provide victims with accommodation and a mobile phone due to no recourse to public funding (police officers k, j); coupled with the delays and/or difficulties in other services providing support:

> But it's been that 'battle' with them [local authority] and that urgency to put them somewhere safe. You know you can be on the phone for hours with them [CSC] ..//.."have they got any money" ..//..And we've [police] ended up footing the bill (police officer k)

Funding pressures are certainly relevant, with 89% of children's social service directors finding it difficult to fulfil statutory duties under the Children Act 1989 (Cromarty et al. 2018). Due to the cost implications, local authorities are under significant financial pressure to restrict the numbers of children in care or accommodation (Ward et al. 2005: 15). This is because the yearly cost of placing a child in care is £61,614, compared with supporting a reunified child back home, which is just over £5627 (Holmes 2014). The chronic state of social care adversely impacts child safeguarding, with children "drifting" within the system. This research supports extant research that social workers are prematurely "putting them back [home] too quickly," with children returned to risk predicaments without any appropriate support and no strategic care plan in place:

> You can get parents—"Oh no, everything's fine, let my son or daughter back, we're happy to have them back" and the next thing you hear is they're not in school, they're not in college and they've disappeared. Or they've

> gone abroad and when they come back and say—"Well, yeah, actually I've married" or they've been assaulted as such. To me if you've got a child who's fled a property, that risk is there heightened and will always be there..//.. it's got to be a long assessment ..//..they're [CSC] putting them back [home] too quickly I think (police officer k)

Reconciling children home is only effective when the underlying family issues that led to them entering care have been addressed (Farmer et al. 2011). Numerous studies indicate that reconciling children home is inappropriate and premature. In Farmer et al.'s study of 180 children that were returned from local authority care back to families, a third of them experienced two or more failed returns home (2011). In a different study, of the 10,270 children living in England that were sent home to family (2006–2007), almost a third (30%) had been placed *back* into care in the five years up to March 2012 (Department for Education 2013: 36). A National Society for the Prevention of Cruelty to Children (NSPCC) study found that in the year up to March 2014, there were 68,840 children in care. And although 30,430 left the care system, 50% of those children were returned back into care due to a breakdown in the family relationship (2015). Such findings reinforce this research in suggesting that children are stuck in a "revolving door..//..in a cycle of referral and assessment, but only receive help if their needs escalate to a crisis point" (Action for Children 2017: 6). The total estimated cost to the tax payer of failed reunifications is £300 million a year, compared with providing adequate support and services to those leaving care, which represents a significant cost saving of £56 million a year (Holmes 2014). Addressing the issue of early and effective state intervention would therefore not only safeguard child victims but would alleviate the financial burden on the state. Preoccupation with cost can also result in increased risk management of cases. This is evident in the following extract where social workers appear to play Russian roulette by employing a "wait and see" strategy of placing children back home in order to collate further evidence of abuse:

> You can see these children shouldn't be with their parents..//.. they get the crystal ball out and they are usually right [CSC]. And there will, maybe, be another incident leading up to that removal, that then speeds that process up where we [police] become involved again (police officer m)

> Researcher: But again, we are leaving children at risk, aren't we? It's almost like 'Let's just wait and see'
>
> Well, yes, will it get better, will it get worse—and then we've got our 'back-up' (police officer m)
>
> Researcher: Evidence
>
> (m) We've made it right—we made the right decision because it happened again—but that could be too late, couldn't it, in some children's cases? (police officer m)

Indeed, it is hard not to reflect back on some serious case reviews when reading the above narrative as to whether professionals adopted this approach. Whether a case is progressed or filed as "no further action" appears to be determined by a number of factors including cost, practitioner workload and the subjective judgements of professionals:

> Is a definite consideration-funding—and sometimes it may get in the way of safeguarding—I don't think it should but, practicalities, in the real world. It's just strange how sometimes you get a person who is able to be put into a hotel, a week, 2 weeks or longer. Then other people who they [CSC] are fighting for to have put with a family member—is that a difference in opinion of the management? Difference in opinion in the social worker? ..//..They are thinking, "If I come in at green I am under budget—I'll have more money at the end of the year to make easier decisions—take them out, take them out [remove from parents]; yet at the start of the year maybe when it's tight [money] would that have an influence—would we see that in the numbers of children removed maybe? (police officer m)
>
> Sometimes there are social workers who get that gut feelings who say "Well, actually no—it's not right this, we need to do a little bit more with this" but we've got… because of their caseloads—and to look at getting a family back together and once they've done an assessment they see it as, everything is "happy as Larry" and they look at closing that case—then that's when those alarm bells start ringing again (police officer k)

Four in five children's social workers certainly consider their caseloads as unmanageable (Purvis 2018). Evidence of large volumes of referrals being filed without children's services statutory agency intervention leads one to the contention that the imperative is to reduce workload. This is illustrated in Stanley et al.'s examination of domestic abuse referrals from police to CSC, which highlight that 60% of cases were immediately filed with no action taken. Only 15% of cases involved a direct intervention (the remainder received a letter) (2011). The current picture is equally bleak. Of the 646,120 child cases referred to CSC by police, education, health and other bodies, 10.2% were immediately filed as no further action, whilst a further 160,000 child cases (27.8%) were assessed but also filed as "no further action" (Department for Education 2017). Policy from the Department of Health appears to have germinated this approach. They proffered that too many cases came under the banner of child protection and therefore advised social workers to sift or screen out cases to avoid catching too many "minnows" in a net widening system (Department of Health 1995: 32–34). The impact of this means that children at risk have been reframed as "children in need" (Littlechild 1998: 116–118). Prematurely screening out cases at an early stage is problematic, as it is not always possible to know at the referral stage what is serious and what is not until an investigation takes place (ibid.). This predicament of filing referrals appears to replicate the central argument of Chap. 4, in which many reported police incidents are filed as "no crime," thereby substantially reducing demand.

It is argued that the policy approach, based on prescriptively grading risks[14] rather than applying personal judgement (Munro 2011), has led to high-risk HBA cases (and many other child protection cases) being prematurely "screened out" at an early stage by both social workers and police officers, in which these are underestimated as false negatives. This dire predicament can only have worsened since this study was undertaken,[15] as local authorities face an unprecedented surge in demand. Between 2010 and 2017, section 47 enquiries increased by 108%, with the number of child case conferences increasing by 75%. Those on child protection plans has also increased year on year since 2010 (Cromarty et al. 2018).

The Cost Implication of Siblings at Risk

Despite police systems being effective in showing a longitudinal picture of offending and highlighting links between victims and offenders, there is evidence of siblings being managed in isolation[16] by some police and social workers. In one case, a 15-year-old Pakistani girl was being hit by her father, was not allowed to attend school and was being over policed by her sisters. There were six other children living at that address aged between 4 and 19 years that were not risk assessed. A child in the same household had already reported in 2013 being "hit with a mop on her arm, neck and hand," and yet despite the bruising, the officer did not input a crime report on the basis that the child did not want to prosecute (case 74). A further case illustrates how one family of three siblings were separately logged on police systems as victims of HBA within the same month. Less than two weeks earlier the victim's older sister had admitted that her father had committed a crime against her. Her 17-year-old brother, as a high-risk HBA victim, had already been referred to MARAC that same month (case 43). Such information should have been discussed at a joint agency strategy meeting. Yet despite the relevant information being written on the incident logs, with a PPI system able to cluster such information together, no professional appeared to "join the dots" and thus no strategy was considered to manage all siblings. This runs contrary to interagency guidelines on safeguarding, which suggest that professionals should consider whether protection arrangements are required for other siblings rather than solely the identified victim (HMIC 2015: 167; HM Government 2018). If the police act to protect one child, the risk to all siblings must be considered (police officers k, m, o):

> We can't leave the siblings there if we think—I know social services are quick to say "the family have said it's always John/Amy that gets it, they're the one that misbehave; they are the eldest—they are the one that always get the punishment, so we can leave the rest [other children] there"—Realistically, can we do that? If the punch bag isn't there—who are they going to take it out on? Imagine the criticism if they are the next (police officer m)

One officer suggests it is logistically difficult to place siblings in care:

> They don't particularly want to split the children..//..or how do they get three foster placements for one family? (police officer o)

Yet, police interviews also identify that placing multiple siblings in care has an important financial implication for local authorities. In one such case, a father offered to marry his 14-year-old daughter, a Romanian national, to a 37-year-old male for £10,000. Although there was allegedly "no relationship" going on, when the male refused, the father reported him to the police. It came to the police child sexual exploitation (CSE) team to investigate (headed by police officer h), who in turn raised it as a concern with CSC. There were no arrests as the girl and her family refused to cooperate (police officer h). Five months later, the victim was reported missing (MFH) and, after much police resource, was tracked to Spain, where the 37-year-old had facilitated the victim's travel there. The victim was not a British national and her Romanian travel documents were out of date. The Romanian embassy agreed that either a family member or the authorities (police and/or CSC), with the written consent of the parents, could travel to recover the victim. The police wanted to recover the victim due to concerns about the father trying to sell his daughter. Against this judgement, CSC argued there was "no evidence" that he posed a threat and so they opted to send the father to recover his own daughter. Heavily involved in discussions with CSC, the police officer considered that the decision of CSC not to aid police in recovering the victim was attributed to finances, rather than the safeguarding needs of the child—"they [CSC] decided that [sending the father] was the cheapest option" (police officer h). On her return from Spain, the girl continuously went missing from home and told officers that she had run off to meet a 15-year-old she had met online. After 12 months, the victim disclosed to police that the father was "controlling and trying to sell her to other people" for marriage, that he "withholds food from her" and her mother, and that he will not permit her out of the house without his consent (police officer h). In this case the victim had six other siblings. The police implemented a Domestic Violence Protection Notice (DVPN)[17] to allow the mother some time away from her controlling husband and facilitated an Independent Domestic Violence Adviser (IDVA) who was working with her. However, the mother supported her husband rather than the police:

> I wanted them removed from the household but social services said we didn't have enough to remove them from the household. I don't think they want to accept responsibility for 7 kids.//..They're saying if he's a risk, then

> he's a risk to all of them. If we're saying that mum can't protect—then she can't protect any of them so they [CSC] don't want responsibility for 7 kids. Because mum won't make a disclosure and they say [CSC]—all the other children are a lot younger—they've done enquiries with education who've said they've got no concerns about these kids, there's never been any disclosures..//..it's took her [victim] 12 months to finally tell us what's going on in the household (police officer h)

The officer perceived that for CSC to admit the father was a risk meant accepting that he was a risk to *all* the siblings, which would cause an adverse financial burden on the state. CSC acted in a similar vein towards the mother, by denying risk and criminality. The cost implication of *all* siblings needing safeguarding was raised by another police officer:

> We could, in some families, be removing 5-6-7 children..//.. I don't know whether it's actually goes down in writing but there's definitely been conversations—"my manager won't pay for six kids to put somewhere tonight—if you are saying that he is the only one that has been hit; we can put him with Grandma—or he can go whatever"—because of the considerations to the costs. I think, again, being influenced by previous jobs; they [CSC] are looking maybe a couple of days down the line, this lad isn't going to make a complaint; we're going to be taking him back home again and maybe second guessing what is going to happen (police officer m)

This indication that managers downgrade cases or offer no social work support at all is apparent in wider child protection studies, which suggest that the threshold for victims being able to access services is now much higher than it was previously (Thompson 2016; Cromarty et al. 2018). Findings illustrate how CSC spend time justifying why a family of siblings are *not* at risk and integrating victims home due to the practical and financial difficulties (along with internal increased workload implications for CSC) of finding places in the care system. The cost of placing HBA children in care appears to inhibit a proactive safeguarding response.

Incoherent Strategies, Deflecting and Resisting Workload

Silo working is evident and lack of strategic partnership working causes professionals not only to be unclear on procedures, but ineffectual short-term strategies are applied. In the first case a hospital social worker instigated an FMPO procedure, but unfortunately did not liaise with the police to ensure a safety plan was implemented prior to the victim being reconciled home, which resulted in the victim suffering further physical abuse (case 28). In the second case a social worker obtained only a short-term FMPO which lasted 12 months. Thus, the father phoned children's social care from Pakistan to check that the order had expired before legitimately marrying his 16-year-old daughter to a suitor (case 44). In the final case a 15-year-old child was taken out of school for an intended forced marriage to her cousin in Pakistan. Police held a "garden gate"[18] strategy meeting with CSC and the girl was quickly placed in care. The interviewee was keen to endorse "letting the social services do their job" as "we walk away now..//..our job [police] is done" (police officer d), and as a result CSC agreed to obtain an FMPO. Unbeknown to the officer at that time, the FMPO was not correctly served on the parents, as procedurally should have occurred, rendering it "useless." After seven months in care, the girl was sent home with the consent of CSC and the case file was closed (police officer d). On two occasions the victim attended the police station to try and seek out the officer (police officer d) whom she referred to as the "forced marriage Asian guy" who had made her "all these promises" that the FMPO would be on the system and she could not be forcibly removed from the country. The police did not locate the officer. The victim eventually acquiesced to a marriage. At the airport, she sought help from a police officer and was "asked to hang [around]." She believed she would be protected when she showed her passport to airline officials, but because the FMPO had not been served, this meant that there were no warnings noted on the Police National Computer (PNC). The victim got on the plane and was then forced to marry her cousin, all the time waiting for her chance to come back and escape to the UK. She felt "abandoned." The family then told her she could not return to the UK until she got pregnant.

"So, I had sex with him. I didn't want to. I was crying." Once pregnant, she was not allowed to return to the UK for 12 months until she had given birth. The victim's initial thought was "I would have had it aborted." The reason she did not leave her daughter was because "the same thing will happen to her as what happened to me—it wasn't fair on her." She lived with her family but said she was not going to bring her husband back to the UK. The only reason this officer found out about the misfortunes of the girl was because her female cousin was now in the same predicament, having had an "engagement party." The original victim dissuaded her cousin from involving the police due to her bad experience and they both eloped with the baby. Soon after they liaised with a police officer, who dealt with the case "brilliantly" (police officer d) and placed them both in a refuge. However, the interviewee felt that the victim had a hardened attitude towards police officers because of the poor service she had experienced—very much an attitude of "give them two fingers, they [police] won't do anything" (police officer d). In a business context silo working can result in missed opportunities (Hughes 2016), but in a criminal justice context, such insularity by professionals not only results in ineffectual interventions, but agency involvement can actually increase risks to victims.

Findings also illustrate that in an effort to reduce workload, some professionals divert or "deflect[ing] workload elsewhere" (Thompson 2016: 188) to other statutory bodies. Police child protection officers often express frustration at receiving phone calls from CSC at 3 pm on a Friday afternoon, where, outside office hours, the "baton" is proverbially passed to the police to "find" a missing family member so that the local authority CSC can "go home":

> Come Friday 3 pm they [social services] have not managed to get hold of them..//..So that they can go home and the police can go round, and keep on knocking—keep on knocking [police say to social services]—"you've had all week—what attempt have you had all week"? (police officer o)

In resisting workload, professionals sometimes appear to rely on internal policies to justify denying victims access to services. For example, a 17-year-old was subjected to systematic HBA by her father and yet her local housing authority stated they "could only place (the child victim) at accommodation in the (local) area," despite the fact that remaining in the vicinity would heighten her risks. Housing officials in the *adjoining* local authority were also loathe to take on problems from a different jurisdiction:

> Because child victim is from (another area) it is nothing to do with them (case 84)

In a similar housing situation, a 31-year-old Pakistani victim and her husband fled to Pakistan after being subjected to HBA from the family. She had "dishonoured" the family by marrying her love choice partner. Returning to the UK eight months later, she relocated *outside* the area where the perpetrators lived, and yet the "safe" local authority argued they could not rehouse her on the grounds she had previously "made herself homeless":

> The social worker stated that if there were no offences then they would be advising the female to return to [the threat location] (case 29)

This resulted in the victim asking relations for a place to stay, which alerted perpetrators of their return to the UK and rekindled the abuse. Counter-intuitively against the best interests of victims, the victim was returned to the high-risk situation on the advice and approval of three statutory agencies.

The act of making a "referral" itself is also used by some professionals to abrogate responsibility for safeguarding to other professional bodies. This is evident in the case of a 15-year-old, who after an unsuccessful overdose attempt divulges to teachers that her parents are being physically abusive. Education contact CSC, but instead of organising a strategy meeting with child protection police officers, CSC make a referral to the Child and Adolescent Mental Health Services (CAAMHS). This results in CAAMHS sending a letter directly to the perpetrating parents, alerting them of the self-harming disclosure, who in turn do not take the child for medical treatment. The following month, a Forced Marriage Protection Order (FMPO) was issued by the family court and served on the parents whilst the victim was still at school. Police data did not identify *which* agency applied for the order, but a failure by CSC and CAAMHS to alert the police meant that the victim was exposed to several weeks of further violence and psychological abuse by the parents,[19] who persuaded her to cancel the FMPO as they had a marriage planned for her abroad. The victim again reached out to public bodies, the police, who took her into police protection when she disclosed that her parents had been "hitting her for months." Although the father was arrested for assault, he denied the offence and attributed her overdose to "taking tablets for a headache." Soon after, the police suggest that the victim's testimony was not "consistent," and within a month, she had been returned with the agreement of CSC and police back to the alleged perpetrators (case 26). The act of "referring" from one agency to another appears to signify a bureaucratic box ticked "resolution" to the problem of the demands placed on that organisation—without applying any resources to fully address the issue.

In summary, these extracts first illustrate how professionals sometimes tackle HBA and forced marriage as a single agency, working in isolated silos rather than through multi-agency working. Perhaps this is why there is no concrete evidence to show that multi-agency work in the domestic abuse sphere is effective (Humphreys and Stanley 2006). Second, working in isolation and lack of fluent communication between agencies generates ineffectual short-term fixes, such as FMPOs that expire without safety plans being considered, as well as incoherent interventions which increase risks to victims. Such actions are seen as ends in themselves, with little cognisance that family members will persevere to ensure the demands of the collective are met. Third, such errors are rarely identified by other partners, as agencies all operate on different systems. Finally, agencies appear overly preoccupied with their own internal workload and focused on justifying why it is *not* in their remit to assist, instead of prioritising the needs and safety of victims.

Child HBA Cases: Professional Responsibilities and Ownership

Child Protection or Domestic Abuse?

The recognition that domestic abuse is a child protection issue has mixed and problematic impacts (Featherstone et al. 2018). Yet, this should not be the case as the most common reason for referring children to specialist services is domestic abuse (Action for Children 2017; Department for Education 2017). An identified problem in police operational management is that, first, a third of police specialists in HBA, including supervisors, have no knowledge or experience of investigating *child* cases,[20] despite being highly conversant with HBA as a specialism. Adult victims of HBA are dealt with by specialist experts in HBA and domestic abuse. Yet problematically, cases involving victims under 18 years are categorised as "child protection" (HBA and FM Policy and Procedure 2013) and are thus allocated to child protection experts. When a victim's needs incorporate both specialisms of domestic abuse and child protection, it becomes problematic for practitioners, who often tend to be expert in one or the other field. This is recognised by other academics, who suggest that there is too much disparate separation between violence against women and violence against children and young people (Humphreys and Stanley 2006; Broadhurst et al. 2010). Moreover, this factor adversely impacts the effective safeguarding of victims. Lack of understanding around honour abuse is apparent, with one officer conceding that child abuse officers often sought advice from domestic abuse sergeants (police officer j). The contention is that only officers who are omni-competent in child protection *and* HBA should liaise with partners and actively manage child HBA cases.

Second, allocating child HBA cases to child protection experts implicitly suggests that methods for managing "traditional" child abuse cases are effective in an HBA context, which is not necessarily the case. As Roberts et al. argue, tried and tested methods of managing child abuse do not work in an HBA context and place children at increased risk, such as involving the family in child protection decisions, or moving children to a different area with a similar cultural mix (2014). A traditional child protection tactic is of social workers insisting on informing families where victims are going to be housed, which, as extracts show, results in HBA perpetrators recovering victims and exposing them to further long-term abuse, accomplished through the use of section 20 arrangements.

Third, there are criticisms for the fragmented approach to case management, with domestic abuse supervisors managing "safeguarding" and child protection supervisors managing the "crime investigation" (a practice occurring in the force investigated), which results in some counter-intuitive decision-making. For instance, the practice of reunifying children home with perpetrating family members whilst suspects are on bail awaiting a prosecution decision results in undue pressure being placed on child victims (and their witnesses) to retract their evidence, which transpired in some cases. Had domestic abuse supervisors been responsible for safeguarding *and* crime investigation, such counter-intuitive decisions may not have been considered.

Information Sharing and "Ownership" of Child Protection

Key factors impeding information sharing, particularly in child protection, are that social workers fail to communicate effectively; they are either unable to make links between incidents or they fail to record and/or share information to other agencies through referrals (Reder and Duncan 2003; Thompson 2016). Due to silo mentalities, professionals can intentionally withhold information, resulting in other departments working with out-of-date or inaccurate information (Investopedia 2018). This is apparent in the following extract, whereby CSC withheld information from the police, divulging it only at a critical stage:

> I've found "can we have a strategy meeting tomorrow?" And then you speak to them [CSC] and you find that "Well, last week this child said 'Mum hit me with a stick.'" "Well, if you knew about it last week, why didn't you tell us?" (police officer b)

Had officers been privy to the information, a different more proactive course of action may have been pursued by the police (i.e. a PPP). Wider child protection research explores this phenomenon by suggesting that CSC often fear that police officers, armed with such information, will pursue punitive interventions and in doing so will interfere with their attempts to "repair" families (Cross et al. 2005). Conversely, another tactic is for CSC to seek active police involvement in mediation, seemingly to ratify a decision to reconcile children home:

> I get many, many phone calls on a weekly basis from officers saying "right we've got this case—social workers or whoever else want to get together, the girl wants—just speak to the parents" (police officer a)
>
> I wouldn't feel comfortable with [mediation] that, because they [CSC] would be too quick to say "the police were here, police have OK'd this; done it with the consent of the police"—and if it all goes wrong—then, well, no—"you asked me to attend and sit there while you have a chat with them" [victim and perpetrators] (police officer m)

These conflicting approaches illustrate the inherent problems associated with partnership working, with police and CSC pursuing different agendas that appear far from victim centred. As Thompson suggests, the problem with information sharing is that each agency has its own piece of "jigsaw" along with its own organisational constraints (2016: 113). Therefore, what is seen as relevant or "within the remit" of one organisation is not seen from the same perspective in another statutory body.

Moreover, if safeguarding is seemingly "everyone's responsibility" (Munro 2011), no one has overall ownership of the problem. This is evident in the case of Peter Connelly, when the General Practitioner Doctor (GP) had concerns about the child prior to his death but assumed that "others would be in a better position to take action" (Haringey LSCB 2009 as cited in Thompson 2016: 32). US research addresses this by suggesting that the "partnership" approach is problematic because it reduces individual responsibility and ownership of certain agencies, particularly if the roles and responsibilities are unclear (Bickman et al. 1997 as cited in Broadhurst et al. 2010). It is suggested that roles and responsibilities need to be more clearly defined, but with *one* agency having clear overall ownership of child safeguarding. Current findings indicate that in cases of heightened vulnerability, once children are taken into police protection (and particularly when victims are discredited or "retract"), police officers abdicate responsibility by taking a "back seat" function in safeguarding. Crucially, over half the interviewees expect CSC to take the lead in safeguarding[21] (8/15):

> Although a big part of our job, it's *all* (emphasis added) social services job. That's what they do." [After the PPP]..//.. it's then over to social services to decide what happens to that child ..//..whether they go back home or not. It's their decision (police officer c)

> If you've got a 15-year-old being abused by parents because obviously it comes in child protection definition, it's very much children's services led—it's very much they will take the lead, we'll take the lead with the investigation but to safeguard that child, it's children's services (police officer j)

Conversely, it is argued here that the police should take primacy in these cases, as they have the skills to minimise the risks to victims (Roberts et al. 2014: 135). Child protection research supports this by suggesting that when police *fail* to take the lead, the perpetrator is more likely to destroy evidence or pressure the child to redact the testimony (Cross et al. 2005). Research has shown that police involvement in child protection matters positively strengthens the interventions of social workers compared to cases in which there is no police involvement (ibid.). The development of multi-agency safeguarding hubs (MASH) has greatly improved information sharing, joint decision-making and better partnership working (Thompson 2016) and this hub may be an opportunity to develop more effective joint working arrangements between police and CSC.

However, some academics suggest that the issue is not about information *sharing* per se, but about the way information is interpreted and then managed by individual professional bodies. Taylor and White argue that individuals tend to selectively prioritise some information over other data when making decisions, which allows professionals to establish a degree of certainty (Taylor and White 2006). It is argued that in order to reduce service demand (Lipsky 2010 [1980]), professionals (including police officers) tend to seek information that supports their own *preferred* hypothesis rather than searching for disconfirming evidence, which is termed confirmation bias (Wolf et al. 1985 as cited in Taylor and White 2006; Munro 1999; Broadhurst et al. 2010). For instance, once CSC glean positive impressions of a caregiver, contrary evidence is ignored or rationalised by social workers so that this does not undermine the originally held view (Reder et al. 1993). This is particularly evident in Chap. 5 when exploring police officers carefully crafted write-ups. This fixed perspective is evident in Munro's review of 45 child abuse (deaths) inquiry reports (1973 to 1994) where social workers were slow to revise their judgement, even on receipt of new information provided by other practitioners (1999). Taylor and White conclude that when making decisions, professionals need to stay in uncertainty for longer in order to avoid making quick judgements and wrongly interpreting situations (2006). However, the contention is that accurately interpreting victim's needs can only be realised if police and social workers focus on the best interests of victims rather than on the internal workload demands of their organisation.

A Relationship Between "No Prosecution" Decisions and Child Reconciliation

Police extracts (and incident data to a lesser extent) illustrate a tacit relationship between the "no prosecution" decisions of police officers and child reconciliation decisions by CSC. For example, in the case of the child who was assaulted, falsely imprisoned and had her hair cut off by female relatives (Chap. 6), police immediately placed both her and her sister (the witness to the offence) in police protection and an EPO was instigated (police officer m). Within several weeks, the other sibling was returned home by CSC. First, no multi-agency meeting was convened to decide the strategy. Second, no one considered the inordinate pressure this placed on the child witness to retract her statement in support of the perpetrating mother and grandmother, which is ultimately what happened. The victim remained in care, was ostracised from the family and went on to commit offences of shoplifting as well as being a victim of child sexual exploitation.

Data findings also indicate that effective safeguarding by CSC heavily relies on evidence to support police prosecutions in the form of physical injuries:

> [Social worker] was quite defensive and said she was 100% [sure] that (victim) was not in any danger at home. She reiterated that (victim) had no injuries. I pointed out [police officer] that injuries are not a prerequisite for a criminal assault to have taken place (case 32)

The primacy of victims "needing" physical injuries reflects the practical difficulties police practitioners have in prosecuting cases of coercive control. As highlighted by Stark (2012) and Wiener (2017), police officers respond to abuse in a very pragmatic way within a "violent incident model" with physical injuries hierarchically graded against specific legislation (GBH, ABH, common assault). This approach tends to trivialise harassment and psychological abuse as "low level" with events evaluated (and recorded in DASH[22]) in isolation (Wiener 2017), rather than recognise activity within the context of an ongoing pattern of behaviour. Whether CSC safeguard children appears to paradoxically hinge on whether there is a police prosecution, with an overreliance on injuries, a complaint or other evidence. This was certainly the perspective of some officers[23] who explored victims being reconciled back to the abuse when there was no police prosecution:

> Social services I think rely on a prosecution or bail conditions sometimes (police officer g)
>
> Despite a 13-year-old Pakistani girl being pulled downstairs by her hair by the uncle and threatened with a knife, children's social care argued they had "no grounding to keep her out of the house" or implement an EPO, and so the victim was returned to the risk (case 43)
>
> They [CSC] sometimes rely on the prosecution, so for an honour-based violence/FM whichever—I think that sort of takes it further down the line that they'd still expect a prosecution for them to have the safeguarding (police officer g)
>
> The social worker stated that if there were 'no offences' then they would be advising the female to return to (the location of the threat) (case 29)
>
> He has to go back—without a complaint the police investigation ends and the child is then returned back to parents (police officer m)

The apparent overreliance on police prosecutions, witness testimony and evidence of physical injuries as some type of threshold and basis upon which CSC effectively safeguard children is evident in prior child protection studies (Humphreys 2006; Broadhurst et al. 2010). Indeed, Parton highlights that since the 1990s, a shift to legal expertise has taken pre-eminence. He suggests that although medical evidence is important, it should not substitute the professional judgements of social workers (Parton 1991; Munro 2011). Such prioritisation of evidence over child safeguarding conflicts with the basic tenets of the social care profession.

Concluding Remarks

The incident sample highlights that 22% (22/100) of all HBA victims are children under 18. Although quantitative data reveal the key risk group are young adults (18–22 years), qualitative findings identify that child victims are exposed to prolonged and high risks. Given that they are vulnerable, child victims should receive an enhanced level of service. Yet, largely due to interventions by CSC, 73% (16/22) of children were retained or returned back to the risk predicaments within 72 hours of the complaint. In a further 9% of cases, it was unclear whether children were safe. The two main concepts impacting the reconciliation decision were children being discredited as blameworthy or telling lies (see Chap. 3) and to a lesser extent being depicted as reluctant to prosecute (see Chap. 4). Such qualitative data evokes a sad indictment of local authority safeguarding, particularly given that social work is "institutionally constructed to protect children" (Radford et al. 2006: 177) and improve outcomes in their lives (The British Association of Social Workers 2016).

Professionals "mediating" with parents is intended to keep families together: whether that is through the use of working agreements to "work with" the family; section 20 arrangements; accommodating the wishes and feelings of the victim or discrediting the victim in support of the perpetrators' perspectives. Although mediation and reconciliation are distinct concepts, the extracts show that they led to the same outcome, which was to decriminalise and informally resolve discord between victims and perpetrating relatives and avoid [predominantly] children entering the social care system. The impact of this is reflected across the findings. The high-risk children in these findings were only permanently removed into care after suffering several years of abuse. Such findings reiterate a HMIC report which concludes that, through their interventions, authorities took the wrong course of action and inadvertently increased the threat of harm to victims (HMIC 2015: 14). Working agreements set by professionals appear to legitimate the controls already established by perpetrators, which unintentionally provides state sanction for continued abuse and gives mixed messages to victims. Given the prevalent use of mediation which is evident in the findings, particularly by CSC, the position as to whether such practices should continue or desist requires clarification in NPCC strategy and associated to child protection guidance.

These outcomes challenge the proposition that children are sent home by police and social workers because it is in their best interests. The genuine wishes of children to reconcile with relatives was difficult to confirm in some cases; these wishes also contradict the overarching findings which illustrate that children's views were overridden in 59% of cases, as they feared death or injury should they return home. Those children with longstanding social service involvement were particularly retained at risk. The wishes of the child, however genuine, should not be the foundation for decriminalising incidents, expediting investigations and "ending" safeguarding provision. One would not apply this strategy when children allege sexual abuse by a parent or carer.

Cumulative factors serve to disadvantage child victims and these include the cost and workload associated with safeguarding, the subjective judgements of some officials and the silo working of professionals in different agencies. Cost and workload appear integral to the decision-making process. Such practices invoked predominantly by children's social care, but on occasion by police officers, not only close cases and reduce workload for practitioners but divert children away from the care system. Screening out cases prematurely before an investigation is underway underestimates the volume of victims and the ongoing risks they face. Equally, when investigations are pursued, the absence of physical injuries and police prosecutions supports the CSC rationale for case closure—when arguably victims still require safeguarding provision. The demand for service is stifled, reflecting back on the crime-recording concerns raised in Chap. 4. The cost and resource implications attached to assessing *multiple* siblings mean that government policy guidelines are seldom followed. It is clear that public bodies do not have the resources to place all children that are at risk in long-term foster- or child care placements. They therefore only manage those in absolute dire need. In the process of joint working, professionals withhold information, mistrust and sometimes disregard the views that conflict with their own organisational priorities, remits and resource constraints. This results in incoherent rather than fully rationalised strategies and is an aggravating feature that exacerbates the risks to victims of crime.

Reminiscent of Lipsky's work on bureaucratic organisations, "referring" cases to other agencies is a mechanism by which professionals can and do reduce workload demand (Lipsky 2010 [1980]; Broadhurst et al. 2010; Stanley et al. 2011; Thompson 2016). Instead of focusing on a quality of service to child victims, the act of referral constitutes a proverbial box "ticked" and a "case closed" resolution for some officials. This is the resounding concern raised by Munro's child protection review (2011). Essentially, the practice of making referrals facilitates "load shedding" (Varano et al. 2009: 554) by public bodies.

When accepting the seemingly illogical narratives of some perpetrating family members, there is an assumption, rather than clear evidence, that professionals may "misread cases" (Thompson 2016: 185). Rather than suggest professionals prioritise the rights of perpetrating family members over victims, the contention is that some children are retained with perpetrators (or inappropriate relatives) because CSC's selective preferences appear to be driven by *internal* imperatives (such as the shortage of foster placements) (Taylor and White 2006) with the need to reduce volume in an overburdened system. Rather than focusing on the internal resources problems of public bodies, decision-making should be based on a robust assessment (Broadhurst et al. 2010) of children's needs, and whether returning them home really is in their best interests (Farmer et al. 2011; Wade et al. 2011).

Acknowledgements Sincere thanks go to Emeritus Professor Terry Thomas for providing helpful insights on an earlier draft of this chapter.

Notes

1. Predominantly local authority CSC social workers and police officers, and to a lesser extent, housing officers, teachers and healthcare workers.
2. A PPP is a power exercisable by a police officer under section 46 of the Children Act 1989 to remove a child to a place of safety for a period of 72 hours if the child is considered to be at risk of significant harm.
3. Under a section 20 Children Act 1989 arrangement those with parental responsibility voluntarily consent for their child to be accommodated elsewhere for a short period.

4. The 1988 inquiry remit by Butler-Sloss was not set up to establish whether the 121 children had in fact been abused, but to examine how the cases were managed (Channel 4 1997; Richardson and Bacon 2018). However, independent experts have since concluded that at least 70% (93/121) of the original diagnoses were correct (Channel 4 1997).
5. A civil protection order to protect people at risk of being forced into a marriage is made under the Forced Marriage (Civil protection) Act 2007. Breach of a FMPO is now a criminal offence under s120 of the Anti-Social Behaviour, Crime and Policing Act 2014.
6. Exceptions are cases 36 and 74.
7. Cases 13, 18, 20, 26, 32, 43, 44, 45, 50, 74, 93, 94 and 96.
8. Cases 10, 18, 20, 22, 26, 32, 39, 43, 50, 57, 64, 84, 94 and case 44, in which an EPO was instigated by officers on attendance.
9. A court will only make the order if they are satisfied there is reasonable cause to believe that the child is likely to suffer significant harm if the child is not removed to accommodation provided by the local authority, or the child does not remain in the place where he is currently being accommodated, for example, in hospital (Children Act 1989 s.44).
10. Cases 20, 22, 26, 81, 96 and 74.
11. Cases 10, 18, 26, 32, 39, 43, 44, 50, 64, 74, 93, 94 and 96.
12. Evident in only one adult case (case 47).
13. A silo is a system, process or department that operates in isolation from others (English Oxford Living Dictionaries 2019). Silos occur because of how organisations are structured (Beal n.d.).
14. One could argue that DASH has precipitated a similar approach.
15. Police interviews took place in 2016.
16. Cases 69, 70, 74, 43, police officers o, k, h and m.
17. A Domestic Violence Protection Notice (Crime and Security Act 2010) requires the authority of a superintendent. These are useful to apply if the perpetrator is free to return to an address and could put the victim at further risk of harm. This notice, followed by an order made by the magistrate's court (DVPO), provides the victim with time (14–28 days) to make decisions to consider victim safety such as a restraining order or non-molestation order.
18. This is a quick meeting conducted between agencies, either over the phone or face to face, with little time to schedule a meeting due to the urgency.

19. Before or at the time the order was served by a bailiff, a safety plan and/or PPP should have been considered. The police were only informed when the child had already suffered abuse.
20. Police officers g, j, e, i and p.
21. Police officers b, c, d, e, h, j, k, p.
22. Domestic Abuse, Stalking and Harassment and Honour Based Violence (DASH) Risk Identification and Assessment and Management Model (2009).
23. Police officers c, g, m; cases 32, 41, 43, 44, 29, 93, 94, 96.

References

Action for Children. (2017). *Revolving Door part 1: Are vulnerable children being overlooked?* [Online]. Retrieved November 22, 2018, from https://www.actionforchildren.org.uk.

Beal, V. (n.d.). *Information Silo*. [Online]. Retrieved January 15, 2019, from www.webopedia.com.

Brandon, M., Belderson, P., Warren, C., Howe, D., Gardner, R., Dodsworth, J., & Black, J. (2008). *Analysing child deaths and serious injury through abuse and neglect: What can we learn? A biennial analysis of serious case reviews 2003–2005*. London: University of East Anglia, Department for Education and Skills (DCSF).

Breckenridge, J., & Ralfs, C. (2006). Point of contact for frontline workers responding to children living with domestic violence. In C. Humphries & N. Stanley (Eds.), *Domestic violence and child protection: Directions for good practice* (pp. 110–123). London: Jessica Kingsley.

Broadhurst, K., White, S., Fish, S., Munro, E., Fletcher, K., & Lincoln, H. (2010). *Ten pitfalls and how to avoid them: What research tells us* (pp. 1–41). [Online]. Retrieved January 16, 2017, from www.nspcc.org.uk.

Cameron, A., Lart, R., Bostock, L., & Coomber, C. (2012). Factors that promote and hinder joint and integrated working between health and social care services. *Social Care Institute for Excellence*. Research Briefing 41 (pp. 1–24). [Online]. Retrieved January 21, 2019, from www.scie.org.uk.

Channel 4. (1997). *The Death of Childhood-Cleveland: Unspeakable Truths*. Interesting Film Company for Channel 4, 27 May, 21.00–22.00, Channel 4. [Online]. Retrieved January 5, 2019, from https://spotlightonabuse.wordpress.com.

Children Act 1989 (c.41) [Online]. Retrieved September 1, 2016, from http://www.legislation.gov.uk.

Children Act 2004 (c.31) [Online]. Retrieved September 16, 2016, from http://www.legislation.gov.uk.

Clapton, G., Cree, V., & Smith, M. (2013). Moral panics, claims-making and child protection in the UK. *British Journal of Social Work, 43*(4), 803–812.

Cleveland Report. (1988). By Butler Sloss, E. *Report of the Inquiry into Child Abuse in Cleveland, 1987.* Presented to Parliament by the Secretary of State for Social Services by command of Her Majesty, July 1988. Cm. (Series) 412. London: HMSO.

College of Policing. (n.d.). [Online]. Retrieved January 20, 2019, from https://www.college.police.uk.

Colwell Report. (1974). *Report of the Committee of inquiry into the case and supervision provided in relation to Maria Colwell.* London: HMSO.

Cromarty, H., Bellis, A., & Harker, R. (2018). *Children's social care in England.* House of Commons Library. [Online]. Retrieved January 16, 2019, from https://researchbriefings.parliament.uk.

Cross, T. P., Finkelhor, D., & Ormrod, R. (2005). Police involvement in child protective services investigations: Literature review and secondary data analysis. *Child Maltreatment, 10*(3), 224–244.

Department for Education. (2013). *Data pack: Improving permanence for looked after children.* London: TSO.

Department for Education. (2017). *Characteristics of children in need: 2016 to 2017. Children referred to and assessed by children's social services for the year ending 31 March 2017.* SFR 61/2017, 2 November 2017 [Online]. Retrieved November 22, 2018, from https://www.gov.uk/government.

Department of Health. (1995). *Child protection: Messages from research* (pp. 1–120). London: HMSO.

English Oxford Living Dictionaries. (2016). [Online]. Retrieved November 11, 2016, from https://en.oxforddictionaries.com/definition/mediation.

English Oxford Living Dictionaries. (2019). [Online]. Retrieved January 15, 2019, from https://en.oxforddictionaries.com/definition/silo.

Farmer, E., & Lutman, E. (2012). *Effective working with neglected children and their families: Linking interventions to long-term outcomes.* London: Jessica Kingsley.

Farmer, E., Sturgess, W., O'Neill, T., & Wijedasa, D. (2011). *Achieving successful returns from care: What makes reunification work?* London: BAAF.

Featherstone, B., Gupta, A., Morris, K., & White, S. (2018). *Protecting children: A social model.* Bristol: Policy Press.

Forrester, D., McCambridge, J., Waissbein, C., & Rollnick, S. (2008). How do child and family social workers talk to parents about child welfare concerns? *Child Abuse Review, 17*(1), 23–35.

Garrity, R. (1998). *Mediation and domestic violence: What domestic violence looks like*. [Online]. Retrieved May 5, 2016, from http://www.biscmi.org.

Grace, S. (1995). *Policing domestic violence in the 1990s*. Home Office Research Study No. 139. London: HMSO.

Hanmer, J. (2013 [1989]). Women and policing in Britain. In J. Hanmer, J. Radford, & E. Stanko (Eds.), *Women, policing, and male violence: International perspectives* (pp. 90–124). London: Routledge.

Harne, L., & Radford, J. (2008). *Tackling domestic violence: Theories, policies and practice*. Maidenhead: McGraw-Hill; Open University Press.

HBA and FM Policy and Procedure. (2013). [This anonymised police force].

Her Majesty's Inspectorate of Constabulary (HMIC). (2015). *The depths of dishonour: Hidden voices and shameful crimes. An inspection of the police response to honour-based violence, forced marriage and female genital mutilation*. London: TSO.

HM Government. (2018). *Working together to safeguard children: A guide to inter-agency working to safeguard and promote the welfare of children*. London: TSO.

Holmes, L. (2014). *Supporting children and families returning home from care: Counting the costs*. Loughborough University, Centre for Child and Family Research.

Hughes, D. (2016, February 24). *What do we mean by working in silos?* [Online]. Retrieved January 15, 2019, from https://www.linkedin.com/pulse.

Humphreys, C. (2006). Relevant evidence for practice. In C. Humphreys & N. Stanley (Eds.), *Domestic violence and child protection: Directions for good practice* (pp. 19–35). London: Jessica Kingsley.

Humphreys, C., & Stanley, N. (2006). *Domestic violence and child protection: Directions for good practice*. London: Jessica Kingsley.

Iranian and Kurdish Women's Rights Organisation (IKWRO). (2014). *Postcode lottery: Police recording of reported 'honour' based violence*.

International Federation of Social Workers. (2002). *IFSW manual: Social work and the rights of the child: A professional training manual on the un convention*. Münsingen, Switzerland.

Investopedia. (2018, March 21). *Silo mentality* [Online]. Retrieved January 15, 2019, from https://www.investopedia.com/terms/s/silo-mentality.asp.

Jones, R. (2014). *The story of Baby P: Setting the record straight*. Bristol: Policy Press.

Kitzinger, J. (2000). Media templates: Patterns of association and the (re)construction of meaning over time. *Media Culture and Society, 22*(1), 61–84.
Laming, L. (2003). *The Victoria Climbie inquiry: Report of an inquiry by Lord Laming* (pp. 1–405). London: TSO.
Lipsky, M. (2010 [1980]). *Street-level bureaucracy: Dilemmas of the individual in public services* (Expanded ed.). New York, NY: Russell Sage Foundation.
Littlechild, B. (1998). Does family support ensure the protection of children? Messages from child protection research. *Child Abuse Review, 7*(2), 116–128.
London Borough of Brent. (1985). *A child in trust: The report of the panel of inquiry into the circumstances surrounding the death of Jasmine Beckford.* Wembley, Middlesex: London Borough of Brent.
Mental Capacity Act 2005: Codes of Practice. (2013, July). UK Department for Constitutional Affairs (pp. 1–301) [Online]. Retrieved January 12, 2016, from https://www.gov.uk.
Moore, R., & Hamilton, P. (2016). 'Silo Mentalities' and their impact on service delivery in Prison-community transitions: A case study of resettlement provision at a male open prison. *The Howard Journal, 55*(1–2), 111–130.
Morgan, R. (2006). *About social workers: A children's view report.* Newcastle upon Tyne: Commission for Social Care Inspection.
Munro, E. (1999). Common errors of reasoning in child protection work. *Child Abuse and Neglect, 23*(8), 745–758.
Munro, E. (2011). *The Munro review of child protection: Final report: A child-centred system* (pp. 1–173). London: Department for Education, TSO.
National Police Chiefs' Council (NPCC). (2015). *Honour-based abuse, forced marriage and female genital mutilation: A policing strategy for England, Wales and Northern Ireland-eradicating honour-based abuse, forced marriage and female genital mutilation together.* London: Home Office.
National Police Chiefs' Council (NPCC). (2018). National Policing Vulnerability Coordination Centre (VCC) Briefing. [Online]. Retrieved January 20, 2019, from https://whatworks.college.police.uk/Research.
National Society for the Prevention of Cruelty to Children (NSPCC). (2015). *Achieving positive outcomes for children in relation to return home from care.* [Online]. Retrieved November 3, 2016, from https://www.nspcc.org.uk.
Ofsted. (2010). *The voice of the child: Learning lessons from serious case reviews. A thematic report of Ofsted's evaluation of serious case reviews from 1 April to 30 September 2010.* [Online]. Retrieved October 3, 2016, from http://www.ofsted.gov.uk.

Oliver, C. (2010). *Children's views and experiences of their contact with social workers: A focused review of the evidence* (pp. 1–39). Leeds: Children's Workforce Development Council.

Parton, N. (1991). *Governing the family: Child care, child protection and the state.* Hampshire: Macmillan Press Ltd.

Police and Criminal Evidence Act 1984 (c.60). [Online]. Retrieved October 26, 2018, from www.gov.uk/government.

Purvis, K. (2018, April 2018). Why are more social work assessments leading to no further action? *Community Care*. Retrieved November 22, 2018, from https://www.communitycare.co.uk.

Radford, L., Blacklock, N., & Iwi, K. (2006). Domestic abuse risk assessment and safety planning in child protection—Assessing perpetrators. In C. Humphries & N. Stanley (Eds.), *Domestic violence and child protection: Directions for good practice* (pp. 171–189). London: Jessica Kingsley.

Reder, P., & Duncan, S. (2003). Understanding communication in child protection networks. *Child Abuse Review, 12*, 82–100.

Reder, P., Duncan, S., & Gray, M. (1993). *Beyond blame: Child abuse tragedies revisited.* London: Routledge.

Richardson, S., & Bacon, H. (2018). *Child sexual abuse whose problem? Reflections from Cleveland* (Rev. ed.). Bristol: Policy Press.

Roberts, K., Campbell, G., & Lloyd, G. (2014). *Honor-based violence: Policing and prevention* (Advances in Police Theory and Practice Series). London: CRC Press; Taylor and Francis Group.

Stark, E. (2012). Looking beyond domestic violence: Policing coercive control. *Journal of Police Crisis Negotiations, 12*, 199–217.

Stanley, N., Miller, P., Foster, H., & Thomson, G. (2011). Children's experiences of domestic violence: Developing an integrated response from police and child protection services. *Journal of Interpersonal Violence, 26*(12), 2372–2391.

Stevenson, O. (1976). Some dilemmas in social work education. *Oxford Review of Education, 2*(2), 149–155.

Stevenson, L. (2015, November 10). Social workers given new guidance for section 20 arrangements amid misuse and abuse. *Community care: Children, family justice, fostering and adoption.* [Online]. Retrieved October 5, 2016, from http://www.communitycare.co.uk.

Taylor, C., & White, S. (2006). Knowledge and reasoning in social work: Educating for humane judgement. *British Journal of Social Work, 36*(6), 937–954.

The Blueprint Project. (2005). *Start with the child, stay with the child: A blueprint for a child-centred approach to children and young people in public care* (pp. 1–75). National Children's Bureau.

The British Association of Social Workers. (2016). *What is social work?* [Online]. Retrieved September 1, 2016, from https://www.basw.co.uk.

The United Nations Convention on the Rights of the Child (UNCRC). (1989). (pp. 1–14). [Online]. Retrieved October 3, 2016, from https://downloads.unicef.org.uk.

Thomas, T. (1988, June). The police and social workers: Creativity or conflict? *Practice, 2*(2), 120–129.

Thompson, K. (2016). *Strengthening child protection: Sharing information in multi-agency settings*. Bristol: Policy Press.

Timms, J. E., & Thoburn, J. (2003). *Your shout! A survey of the views of 706 children and young people in public care*. London: NSPCC.

Varano, S., Schafer, J., Cancino, J., & Swatt, M. (2009). Constructing crime: Neighborhood characteristics and police recording behavior. *Journal of Criminal Justice, 37*(6), 553–563.

Wade, J., Biehal, N., Farrelly, N., & Sinclair, I. (2011). *Caring for abused and neglected children: Making the right decisions for reunification or long-term care*. London: Jessica Kingsley.

Ward, H., Skuse, T., & Munro, E. R. (2005, Spring). The best of times, the worst of times. *Adoption & Fostering, 29*(1), 8–17.

Wiener, C. (2017). Seeing what is 'invisible in plain sight': Policing coercive control. *The Howard Journal of Crime and Justice, 00*(0), 1–16.

Youth Justice and Criminal Evidence Act 1999 (c.23). [Online]. Retrieved September 26, 2017, from www.gov.uk/government.

8

Conclusions

This chapter distillates the 12 key discretionary practices of professionals and then moves on to synthesise the central findings across empirical chapters, in particular answering the three objectives of the research. The concluding sections consider the research credibility and limitations of the study, the advantages of analysing police incident data and areas for future research. Finally, recommendations are made for both police and social service practitioners involved in honour-based abuse (HBA) safeguarding and investigations.

HBA Investigations: Discretionary Practices of Professionals, Their Influence and Impact

Discretionary police practices were unearthed by examining the contradictions and/or omissions between the subsequent secondary investigation documents (PPI, DASH, crime reports) and the allegations made to call handlers in the initial incident report, in which the former bore little resemblance to the latter. Furthermore, interviews with specialist officers aided in consolidating the documentary analysis. It is useful at this

R. Aplin, *Policing UK Honour-Based Abuse Crime*,
https://doi.org/10.1007/978-3-030-18430-8_8

juncture to restate the purpose of the study, which was to critically explore discretionary policing practices when investigating honour-based abuse incidents, achieved through three objectives:

Objectives:

1. To examine police decision-making, behaviours and discretionary practices when investigating honour-based abuse incidents
2. To determine the factors that influence and shape those policing decisions and practices
3. To assess the impact of those practices on service provision to victims of crime

Figure 8.1 assists in providing an overarching relationship between discretionary decision-making, factors influencing professional decision-making and the impact of these on victim service provision, which shall be holistically assessed below. Twelve key discretionary practices of some professionals were identified:

1. An "acceptance" of perpetrator narratives
2. A reluctance to define relatives, including females, as criminal
3. The reasonableness of perpetrators, as acting in victims' best interests
4. Victim blaming, that victims are "wayward," "cry wolf" and "use the system"
5. Discrediting victims through the theme of mental health
6. Abrogating workload to other departments, agencies and forces, which sometimes generates incoherent strategies
7. Goal displacement, which deflects the crime away from perpetrators, focusing on bureaucracy and the victim (demonisation, medicalisation and mental health), or sees protective influences as a potential "threat"
8. Diluting the seriousness of the incident through data omission, trivialisation, distortion and alteration (also includes omitting to use interpreters)
9. Using legal rules and procedures (and quasi-legal) as convincing props to justify no further action

10. Poor recording of adult vulnerability and female perpetration.
11. Freewill and choice ascribed to children and vulnerable adults that lack capacity
12. Victims portrayed as reluctant to disclose

Although elements of officer cynicism with their distinctly "jaundiced view of the world" (Waddington 1999: 101) are evident, the most salient trait reverberating across empirical findings is the pragmatism of professionals in their preoccupation with personal "internal" workload reduction, often at the expense of the "external" needs of the victim. Such findings are reminiscent of Brown's research (1981). It is suggested that "police officers recognise that to make something into a crime requires work" (Sumner 1994: 218). The contention is that the key driver *influencing* discretionary practices involves circumventing the formal paradigm of the crime recording process, thereby reducing or eliminating workload. This is because almost all the discretionary practices identified are instrumental in deconstructing the crime process and informally resolving incidents as "no-crime." There is only deflection and goal displacement that re-channels workload to other agencies or departments, albeit the outcome still results in the easing of workload and enquiries being filed. Such practices result in premature case closure, no further action by the police and victims being reunified with perpetrating relatives, predominantly by children's social care.

Deconstructing "Crime" and Informally Resolving Incidents

Findings dispel the contention that there has been a broad decline in "cuffing" practices by police officers (Coleman and Moynihan 1996: 34). Inappropriately "writing off" incidents as "no-crime" when offences are apparent is an enduring and central police discretionary practice. Although it is acknowledged that not all incidents necessitate a crime report, the findings identify poor HBA incident to crime conversion rates, amounting to 90% of filed incidents over a three-year period (2011–2013) that were not further investigated by the police. This supports the view that crime statistics are not firm evidence of what they report (Atkinson and Coffey 2011) but are products of police decision-making (Black 1980), reflecting the tip of a large iceberg. Such findings evoke the work of Black (1980), Young (1991), and Coleman and Moynihan (1996) and particularly identify with key home office reports (HMIC 1999, 2014a, b; House of Commons PASC report 2014). Of the 30 incidents in the sample that breached crime recording rules, 77% constituted crimes of violence. This finding contradicts previous research suggesting that cuffing is limited to low-level and less serious crimes (Roberts et al. 2014; HMIC 2014a). It is concluded that HBA as a crime type appears very much the 'poor relation' when compared with traditional domestic abuse. The incident to crime conversion rate for HBA in this study averaged 11% compared to the national average for traditional domestic abuse, which currently stands at 50% (ONS 2018: 2).

The importance of recording crimes should not be underestimated, as extant research confirms that victims get a "better service" once a crime is recorded (HMIC 2014a: 56). Failing to crime an incident when it fits the criteria has adverse ramifications for victims and justice itself. At a basic level, some officers breach National Crime Recording Standards (NCRS). At a strategic level, the grey figure of filing incidents as "no further action" serves to mask the true extent of HBA. Crucially, if it is not crimed, it has not happened. Therefore, the government will not allocate funds to manage a crime that "on paper" does not technically exist. Neither is there any deterrent for perpetrators who are rarely arrested and continue to operate under the gaze of law enforcement. This results in numerous calls for service that were not dealt by officers effectively the first time. Victims remain under-protected and at risk. Discretionary and fundamentally dysfunctional police practices adversely impact victim confidence, creating a vicious circle in which there is less victim reporting, which is reflected in the longitudinal data on crime recording (Chart 4.1).

Findings identify two central mechanisms facilitating crime deconstruction. The first is particularly evident in Chap. 4, and involves officers breaching NSIR compliance by providing no rationale in the incident write-up to justify "no-crime" decisions. The second mechanism is accomplished through the creative carving of a linguistic narrative in the summary write-up, whereby some officers convey biased, selective and inaccurate information to persuade supervisors of the appropriateness of a decision. This is reminiscent of Manning's "front work" (1978a), which is explored in Chap. 5. Such creative writing stratagems justify "no-crime" decisions and are effective in reconstructing an alternative documentary version of reality—that which is "filtered through paperwork" (Hobbs 1989: 175). Many such presentations conflict sharply with the initial victim reports but are effective in justifying case closure, no-crime report and no further police action (NFA).

Officers dismantle the crime process through distortion, alteration and the trivialisation of language, along with significant levels of data omission. Such findings reinforce research conducted by Manning (1977), Brown (1981), Holdaway (1983) and Shearing and Ericson (1991). In omitting data, officers present artificially constructed compressed summaries in a closed answer format, which are effective in cauterising all further lines of enquiry. An analysis of HBA DASH risk assessments highlights data omission as a prevalent discretionary practice, with 71% of DASH reports containing incomplete or missing data. Rather than DASH being used to measure risk, the overriding impetus for some officers appears to be the additional workload created by the DASH process itself. Akin to other bureaucratic behaviours evident in the findings, DASH is seen as an "end" in itself (Knott and Miller 1987: 110), a burdensome imposition that detracts from "real" police work, with some not seeing the point of expending effort if little is done with the information. The alleged non-cooperation of cagey reluctant victims is also relied on to rationalise *why* such data might be missing.

Officer practices include downplaying or trivialising cases by presenting victims as "not concerned," "fazed" or "bothered" about returning to the risk situation. Trivialisation is evident in the practice of resolving incidents as a "family dispute(s)" or "longstanding family feud(s)." Such write-offs are highly reminiscent of "classic" domestic abuse incidents, often categorised as a "civil dispute" (Edwards 1986; Hanmer 2013 [1989]; Grace 1995; Lynn and Lea 2012). Such cases are erroneously justified as constituting a private matter between individuals and therefore outside the remit of the criminal law. The impact of these narrative practices dilutes the seriousness of the HBA allegation (albeit only on paper) and causes incidents to be filed as no further action rather than crimed and investigated. Crucially, there is no signposting to support services, such as Women's Aid, children's social care and IDAA, and no MARAC due to the case not being deemed as "high risk." Rather than victims being unable to communicate their abuse and not being listened to, victims are portrayed as reticent.

Patterns in documentary analysis expose two distinctly different realities, a dichotomy between what victims report and the subsequent presentational write-offs advanced by some officers. Such a disparity in narratives is ordinarily difficult for the public to excavate. Compressed summary "write-offs" appear to be manufactured presentations of a reality that officers advance, rather than a mirrored reflection of victim testimony. It is argued that due to the nature of police work, supervisors are not routinely aware of the interactional realities of officers' daily encounters, as they are presented with a persuasive narrative that is often difficult to counteract in the physical absence of victims. Findings indicate that some unscrupulous officers "put (ting) words in people's mouths" (Holdaway 1983: 112). Yet moreover, the findings also highlight that officers are particularly adept at *removing* or radically *altering* those words. The impact of such practices is that victim testimony becomes diluted and, in some cases, entirely drowned out by a dominant officer narrative that shapes and dictates the discourse.

The trading of labels, apparent in Chaps. 3 and 7, heavily contributes to the crime deconstruction process. Problematically, findings show that professionals often overlook the voice of the victim, particularly children and disabled victims, decriminalising relatives by portraying them as trusted appropriate adults rather than perpetrators. Accepting perpetrator narratives often coincides with the theme of victim blaming and lack of police action, which is the second-highest case outcome for adults (22%) in the incident data. Professionals too readily, and arguably illogically, align to the views of perpetrators when making decisions at scenes. Doing so decriminalises and neutralises the actions of perpetrating relatives as being in the best interests of victims. Perpetrators amplify and sometimes entirely fabricate the poor mental health of victims during interactions with professionals. Akin to behaviours towards child victims, perpetrators package control as a necessity, that victims need protecting from themselves and lack the capacity to make coherent decisions. Yet in all cases there was no evidence of any diagnosed condition. Equally, there is evidence of some professionals latching onto and *cultivating* the mental illness labels advanced by perpetrators, using victim impairments as props by which to discredit and undermine victim testimony, suggesting victims were delusional, suffering breakdowns or struggling to recall information due to the effects of medication. Ironically, perceived impairments should result in an enhanced service, and yet only one case reflected the pro-active protection of a mentally ill victim. Perpetrators only had to apply some stereotypical labels when police attended (e.g. boyfriends were "criminal" "drug dealers," "extremists" or "terrorists") in order to successfully divert police attention away from perpetrators and towards perceiving protective influences (such as boyfriends) as a "threat" to victims. Such practices were often evident in traditional child abuse settings (Farmer 2006). The impact on victims is the trading of labels, with victims being portrayed as perpetrators and perpetrators delineated as victims. Moreover, the outcome was that enquiries were expedited and "no-crimed" by some officers.

When making decisions, professionals appear influenced by gut subjective judgements rather than the law, which is consistent with police culture(s) research. Officers quickly move to a victim-blaming discourse, particularly if they are unable to rationalise the ambivalent or petulant behaviours of victims coupled with a situation that appears to be incongruent. In 69% (9/13) of child cases, professionals exhibited victim-blaming attitudes. Child victims were not listened to and not believed. The belief that officers can distinguish between "genuine" and "non-genuine" victims appears overstated, as officers misread victims and situations, and this leads to flawed decisions based on faulty logic. The level of victim blaming and adverse outcomes across the two data sets highlights the difficulty police officers and other professionals have in determining *who* the perpetrator is. The effect of this grossly miscalculates risks to victims and impacts victim safeguarding.

The implication of accepting perpetrator narratives and discrediting the testimony of victims is that in 73% (16/22) of cases HBA child victims were returned to (often within 72 hours of the complaint) or retained in the risk predicament. Crucially, in 59% (13/22) of those cases, police officers had already taken child victims into police protection and categorised them as at risk of suffering significant harm (Children's Act 1989 s.46). Moreover, the findings also indicate that the misjudgements of professionals in one agency tend to taint the attitudes and responses of other professionals (police and CSC), as these become set reliable "scripts" for dictating future action/inaction. This situation was particularly apparent in the qualitative data concerning child reconciliation. Professionals have the power to determine victim and perpetrator status, and those labels, however undeserving, are durable and can adversely impact future policing incidents. A further indication that professionals are heavily influenced by other agency assessments is evident when officers do not submit crime reports. The absence of a crime report (often associated with a filed investigation) correlates with a lack of preventative or safeguarding measures for vulnerable victims in the social services sphere. CSC trivialised and decriminalised reports of abuse particularly when children lacked physical injuries. Counterintuitively, social services rely on crime reports, evidence of injuries and prosecutions in order for victims to receive an appropriate level of safeguarding.

Continuing with the theme of child protection, the cost of care is identified by police officers as a key and influential driver for CSC, which leads to premature reconciliation of child victims with perpetrating family members. Premature child reconciliation, explored in Chap. 7, is achieved through victim blaming, child reluctance, misjudgements about victims and an unwillingness to define relatives, including mothers, as perpetrators. Keeping victims out of the care system generates a misuse of section 20 voluntary arrangements and the application of working agreements, in which social workers expect victims to subscribe to the stifling controls determined by parents (such as removal of mobile phones, going late to school). The conciliatory approach of social workers not only provides mixed messages to victims but promotes the perception that public bodies collude with perpetrating family members. Although 60% of specialist officers deem mediation to be "dangerous," CSC rely on this practice to reconcile children back home. Crucially, this fosters a lack of trust and confidence in professionals by HBA victims, particularly children, whose fears about returning home are largely overridden by CSC. These findings support many child protection research studies which highlight how children were retained in risk predicaments, and having been prematurely "screened out" from professional caseloads (Littlechild 1998), they were returned home from local authority care (NSPCC 2015), with parents given far too many chances to "do the right thing" (Farmer and Lutman 2012). The implications of such practices are premature case closure, the reduction of workload and the diversion of children out of the care system. Like the discretionary practices of police officers, managing and reducing the internal workload of social services appears to dominate the decision-making process of professionals to the detriment of victim safeguarding and effective crime investigation.

Decision-making by some frontline officers highlights a reluctance to label and implicate women as perpetrators. This is evident in 12% of cases where victims implicate mothers as perpetrators on the incident log, yet officers only formally logged male relatives as perpetrators on police systems. This reluctance to implicate is borne out in that a third of HBA specialists had never investigated a female perpetrator of HBA. It is suggested that officers adhere to traditional gender role expectations of women as victims, nurturing and non-criminal and males as perpetrators. This contention is supported in UK prosecution rates, which appear low for females (35/225) (15.6%) when compared with male perpetrators (190/225) (84.4%) (CPS 2015: 73). Findings highlight that specialists fluctuate uncertainly in their decision-making, between perceiving mothers as either secondary victims or as culpable "villains" who fail to protect their children. Either view adopted is contingent on the situation and crucially on how victims perceive and portray their mothers to attendant officers. Where mothers are portrayed in a sympathetic light, as equally oppressed, this influences officers and creates a reluctance in labelling mothers as perpetrators. However, if we consider poor rates of recording female perpetration against all the police discretionary practices in these findings, it is argued that this does not necessarily mean officers do not *recognise* abuse by women. It is proffered that some officers utilise the "wishes," misplaced trust and naivety of victims in order to justify both the non-recording of crimes and the selective non-enforcement that follows. As these findings already highlight, professionals advancing the view that they act in accordance with a victim's wishes does not necessarily mean that they act in a victim's best interests. The implications of these discretionary practices are not only the under-recording of female perpetration, but of professionals sanctioning the return or retention of young women and children at home and at risk, based on the presupposition that mothers will nurture and protect their children.

A further discretionary practice contributing to crime deconstruction and case closure is the freewill argument, whereby professionals deny victim vulnerability by advocating that vulnerable adults and children (under 18 years) consent to marriages abroad of their own wishes and freewill. First, this proposition is legally flawed as vulnerable victims do not have the capacity to consent. Second, suggesting that victims' consent places the onus for a course of action squarely on those victims, which negates any requirement for police action, reduces police accountability and functions as a self-protecting "back-covering" veneer should anything subsequently happen to the victim. Third, for professionals to admit and record victim vulnerability makes any subsequent inaction by the authorities untenable, which is precisely why some professionals deny and fail to record victim vulnerability. The outcome of such a practice is of disabled HBA victims, with the awareness of agencies in some cases, being sent abroad to be married; some had medication removed or were left in the "care" of perpetrators. The strategic implications of these practices are that shortfalls in recording victim vulnerability fail to trigger policies that are designed to meet vulnerable people's needs. Without professionals identifying vulnerability, victims of crime cannot be sign-posted to support agencies nor given the special measures that they are entitled to, resulting in unmet needs and under-protection by the state. Understandably, some of these crimes are difficult to prosecute due to the difficulties in obtaining evidence via witness testimony. Furthermore, this situation is further exacerbated, as professionals paradoxically have to seek consent from perpetrating family members to have vulnerable people examined or formally interviewed when a crime allegation is made. It is argued that the complexity of these cases inclines some professionals to adopt dysfunctional avoidance practices that informally resolve situations and reduces professional workload, rather than boldly tackling crime and safeguarding considerations. There appears to be a risky "wait and see" mentality adopted in child and vulnerable adult cases, particularly from social services, which justifies inaction on the basis of professionals waiting for full victim "disclosures" in order to collate more "evidence" from vulnerable victims that do not have the capacity for self-help. This prioritises prosecution over safeguarding and results in agencies "treading water" seemingly transfixed in inertia, waiting for other agencies to respond.

The overlapping discretionary practices of goal displacement and deflection of workload were apparent in the findings. Goal displacement (Lipsky 2010 [1980]) involves professionals refocusing and deflecting the response away from the HBA crime itself and towards managing the victim and their alleged or real impairments or questioning individuals attempting to protect victims. Instead of investigating the abuse or safeguarding, professionals were busy sending letters; organising meetings; applying for FMPOs but failing to implement them properly; managing a teenager's perceived problematic behaviour in the form of "working agreements"; investigating the alleged "criminality" of the boyfriend and/or dealing with ancillary health issues or medicalising victims. In this way, cases are decriminalised, as the HBA allegation becomes superseded and replaced with short-term goals that are often ineffectual yet more manageable for professionals to achieve. Professionals did not merely "engage(ing) in ritualistic behaviours" (Manning 1978b: 21); they appeared to *rely* on such "inefficient bureaucratic routines" (Knott and Miller 1987: 167) as a means of justifying inaction. These short-term "sticking plaster" responses render a bureaucratic "box ticked" but are ineffectual in minimising the risks to victims.

A further "avoidance strategy" (Knott and Miller 1987: 110) is of professionals retreating behind the process of rules and regulations (including quasi-legal rules) as a means of justifying no further action. The deflection of workload to other agencies or departments is particularly evident in Chaps. 5 and 7, with agencies (police, social services, CAAMHS and local authority housing) suggesting cases were inappropriate, not in their remit or outside their jurisdiction. Professionals rely on formal bureaucratic rules to justify abrogating workload to other public bodies, the effect of which increases risks to victims. This is evident in the section exploring incoherent strategies (Chap. 7). Such a compliance culture of checklists and targets provides "cover for wary professionals" but does not necessarily mean victims are better protected (Campbell 2013). There was sometimes a requirement to "back-cover" by suggesting something needed to be done, but by someone else. For example, in Chap. 5, there was evidence of officers "guesstimating" risks, despite not even completing a DASH risk assessment. Officers inflating DASH risks to "high" necessitated specialist units having to deal with the workload. A further iterative theme, identified in Chap. 4, was of officers using quasi-legal rules to justify "no-criming" threats to kill offences, even though the basis for these decisions (concerning immediacy and third-party indirect threats) transpired to be legally inaccurate. NCRS rules were relied on by some officers to bypass the crime recording system and informally resolve cases, suggesting that because there was no "victim confirmation" of a crime, there was no requirement to submit a crime report. Such creative rule bending has resulted in further changes to NCRS, which now demands that crimes must be recorded even for "unwilling victims" (HOCR 2016: 4).

Some officers use their knowledge of the law and procedures to modify the original allegation and this is specific to the offence of "threats to kill." It involves the subtle and hard-to-detect practice of removing key words in the write-up such as "kill" or "death," rendering cases non-criminal because they no longer fit the criminal "points to prove." Specificities within legislation are also used by some professionals to distort parliament's original intentions. For example, under the Mental Capacity Act (2005), it must be assumed a person *has* capacity unless it is established otherwise. Professionals leaving this point (capacity) shrouded in uncertainty renders vulnerable adults as "consenting" to marriages and arguably is the reason why adult vulnerability is denied.

Along with victim blaming, the reluctant-to-prosecute theme is the most prevalent justification supporting an officer's "no-crime" decision, apparent across Chaps. 4, 6 and 7. Findings demonstrate that officers did not "dig deeper" to investigate and pragmatically moved to expedite enquiries due to victim reluctance. Yet conversely, iterative findings depict victim cooperation rather than reluctance. There are manifestations of alleged "U turns" in victim behaviours that are simply incompatible with genuine reluctant victims. For example, victims with language barriers (therefore requiring interpreters) providing written notes of death threats were suddenly able to elucidate to officers a reluctance to prosecute; victims waiting days to speak to operational officers having provided full accounts of physical abuse and false imprisonment, or even a rape in the initial call, inexplicably refuse to divulge information, or provide "no" answers within formulaic compressed summaries. In 12% of DASH cases, officers allege that victims "refuse" to respond, only to find that a common ploy amongst some officers is not to ask victims the DASH questions, with this manoeuvre apparent in wider literature (Robinson et al. 2016). Given that a third (31%) of HBA victims in the incident data return home of their own volition (the highest outcome in adult cases), it is inherently difficult to delineate the "impostor's performance" (Goffman 1990: 59) from the bona fide reluctant victim, which is arguably why "victim reluctance" is a convincing stratagem relied on by some unscrupulous officers to "cuff" crimes. These findings support extant research (Brown 1981) suggesting that in some cases victim reluctance is manufactured by officers in order to file the incident as no further action.

Heavily interwoven with the reluctance theme is the overriding preoccupation officers have in restricting workload and limiting demand in order to "make tasks more manageable" (Lipsky 2010 [1980]: 83). Particularly when victims "waver" as to whether to prosecute, officers strategise as to whether a case is worthy of time investment, as submitting a crime report might precipitate expected actions that could be considered "wasteful" (Brown 1981: 205) and "for nothing" (police officer i) if there is no tangible outcome to justify the effort. In the "investigate to record" era, there was a culture of managers expecting officers to revisit victims and put pressure on them to negate the crime, particularly if victims were uncertain about prosecution. Findings here reinforce both classical and contemporary police culture(s) research in highlighting a relationship between the reluctant victim and workload reduction, which influences officer decision-making. This is apparent in the work of Goldstein, where it transpired that officers dealing with a large number of stabbing cases (38/43) dissuaded victims from signing their complainant statements, giving a false impression of reluctance because it "reduces the pressure of work" (1960: 574). Equally, a recent HMIC report on the policing domestic abuse suggests that in instances of anticipated retraction it is "sometimes deemed a waste of everyone's time to have to complete paperwork" (Robinson et al. 2016: 13); so consequently, the pragmatic resolution is for officers to circumvent formal paradigms.

Further indication that managing and reducing workload is an important influence for officers is apparent in the pragmatic organisational imperative of simplifying and "satisficing" (Simon 1976), which, it is suggested, is more apparent in the aftermath of public service cuts. There is evidence within Chaps. 4 and 6 of officers reducing crimes to less serious offences, what Bourlet terms "criming down" (1990); choosing one crime (or no crime) or one charge; or reducing complicated cases of multiple perpetration into processing a single perpetrator. Equally, offences like "threats to kill" are deemed as notoriously difficult to prosecute and officers, having anticipated a "no charge" decision from the CPS, are expedient in reducing unnecessary workload by avoiding crime submission in 78% of cases. Such reductionism could be considered pragmatic, yet the implication of such practices may encourage officers to aim for the "low hanging fruit" in which other crimes and multiple perpetrators, including female perpetrators, could be overlooked, resulting in the under-protection of victims and impoverished justice.

Concluding Remarks

Undoubtedly, the burgeoning of managerial efficiency (bureaucracy) in a climate of reduced public spending is a feature of the public sector that is considered to be a "great leap backwards" (Featherstone et al. 2018: 28). Yet, several government reports on policing and child protection suggest that because of increased bureaucracy and a blame culture, professionals are unduly risk averse and follow "rules and procedures to the letter" (Berry 2009: 61). This, in turn, is said to *reduce* officer discretion and professional judgement at incidents (Flanagan 2008; Heaton 2010; Munro 2011). Findings show limited evidence[1] of this assertion, with officers sometimes acting on the basis of "worst case scenario" (Flanagan

2008: 50), more preoccupied with self-preservation and the need to "back-cover" rather than borne out of an intrinsic duty to pursue a quality investigation. Although bureaucracy and servicing the information "machine" (Parton 2008) have taken primacy at the expense of professionals focusing on victims and families (Munro 2011; Thompson 2016), these findings contradict the view that professional discretion has been reduced due to excessive adherence to bureaucracy. Reinforcing Manning's research (1978b), the findings support the contention that corporate controls such as procedures, rules and even legislation are consistently subverted and reinterpreted by officers to *avoid bureaucracy* in the overall pursuit of workload reduction.

One of the difficulties encountered was interpreting whether professionals were *wholly* duped by perpetrator explanations, or whether this in itself is a stratagem used by professionals to expedite seemingly complex crime enquiries. Based on the overall findings, it is hypothesised that some unscrupulous professionals (in this study, police officers and social workers) take the path of least resistance by appearing to accept illogical perpetrator narratives, because it fits their self-interested preferences to do so. In line with the Rational Choice Model of Ignorance and Bias (Knott and Miller 1987), it is proffered that some professionals are selective in their interpretation of information, not only prematurely screening out information that supports their preferred hypothesis (Reder et al. 1993; Munro 1999; Taylor and White 2006) but ignoring or altering information that might lead them to make decisions that they do not want to make. Professionals not only "inject caring narratives" as an impetus for decision-making, but under the pressure to expedite cases they are driven by *different* imperatives (Taylor and White 2006) that are not victim focused, which predisposes them to lean towards their own biases. This certainly conflicts with Klockars proposition that action/inaction is prompted out of respect for victims' wishes (1985). It is considered that it is a mistake to assume that officers exhibiting poor crime recording practices simply do not comprehend the risks (Myhill and Johnson 2016) or that professionals "misread cases" (Thompson 2016: 185). Those advancing this argument do not factor in the prominent role played by organisational culture. Rather than accept these are the isolated aberrant judgements of a poorly trained few, the researcher suggests these patterned practices should be recognised as *functional* strategies, applied by unscrupulous officials in order to deconstruct the crime process, informally resolve incidents and reduce personal workload.

Although classic characterisations and typologies of police officers (Muir 1977; Reiner 2010) are useful reference points, these appear outdated in the current research context, as they straitjacket officers into overly prescriptive and two-dimensional caricatures which fail to reflect the nuanced reality of interactions between police officers and the public. Although the findings highlight dysfunctional practices by some professionals, these are certainly not monolithic and nor are they universally applied by all state agents. It is acknowledged that competent professionals of high ethical integrity committed to public service values can recognise dysfunctional subculture(s) without subscribing to them (Lipsky 2010 [1980]: xviii; Shearing 1981). Such discretionary practices illustrate that the corporate vision and mission statements of the policing organisation are misaligned with the reality, creating "strategic drift" (Handy 1999). The overarching implications of such practices are the rationing of service provision, under-policing, under-protection and the stifling of unmet needs which occasions secondary victimisation by the state.

Research Credibility and Limitations

Although the research was limited to one police force, making findings difficult to generalise across England and Wales, the application of this predominantly qualitative grounded theory mixed method study enabled a deep and holistic understanding of the research problem. Through unique access and examination of 100 classified electronic police incident records (and associated electronic supporting documentation) and bolstered by the semi-structured interviewing of 15 specialist HBA police investigators with a collective 228 years policing experience, the endeavour has been to provide implicit quantification of qualitative data (Strauss and Corbin 1998). The aim has been to make defensible knowledge claims about the policing of honour-based abuse. The method of using findings from one data set to corroborate, double check and compare findings against the other data set increases the weight and validity of the findings (Creswell 2014; Berg and Lune 2012). The inclusion of three police participants from ethnic minority origins is beneficial. Equally, 11 of the 15 officers are female, a ratio which is purely incidental and based on those officers' volunteering to be involved in the research. Consequently, the interview sample is much more diverse than the current police workforce configuration of England and Wales, which is currently made up of 29% female officers and only 6.3% of Black and Minority Ethnic (BME) officers (Home Office 2017: 6).

Future Research

Police incident data analysis rather than the examination of crime reports is considered an untapped but crucial resource and method for future researchers. This method aided not only in highlighting the disparities between victim accounts and officers' write-ups but also in excavating many hidden unrecorded crimes. As explored, police force analysts do not currently examine incident data. Coupled with this, given that the current findings suggest that breaches to crime recording rules are not distinctive to HBA, by applying the current methodology to other crime types there is a potential for police forces and academics to pursue projects that could lead to all-embracing policing improvements.

The current research identifies overlapping commonalities in the way DASH risk assessments are operationally completed in an HBA context that could support future work in the traditional domestic abuse, stalking and harassment fields. Furthermore, there are a number of embryonic themes which the researcher did not have the opportunity to theoretically develop within the current study—most notably, a correlation between HBA victims and child sexual exploitation, particularly when those victims spent time in the care system. Another emergent theme is how officers of Asian heritage negotiate their own culture and the benefits and challenges this poses within an operational policing context.

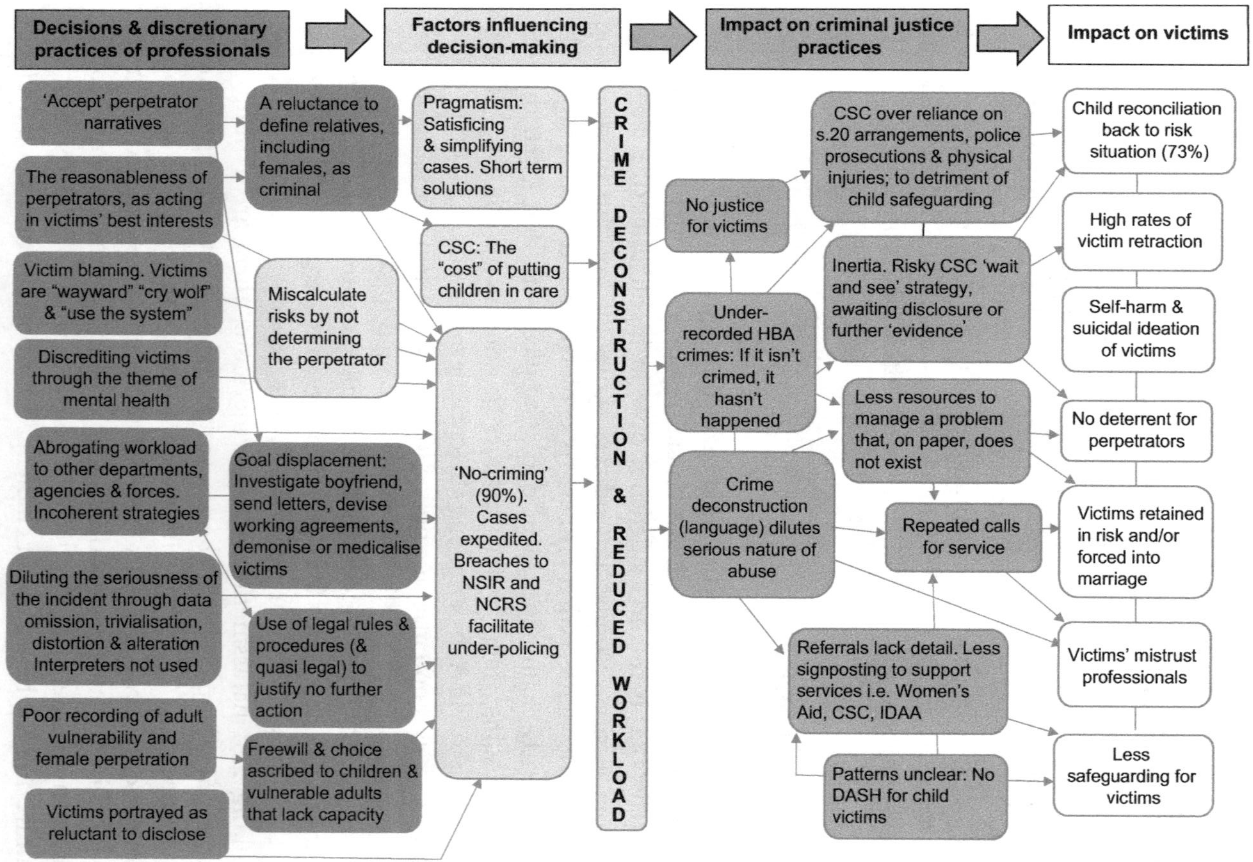

Fig. 8.1 HBA investigations: discretionary practices of professionals, their influence and impact

Recommendations

Recommendations for Police

Crime Recording

8.1. The Scale of HBA

To identify the scale of honour-based abuse in England and Wales, each Force Intelligence Branch should send HBA crime and incident figures to the Home Office on a routine basis.

8.2. Auditing HBA

To drive higher standards and identify blockages to crime recording practices in each force area, each force crime audit unit should routinely sample HBA incident data, rather than crime data. Such findings should be interpreted and published by force intelligence analysts for the benefit of Public Protection Divisions.

8.3. NSIR and NCRS Compliance

Before closing an incident, divisional supervisors must ensure NSIR compliance and either that a crime report is submitted or that the rationale for a "no-crime" report is appended to the incident. The practice of supervisors writing "NCRS compliant" without checking that that is the case must cease. Communications operators must avoid closing an incident in order to reduce the queues.

8.4. Supervisory Oversight

Where discrepancies are found between incidents reported by victims and the subsequent summary write-ups provided by officers, supervisors in all departments should actively challenge such discrepancies and hold officers to account.

Such recommendations will ensure that incidents are NSIR compliant and improve police crime recording practices in this and other crime types. The creation of the crime report ensures that officers' actions are placed under direct supervisory scrutiny, which can only assist in benefitting victims of crime.

Child and Vulnerable Adult Safeguarding

8.5. Listen to Victims

There is a misguided assumption by professionals that relatives automatically pursue the "best interests" of children or vulnerable adult victims. In drawing out the distinction between relatives who "protect" and relatives who "control," professionals should listen to, centralise and prioritise the needs of victims as paramount, rather than accede to perpetrator narratives.

8.6. Recording and Disseminating risks to Vulnerable victims

Current risks to vulnerable adults and children are not appropriately recorded and/or disseminated through partnership working arrangements. Consequently, victims are reunified with inappropriate or direct perpetrating family members. It is recommended that a simplified version of the DASH risk assessment be applied to child and vulnerable adult groups. This will improve both the recording of vulnerability and the detailed nature of the abuse to support quality intelligence sharing between agencies in order to enhance safeguarding provision.

8.7. HBA Against Siblings

Despite advanced systems that were able to highlight recurring HBA issues in the same families, there is evidence of a failure by police and social services to "join the dots" in responding to siblings at risk. Professionals should strategically consider the risks posed to siblings in a family unit, rather than assessing cases in isolation.

8.8. HBA as Domestic Abuse, Not Child Protection

Some uniformed policing responses to child HBA are derived from traditional child safeguarding police tactics, such as a clean home and other siblings not reporting any abuse. The risks and triggers of HBA demand a different more nuanced cultural understanding of HBA. For this reason, like adult HBA investigations, child HBA investigations and safeguarding should be placed under the ownership of specialist police experts in HBA (and domestic abuse more broadly), rather than with police child protection officers.

8.9. Police Ownership of HBA Safeguarding and Investigation

Findings show that when agencies are working in partnership, roles and responsibilities are unclear, resulting in a lack of action and, in some cases, inertia by several agencies. It is recommended that the police should take primacy in investigating and safeguarding child and vulnerable adult cases of HBA. This will reduce the number of victims slipping between the cracks of service provision.

Interpreters

8.10. Use Interpreters

Findings illustrate how officers actively avoid enlisting interpreters and, in some cases, use perpetrating or sympathising family members to translate for victims that are non-English speakers. Authorised and accredited interpreters must be used by officers to both capture victim/witness testimony and complete the DASH report. Police supervisors must ensure that this is reinforced.

8.11. Use Interpreters When Serving Orders

Some perpetrators exploit language barriers and thus evade criminal justice sanction in suggesting they do not understand the conditions set by court judges regarding Forced Marriage Protection Orders (FMPOs) when these went onto be breached. To ensure this loophole is closed, bailiffs and police officers should employ the services of an interpreter when serving FMPOs in order to explain in the perpetrators' native tongue the conditions of an FMPO.

8.12. Provide Guidance on Interpreters

Guidance on interpreters and the use of friends and relatives exists at local force policy level, yet such advice is entirely absent from the NPCC strategy. The overarching NPCC strategy on HBA (2015) must provide guidance concerning the use of interpreters.

Education and Training

8.13

There must be raised awareness amongst police forces that discrediting victims, feigning or exaggerating the mental or physical illness of victims, accusing well-meaning boyfriends of terrorism or other criminality are all mechanisms used by perpetrators to deflect professional attention away from the HBA allegation.

8.14

All specialist police officers and other practitioners (adult and children's social care) involved in the investigation and/or safeguarding of those at risk of HBA must receive accredited training on HBA, ideally integrated within domestic abuse training.

8.15

To improve the understanding and training of HBA, the domestic abuse sergeant on each division and/or HBA lead (Inspector) should adhere to

Nationally accredited guidelines and cascade this to frontline uniformed officers, educating them on the signs, triggers and cultural nuances of HBA and related forced marriage issues.

Recommendations for Social Services

8.16. Working Agreements and s.20 Arrangements

Social services should urgently review the current practices around using working agreements and section 20 arrangements, which portray professionals as colluding with perpetrators to the detriment of listening to the needs of child victims.

8.17. Inappropriate Implementation of FMPOs

Findings illustrate that FMPOs are not appropriately implemented by partner agencies (CSC and health), that is, not properly served and thus not entered on the Police National Computer (PNC) system, with several victims being provided with a short-term 12-month order. Furthermore, family members often persevere to ensure victims are already abroad and ready to be married once a Forced Marriage Protection Order (FMPO) is close to expiry. Professionals should ensure FMPOs are procedurally implemented correctly and that these adequately protect victims in the long term (i.e. an unlimited order). This includes ensuring such applications are communicated to the police in order that a safety plan can be devised with the victim.

Mediation

8.18

To avoid the premature reconciliation of children with perpetrating family members, social service policy and practice guidelines should explicitly prohibit the practice of mediation by professionals.

8.19

The dangers of mediation should be made explicit in the national policing strategy (2015), and adult social care and child protection guidelines for social service professionals.

8.20

As part of a mediation process, CSC and some police officers appear to place victims (including child and vulnerable adult victims) in a difficult predicament by expecting them to disclose abuse in the presence of potentially perpetrating family members. To ensure that children and vulnerable adults have the opportunity to disclose abuse away from perpetrators and sympathisers, social services should legally act as "appropriate adult," particularly when victims undertake formal procedures such as medical examinations or give preliminary first accounts of abuse to police (and proceeding video interviews).

Recommendations for All Professionals

8.21. Raise Awareness Amongst Teenage Victims

Findings demonstrate that HBA is quantitatively concentrated against teenage daughters pre-marriage (63%), compared to post-marriage abuse, which is a considerably smaller proportion (26%) (Chart 6.6). Furthermore, HBA as a phenomenon is linked to marriage in 64% of cases. Therefore, it is argued that forced marriage is deemed by perpetrators to be the resolution to the problem of a perceived "wayward" daughter. Therefore, any future HBA strategy should focus on the safeguarding and education of HBA to young teenagers.

8.22. "Westernisation" Trigger Not Recognised

Professionals apply a culture-blind yardstick when receiving reports of the perceived "westernisation" of children, which leads to trivialisation and a failure to recognise these manifestations as precursors to HBA. This facet requires inclusion within multi-agency police guidelines and DASH risk assessments (for children) to assess whether child HBA victims are at risk of "significant harm."

8.23. Confidential Settings

To aid victims in disclosing abuse, health professionals should prevent family members from using the justification of honour and culture in order to access confidential consultations between the patient and the doctor.

8.24. Education

Government policy in HBA should focus on educating communities, specifically young women, of the dangers of subscribing to honour codes which impede life choices and contravene the rights of young people to marry/not to marry. Only through education will communities be empowered to renounce patriarchal pressures.

8.25. Working Together

Professionals appear unduly preoccupied with their own organisational goals, resourcing and financial constraints, which often conflicts with the overarching goal of victim safeguarding. Decisions made by social services to reunify children with perpetrators must not be taken in isolation from any ongoing police investigation. Joint strategy meetings between police and other agencies (CSC, adult social care) must be documented to include the rationale for an agreed course of action between agencies.

Note

1. One officer spent time "back-covering" through comprehensive "write-ups" on the system catering for the "worst case scenario" (death). Conversely, another officer disbelieved a victim but still "back-covered" to present an impression of service even though "less is done" with those cases.

References

Atkinson, P., & Coffey, A. (2011). Analyzing documentary realities. In D. Silverman (Ed.), *Qualitative research: Issues of theory, method and practice* (3rd ed., pp. 77–92). London: Sage Publications.

Berg, B., & Lune, H. (2012). *Qualitative research methods for the social sciences* (8th ed.). Upper Saddle River, NJ: Pearson Education Limited.

Berry, J. (2009). *Reducing bureaucracy in policing: Full report.* London: Home Office.

Black, D. (1980). Production of crime rates. In D. Black (Ed.), *The manners and customs of the police.* New York, NY: Academic Press.

Bourlet, A. (1990). *Police intervention in marital violence.* Milton Keynes, UK: Open University Press.

Brown, M. (1981). *Working the street: Police discretion and the dilemmas of reform.* New York, NY: Russell Sage Foundation.

Campbell, B. (2013, September 17). From Jasmine Beckford to Daniel Pelka: A history of chaos and calumny. *The Guardian.* [Online]. Retrieved November 4, 2018, from https://www.theguardian.com.

Children Act 1989. (c.41). [Online]. Retrieved September 1, 2016, from http://www.legislation.gov.uk.

Coleman, C., & Moynihan, J. (1996). Understanding crime data: Haunted by the dark figure. In M. Maguire (Ed.), *Crime and justice.* Buckingham: Open University Press.

Creswell, J. (2014). *Research design: International student edition. Qualitative, quantitative, and mixed methods approaches* (4th ed.). London: Sage Publications.

Crown Prosecution Service. (2015). *Violence against women and girls crime report (2014–2015).* London: CPS.

Edwards, S. (1986). Police attitudes and dispositions in domestic disputes: The London study. *Police Journal, 59*(3), 230–241.

Farmer, E. (2006). Using research to develop practice in child protection and childcare. In C. Humphries & N. Stanley (Eds.), *Domestic violence and child protection: Directions for good practice* (pp. 124–136). London: Jessica Kingsley.

Farmer, E., & Lutman, E. (2012). *Effective working with neglected children and their families: Linking interventions to long-term outcomes.* London: Jessica Kingsley.

Featherstone, B., Gupta, A., Morris, K., & White, S. (2018). *Protecting children: A social model.* Bristol: Policy Press.

Flanagan, R. (2008). *The review of policing: Final report*. London: HMSO.
Goffman, E. (1990 [1959]). *The presentation of the self in everyday life*. Harmondsworth: Penguin.
Goldstein, J. (1960). Police discretion not to invoke the criminal process: Low-visibility decisions in the administration of justice. *The Yale Law Journal, 69*(4), 543–594.
Grace, S. (1995). *Policing domestic violence in the 1990s*. Home Office Research Study No. 139. London: HMSO.
Handy, C. (1999). *Understanding organisations* (4th ed.). London: Penguin Books Limited.
Hanmer, J. (2013 [1989]). Women and policing in Britain. In J. Hanmer, J. Radford, & E. Stanko (Eds.), *Women, policing, and male violence: International perspectives* (pp. 90–124). London: Routledge.
Heaton, R. (2010). We could be criticized! Policing and risk aversion. *Policing: A Journal of Policy and Practice, 5*(1), 75–86.
Her Majesties Inspectorate of Constabulary (HMIC). (1999). *Police integrity England, Wales and Northern Ireland. Securing and maintaining public confidence*. Swindon: Swindon Press.
Her Majesty's Inspectorate of Constabulary (HMIC). (2014a). *Crime-recording: Making the victim count. The final report of an inspection of crime data integrity in police forces in England and Wales*. London: TSO.
Her Majesty's Inspectorate of Constabulary (HMIC). (2014b). *Everyone's business: Improving the police response to domestic abuse*. London: TSO.
Hobbs, D. (1989). Policing in the vernacular. In D. E. Downes (Ed.), *Crime and the city* (pp. 154–181). London: Macmillan.
Holdaway, S. (1983). *Inside the British police*. Oxford: Basil Blackwell Publisher Limited.
Home Office. (2016). *Home Office counting rules for recorded crime*. London: TSO.
Home Office. (2017). *Police workforce, England and Wales, 31 March 2017*. London: TSO.
House of Commons Public Administration Select Committee (PASC). (2014). *Caught red-handed: Why we can't count on police-recorded crime statistics*. Thirteenth Report of Session 2013–14, HC 760.
Klockars, C. (1985). *The idea of police*. Beverley Hills, CA: Sage Publications.
Knott, J., & Miller, G. (1987). *Reforming bureaucracy: The politics of institutional choice*. Englewood Cliffs, NJ: Prentice Hall.
Lipsky, M. (2010 [1980]). *Street-level bureaucracy: Dilemmas of the individual in public services* (Expanded ed.). New York, NY: Russell Sage Foundation.

Littlechild, B. (1998). Does family support ensure the protection of children? Messages from child protection research. *Child Abuse Review, 7*(2), 116–128.
Lynn, N., & Lea, S. (2012, March). Civil disputes and crime recording refusals, disinterest and power in police witcraft. *British Journal of Criminology, 52*(2), 361–380.
Manning, P. (1977). *The social organisation of policing*. Cambridge, MA: MIT Press.
Manning, P. (1978a). Lying, secrecy and social control. In P. Manning & J. Van Maanen (Eds.), *Policing: A view from the street* (pp. 238–255). Santa Monica, CA: Goodyear Publishing Company Inc..
Manning, P. (1978b). The police: Mandate, strategies and appearances. In P. Manning & J. Van Maanen (Eds.), *Policing: A view from the street* (pp. 7–31). Santa Monica, CA: Goodyear Publishing Company Inc.
Mental Capacity Act 2005: Codes of practice. (2013, July). UK Department for Constitutional Affairs (pp. 1–301). [Online]. Retrieved January 12, 2016, from https://www.gov.uk.
Muir, W. (1977). *Police: Streetcorner politicians*. Chicago: University of Chicago Press.
Munro, E. (1999). Common errors of reasoning in child protection work. *Child Abuse and Neglect, 23*(8), 745–758.
Munro, E. (2011). *The Munro review of child protection: Final report: A child-centred system* (pp. 1–173). London: Department for Education, TSO.
Myhill, A., & Johnson, K. (2016). Police use of discretion in response to domestic violence. *Criminology and Criminal Justice: An International Journal, 16*(1), 3–20.
NSPCC. (2015). *Achieving positive outcomes for children in relation to return home from care*. [Online]. Retrieved November 3, 2016, from https://www.nspcc.org.uk.
Office for National Statistics (ONS). (2018). *Statistical bulletin: Domestic abuse in England and Wales, year ending March 2018*. Released 22 November 2018. [Online]. Retrieved February 1, 2019, from https://www.ons.gov.uk.
Parton, N. (2008). Changes in the form of knowledge in social work: From the social to the informational. *British Journal of Social Work, 38*(2), 253–269.
Reder, P., Duncan, S., & Gray, M. (1993). *Beyond blame: Child abuse tragedies revisited.* London: Routledge.
Reiner, R. (2010). *The politics of the police* (4th ed.). Oxford: Oxford University Press.

Roberts, K., Campbell, G., & Lloyd, G. (2014). *Honor-based violence: Policing and prevention* (Advances in Police Theory and Practice Series). London: CRC Press; Taylor and Francis Group.

Robinson, A., Myhill, A., Roberts, J., & Tilley, N. (2016). *Risk-led policing of domestic abuse and the dash risk model* (pp. 1–46). [Online]. Retrieved November 23, 2016, from http://www.college.police.uk.

Shearing, C. (1981). *Organisational police deviance: Its structure and control.* London: Butterworth and Co Ltd.

Shearing, C., & Ericson, R. (1991). Culture as figurative action. *British Journal of Sociology, 42*(4), 481–506.

Simon, H. (1976). *Administrative behavior: A study of decision-making processes in administrative organisations* (3rd ed.). London: The Free Press; Collier Macmillan Publishers.

Strauss, A., & Corbin, J. (1998). *Basics of qualitative research: Techniques and procedures for producing grounded theory* (2nd ed.). London: Sage Publishing.

Sumner, C. (1994). *The sociology of deviance: An obituary.* Buckingham: Open University Press.

Taylor, C., & White, S. (2006). Knowledge and reasoning in social work: Educating for humane judgement. *British Journal of Social Work, 36*(6), 937–954.

Thompson, K. (2016). *Strengthening child protection: Sharing information in multi-agency settings.* Bristol: Policy Press.

Waddington, P. (1999). *Policing citizens.* London: Routledge.

Young, M. (1991). *An inside job: Policing and police culture in Britain.* Oxford: Clarendon Press.

Index[1]

[1] Note: Page numbers followed by 'n' refer to notes.

R. Aplin, *Policing UK Honour-Based Abuse Crime*,
https://doi.org/10.1007/978-3-030-18430-8

FSC
www.fsc.org
MIX
Papier | Fördert gute Waldnutzung
FSC® C083411

Kolibri 360 GmbH
Ferdinand-Jühlke-Straße 7
99095 Erfurt, Deutschland
produktsicherheit@kolibri360.de